THE DARTMOUTH REVIEW
PLEADS INNOCENT

THE DARTMOUTH REVIEW PLEADS INNOCENT

TWENTY-FIVE YEARS OF BEING THREATENED,
IMPUGNED, VANDALIZED, SUED, SUSPENDED,
AND BITTEN AT THE IVY LEAGUE'S MOST
CONTROVERSIAL CONSERVATIVE NEWSPAPER

Edited with an Introduction by

JAMES PANERO

and

STEFAN BECK

ISI Books
Wilmington, Delaware
2006

The Dartmouth review pleads innocent : twenty-five years of being threatened,
impugned, vandalized, sued, suspended, and bitten at the Ivy League's most controversial
conservative newspaper / edited by James Panero and Stefan Beck. — Wilmington, DE :
ISI Books, 2006.

    p. ; cm.

    ISBN-13: 978-1-932236-93-4
    ISBN-10: 1-932236-93-7
    Includes index

    1. Dartmouth Review. 2. Dartmouth College—History. 3. Universities and
colleges—United States—Newspapers—History. 4. Conservative literature—United
States—History. 5. Conservatism—United States. 6. Education, Higher—Political
aspects—United States. I. Panero, James 1975–. II. Beck, Stefan 1982–.

LD1438.8 .D37 2006
378.73—dc22   0603

Published in the United States by:

    ISI Books
    Intercollegiate Studies Institute
    Post Office Box 4431
    Wilmington, DE 19807-0431

Cover design by Kevin van der Leek Design, Inc.

Interior design by James Panero and Stefan Beck

Manufactured in the United States of America

For Jeffrey Hart

Contents

Introduction   *ix*

The Man of Steel
In the beginning: Reagan, John Steel, and the Review.   *3*

Take Five
Review *editor Dinesh D'Souza says "time out."*   *16*

The First Case
A Review *founder lands in kangaroo court.*   *18*

No Jive
The bad language of affirmative action.   *30*

Once Bitten
A Review *opponent breaks the skin.*   *35*

Bill Cole
A music professor strikes a sour note.   *43*

An Inside Look
Sex, lies, and audiotape.   *59*

The Indian Wars
The meaning of a symbol.   *71*

Divestment
The beautification of the Green before Winter Carnival.   *88*

Bill Cole Strikes Back
A music professor tries to break the Review *editorship.*   *122*

Sex Ed
Our bodies, ourselves, our liberal pieties.   *166*

The First Stone
Jeffrey Hart sues the College over a Hitler quote.   *176*

Liberal Fascism
Gestapo tactics and a Review *column.*   *180*

Sabotage
Hate upon hate in Dartmouth's darkest hour.   *192*

The Freedman Legacy
All the president's men.   *226*

The Freedom of Assembly
Greek life, the "Student Life Initiative," and liberty.   *240*

Deviance on Tap
The Big Green goes blue.   *268*

God & Man at Dartmouth
What would Buckley do?   *282*

Rebel Yell
Conservative vindication at Dartmouth.   *298*

---

*Seven specially commissioned essays on
twenty-five years of* The Dartmouth Review

Dartmouth's J-School
by Jeffrey Hart   *315*

Lessons from Jeffrey Hart
by Peter Robinson   *320*

The Early Days
by Dinesh D'Souza   *323*

The *Review* & the Olin Foundation
by James Piereson   *328*

Delhi, *Deliverance* & Dartmouth
by Harmeet Dhillon   *334*

Shut Up, I Explained
by Joseph Rago   *337*

The *Review* Today
by Michael Ellis   *339*

Contributors   *343*

Acknowledgments   *347*

Index   *349*

Introduction

"I EXPECTED YOU to make mistakes your first year. We all do." So begins Jasper's Grand Remonstrance of his younger cousin, Charles Ryder, the hero of Evelyn Waugh's *Brideshead Revisited*. At issue is Charles's louche coterie at Oxford. Jasper goes on: "But you, my dear Charles, whether you realize it or not, have gone straight, hook, line and sinker, into the *very worst set in the University*. You may think that, living in digs, I don't know what goes on in college; but I hear things. In fact, I hear all too much. I find that I've become a figure of mockery on your account at the Dining Club."

For twenty-five years, the undergraduate editors of *The Dartmouth Review* have been, for the Jaspers of Dartmouth, the "very worst set" in the College on the Hill. To their supporters, through a blend of activism and journalism, they have shown Dartmouth to be an institution that celebrates free expression while maintaining a byzantine code of permissible conduct and thought. To their detractors, they have made Dartmouth a figure of mockery at the Dining Club of progressive academia.

The editors of *The Dartmouth Review* have been a public embarrassment, willfully so, to the good name of Dartmouth's liberal administrators, faculty, and trustees. This book is the story of *The Dartmouth Review* in its own words. It does not take a Dartmouth Man to draw a lesson from it. The experience of the *Review* is a chapter in the struggle of youth against intellectual ossification, as youth has perceived it. Its story illustrates what happens when you give precocious twenty-year-olds unfettered control of a six-figure-a-year media operation, and what can come of the combination of indiscretion, energy, and insight.

In 1955, the conservative counter-reformation of American universities took shape with the publication of *God and Man at Yale*, William F. Buckley Jr.'s challenge to the secular pieties of his alma mater. In the years to follow, conservative displeasure on campus, which Buckley's book gave voice to, was galvanized as the radicals of the 1960s found tenure in the increasingly progressive universities of the 1970s and 1980s.

In 1980, a small college in New Hampshire, population 4,000 undergraduates, suddenly found itself front and center in this confrontation. A few editors of the official student daily, shackled by the political diktats of a liberal college administration, decamped to Main Street and hung out a shingle for their own independent newspaper.

Financial and moral support came from organizations like the Collegiate Network and those alumni who felt rejected by a college ashamed of its history. At any college, at any time, such support might be expected. But at Dartmouth, by 1980, there had emerged such a stark divide between conservative alumni and an administration that sought at all costs to advertise its left-liberal credentials that this support was swift and overwhelming. The newspaper, available by subscription and distributed door-to-door on campus, forged a direct, immediate, and powerful connection between once-marginalized students and their supporters. "I look at us as being the first real example of *God and Man at Yale* in practice," noted *Review* founder Gregory Fossedal '81. From its first issue, the *Review* was able to draw a significant source of revenue from alumni, who perceived the newspaper's not-for-profit cause as an alternative to the College Fund.

At the outset, *The Dartmouth Review* broadcast the message of a conservative candidate, John Steel, who ran successfully for the Dartmouth Board of Trustees by means of a petition ballot, bypassing the liberal Alumni Council. At the same time, the newspaper became the home of the 1980s brand of Ivy League misfit: super-smart students who supported the candidacy of Ronald Reagan, who found communion in the deathbed conversion of Lord Brideshead, and who sought their role models not in Karl Marx or Che Guevara but in Alexander Pope, Stanford White, and the gentleman tennis player Bill Tilden.

Beyond mere reporting, the editors of *The Dartmouth Review* also perceived their journalistic mandate as a call to arms: to force the dominant culture of Dartmouth, the "party of resentment," as Harold Bloom called it, to contend with their own conservative ideas. Former Editor-in-Chief Dinesh D'Souza '83 described such an animating principle in this way:

> Typically, the conservative attempts to conserve, to hold on to the values of the existing society. But what if the existing society is liberal? What if the existing society is inherently hostile to conservative beliefs? It is foolish for a conservative to attempt to conserve that culture. Rather, he must seek to undermine it, to thwart it, to destroy it at the root level. This means that the conservative must stop being conservative. More precisely, he must be philosophically conservative but temperamentally radical. This is what we quickly understood at the *Review*. We recognized that to confront liberalism

fully we could not be content with rebutting liberal arguments. We also had to subvert liberal culture, and this meant disrupting the etiquette of liberalism. In other words, we had to become social guerillas. And this we set out to do with a vengeance.

Another former Editor-in-Chief, Harmeet Dhillon '89, put it simply when she wrote that *"The Dartmouth Review* has, several times in its history, gone too far in its criticism of College policies so that other people will feel compelled to go far enough."

The *Review* today still fills this role as an example and an encouragement to Dartmouth's conservative-minded students. It continues to thrive. This book is in no way meant to be a final say: It does not signal the end of a story but rather a mid-course report. The *Review* has succeeded for a quarter-century through vigorous, sometimes vicious, opposition; there is little doubt that it will continue writing its own history well into the future. As we complete this anthology, new issues of *The Dartmouth Review* are landing outside the doorways of Dartmouth dorm rooms; the *Review*'s alumni circulation continues to be thousands strong, bolstered now by a public website at www.dartreview.com that has become a digital clearinghouse for the conservative voice on campus.

The process of creating this book, on the suggestion of the board of *The Dartmouth Review*, afforded us a long look at what the *Review* has done well. Below the surface of provocative antics, with which we ourselves were well acquainted as student editors, we discovered a coherence and narrative arc. That narrative is the story of a college's methodical campaign against student liberties, in an ironic appeal to tolerance and the "principles of community." This initiative can be tracked through five Dartmouth presidencies: those of John G. Kemeny (1970–1981), David McLaughlin (1981–1987), James O. Freedman (1987–1998), and now James Wright. In the first ten years of the newspaper, this effort manifested itself in nearly annual attempts to suspend *Review* editors and writers. From 1990 on, this campaign broadened to take on student liberties in many areas of campus life, not only in the freedom of student assembly but in the freedom of student behavior. In the past ten years especially, the Dartmouth student body has felt the scrutiny of an administration once reserved only for Dartmouth Reviewers. Dartmouth students are now perceived as guilty for merely matriculating at Dartmouth. Through proposals like the Student Life Initiative, and a circus of college programming, the administration has sought to undertake their political reeducation.

The Dartmouth Review has been in a unique position to report on all of these developments. As editors of this anthology, we have isolated these episodes into thematic chapters, single stories made up of multiple articles that we present in general chronological order.

Separated by a quarter century, and framing this story of the *Review*, has been the election of Dartmouth trustees by means of petition ballot. *The Dartmouth Review* has never fallen under the system of controls that the College maintains to "de-politicize" contentious petition elections. In this regard, the *Review*'s independent voice poses the greatest challenge to the status quo. Inaugurating its first issue with the candidacy of John Steel, documented in the chapter "The Man of Steel," *The Dartmouth Review* consistently reported on petition candidates up through the latest 2004 and 2005 elections. In these cases, documented in "Rebel Yell," three new petition trustees were elected in succession by direct alumni vote: T. J. Rogers, Todd Zywicki, and Peter Robinson. The fact that Robinson, an early contributor to *The Dartmouth Review*, could one day be elected to the Dartmouth Board of Trustees testifies to the newspaper's transformation from a fringe element of college culture into a powerful voice of the mainstream. Over twenty-five years, the newspaper has changed the terms of campus debate. Dartmouth is finally catching up with *The Dartmouth Review*.

What occurred between these election victories is the rest of the story. From "The First Case," an episode in which a *Review* founder defended himself before biased administrative jurors, the stakes of contention between the College and the newspaper quickly escalated. "No Jive" and "Once Bitten" start with a controversial and deliberately offensive column arguing against affirmative action, and end with a college administrator biting another *Review* founder as he distributed issues. These chapters also document the national notoriety the *Review* attained early on.

"Bill Cole" and "An Inside Look" begin with offending articles of their own—one concerning the teaching habits of the chairman of the music department, the other a meeting of an association of gay students—and go on to describe the multi-year fallouts from each episode. "The Indian Wars" challenges a basic assumption of a progressive institution: the offensiveness of its once-accepted symbol. At the time of the founding of *The Dartmouth Review*, the mere appearance of the Dartmouth Indian symbol, or the expression of Indian-related school spirit, was grounds for College discipline. By the middle of the 1980s, following a survey of tribal leaders conducted by *The Dartmouth Review*, and repeated editorials about the issues of free expression, freshmen students felt emboldened to unfurl Indian banners at College football games.

The strategy of ideas put into action reached its apogee over the issue of South African divestment. As documented in the chapter "Divestment," several *Review* editors performed the most famous act of right-wing guerilla art of the 1980s. They first challenged, in print, the illegal construction of protest "shanties" on the college Green, as well as contesting the wisdom of the cause of divestment. Following College inaction, the editors then set about removing the protest structures themselves.

Introduction

With each new episode, College sanctions against *Review* editors increased. In "Bill Cole Strikes Back," the multi-term suspension of Reviewers, over another altercation with the chairman of the music department, was overturned by state court. The defense of these students cost over a quarter of a million dollars. The *Review* was able to pay its legal bills through a special grant from the Olin Foundation, which not only saw college justice reversed, but also faced down future threats. While this was merely the penultimate great confrontation between the college and the newspaper, it became the final episode thus far in which Dartmouth College attempted to undermine the *Review* by attacking its editorship.

Following "Sex Ed," a chapter on the College's early inclinations toward student reeducation, several chapters document the lead-up to and fall-out from *The Dartmouth Review*'s most serious test to date. "The First Stone," "Liberal Fascism," "Sabotage," and "The Freedman Legacy" follow the College's decade-long direction under President James O. Freedman, as he manipulated the charge of anti-Semitism into a blanket campaign that nearly devastated *The Dartmouth Review* through false charges. So strong was Freedman's desire to eliminate the *Review*, in fact, that he risked damaging the reputation of Dartmouth to accomplish it. William F. Buckley Jr. wrote at the time, "There is nothing Dartmouth President James Freedman is better at doing than calling the attention of the whole world to the putative delinquencies of his own college."

Following the high tensions of what has become known as the "Hitler Quote incident," which sparked national controversy and even a parody of *The Dartmouth Review* by the *Harvard Lampoon*, Dartmouth broadened its campaign against student freedoms. From freedom of the press, the College went after the freedom of association in Dartmouth's fraternity system, documented in "The Freedom of Assembly," and the freedom of religious expression, documented in "God & Man at Dartmouth." In its place, Dartmouth proposed an alternative, progressive student culture in the form of programming and diversity deans, as reported in "Deviance on Tap." It was these recent campaigns against student life that motivated alumni dissatisfaction over college governance to the point where Rogers, Zywicki, and Robinson could be elected in succession.

Finally, in this anthology, on the occasion of the *Review*'s twenty-fifth anniversary, we have collected seven new essays on the history of the newspaper, written by the people who shaped it. All of these articles have appeared, or are slated to appear, in issues of *The Dartmouth Review*.

An unfortunate but unavoidable consequence of our editorial selection has been the omission of material that has often defined the newspaper's style. A word on those omissions is in order. The *Review* covers a wide variety of campus matters, from courses and faculty to new campus architecture to sports. It has demonstrated an abiding interest in culture and the arts, publishing reviews of books, music, and campus events. The newspaper has conducted regular interviews with an array of public figures, including Betty Friedan, Ralph Nader, Czeslaw Milosz, Abbie Hoffman, Richard Nixon, Donald Rumsfeld, Bobby Seale, Charlton Heston, Allen Ginsberg, Charlie Daniels, Gennifer Flowers, and Norman Podhoretz. Particularly indicative of the newspaper's jaunty tone are the Last Word (a collection of famous quotations compiled on the last page of each issue, an editorial tradition inaugurated by *Review* founder Gordon Haff) and the Week in Review (jocular notes on campus and extramural affairs). While notice of these sections has been precluded by the narrative form we have adopted for this anthology, we do not intend for these contributions to be regarded as any less vital to *Review* history.

It is with such jocularity in mind that we present to you the title of this anthology. *The Dartmouth Review Pleads Innocent* is not intended as a victimology. Impugned and bitten though it may have been, the newspaper has found its greatest successes through adversity, not in spite of it. The *Review* is at its best when it is both writing about and making the news.

In order to add perspective to this dynamic, we have included commentary from other newspapers and magazines, occasioned by events at Dartmouth involving *The Dartmouth Review*.

The masthead of *The Dartmouth Review* includes the phrase "Special Thanks to William F. Buckley Jr." We reiterate these thanks for his allowing us to reprint his syndicated columns on *The Dartmouth Review*. Mr. Buckley once wrote, "students of liberal behavior should be as interested in Dartmouth College these days as Charles Darwin was in the Galapagos." No outside observer can rival Mr. Buckley's scientific insight into the odd situations in which *The Dartmouth Review* often found itself.

Through nature and nurture, the environment of Dartmouth sustained *The Dartmouth Review*. Yet this newspaper would never have germinated, much less thrived, without the care of one man, to whom this anthology is dedicated. A beloved professor of English at Dartmouth College, not to say mentor to a generation of students, Jeffrey Hart has lent more than his advisement to the *Review*. With a joy for confrontation and a deep interest in literature, Jeffrey Hart has provided a model for gentlemanly behavior and the life of the mind that is otherwise absent from College life. *The Dartmouth Review* represents the institutionalization of his qualities.

The *Review* has been an education. We hope this anthology will instruct a future generation of Reviewers, wherever they may be.

James Panero & Stefan Beck
New York, New York
& Hanover, New Hampshire
January 2006

THE DARTMOUTH REVIEW
PLEADS INNOCENT

The Man of Steel

Steeling the Election
by Gregory Fossedal

Volume One, Issue One: Commencement 1980

L AST MONTH, twelve thousand ballots flowed into the office of Michael McGeehan, secretary of the College, in the second trustee election in Dartmouth history. Seven thousand of those ballots were cast for petition candidate Dr. John Steel. Assuming Steel is rubber-stamped by the board when they meet this weekend, Steel is the next trustee of Dartmouth College.

Throughout the balloting in this race against Raymond Rasenberger, the official Alumni Council candidate, Dr. Steel, a California surgeon, attracted wide attention. His controversial official statement drew immediate fire from the administration, and from students who feared a vote for Steel was a vote against minorities, women, tolerance, and, indeed, progress.

The *Review* contacted Steel at his home in La Jolla for comment:

THE DARTMOUTH REVIEW: What does the Steel victory mean for alumni?
JOHN STEEL: The trustees should make a reappraisal of how things are going. This is the first clear-cut sample of the alumni both in vote form and in message form.

TDR: What specific areas of the College's operation would you like them to re-evaluate?
JS: The most important consideration facing the trustees is obvious to everyone, and that is in the selection of the next president and chief administrator of the College.

TDR: And what sort of qualities would that person have?
JS: I think that certainly it should be someone who has lived and has felt the Dartmouth experience in Hanover. From my standpoint and that of

many of the alumni, that would mean a Dartmouth man—somebody who has that feeling of having been through Dartmouth and therefore has an understanding and a respect for the traditions of the College, its place in history, and, most importantly, where that might be taking us in the future.

TDR: You've placed quite a bit of emphasis on the Indian, the Dartmouth symbol banned by outgoing president John Kemeny in 1974. That emphasis has alienated some people who might well be with you in other areas. What do you see in the symbol that makes it so important?
JS: The Indian symbol represents strength and leadership; those of us who admire the Indian symbol have never meant to offend anybody.

TDR: But you have offended people by supporting the symbol.
JS: Freedom of expression is very important in this business of the symbol. I don't think that anyone should have their feeling suppressed, nor should one be told that they should or should not sing songs, nor should artwork be covered up. I am also a very loyal son of Dartmouth College, and certainly I am going to protect her traditions and try to maintain Dartmouth's position among the outstanding educational institutions of this country. These historic concepts of this college should be preserved; these are legacies from those who have been to Hanover before us. So I think that before we abandon significant traditions, we should take a good look at them and see what they really mean.

TDR: Are you merely saying that you oppose administrative attempts to suppress expression in favor of the symbol, or are you arguing further that the trustees should vote to establish it as an official College symbol?
JS: If the symbol were to return, the students would have to return it themselves. They themselves should be the ones that demonstrate their right to freedom of expression and their affection for the symbol. That is the one way for the symbol to be returned. I certainly wouldn't want it returned and then demand that everybody wear an Indian. It requires freedom, and if you want it, fine; if you don't want it, fine. This is one of the vital areas that the College needs to re-examine, in terms of not only the symbol but freedom of expression.

TDR: You have a son and a daughter here. What do they tell you about what's going on at the College?
JS: My daughter and her classmates received a letter from an administrator saying that it would be in bad taste to have any clothes with Indian markings on it, or any jewelry with the same. That's treading off onto personal freedoms. I'm in favor of saying that people are free and responsible for their freedom, and that they should conduct their lives as such. They

don't need an administrator to suggest what kind of jewelry they should have on. My son has told me of the threat to fraternities if they don't comply and get rid of their Indian jackets. I'm not against change, certainly, but I think that if one looks back over the years, we haven't turned out all that bad. There must be something good about what happened there.

TDR: You were in Alpha Delta. What's your sense of the state of the fraternity system?
JS: The fraternities that I have seen have not only done some good things in the community and on campus, but have done a lot for the social patterns at the College. I'm sure there are abuses and there always have been. I don't think that one can eliminate an occasional abuse. I've been impressed with what I've seen of the fraternities; I've seen news recently about the rushes and the renewed interest in belonging to a fraternity.

TDR: How do you think the average student sees the average alumnus?
JS: When I was an undergraduate, I felt very close to the alumni, very involved, and felt that they were pillars of strength for the College. I have the feeling now, though, that that's no longer true, that many of the undergraduates are in a vacuum in terms of the alumni. We should be closer.

TDR: What would help bring that closeness about?
JS: I hope that we could get some of the undergraduate news media to the alumni. Most of these alumni get only the bulletins or the *Dartmouth Alumni Magazine* or the letters that come out from the administrator's office. It would be nice if some of the undergraduate publications could get into more alumni hands.

June 7, 1980

The Steel Affair: Who Really Cheated?
by Gregory Fossedal, Benjamin Hart & the Editors

AFTER MONTHS OF DEBATE, John Steel '54 has been officially seated as a Trustee of Dartmouth College. The results, however—broken agreements by College employees, an embarrassing investigation into the Steel ballot statement, conflicting administration accounts of the involvement of high Parkhurst officials—have left both Steel supporters and Steel opponents grumbling.

The just-released investigation report, compiled by a special Alumni Association committee, resolves few of these issues. In question is the conduct of five men: Steel, Alumni Association President John French,

College Secretary Michael McGean, Steel supporter Avery Raube, and President of the College John G. Kemeny.

French complains that the Trustees did not grant the investigative committee sufficient authority to address the central question: "Was Steel's conduct dishonest?" Raube counters that the real questions center around French, McGean, and Kemeny: Did the administration break numerous agreements by chance, or as a result of a central strategy to discredit Steel? And if there was such a strategy, by whom was it directed?

The Dartmouth Review, granted access to several heretofore confidential documents, compiled a series of charges and facts that shed new light on the Steel affair. They raise the question: who really cheated?

Charge: McGean, who collected and counted the ballots, broke several agreements between his office and Steel regarding vote tallying, opening the possibility of tampering with several thousand alumni votes.

The Alumni Committee Report: does not comment on the alleged violations.

Facts: McGean opened and counted the first four thousand ballots to arrive back from the alumni ballot mailing of nearly 40,000. McGean says he had established that procedure in a prior Trustee election (1977), and that "once Steel objected to that procedure, it was changed."

Yet Steel cites three conversations—one in November, one in December, one in April—in which McGean agreed to open ballots only after Steel representatives arrived to participate in the counting. McGean told Steel he would "not consider opening any envelopes containing ballots until your representatives are here in my office to help count them."

On the first day ballots arrived, though, McGean told Steel observers that they could only count the number of envelopes, not the votes—a procedure he said protected the results of the voting, as final counting would be subject to scrutiny at the May 23, 1980 final counting. When Steel supporters pointed out that votes could be observed through the envelopes—thus enabling McGean to discard Steel votes if he so chose—McGean said he was compelled to count the votes and would continue to do so under "my own constitution." Steel representatives protested, but McGean continued to exclude them from the counting for several days.

Steel flew to Hanover on May 8 and hired counsel to work for an injunction to prevent further opening of the ballots. Gary Clark, the College attorney, was called in to negotiate with Steel. The four thousand opened ballots were placed in Clark's safe and McGean was forced to leave the next eight thousand ballots sealed; McGean set May 23 as the date for opening and counting the ballots in the presence of Steel representatives.

Charge: Kemeny knew about and encouraged efforts to defeat Steel first by altering the ballot statement, then by launching investigations into the Steel statement as released.

The Alumni Committee Report: does not comment on the alleged involvement.

Facts: Alexander Fanelli, assistant to Kemeny, told the *Review* in June that he had never discussed the Steel election with Kemeny. Yet independent sources in Parkhurst says Kemeny and Fanelli spent hours discussing Steel and the implications of his victory.

Moreover, French and McGean could not account for their failure to consult Kemeny's office on any of several matters that were eventually brought before the Trustees. One College official told the *Review* that Kemeny threatened to resign if Steel were approved at the Trustees' June meeting.

Kemeny and Fanelli continue to deny ever having held any position on the Steel candidacy—even though Steel was an outspoken critic of Kemeny's policies on the Indian symbol, the Kemeny Plan of trimester terms and required summer enrollment, and the establishment of separate minority organizations among alumni and on campus.

September 26, 1980

Will the Administration Eliminate Trustee Elections?

by Benjamin Hart

T HERE'S A LOT of talk going around that the procedure for electing Dartmouth trustees is going to be changed in some as-yet-undefined way. A letter has been circulated among the trustees hinting strongly at such a design, and in September an editorial in the *Daily Dartmouth* arrived "independently" at the conclusion that trustee elections ought to be "de-politicized."

This anxiety about elections clearly proceeds from the fact that in the last election the liberals lost in a landslide. Now the same people who for years have denounced the governments of Pinochet, Franco, and the Shah are leaning towards having no elections at all. Some of the more conscientious say, however, that eliminating elections completely from the process of selecting new trustees would be going too far. They say we should permit elections, but prevent the candidates from making any positional statements on the ballot.

To those busily canvassing these and other options on how new trustees can be selected, and at the same time preventing the future election on someone who holds the same views as Steel, the opinions and votes of Dartmouth alumni are obviously a nuisance.

What does "de-politicization" of trustee elections really mean? It means that if someone agrees with the prevailing drift of things at Dartmouth, that is "not political." If he disagrees—he's being obnoxiously "political."

If you think that the Hovey Grill murals of college founder Eleazar Wheelock are obnoxious and racist, but that the Orozco murals in Baker Library have no ethnic content, then you are not political. If you reverse those judgments, well, I'm afraid that you're being political.

Steel's election sent shock waves through the entire officialdom here.

Under the current rules, it is possible to nominate a candidate by petition to run against the choice of the Alumni Council which, on this occasion, was Raymond Rassenberger. Steel received the required number of signatures and his name was placed on the ballot, which was mailed to all Dartmouth alumni. Steel was generally perceived as the more traditional of the two candidates, supporting freedom of speech on even such sensitive issues as whether or not students should be allowed to look at the Hovey Grill murals, covered up by the Kemeny administration in 1979.

Kemeny has correctly interpreted the election of Steel as a renunciation of at least some of his policies. "Different opinions," I am told by College attorney Gary Clark, "can be divisive." That is the party line at Dartmouth, a liberal arts college devoted to free expression and open debate.

Our local administrators must have a very low opinion of the alumni if they think that a Dartmouth graduate is incapable of choosing between more than one candidate in an election, or more than one point of view on what is taking place at the College.

Suppose President Carter goes on television to announce that there can be no more elections because he does not trust the ability of the American people to make a decision; all members of Congress from now on will be chosen by the president.

Suppose President Carter announced that Ronald Reagan's and John Anderson's opinions "are divisive" because they disagree with his; therefore we can have no more elections.

Suppose President Carter announces that the whole process of selecting our governing officials "should be de-politicized."

If he said that, he wouldn't be president for long. It is not surprising, however, that some people want to eliminate the possibility of ever having another trustee election.

Devotion to democratic procedures is not always as firm as it may appear. An article in the magazine *Technology Review* by President Kemeny has raised some questions about his own commitment to the vote. What he calls "Jeffersonian democracy," he says, cannot work in the complicated world of the 1980s:

> My last point, and the most important one, is for our nation to recognize that
> the present system does not work. It was designed for a much earlier and

simpler age. Even 200 years ago, the founding fathers made choices. They opted for democracy, but they did not opt for Athenian democracy. It would have been totally impractical to use an antiquated model that called citizens into the market place to vote on every issue as it occurred. And yet today we have essentially the same system, now itself outmoded, that we had 200 years ago. It is time to rethink the issue, because I believe that Jeffersonian democracy cannot work in the year 1980—the world has become too complex.

The desire manifested throughout this piece is for a government by "experts." Only expert opinion counts. It seems clear that at Dartmouth the opinion of "non-experts"—that is, Dartmouth alumni—is an official embarrassment.

Just why are alumni regarded with such suspicion and hostility? After all, they are products of a Dartmouth liberal arts education.

There seems to be a fear that alumni will "intervene"—interesting word—in the affairs of the College. Actually the opposite is true.

The alumni have been remarkably reluctant to intervene in the policy-making process of the administration. In the 200-year history of Dartmouth College, there have been only two legitimate trustee elections. On 188 occasions, the alumni have mutely accepted the choice of the Alumni Council.

The fact that on this occasion the alumni felt they could not accept the decision of the Alumni Council to nominate Raymond Rasenberger for trustee shows that there is something seriously wrong with their perception of Dartmouth College. For only the second time in Dartmouth's history a trustee election was held. Steel won. The bureaucrats lost.

They would prefer that no one knew—especially the alumni—what was happening behind those closed doors upstairs in the administration offices of Parkhurst Hall, because what is happening up there can't stand the light of day.

October 17, 1980

The Role of Alumni:
An Interview with William F. Buckley Jr.
by Dinesh D'Souza

T HE DARTMOUTH REVIEW: You wrote *God and Man at Yale* in 1951. Here you documented the fundamental assumptions at the time behind the Ivy League education, assumptions that, far from assigning equal weight to different doctrines, were demonstrably biased in favor of an anti-Christian, anti-free-market doctrine. Would you comment on the role of the alumni in a college like Dartmouth today, in view of the conservative movement at the College, the upcoming trustee elections, and a possible fruition of the solutions outlined in your famous book?

WILLIAM F. BUCKLEY JR.: I felt a very distinctive condescension, when I wrote my book, toward anybody who sought to argue about what it was like to sustain an undergraduate experience. That was something quite sacrosanct, and I would not dream of asking an alumnus about it. The principles which are at stake, for instance, in your alumni election, however, are general in their application: namely, a college, to a relevant extent, is an instrument for the preservation of the values which its alumni hold and foster. You have got to answer yes to this, because if you answer no, I am at a loss to come up with another reason for private colleges existing, as opposed to state colleges. If alumni are going to finance the College, they cannot be perceived as inactive agents who visit the area once a year for the annual stimulation of their philanthropic glands.

TDR: You think private colleges should be a weighted average of the opinions of its alumni?

WFB: I wouldn't make it that mechanical. What I would say is that the opinion of the alumni of the College should figure, and that a private college should buff the zeitgeist. Its policies are thus determined by whoever wins the elected governorship, who appoints trustees under him, who appoints officers to serve them, and so on.

TDR: We are quite popular with alumni, but students and administration at the College often react to the *Review* with outrage, which we admittedly often enjoy. But as an outsider to Dartmouth, do you read the paper, and if so, what do you think of its style and content?

WFB: I am a professional editor, and the way I edit could very well be a little different from the way that you edit. If you are asking me whether I would find anything in *The Dartmouth Review* worth revising, I would say, sure. But my impression of it is that it is serious—in the best sense of the word, not in the pompous sense of the word—it is lively; it has spirit; and it has a considerable capacity to meditate its own weaknesses. The fact that you publish an awful lot of letters that almost always say unpleasant things about you—I think that's always healthy. It's something completely alien to the totalitarian and Nazi experiences.

I think *The Dartmouth Review* is an exciting and lively publication. I would hope that the Dartmouth administration would welcome the paper, especially as its rhetoric pays so much attention to the vigorous exchange of ideas.

April 13, 1981

ON THE RIGHT
Carnival Time in Dartmouth
by William F. Buckley Jr.

A SEASON OR TWO BACK Dartmouth College was in the news when two or three students, in a moment of high exuberance, skated across the ice between periods at a hockey game, wearing Indian feathers and whooping a war cry. The crowd loved it, the Indian having, of course, been the totemic symbol of Dartmouth for a couple of hundred years. The authorities, on the other hand, all but assembled the Nuremberg Tribunal to try the students for genocide. If you have lost the point, it is this: that the perpetuation of the Indian symbol is deemed offensive by official Dartmouth to an ethnic minority. Since no alumnus of Dartmouth has been known to have harbored an unfriendly thought against Indians since Sitting Bull's excesses at Little Big Horn faded from memory, the alumni began to fidget, wondering whether the administration at Dartmouth had adopted fresh and trendy totemic symbols of their own, far more mischievous than the innocent Indian head.

Enter a Californian alumnus: Dr. John Steel, who announced himself as a candidate for trustee on a petition ballot. The administration hurled its considerable resources against Steel, but he won in a walk and survived easily against a procedural challenge. Dr. Steel came in determined that Dartmouth should not succumb to modernist trends of which examples in most progressive institutions of higher learning abound, where tradition and piety are scorned, injustices sociologized, and the state glorified, patriotism patronized.

Meanwhile, the undergraduates had become restive. Most colleges are deeply influenced by the presence of forceful men who are concerned with public issues and willing to give students their time. Mostly, in the past period, such professors have been active on the civil rights front, in denouncing the Vietnam war, nuclear energy, McCarthyism, or whatever. At Dartmouth, Professor Jeffrey Hart not only teaches profound and popular courses in English; he is ubiquitous in challenging the modernist icons by writing books, a syndicated column, and making himself available to any Dartmouth students who want academic or political advice and encouragement. His presence has catalyzed an entire generation of Dartmouth students, whose turn to the right anticipated the Republic's last November.

Recently, these students founded their own weekly newspaper, which is a vibrant, joyful, provocative challenge to the regnant but brittle liberalism for which American colleges are renowned. The Dartmouth administration foolishly attempted to deprive the journal of the right to use the name "Dartmouth" on its logo, such was its desperation.

But there was more on the horizon. A few weeks ago, two young graduates, who have already distinguished themselves in their respective fields, announced that they would run for trustee. The conservative weekly undertook to arrange to interview the two candidates in order to ask them questions about their educational philosophy.

Now it is widely known but seldom enunciated that college trustees are supposed to attend meetings, purr as orchestrated by the president, and then go home and raise money. The administration, learning that two men were actually proposing to advise the alumni of Dartmouth on their views of educational policy, had yet another legal fit, advising candidates that any such ventilation of their views would disqualify them under the by-laws for consideration. A lawyer for the dissidents replied, in a rather energetic letter, that the administration should acquaint itself with the First Amendment to the Constitution before seeking to deny Dartmouth alumni the right to advise other Dartmouth alumni of their views, the better to inform them who to vote for.

The ballots will be sent out in due course, and it is just possible that Dartmouth will do for the academic world what Reagan has done for the political world, and incidentally avenge poor General Custer.

April 11, 1981; printed in The Dartmouth Review *April 20, 1981*

Shysters

The Week in Review

HERE'S A REFRESHER COURSE on how the College strenuously avoids conflict of interest: One of Dartmouth's leading consulting firms, Orr and Reno, is based in Concord, New Hampshire. The College has refused to disclose the amount of money it spends with the firm, but sources at the firm admit it is in the hundreds of thousands of dollars.

When the Steel election erupted into a major controversy last year, the trustees decided to hire an "independent firm" to conduct an investigation of improprieties in the campaign. The firm? Orr and Reno.

During that investigation, Dartmouth professor Jeffrey Hart received a phone call informing him that his signed confirmation of support for Steel was unacceptable. The call came from a young lawyer named Thomas Rath. Rath's firm? Orr and Reno.

In November of 1980, *The Dartmouth Review* attempted to incorporate in the state of New Hampshire under the name, of all things, "The Dartmouth Review, Inc." The request was refused by a New Hampshire official named, of all things, Thomas Rath, of Orr and Reno.

Just this April, Dartmouth began another controversial trustee election—so controversial that the secretary of its ballot committee, Ed Scheu, resigned. The College needed a new secretary, and the situation seemed desperate until someone suggested the name of an aggressive young impartial attorney down in Concord. His name? Thomas Rath. His firm? Orr and Reno.

May 25, 1981

Trustee Candidate Announcements
by Gerald Hughes

FOR THE FOURTH TIME in Dartmouth's history a group of alumni will be challenging the College's chosen candidates in a trustee election. Two of the present trustees, Robert Field '43 and Ronald Schram '64, will be seeking reelection for their seats this spring. They will be opposed by Daniel E. Provost III '42 and Steve Kelley '81, two candidates who have been chosen by the Alumni Committee for a Strong Dartmouth, a group that feels that the College's candidates do not effectively represent the interests of the alumni.

Provost is a former senior executive of Grand Met Inc., and is now retired. Kelley is a former cartoonist for the *Daily Dartmouth* and *The Dartmouth Review*, and is now on the editorial staff of *The San Diego Union*. His cartoons are syndicated nationwide in over 100 papers.

The Alumni Committee will attempt to secure nomination petitions of 250 signatures for each of its candidates by April 5, 1986 in order to add the candidates to the ballots that will be mailed to forty thousand alumni on April 21. One of the founders of the committee, Avery Raube '30, is confident from the support that the group has already received that the signatures will be collected without difficulty.

Raube, who was involved in the election of Dr. John Steel as a challenge nominee in 1980, first spoke to Provost and Kelley of the need for two alternate candidates in the election. According to Raube, "The cause of all of Dartmouth's problems is fundamental. It is suffering because its supreme authority has not been providing strong and decisive leadership." He feels that Provost and Kelley are the "good, top people who will make the sensible decisions" that will strengthen the leadership in the Board of Trustees.

The two challenging candidates question the actions of the College on a number of specific issues, most of which are directly related to the effectiveness of the trustees in exercising their authority at the College. Kelley cites as one of the main problems the administration's reacting to crises, but not taking the initiative itself to guide the College. "The College," he says, "needs to spend less time reacting to crises and more time seeking out clear, cogent positions which will prevent the crises of the past."

Provost also cites as one of his major concerns the quality of the Dartmouth education, which he thinks "could be much better." Specifically, he would like to see the elimination of "frivolous courses," such as women's and black studies, and of lowered standards adopted to fulfill goals of minority admissions.

According to Kelley, the way that the College has implemented the Principle of Community has also hurt the intellectual quality of life at Dartmouth. He claims that the administration is turning Dartmouth into a "non-entity with no character" by implementing a policy that says no one can do anything that might offend anyone.

The group supporting Provost and Kelley are also concerned that the College has failed to attempt to maintain good relations with the alumni. Raube calls for "the Board to end the longest and most divisive issue on campus by bringing back the Indian symbol, an issue that has assumed great magnitude for thousands of alumni."

Raube feels that the Alumni Committee for a Strong Dartmouth is representative of a vast segment of the Dartmouth alumni. It includes members of fifty-five classes, among whom are former trustees and Alumni council members, college professors and presidents, elected officials at the state and federal levels, members of the national judiciary, and members of the major ethnic groups, including Native Americans.

The challenging of candidates chosen for election by the Alumni Council has in the past been a rare and controversial event. While the provision is made for other alumni candidates to be entered onto the ballot by a petition of 250 signatures, it is something that has been openly fought by the College administrators concerned with dealing with the alumni. In 1980 Dr. John Steel was put forward by a group called the Committee of Concerned Dartmouth Alumni as an alternate candidate to the Alumni Council's choice of Raymond Rasenburger '49. Steel was elected by a large margin of a substantial alumni vote, and the trustees attempted, unsuccessfully, to refuse to sit him on the Board. He has since served as a responsible spokesman of alumni concerns.

Again in 1981, two of the council's candidates, Schram and Field in their first election, were challenged by Malcolm Beard '68 and T. Coleman Andrews '76. The Alumni Council was accused of mailing letters biased against the two challengers to alumni. Beard and Andrews were charged with violating a regulation that was adopted after the election of Steel against organized campaigning for trustee elections. Schram and Field won the election, but their victory was protested by the resignation of Edmund Scheu '46 as acting secretary of the election balloting committee.

Again, some trustees are making an issue out of the challenge process.

Field, one of the challenged trustees, said to the *Review*, "I don't feel that it is good for the College; I don't feel that it is good for the Alumni Association." He feels that because the Alumni Council's process of choosing a candidate seeks extensively to determine the needs of the alumni and the Board, it is harmful and divisive for an outside candidate to run. The provision exists "as a reasonable safety valve" to protect against the Council doing anything drastically wrong, but otherwise "the process is not conducive to harmony on the Dartmouth campus."

Kelley's view is quite different. He believes that "it is ironic that challenging candidates are something that the College doesn't like." For Kelley, an open election is a healthy process, and to oppose it defies American democratic traditions.

February 26, 1986

Following the election of John Steel, no petition candidate ran successfully against the Dartmouth Alumni Council slate for over twenty years.

Take Five

Reviewing the *Review:*
An Editor's Assessment
by Dinesh D'Souza

I T IS UNCOMMON for an editor to criticize his own paper. I have never seen it done before, and I suppose it would be considered inappropriate, self-deprecating, maniacal.

And yet *The Dartmouth Review* has strayed so far from its original goals and perspectives and is steam-rolling ahead with such impetuosity that I am compelled to issue a warning.

The *Review* has published five issues now, and it has yet to approve a statement of newspaper policy. Top editors argue such a policy is, by its nature, restrictive. They say the *Review* should be a "champion of free speech."

This is a specious and irresponsible stance. Freedom is the right of exemption from external control, and I will defend it. But the word for liberating oneself from internal control is not freedom but anarchy. Freedom says you can go out and shout nonsense if you want to, but having the right to do so doesn't mean you should; doing so just because you can reflects childishness and irresponsibility. In other words, freedom tolerates contradiction and confusion, but the *Review* doesn't have to.

The *Review* has chosen a conservative perspective, and that is fine. In its zeal to aggressively push this conservative philosophy, however, the *Review* is unfortunately compromising both accuracy and journalistic taste.

Point of accuracy: In a follow-up quip to the infamous John Steel story, the October 2, 1980 issue of the *Review* claimed John French controlled and chaired the Alumni Council. The fact is, John French is not even a member of the Alumni Council, but rather the chairman of an obscure committee, The General Association of Dartmouth Alumni, which supervised the election. French had no control whatsoever of the Alumni Council nominee election process.

The *Review* is going to change. It cannot proceed with this barrage of proselytizing ultra-rightist garbage. It has got to become what it was set up to become: a responsible, bold publication of conservative opinion.

The paper's other function—to report courageously and aggressively—has been well served. The *Review*, despite being a weekly, has on several occasions scooped the *Daily Dartmouth*, which seems to bleed from the competition. Point in question: Our story on the Foley House fraternity's apparent victimization by the College under the guise of "procedural application," unearthed by Joanne McMullen, took the *Daily Dartmouth* by surprise.

The *Review* has additionally submitted many constructive criticisms of the College institution—staggered lunch breaks, Saturday Hinman delivery, the Hopkins Center's stifling of competitive events, etc.—although these have often been lost under a veneer of ideological rhetoric.

What the *Review* is not here to be: a political tool of ultra-conservative alumni; a force for bringing back the Indian symbol (I don't give a damn about the symbol); unseating President Kemeny; selecting a conservative president; electing Ronald Reagan; or maligning John French (believe it or not).

What the *Review* is here to do: Publish unbiased, reliable articles without fear of administration clamps; run reasonable conservative columns; criticize constructively; establish coherent editorial policy; avoid fun at the expense of others (some items in the Week in Review); and settle disputes with the College amiably.

The *Review* is going to have to change course.

October 17, 1980

The First Case

CCSC Takes Fossedal to Task
by Dinesh D'Souza

IF YOU WERE before a tribunal at which the charges were not specified; at which challenges to the competence of the tribunal were voted on by the tribunal itself; at which clear contradictions in the testimony of key witnesses were not explored; at which apparent lies were told, but were ignored; at which no offense was established; and which handed down a verdict of guilty after a half-hour confab—you would be, well, where, at a trial in Bulgaria? Up on charges before the Ayatollah?

Wrong. You're facing the College Committee on Standing and Conduct (CCSC) at Dartmouth College. Where your rights are suspended. And where you can be kicked out of college on the say-so of demonstrably unreliable witnesses.

Greg Fossedal, editor of *The Dartmouth Review* facing this remarkable tribunal, had some advantages. He had a lawyer. He had the advantage of public notice and an open hearing, covered by the press. Most students who go before the CCSC go alone, without a lawyer, and have their fates decided in closed and, by regulation, secret, hearings.

In what follows, some of the most outrageous features of the Fossedal hearing are documented.

You are not reading Kafka. You are not reading Orwell. You are reading about the facts of current Dartmouth history.

The Date: February 25, 1981.
The Time: 3:30 p.m. until 12:30 a.m. the next day.
The Defendant: Gregory A. Fossedal '81.
The Prosecution: College Committee on Standing and Conduct.
The Judges: College Committee on Standing and Conduct.
The Charge: CCSC Chairman Michael Green refused to specify or clarify charges. The charges were later identified as Misappropriation and Violation of the Honor Principle.

The Verdict: Fossedal was ruled innocent of Honor Principle Violations for insufficient evidence, and guilty of Misappropriation.

The Penalty: College Discipline. A letter of complaint will be sent to Fossedal's parents, and he may be kept from participation in College-sponsored activities. Notice of his conviction will remain on his records until his graduation this spring. Fossedal has appealed the decision to Dean Manuel.

Sometime between January 15 and 18, Fossedal allegedly entered the Office of Information Services to visit the student intern, during which time he saw a news release concerning a possible cancer discovery by a faculty member of the Dartmouth Medical School hanging on a hook marked "cleared for release."

The release, which Information Services Director Robert Graham later claimed was confidential and being held until the publication of the researcher's findings in a prestigious medical journal, supposedly interested Fossedal, a correspondent for the *Union Leader*, who made a photocopy of the release. The rewritten story was sent down the following Monday to the *Union Leader* on the telecopying machine in the Information Services office.

Publication of the release in the *Union Leader* angered Dr. Leo Zacharski, the researcher who claimed to have discovered that a blood coagulant called Warfarin helped cure lung cancer. Zacharski, in conjunction with two of his supervisors, wrote letters to College authorities claiming that the effect of Fossedal's premature publication of a sensitive discovery in a popular newspaper was to jeopardize both Zacharski's professional career and research funding for the medical profession. The doctors called for Fossedal's dismissal from the College.

Before the testimony of the hearing, Fossedal's attorney Clauson challenged the impartiality of six members of the committee: Chairman Green, Acting Dean of Freshmen Almon Ives, Assistant Dean of Students Ann Smallwood, Professor of Physics Elisha Huggins, Philippa Guthrie '82, and Cynthia Woodward '82. The committee voted separately on each challenge, and refused to sustain any of the objections.

In one particularly surprising challenge:

> CLAUSON: The challenge would be to Professor Green.
>
> GREEN: Excuse me. The vice-chairman will sit in this chair.
>
> CLAUSON: I am amazed that Mr. Green has not already disqualified himself. The relationship between *The Dartmouth Review* and Professor Green has been probably the worst of any of the members of the Committee, which is to say something, because it's not been good with the Committee in general . . .

I had the privilege to read a long article in last week's *Dartmouth Review*, which in essence explained how badly this Committee has been run under the chairmanship of Professor Green, and went through any number of specific cases and attempted to state exactly what the Committee has done which is offensive to most of our notions of fair play.

Certainly if anything in the article in *The Dartmouth Review* is anywhere close to being true on any occasions, then my notions of free play—everything I have ever learned about due process—is offended . . .

HUGGINS: Do you wish to disqualify yourself?

GREEN: I believe I can sit. [Laughter.]

Though Attorney Clauson protested Dean Smallwood's animosity toward the *Review*, the dean said, "I see no reason why I can't be objective."

Clauson also attacked the procedure of challenged members of the Committee voting on other members. "I can tell you that in no judicial proceeding would judges who have been attacked because of their impartiality leave the room and vote on whether the remaining judge gets to sit as part of the hearing." Green defended the procedure on the grounds that the CCSC is not judicial, but rather an administrative committee.

The charges facing Fossedal were contained in six letters: a letter dated January 20, from Zacharski to Dean Russell Stearns; a letter dated January 22, from Dr. Bush to Stearns; a letter dated January 22, from Dr. Green to Stearns; a letter dated January 26, from Graham to Stearns; and two statements of charge from Stearns to Attorney Clauson, which incorporated the above four letters.

Dean Stearns announced the formal charges of misappropriation and violation of the honor principle. Green, however, said these were by no means all the charges facing Fossedal. "It's going to be necessary for you to interpret the charges for your client; we will proceed with the hearing," he said. Steven Godcheaux '81, CCSC member, said, "If you feel that your violation or alleged violation is a grievous act of some sort, I suggest that you address yourself to that." His remark was met with laughter from the audience.

Witnesses in the hearing included Dr. Zacharski, Graham, the student intern, Dr. Bush, and Dr. Green. The three doctors attempted to explain why they believed the premature publication of the news release could be detrimental to the scientific community and Dr. Zacharski's career. Graham described his understanding that Fossedal entered the Information Office on Sunday, January 18, and helped himself to the release marked "hold" on the wall. The student intern denied any particular knowledge of the circumstances under which the release had been taken.

Fossedal spoke last and claimed that on Thursday or Friday afternoon he had walked into the Information Office, and while waiting to talk to

Graham spotted the news release on the wall. "I didn't think much of it, because I have seen a lot of press offices; they are public offices, and press releases are like toilet paper," Fossedal said. After allegedly obtaining permission from a secretary to use the photocopier, Fossedal said he copied the release and left it in his room for a few days.

On Monday, January 19, Fossedal said he rewrote the release, returned to the Information Office, and sent it over the teletype to the *Union Leader*. Graham's secretary helped him use the teletype machine, because he was not accustomed to the magnetic device, Fossedal said.

When the uproar arose following publication of the release, which was being held in the Information Office until the publication of Dr. Zacharski's research in the *Journal of the American Medical Association*, Fossedal said he was very surprised because "it would never occur to me that someone who wanted something kept secret would hang it up on a wall, on a peg marked 'ready for release.'"

On just which peg the release was hanging at the time it was photocopied by Fossedal was a matter of debate. Graham said the release was attached to a pink slip marked "hold" and "cleared by Zacharski."

Both Zacharski and Graham denied that the release was scheduled for any special concealment. Graham said no reporter had ever used a pending release from the wall without his permission in the past. Zacharski testified that the release was a "very preliminary draft" that was not ready for publication, and needed further scrutiny and approval. Clauson raised the question with Graham:

> CLAUSON: Then you do remember that the slip said "cleared by Dr. Zacharski." My impression of the way you guys deal with that means that Dr. Zacharski had read this draft and this draft is set to go out once the publication comes out.
>
> GRAHAM: That is correct.
>
> CLAUSON: Dr. Zacharski told us that the draft wasn't ready to go out, he hadn't cleared it. In fact, he was somewhat unhappy with the way it was written, and it was going to have to be rewritten before it is published. Can you comment on that?
>
> GRAHAM: No, I can't. It's the first I've ever heard of . . .

Clauson pointed out later that Zacharski's testimony contained several contradictions, including his claim that he did not discuss the writing of letters calling for Fossedal's dismissal with Dr. Bush, and a statement that he had not helped Julia King of the *Valley News* write her news story concerning the cancer discovery.

> CLAUSON: Now, you know Dr. Bush and Dr. Green have also written

letters to Dean Stearns supporting your request and your views of all this. Did you discuss with them writing letters?

ZACHARSKI: No.

CLAUSON: Did you know they wrote letters?

ZACHARSKI: Afterwards I found out that they did.

[Four hours elapse.]

CLAUSON: You sent a copy of your letter to Dean Ralph Manuel?

BUSH: Correct.

CLAUSON: Why'd you send a copy to Dean Manuel?

BUSH: Zacharski sent a copy to Dean Manuel, and he suggested it would be appropriate for me to do so too.

CLAUSON: Did you discuss the sending of your letter with Dr. Zacharski?

BUSH: Indeed.

CLAUSON: So you had a chance to review his letter, and then you had a chance to draft yours and discuss the matter with him?

BUSH: Correct.

Dr. Ian Bush claimed that the article in the *Union Leader* was not inaccurate in substance, but was deceptive because "it is written in a style that implies that Dr. Zacharski released material in the form of an interview to the correspondent writing the article." Fossedal claimed that the draft he sent down to the *Union Leader* credited the Office of Information Services, but an editorial misunderstanding had led to his byline appearing below the column, a statement confirmed by sources at the *Union Leader*.

Bush said in addition to Fossedal's dismissal he wanted a disclaimer in the *Union Leader* claiming that Dr. Zacharski had nothing to do with the publication of the release. Bush said separation from the College was not too serious a penalty for Fossedal because, "when one considers the value of the object stolen, when one considers the responsibility or degree of the person involved, when one considers the use of the stolen material—you can take all those three as a pretty serious grievance."

Professor Jeffrey Hart, an advisor to Fossedal, took up the matter:

HART: Dr. Bush, you have used the word "stolen." What knowledge do you have of the circumstances under which the story passed into the hands of Greg Fossedal?

BUSH: I said, I understood from Dr. Zacharski that it had been stolen, and I understood from the beginning of this proceeding that the specific complaint against Mr. Fossedal involved misappropriation.

HART: You knew nothing of the actual circumstances?

BUSH: I am not a detective, and I told you quite clearly where I got my information and what my understanding was.

HART: Do you habitually reach conclusions in the absence of facts?

The College's attorney, Sherman Horton of Nashua, confessed toward the end of the hearing that he did not believe Fossedal would be found guilty. "Why are you asking all these legalistic questions? They aren't going to find him guilty," Horton told a reporter for the *Review*.

Contacted the next day in Nashua, however, Horton denied the statement. He was partially intoxicated at the time, and had no recollection of the substance of the conversation, he said. "I did tell Clauson that, based on the evidence, I would be very surprised if Greg had been kicked out of school," Horton said. Overall, he said, the verdict had been fair and "I was able to rationalize in my mind all the testimony."

The student intern in the Information Office denied any knowledge of the circumstances under which the release was taken. "The first I heard of the missing release was Tuesday morning when it appeared in the *Union Leader*," he said.

As a reporter, however, he said it is neither uncommon nor unethical to use information publicly displayed in a public office, even without permission. "A smart reporter who came into Dr. Graham's office, looks over Maureen's desk, and sees a release that says the next President of the College is David McLaughlin would not hesitate to go back and put that in the paper . . . after confirming it by other sources."

The intern said he was embarrassed by the incident, however, because he had a specific agreement that information disseminated by the Information Services would be held confidential prior to release. "If I were just an editor, I would consider it good reporting. As an intern, I would not use it because of the confidentiality agreement between me and Mr. Graham," he said.

After the hearing, CCSC chairman Green clarified some terms for the *Review*. Earlier Clauson said Fossedal could not be guilty of misappropriation because information in a news release did not constitute property. Green said, "Misappropriation is taking something and converting it to a use for which it was not immediately intended."

THE DARTMOUTH REVIEW: I guess the handbook establishes the criterion of guilt or innocence as being "preponderance of evidence." How do you define "preponderance" in this case?

GREEN: Well, I guess "preponderance" means being more than half.

TDR: Doesn't that make the probability that an innocent person will be judged guilty to be very high?

GREEN: Well, I don't know, in an abstract sense. In practice, almost no one appearing before the CCSC denies having done what the deans have charged them with doing.

Green said he did not think the CCSC had lost trust among the students. "I really don't know," he said, "I am concerned about the breach of confidentiality (in the *Review*'s article two weeks ago). The committee as a fair institution within the campus community is jeopardized because if a student chooses to have a closed hearing, he makes that choice because he does not want his case known. If the principle of confidentiality has been breached, his rights to privacy have been violated."

Commenting on the hearing, Green said, "One of the things you have to realize is that what Mr. Clauson was doing was trying to bring in to a non-judicial system a set of values that prevail in a judicial system."

The student handbook states that the rights and obligations of a student before the CCSC do not abrogate his constitutional rights and obligations.

March 9, 1981

Fossedal on Trial
by Benjamin Hart

G REG FOSSEDAL'S CCSC hearing reached a critical turning point less than half an hour into the proceedings when he personally challenged the objectivity of Committee chairman Michael Green. Anyone who was at the hearing—and those who weren't should have been—knew that it was all downhill from there.

Acting in concert with his attorney, Bill Clauson, Fossedal had challenged several Committee members. Predictably, each professed objectivity; then the rest of the challenged members left the room for a secret vote and, surprise surprise, they found that their friend could, after all, sit in judgment of Fossedal.

Still, an expectant hush came across the room when Fossedal called the Committee chairman to task. Would Green really have the nerve to assert his own objectivity? And if he did, would the Committee back him up?

Green's relationship with Fossedal began February 25, 1979—exactly two years before Fossedal's roasting at the hands of Green's Committee, and over an incident that would lead the CCSC to vote to expel two students: the Indian skater protest.

On the Sunday afternoon that Shaun Teevens skated into Dartmouth history, Fossedal was working as sports editor for the *Daily Dartmouth*.

"I was laying out my page and helping with the news editing," Fossedal remembers. "Then in came one of my photographers who said he had a great picture of the Indian skaters. I told Judy Reardon, the layout editor, it should run front page. She didn't want to at first, but I convinced her. We even put in the Indian cheer as quote of the day.

"It was a simple decision. News is news." But not so to the emotionally charged Native American contingent at Dartmouth. Already angry over the mere appearance of the skaters, Native Americans at Dartmouth (NAD) penned a letter to the *Daily Dartmouth* blasting the paper's editorial judgment in printing the picture and the story. The letter was signed by, among others, Michael Green:

> That Dartmouth students choose to present themselves as racist caricatures is unfortunate; that the College newspaper elects to publicize this example of crass insensitivity without critical judgment is appalling. . . . Either the [*Daily*] *Dartmouth* should make a public explanation and apology for selecting this picture for the front page (and the "Indian cheer" for the quote of the day), or cease to pretend that it is a publication for all segments of the Dartmouth population.

The letter went on to call the paper's editors guilty of "blatant racism" and lashed out at its "anti-feminist and anti-semitic cartoons."

Things heated up in the spring following the incident. Lennie Pickard and Green were outspoken critics of John Kemeny's decision to keep the College out of a major lawsuit and avoid embarrassing national publicity by pardoning Teevens and the skaters, overturning the CCSC's vote to suspend. Pickard called the pardon the "most heinous and racist act" of any Dartmouth president.

In the summer of '79, Fossedal twice incurred the wrath of Native Americans at the College—first for a controversial interview with Indian symbol activist Jack Herpel '28, then for his work as editor of the *Daily Dartmouth*'s annual freshman issue, which is mailed out to matriculants each August.

"I was told our selection of photographs was abominable, clearly racist," Fossedal explains. "There were letters, telephone calls. Again, the lack of minority photos was seen as deliberate. Actually, it's the kind of thing I would never think of one way or the other. Who has time to count up pictures for ethnic content? I had courses to take."

Another small incident occurred in the spring of 1980 when Fossedal was in the middle of his controversial tenure as editor-in-chief of the *Daily Dartmouth*. Cathy Camp, a news editor for the paper, released excerpts from interviews with several minority students who alleged pervasive peer pressuring on the part of NAD and its black equivalent, the Afro-American Society. Fossedal and his executive editor decided to print the article after some agonizing and much editorial revising.

Even in its watered-down version, Camp's piece proved to be dynamite. Angry letters gushed in, and for Fossedal and the NADs, it was powwow time once again.

The formation of *The Dartmouth Review* sparked a renewal of the acrimony in the fall of 1980. In its first issue that term, the *Review* ran a cover collage of fifty years of Dartmouth football programs; the dominant motif was Indian-related. Green and other Native American leaders complained to the offices of Dean Ralph Manuel and John Hanson, who politely explained that there was nothing the College could do if the *Review* chose to revive the Dartmouth Indian.

At this point, things began to get nasty. On October 10, Fossedal wrote an editorial blasting the very existence of NAD as constituting "institutional racism." The editorial called for an end to affirmative action programs and urged the elimination of minority study departments and courses. Green is chairman of the Native American Studies department and depends for his livelihood on its existence. Green was not happy with the editorial.

The next week, Fossedal's editorial attacked Green personally for playing a leading role in the persecution of a student before the CCSC on charges of illegal possession of alcohol.

"I'll never forget walking into that meeting," Fossedal says. "There were at least fifty people packed into that little room in Blunt Alumni Center where they usually meet. Green kept giving me nasty glances and finally noticed I was taking notes. The exchange went something like this:

> GREEN: May I ask you to identify yourself?
>
> ME: My name is Greg Fossedal. I'm a reporter for *The Dartmouth Review*.
>
> GREEN: You're aware that you may not quote Committee members outside of this hearing.
>
> ME: No, I'm not aware of that. I thought this was a public hearing. That means that . . .
>
> ANNE CRAIG: When we wrote you last spring at the [*Daily Dartmouth*] we told you you could send a reporter but . . .
>
> ME: Look, this is a public hearing. That means everything is for the record. The choice of whether or not a hearing is public is to protect the defendant, not you. A public hearing means, by definition, that everything is for the record. And I'm going to quote what you say. If you want to amend your laws and not allow public hearings, that's fine, but I can report what I want as long as this is open.
>
> GREEN (still scowling): Well, we'll have to check the record on that.
>
> ME: Go ahead. You sent me a letter when I was at the [*Daily Dartmouth*] last year. You can't change the rules for a public hearing.
>
> GREEN: We operate under our own rules.

If Green was scowling at the meeting, he must have been steaming after reading Fossedal's editorial on October 17. The article quotes Green as saying, "We operate under our own rules," and concludes:

> Green's explanation of the CCSC's operating procedures is both accurate and enlightening. That his committee on student conduct operates with wide discretion, little restraint, and a great deal of vindictiveness is taken as a given on campus. That it has terrorized thousands of students and bullied those who come before it is fact.

Noting an editorial error under which his first name was incorrectly reported as Ronald, Green wrote:

"My name is Michael Green, not Ronald Green. The balance of your remarks on the CCSC in *The Review*, like your rendition of my name, is no more than half true." Green's letter appeared in *The Dartmouth Review*'s October 24 edition.

Fossedal issued a characteristic response: "Mr. Green—Your letter is both pompous and stupid. . . . The name of this publication is *The Dartmouth Review*, not *The Review*."

The ribbing between Fossedal and Green's Committee continued right into the new year, culminating in *The Dartmouth Review*'s CCSC issue several days before Fossedal's public trial. In a deep-cover investigative story by Fossedal and another *Review* staff member, Green's leadership of the CCSC was outlined in stark terms. One CCSC member was quoted in the article as saying Green was out to "get Teevens's ass" in a case that went before the CCSC in the fall of 1980 (the Indian skaters case). Another unabashedly referred to Green as a "racist." The day before the CCSC story appeared, Fossedal spoke before the committee in defense of Anthony Desir, another *Review* editor. Fossedal wore an Indian tie.

"I remember hearing that Green once bragged to the committee that he had been out tearing down Indian posters that were popping up on campus. I wanted to see what he would do with a necktie," Fossedal explained.

Other *Review* staff members threatened with trips before the Committee include myself and Steve Kelley, who dressed up as Indians at a pair of fall home football games, and Keeney Jones, who along with Fossedal hired a plane to fly above fans at the Columbia game, tugging a banner that read "The *Review* Says Go Indians!" The move to punish Kelley, myself, and Jones was apparently squashed in the office of Ralph Manuel. And so we waited quietly. Green told the Committee he could sit in impartial judgment on Fossedal. The CCSC went into the next room and voted: "We have decided not to sustain your challenge to Professor Green."

Fossedal sighed.

March 9, 1981

Fossedal Sues College
by Dinesh D'Souza

G REG FOSSEDAL has sued Dartmouth College for "maliciously and willfully" violating his rights of due process in last March's hearing of the College Committee on Standing and Conduct, in which Fossedal was found guilty of misappropriating a press release from the Dartmouth Office of Information Services.

Claiming that the College, witnesses at the hearing, and members of the CCSC were unduly biased against him, Fossedal has sued, in addition to the College, Dr. Leo Zacharski, a doctor whose research was allegedly released prematurely by Fossedal, and CCSC members Dave Shula, Michael Green, Steve Godcheaux, Elisha Huggins, Almon Ives, Ann Smallwood, Keith Walker, Cynthia Woodward, and Philippa Guthrie. The CCSC members are being sued "both as individuals and in their official capacity," according to a complaint document filed by Fossedal's attorney, William Clausen of Hanover, in the U.S. District Court for New Hampshire.

Individuals sued will be served documents by Federal Marshals in the next few days. They will be required to defend themselves against charges of prejudice and malice against Fossedal, which Fossedal claims has severely damaged his reputation and potentially hurt his career.

Fossedal's attorney has asked for a sum of $30,000 in damages, to be divided in a manner determined by the court.

The thirty students contacted by the *Review* had mixed reactions to the suit. Approximately fifteen students said they thought Fossedal received a relatively minor penalty for what they thought was a violation of college rules; some said the trial procedure was a farce. In a recent letter to the [*Daily Dartmouth*], Jim Kirschner '81 accused Fossedal of stealing the press release, and called *Review* staffers "thiefs [sic] and liars."

Charges against the College and members of the CCSC include:

—That they denied Fossedal a hearing before an impartial tribunal. CCSC members refused to disqualify themselves or others who had a special bias against Fossedal from the jury.
—The regulation violated was not reasonably specific.
—Fossedal did not have access to rights of due process.
—Defendant Dr. Zacharski presented exaggerated and untrue evidence for the purpose of blackening the case against Fossedal.

Fossedal said he was "deeply hurt" to have to take this action against Dartmouth College. He said he had heard from over a hundred students and alumni, who were not present at the hearing, claiming that he shouldn't have stolen the release. "There is no question that this has gravely hurt my reputation," Fossedal said, adding, "Even national media like *Newsweek* reported on the event as if it were fact."

Commenting on the suit, Clausen said, "Most students, I think, will have questions about the CCSC, but in view of the fact that Greg was convicted of misappropriation, they will think he is not honest." Clausen said two of Fossedal's constitutional rights—to due process as a citizen, and to First Amendment privileges as a reporter—were willfully denied him by the CCSC. The College has a contractual obligation to grant its students these rights, Clausen said.

Because the case involves First Amendment violations, it will be heard in federal court.

June 15, 1981

No Jive

What's Wrong with Affirmative Action?
by Dinesh D'Souza

THE RATIONALE for affirmative action is intuitively sound. Blacks have suffered environmental disadvantage arising from a history of discrimination and racial abuse, and even today they are accosted by racist provincialists. It seems quite sensible to institute some form of aid to enable blacks to combat the societal retardation they face, and to enjoy the equal opportunity guaranteed them by the Fourteenth Amendment.

Yet the present system of black favoritism has failed. Why do blacks, with few exceptions and without the aid of the Peter Principle, rise to posts of ineptitude, waved along by militant defenders of social justice? Why do competent blacks fare badly at colleges, finally slinking away into the cocoon of protective organizations such as the Afro-American Society? Most of all, why do liberals continue to applaud the screwed-up mechanism of affirmative action?

It must first be said that any social engineering is bound to create problems, because it runs contrary to the Darwinian free-market society we live in. Favoritism may provide a leg up on the social ladder, but anything more than a slight push can be disastrous. Upper rungs demand more from the individual, and those who can't hack it drop out. Thus even an adept black student at Dartmouth may suffer spastic grades and despondency because he is buckling under pressures he cannot endure. Perhaps he would have romped through Swarthmore or Oberlin, but Dartmouth didn't want to get off the honor list of the authorities in Washington, and so Dartmouth it is.

Institutionalized advantage, such as affirmative action, encourages laziness and inefficiency, because there is no incentive to work hard—one is guaranteed of promotion and success. The finesse demanded of other persons in society is not asked of a black, and being almost-good-enough has become a way of life.

Some blacks see affirmative action as a necessary vitamin to allow themselves to rival other people in society. But this dependency on the government—the coercive admissions and token employment—saps their confidence and pride.

Other blacks see the program as an arrogant effort on the part of the capitalists to appease their guilty consciences. This I-have-the-right-to-charity attitude becomes an excuse for social militancy, and failures can easily be blamed on inadequate social compensation for historical abuse.

The affirmative action scenario is abetted by the liberal bureaucracy, which has cajoled blacks into embracing its rationale, and is avidly pursuing the program for its own ends. Ever anxious to take on more social redemption—for a price, of course—the liberal bureaucrats find it in their interest to siphon off the public purse in the name of justice.

Affirmative Action blacks have additionally been hampered by the infiltration of liberal educators into the program. At the forefront of the affirmative action march is that touchy-feely smorgasbord of homosexuals, sociologists, lesbians, and feminists, who seem to believe that the purpose of education is emotional readjustment. Their idle rhetoric and shoddy scholarship have infected the minds of the blacks they woo. Burdened with an environment too arduous to endure, blacks are driven further down the social stratum. The black student must now take courses in feminism from the guy in jeans and ponytail to survive at Dartmouth.

Although affirmative action is always hailed as a "temporary measure," the bureaucracy it nourishes will never let it go. Remember that welfare was once intended to be a "transient" phenomenon.

Moreover, the program does nothing to change the attitudes of the ignorant and racially prejudiced, who only find confirmation of their belief that blacks are inferior to whites, and clearly seeking refuge in government programs.

If there is to be a successful affirmative action program, it must be monetarily, and not racially, based. It must apply to all poor people, not just blacks. It must be at one juncture of social development only, not at every stage. The black student may be admitted to Dartmouth despite his inadequate preparation, because he is bright and will bring variety to Hanover, but if he can't take the heat at an Ivy League school, he must be allowed to flunk out. Only the threat of failure will generate an awareness in blacks that social development is earned through hard work and struggling to overcome past inhibitions, and not by liberation marches and social demonstrations.

An affirmative action program that allows a single-stage leg up to poor people will, in any event, disproportionately help blacks. It will also dispel the notion that blacks as a race cannot survive the demands of modern American society. And the black student, when he chooses to take advantage of the affirmative action option, knows that it asks more, not less, of him. If he does not want to work extra-hard to catch up with preppies from Andover at Dartmouth, the black student will fail; this is a factor he must consider when he picks Dartmouth over Oberlin.

April 13, 1981

Dis Sho' Ain't No Jive, Bro
by Keeney Jones

S HEET! We be bucoo[1] riled, bro. Dem white mo-fo be sayin' 'firmative action ain't no good fo' us, cause it be puttin' down ac-demic standards. Dey be spoutin' 'bout how 'firmative action be no hep to black folk 'cross da nation, on account we be not doin' too well wit da GPAs and sheet.

Got dang! I tink dis be 'scusing the rollin' back of da civil rahts gains of da sixties. White folk be itchin' to be puttin' us back into fettas.[2] Dey be forgettin' we be 'mancipated. Sheet! Today, the 'ministration be slashin' dem free welfare lunches for us po' students. How we be 'posed to be gettin' our GPAs up when we don't be havin' no food? Dem lunch womans be spoonin' our sprigs cat-sup, and makin' racist comments 'bout our ility to work. You be expectin' us to tink, you best be giving us fus[3] dibs on da food line.

White folk be sayin' dat 'firmative action be 'complishin' frightful tings, which for dat not be da purpose. Dey be mouthin' 'bout how 'firmative action be racist, when at da same time dese folk be havin' black boys hodin' lantins[4] luminatin' da driveways up to dere pads. Dey be da mo-fo dat be oppressin' us all dese centuries. Dey be whuppin' us wit dere mouts an' wit da rawhide ta boot! We don't be likin' to see our sisters be sat on. We be risin' up, rallyin', singin' gospel songs, and stagin' de revolution.

Dat racist horro' be right in front cho eyes, yep, it even be in Hanova. It be in da 'guise of dat white boy, Keeney Jones. (By da way, I tink he be latherin' up wit pur Afro-Sheen, fo his light brown friz.) Jones be callin' us "Negroes"; for one ting we ain't be Negroes. We be da united black race. Some of us even be coalitionin' the Black Marti Farabundo Front. But we be smackin' dat Keeney 'pside 'is head, 'fhe keeps dis up.

Dese boys be sayin' that we be comin' here to Dartmut an' not takin' the classics. You know, Homa, Shakesphere, but I hea' dey all be co'd in da ground, six feet unda, and whatchu be askin' us to learn from dem? We be culturally lightened too. We be takin' hard courses in many subjects, like Afro-Am Studies, Women's Studies, and Policy Studies. And who be mouthin' 'bout us not bein' good read? I be practicly knowin' *Roots* cova to cova, til' my mine be boogying to da words! An' I be watchin' "The Jeffersons" on TV til I be blue in da face. Say what, mo-fo? I can't be blue? 'Scuse me. Sheet!

'Firmative action be havin' bad[5] 'fects on us blacks. It be hepin us git equal opp-tunity. Some of us be gettin' into Ivy schools from the inner city, even do we not be bustin' our gizzards doin' work. But where the Ivy be at? Now we be comin' to Dartmut and be up over our 'fros in studies, but we still be not graduatin' Phi Beta Kappa. Maybe dere should be anudda 'firmative action program 'bout dat. Sheet! Citations for blacks wit Cs would be bucoo nice.

But we still be havin' a long way to go. Dere still be many white trash try in' to put us down. We not jus' be referrin' to da Klan, wit dere white robes to match dere faces. Da head honcho of Exxon be a mo-fo racist too, jus like the bosses of udda corporations, 'cept if dey be black, of course. (We not be includin' dat Uncle Tom, Tom Sowell, in dis.) Once mo, I say loud and clear dat 'firmative action be the only pat[6] to our being 'cepted in 'ciety. Got dang!

'Fyu be wantin' to gape at the vantages of 'firmative action, den be lookin' ma way, bro. I be a mo-fo, got dang, bucoo, bad studier. Sheet! I also be makin' myse'f a wuthwhile piece of 'ciety by havin' many extra-curries. I be in the BUTA, a memba of da AAm, an' I also be playin' hoops fo' Alpha Phi. Til now I be writin' a lot, but I not be gettin' published by da campus papa's. Culturally 'oused 'gain! Makes me so mat.[7] What's mo, my birfday is comin' up, an' I be wantin' chocolate cake. But dey not be stockin' any at da Thayer, only vanilla. Mo 'scrimination! Sheet!

Ho'd on, now. I not be settin' out to be brutally 'tackin nobody. I only be hopin' to open a line of speakin' between all da college colors, but da only green we want in da 'scussion is Professa Michael Green. Dis communicatin' has got to be civilized, but at the same it betta be honest injun (no offense to da Native Americans on da campus). I'll be honest. I'll tell da truf. Dat is da fus 'quirement for 'scussion on dis, and I would aks[8] da Dartmut c-munity to do da same. Well, you know, it's like I say—to call a spade a spade.

1 bucoo—really
2 fettas—fetters
3 fus—first
4 lantins—lanterns
5 bad—good
6 pat—path
7 mat—mad
8 aks—ask

March 15, 1982

Don't Be Riled, Bro
The Week in Review

T HE LIBERALS appear to be in a frenzy over a certain item which appeared last term in this paper.

All right, you know what it is. Jones's "jive column," which was a defense of affirmative action written in mock black dialect.

Some observations:

1) The column was intended to be satire. Hence it was exaggerated. Of course, not all blacks talk like that. Some do. If none did no one would be upset.

2) The precedent for using racial dialect is sound. Ring Lardner did in *Damon Runyon*; Mark Twain did in *Huck Finn*. In fact, the most recent issue of *National Lampoon* has a parody about the effect on blacks of the reduction of federal programs—it includes long sections in jive.

3) Just as it is, of course, legitimate for a conservative to criticize affirmative action, it is legitimate to question jive. After all, if jive is—as some blacks claim—a viable alternative to English, what's wrong with a column written in just another language? We're broadening horizons, right?

4) Finally, not as disclaimer but just to reiterate a misunderstood fact, the jive column was just that—a column. It was signed. It did not, per se, represent editorial policy.

June 14, 1982

Charles J. Sykes, in The Hollow Men: Politics and Corruption in Higher Education *(Regnery Gateway, 1990), writes: "The* Review's *'jive' column, though signed by Keeney Jones, was, in fact, not written by him. It was reportedly based on notes taken by another* Review *staffer in her roommate's syntax and vocabulary, and was written into a satire by another senior staffer, and signed by Jones."*

For a detailed history of the first years of The Dartmouth Review, *see* The Hollow Men, *pages 231–306.*

Once Bitten

Another One Bites the Dust
The Week in Review

B ENJAMIN HART, founder of this newspaper, was assaulted and bitten by a black administrator of the College in the Blunt Alumni Center last Friday.

Hart was delivering issues of the newspaper (as he does each week), when Samuel Smith, associate director of the Alumni Fund, approached Hart and told him he could not distribute papers.

When Hart ignored him, Smith attacked Hart from behind, hitting his face and back. Hart held Smith in a headlock to stave him off, at which point Smith bit Hart in the right side.

Hart was treated for injuries at Mary Hitchcock Hospital and given a tetanus shot.

Smith was held back from his assault by Henry Eberhart, director of the Alumni Fund. Eberhart has been instructed by President McLaughlin to conduct an investigation of the incident.

Smith pleaded "no contest" to charges of assault Tuesday in Hanover Court and was convicted. He was fined $250 ($150 suspended) and sentenced to three months of probation.

The Smith attack is the last in a long series of incidents involving this newspaper and black radicals on campus.

The Afro-American society (AAm), Dartmouth's segregated black organization, has distributed a petition to students claiming that "*The Dartmouth Review* does not keep the Principle of Community."

It has mailed letters to alumni and friends charging that the newspaper is "racist and sexist." This is ironic, because the Afro-Am does not have a single white member and actually encourages a strong anti-white attitude on the part of its members.

Last Tuesday, upon urging from the AAm and the all-black fraternity Alpha Phi Alpha, a coterie of black faculty members introduced a petition "deploring" the journalism of *The Dartmouth Review*.

Classics Professor Edward Bradley, who introduced the motion in a faculty meeting, confessed that it was stimulated by the Smith assault.

In other words Bradley's motion to the faculty was intended to justify and balance Smith's attack of Benjamin Hart, which embarrassed the faculty and administration, and divert press attention away from the assault and toward the faculty motion.

The motion passed easily, which suggests that not only did the faculty admit that an environment of hostility toward this newspaper could make an assault like that of Mr. Smith possible, but that the Dartmouth faculty were going to come right out and congratulate Smith on his achievement.

This condonement of violence is not new to our faculty, which egged on radicals in the 1960s. In fact, after the Smith incident, an English professor here praised Smith's action to her dismayed class, arguing that Smith had acted "for higher principles."

We operate in a highly principled community, you see.

May 31, 1982

Reflections on a Crime
by the Editors

L AST FRIDAY MORNING, a Dartmouth senior was physically assaulted by a member of the Dartmouth administration. The assault occurred before many witnesses while the student was in the process of delivering copies of this newspaper to the Blunt Alumni Center.

The student was struck from behind by Samuel Smith, a Dartmouth administrator. Mr. Smith attempted to push the student through a plate glass door. In the fracas, the student's eyeglasses were broken. He was punched, kicked, and bitten. For the latter injury, he was treated at Dick's House.

Fortunately, the student was able to subdue the frenzied administrator before further damage.

A complaint of criminal assault has been filed against Mr. Smith, there may be civil suits, and it no doubt will take some time before the case makes its way through the courts to a legal resolution.

We wish, however, to make some observations that go beyond the legal issues involved.

What has occurred is bizarre and unthinkable, but not unpredictable. We see two principal factors as lying behind this crime, for both of which, we are sorry to say, two Dartmouth administrations bear a large measure of responsibility.

On this campus, over a period of several years, radical blacks have been led to understand that they are in some sense outside the law.

Repeated offenses have been overlooked, e.g., the vandalizing of a Winter Carnival sculpture, implicit threats of violence, as at a recent Undergraduate Council (UGC) meeting, and so forth.

In the local atmosphere, the charge of "racism" has been a catch-all category used to smear anyone who does not, on issues of public policy, go along to get along.

Casual lies about members of the Dartmouth community go unchallenged and uncensored in publications supported by the College.

There thus was created a climate of opinion in which the bizarre crime of Mr. Smith became, to some degree, predictable.

Then there is a second factor. From the beginning, the Dartmouth administration has grotesquely overreacted to *The Dartmouth Review*.

This newspaper has not been treated as another publication expressing its point of view, a publication among many, and, after all, a publication put out by undergraduates.

It has been subjected, from the start, to various kinds of harassment.

There has also been a history of property damage directed at the *Review*—an expensive sign stolen, automobiles vandalized, etc.

None of this has registered in any way on the moral graph of the Dartmouth administration.

The implicit message therefore went out loud and clear to all who cared to hear: morally, it is open season on individuals connected with this newspaper.

Only it is not. The big party is over. There are courts of law in this country, and statutes both criminal and civil.

Tell it all to the judge, gentlemen.

May 31, 1982

The Continuing Problem
by the Editors

T HE ABOVE-MENTIONED act of criminal violence took place on Friday morning. The following Monday, according to information supplied to *The Dartmouth Review*, Professor Patricia McKee of the English Department devoted her seminar on the novel to this incident. Professor McKee sought to justify this violence. The students in her seminar emphatically disagreed.

On Monday afternoon, when awareness of the violence was widespread in the community, the Dartmouth faculty passed a resolution critical not of violence but of the *Review*. Implictly, by that vote, the faculty was endorsing the criminal violence.

These events illustrate precisely the scope of the problem we have here at the College.

Of course it is true that any left-wing position can receive the endorsement of a faculty meeting. The Dartmouth faculty during the 1960s passed one resolution after another hostile to the defense of South Vietnam. It voted to abolish ROTC. No doubt it would support the Salvadorean guerrillas if it had a chance. Intending mischief, but impotent to achieve it, the faculty has voted to abolish fraternities. And so on.

William F. Buckley once remarked that he would rather be governed by the first three hundred names in the Boston phone book than by the faculty of Harvard.

He meant that common sense is more evenly distributed in the general population than among faculty members. The gentleman had a point.

May 31, 1982

Why They Voted

The Week in Review

IN THE LAST MONTH the Undergraduate Council and faculty of Dartmouth College have voted to deplore the "irresponsible" journalism of *The Dartmouth Review*.

The circumstances surrounding their act are revealing.

First, the Undergraduate Council voted with less than half of its members present. Lacking a quorum, it suspended all rules to accommodate the black caucus which presented the motion against the newspaper.

Second, after the motion passed, Keeney Jones, former chairman of the *Review*, challenged any of the council members who voted for the motion to a public debate. All refused.

Third, a recent poll of Dartmouth students revealed that less than 50 percent recognize the Undergraduate Council as representative of them. Many students do not know it exists.

Last Friday, Benjamin Hart, a founder of the *Review* who helps circulate the newspaper, was assaulted by a black college official, Samuel Smith.

Mr. Smith, Associate Director of the Alumni Fund, attacked, kicked, and bit Mr. Hart, who was subsequently treated at a local hospital for injuries. On Tuesday Smith was convicted of assault and sentenced to a $250 fine ($150 suspended) and three months probation.

Naturally this incident greatly embarrassed the college administration and faculty. The administration has remained silent, but faculty members have publicly defended Mr. Smith's violence.

One, English Professor Patricia McKee, said in her class that Smith had acted for "higher principles."

Professor Edward Bradley, who introduced the faculty motion against the *Review*, admitted to the regional daily that his motion was prompted by the Smith assault.

He blamed *The Dartmouth Review* for creating the atmosphere in which an assault could be rendered plausible.

The Dartmouth Review contends that the faculty motion is nothing more than an effort to justify Mr. Smith's violent acts, and divert press attention away from them.

After all, the faculty vote did come just two days after the attack.

We believe that the Dartmouth administration and faculty have not only created a feeling of hostility toward *The Dartmouth Review*, but once such hostility has led to violence they are reacting to it with encouragement.

Blaming *The Dartmouth Review* for causing Mr. Smith to attack and bite a student is analogous to blaming society for all criminal acts.

Of course, the debate on the issue hinges on a couple of sentences published in the newspaper, material by no means representative of our literature.

We print interviews (Milton Friedman, Betty Friedan, Ralph Nader, William Simon), news stories (we won the NEC/Society of Professional Journalists Award for in-depth reporting), syndicated columns, and humor. Ronald Reagan and William F. Buckley have lauded the newspaper.

Finally, in all the acrimony directed at the paper, Ben Hart is ignored. He was the victim; now somehow he has become the perpetrator.

June 14, 1982

Dunkirk for Ivy Liberalism

by Keeney Jones

H AVE YOU BITTEN anyone lately? No. Well, neither have I. Still, it does seem to happen.

About a week ago, a Dartmouth senior was making his rounds delivering copies of *The Dartmouth Review* to various locations on the campus. All of a sudden, in Blunt Alumni Center, he was set upon by an Alumni Fund official, a fifty-three-year-old black gentleman named Samuel Smith. Mr. Smith hit the student from behind, tried to push him through a plate glass door, broke his glasses, and, finally, bit him on the chest.

The student filed complaints with the deans and with the local police. In due course, Smith was found guilty, fined, and given ninety days probation. The student received tetanus shots.

The most interesting part of the story is yet to follow.

A couple of days after Smith's assault, the faculty of Dartmouth College held a meeting, and passed overwhelmingly a vote of censure against . . . *The Dartmouth Review*. Not a word was breathed critical of Mr. Smith's acts of violence. The assumption seemed to be that *The Dartmouth Review* had somehow unhinged the administrator to the point where he went berserk.

Of course, that is ridiculous, but I think something important is going on here, something worth pondering. *The Dartmouth Review* is a feisty, often irreverent paper, and it has won national awards both for its cartoons and for its reporting. In its two years of publication it has printed around 1,100 articles, of which perhaps five or six have been cited by some people as offensive.

I myself wrote one of these offending articles a month or so ago, a satire written in black slang and directed at a number of targets: reverse discrimination, separatist arrogance, cultural impoverishment. A lot of people thought it was funny, a lot didn't, but—after all—the thing was intended as humor, as a lampoon. I was astonished to find that some people were referring to it in terms more suitable to an official statement by Heinrich Himmler. *The Boston Globe*—no doubt to the surprise of its readers—addressed itself to the article in a major editorial; and for the past week the Dartmouth campus has been crawling with reporters and television crews.

It seems to me that *The Dartmouth Review* has come under attack for two main reasons.

One, it was the pioneer nationally of the independent conservative campus newspaper. It was the first. Others have sprung up at Princeton, Columbia, Yale, UCal-San Diego, and I have learned that perhaps a hundred are in the planning stages for next fall. To attack the *Review* is a way of attacking the whole phenomenon.

Second, though George McGovern was buried in 1972 and bounced in 1980, his spirit lives on among many college faculty members—see the faculty vote mentioned above. Furthermore, the spirit of the 1960s lives on as well.

For example, out in the real world we don't hear much anymore about black separatism. The Panthers and the Muslims and all the rest of it are a distant memory. In the real world, blacks hold elective office, occupy executive posts, and have no desire to be isolated. Most Ivy League colleges, however, created segregated black facilities during the 1960s, and these still exist as entrenched campus interests. Ditto the militant feminist institutions. If you attack these stale legacies from the 1960s, you are immediately called a racist or a sexist—language which, among some intellectuals, takes the place of thought.

Well, the *Review* is alive and well, and it cannot be intimidated.

If College administrators feel that it threatens their mental stability, perhaps they should be required to wear muzzles. We try to provide food—for thought, that is. We want to be in good taste, but not literally eaten. And though the Dartmouth faculty could not bring itself to condemn violence, we eschew it—no pun intended.

June 14, 1982

ON THE RIGHT
Fever-Swamp Time
by William F. Buckley Jr.

F OR YEARS I HAVE MADE myself unpopular by insisting, whenever the subject came up, that much more interesting than the behavior of Sen. Joe McCarthy was the behavior of his critics. It is one thing for an unknown senator from Wisconsin to exaggerate charges about communist infiltration of government. Something else for the foremost living philosopher (Bertrand Russell) to report that in America McCarthy had made it so dangerous to read Thomas Jefferson that anyone caught doing so would likely end up behind bars; or for America's leading educator (Robert Hutchins) to report that McCarthy had made it dangerous for any American to give money to Harvard University.

And it was McCarthy, rather than his critics, who was held to be hysterical! One is reminded of the old saw: The man advising his psychiatrist he suffers from the illusion he has grasshoppers on his lap, which he brushes off as he speaks. "Well, don't brush those grasshoppers on me!" the doctor exclaims.

At Dartmouth College for almost a year, there has been much groaning about the excesses of a right-wing student publication called *The Dartmouth Review*. The charge is that the *Review* is ill-managed, bigoted, that it breeds disharmony on campus, etc. Now listen to a letter addressed to the alumni publication of Dartmouth by one of its graduates, Mr. Steve Pennypacker of Phoenixville, Pennsylvania, Class of 1963—back when the Dartmouth campus was uncontaminated by a right-wing student newspaper so that everyone was safely taught his polemical manners. Here is a letter the editor of the *Dartmouth Alumni* chose to lead off the letters column in the current issue.

> Throw those *Review* bums out before I take my lily-white fist and burn a big black hole in their pointy little head! How absolutely embarrassing! Free speech? I suppose that's how Hitler got his start. Well, it ain't going to work in my house, because I learned long ago to exterminate rats whenever and

wherever I find them. Filth and vermin breeds more of the same. Dartmouth, for God's sake, clean up your act!

It was not possible to ascertain from the editor of the *Alumni Magazine* what went through his mind when he decided to publish, in defense of genteel civil discourse, a letter Joseph Goebbels would be proud to have written—because the gentleman in question has been dismissed (though not for publishing this letter). Accordingly, the question was asked of the acting editor, Mr. Peter Smith: "If you had been in charge of the magazine, would you have published the Pennypacker letter?"

Well, Mr. Smith, it transpires, inhabits Evasionville. All very complicated, you know: "It made me think of the time I was at the Alcazar in Toledo. It struck me how brave the defenders must have been. Then I discovered to my surprise that they were the fascists." The moral? "There is no monopoly on any of life's virtues or vices. The editors of *The Dartmouth Review* don't have a monopoly on outrageous statements." Well, but would Mr. Smith have published this letter? The magazine has always "prided itself on sharing an extraordinary variety of points of view. In printing such a letter, or indeed any letter, it doesn't endorse or comment." It is "simply informing the Dartmouth community that such a point of view exists. That somebody could feel thoughts so extreme is perhaps something that should be made known to the community."

Really? I can imagine forwarding Mr. Pennypacker's letter to a psychiatric clinic, perhaps taking up a collection from the class of 1963 for help for its helpless members. I can't see any point in publishing a hysterical letter urging violence.

Dartmouth has got itself some interesting problems, catalyzed by *The Dartmouth Review*, but hardly the *Review*'s responsibility. Last spring, an official of the alumni organization physically attacked and bit an editor of the *Review*. Prompting his dismissal? Suspension? Rebuke?

No, just a denunciation of the student newspaper by the faculty at Dartmouth. The idea, presumably, is that no paper should be published that has the effect on Dartmouth officials of causing them to bite student editors. And now, no doubt, the *Review* will once again be censured, this time on the grounds that it causes certain alumni of Dartmouth to act like the Ku Klux Klan, and alumni magazine editors to publish material normally unpublishable. Thus Versailles is said to have begot Hitler.

December 16, 1982; printed in The Dartmouth Review *January 17, 1983*

For an additional account of the Smith episode, and more on the founding years of The Dartmouth Review, *see* Poisoned Ivy, *by Benjamin Hart (Stein and Day, 1984).*

Bill Cole

Bill Cole's Song & Dance Routine
by Laura Ingraham

C LASS WAS supposed to begin at 2 p.m. Nearly 150 students crowded in the seats and aisles of 54 Hopkins Center. They awaited the master.

But the master was in no hurry. Nothing worries Bill Cole. Not students, not regulations, not teaching. Nothing.

Of course, Professor Cole was late to class. He is Chairman of the Music Department, and tenured; no one keeps his timetable.

Cole sauntered down to center stage. "Lotta people in this class, man," he surmised. "A lot of athletes, aren't there?"

People laughed. Welcome to Music 2, renowned to be the most outrageous gut course on campus, home of the thicknecks.

Professor Cole knows why they signed up, but it is hard to tell if he cares. He is a lean, scruffy fellow, "looks like a used Brillo pad," in the words of one student.

Cole began by trying to write the name of the course, "American Music in an Oral Tradition," on the blackboard. But he forgot the title, and had to consult the book of Officers, Regulations, and Courses (ORC).

Out of the blue, Cole said, "Hey, I know a lot of you are racist or sexist or out to lunch. But that's your problem, not mine." And he began to pace around the room.

During class time, Cole intermittently leaves the classroom. Sometimes he occupies the students by playing a record. As many as ten minutes may pass before Cole returns to class.

A goodly number of Cole's students are black. Some allege that these are "affirmative action" kids looking for a course they can handle.

The main reason seems to be that Cole makes an extra effort to amuse black students. In doing this, he has the whole class rolling on the floor.

Cole devotes at least half his lecture to the "race question," even though this is mostly irrelevant to the course.

In his second class he told about competing for a "token" position as a bank teller. When he got the job, the vice president threw a note pad at him with a dark ink spot in the center.

Cole said, "That's a little black spot." And the VP said, "And that's how inconspicuous you better be around here."

Music 2 is about Afro-American, Native American, and Anglo-American music handed down orally over the generations. It is rich, folksong music: Jayne Cortez, Blind Willie Johnson, Sara Cleveland, and so on.

The syllabus for Music 2 is three lines long. The requirements are: attendance, handing in a journal twice during the term, and a final "listening exam."

The Music 2 journal need not be about music at all. It could be about horseback riding. Or a trip to Malaca. The main object, Cole stresses, is to "think deeply for twenty minutes before writing."

The final listening exam is an exam involving twenty-four pieces of music. Students must memorize them, and be able to identify both the piece and musician.

Last year, Cole employed a unique testing system for the final exam. Cole played a song and identified it. Students who felt he identified it correctly were told to stand up. Those who were right left the room and signed out: they got an A. The rest of the class listened to the second selection, competing for an A minus. And so on.

Professor Cole has some illuminating advice for students in his course. On the first day he handed out "Standard rules for the student" of Music 2. These include:

> Read little, think deeply—and much. Avoid acquiring the grasshopper mind. . . . Avoid mental indigestion at all costs. It is not to be cured merely by going to the Drug Store. . . . If you must lie, lie to others; they will find you out and know you for the fool that you are. . . .
>
> Remember at all times: Nothing belongs to you except your mind has had a hand in its formulation. The moral is obvious: Ensure by every means at your disposal, that your mind is actively functioning on oiled wheels, and that it functions as your servant and not your enslaver.

This pop philosophy is supplemented by Cole's classroom rantings. Often students find this befuddling; some just laugh it off.

For example, on the first day of class, Cole elaborately praised the man who threatened to blow up the Washington Monument. "He had a lot of guts," Cole said. "And look what they did to him: They blew his head off."

"Only one newsman—Bill Moyers—said anything positive about the cat. He was questioning all the stuff that the Congressmen feed you" about nuclear war, Cole said.

On the second day of class, Cole told students his own life story. A Pittsburgh native, he suffered the discrimination prevalent before the civil rights movement. The neighborhood swimming pool let no blacks in. College aid was scarce in general, but nonexistent for black students.

Cole attended the University of Pittsburgh. After a month, he says, he realized he was "totally, I mean totally, unprepared." He failed Chemistry, Biology, and other courses, and was put on academic probation. It took him ten years to graduate.

It was Cole's tremendous interest in music that sustained him. "Music saved me," he admitted to the class. He got As and Bs in Music courses, and today he plays numerous instruments and shares with the class songs from the early 1900s that his mother sang to him.

Cole also performs professionally, playing the musette for a lively group called "Wind and Thunder." The group has played at the Collis Center.

Bill Cole is not, by a long shot, your typical Ivy League professor or department head. There is nothing intrinsically wrong with that; in fact, it can jazz things up quite a bit.

But Cole should be careful about making gratuitous racial allusions in class. He should also cultivate a more serious attitude toward reading and scholarship. That would make Music 2 more than amusing—it would make it a course.

January 17, 1983

Cole Crazed Over *Review* Article
by William Cattan

C HAIRMAN of the Music Department William Cole last Tuesday suspended his Music 2 class for two sessions. He wants *The Dartmouth Review* to publicly apologize for an article criticizing his teaching methods printed last week.

According to several sources in Professor Cole's class, he said, "I will not tolerate any sneaky m*th*rf*ck*r to come into my class to write an article."

Cole told his students that Dean of the Faculty Hans Penner threatened to fire him if he suspended his class. Cole told the *Review* that a public apology was "the only way this situation can be rectified."

Cole did not question the accuracy of the article, which was attested to by numerous students in Music 2.

Dinesh D'Souza, chairman of the *Review*, said Cole's request for an apology was "humorous," because "the article was indisputably accurate."

Early last Saturday Professor Cole himself showed up at *Review* reporter Laura Ingraham's door. He banged on the door for almost twenty minutes, waking up everybody in the hallway.

Ingraham's roommate was sleeping and didn't open the door. She thought it was a drunk friend venting a morning hangover.

Cole returned later and this time rapped even more violently on the door. He tried to force it. The roommate opened up, but was undressed. Cole grudgingly gave her time to put her clothes on.

Cole said he wanted Ingraham to come to his class Tuesday and apologize to all enrolled. He intimidated the roommate by using an "extremely irate" tone of voice.

Later the roommate complained to Dean of the Faculty Hans Penner. After a brief session between Cole and Penner Tuesday, Cole sent a short letter of apology. It was signed "Peace, Bill Cole."

Penner met with Professor Cole on Tuesday morning, and told the *Review* that "I thought he understood me, and the situation was resolved."

Penner said Cole's decision to suspend class "cannot be justified" because "he is taking out his anger on innocent students who signed up in good faith for the course."

Attempting to explain Cole's action, Penner said, "I don't know what it's like to be a black man. He was obviously under emotional stress."

Cole talked to Penner early Tuesday morning. That afternoon he suspended his two-hour class after forty-five minutes when he found out that *The Dartmouth Review* was not going to apologize or retract an accurate article.

In class Tuesday, Cole used words like "bastard" and "m*th*rf*ck*r" to describe the *Review* and Laura Ingraham.

He told his class. "I'm the professor, I have the Ph.D. You all are ignorant. . . . You all are responsible for this, because you are [Ingraham's] peers, and some of you know her or are her accomplices."

In the last fifteen minutes of the shortened class, Cole appealed to black students in his class to confront the administration because his "job's on the line, man." Cole said, "Black people are the only ones who understand freedom and justice."

At the end of Cole's speech, many black students applauded, in a standing ovation, whereas others were "simply stunned" and remained seated. After class some students commented that Cole was willfully and maliciously trying to divide the community along racial lines.

Dean Penner said he deplored Cole's use of language. "I would hope I would not use such words if I was in a similar situation," he said.

Cole told the *Review*, "You c*cks*ck*rs f*ck with everybody. You have f*ck*d with the last person. I'm telling you right now. And just the audacity you m*th*rf*ck*rs have calling me up with this b*llsh*t."

Cole declined space offered to him in *The Dartmouth Review* to list his concerns about the article, or explanation for his behavior. He also dismissed a suggestion to publicly discuss the matter or to meet with *Review* editors.

Penner said the only solution was to try to calm Cole down. Because of the frenzy to which Cole had incited black students in his class, Penner thought at one point about having Ingraham and her roommates sleep at the house of Dean of the College Edward Shanahan.

Finally he advised that the girls sleep in their own room, so as to witness possible acts of vandalism or intimidation by Cole or his students.

The situation has been exacerbated by Cole's attempts to publicize his actions in the local media.

Last Wednesday the *Daily Dartmouth* ran a lead story on the incident, after Cole pressured Brad Hutensky, editor of the *Daily Dartmouth* and a student in Music 2, to write a favorable account of what happened.

Cole's statement to the *Daily Dartmouth* contained several demonstrable lies. Cole said he called Laura Ingraham at 10:30 a.m. on Friday, and went over to her room at 11 a.m.

January 24, 1983

Bill Cole Sues the *Review*
by Dorn Bishop

P ROFESSOR of Music William S. Cole has filed suit for libel in U.S. District Court against the Hanover Review Corporation, Laura Ingraham, Dinesh D'Souza, and E. William Cattan on March 17, 1983.

According to the suit, Professor Cole has accused each of the four defendants of acting "in a malicious, intentional, willful, wanton, reckless, scandalous, outrageous, and defamatory manner" and, in the process, of committing both libel and slander against the plaintiff.

The suit stems from an article published in the January 17, 1983 edition of the *Review*, written by Laura Ingraham and entitled "Bill Cole's Song and Dance Routine," and from subsequent statements printed in the *Valley News* and *Rutland Herald* in which Cattan and D'Souza allegedly presented Professor Cole as "generally incompetent in his profession."

Cole seeks remuneration from each of the four defendants as follows:

1) general damages of $300,000;
2) punitive damages of $300,000;
3) the costs and disbursements incurred from legal fees, etc.;
4) for any further relief the Court may deem appropriate.

The case will be heard in Vermont District Court at Cole's request, rather than in New Hampshire, based on the fact that Cole lives in Vermont and much of the *Review*'s business is located in Vermont. As a result of this venue placement, Cole may sue for punitive damages in addition to general damages (New Hampshire law prohibits such a basis for a suit). As a result, Cole is suing for a total of $2.4 million rather than merely $1.2 million.

According to the complaint, Cole "has been forced to suffer trouble, inconvenience, and loss of time in attempting to seek redress" and "has suffered physical pain, personal humiliation, mental and emotional anguish, suffering and distress, and embarrassment, all to his financial loss and damage." Although both Cole and his lawyer, John L. Long, Jr., declined to expound on the charges, or any matter related to the suit, the three journalists mentioned in the suit as well as their lawyer, William Clauson, denied the allegations.

"Well, obviously the *Review* article was written with the intention of portraying Professor Cole in an unfavorable light," said Clauson. "However, if you look closely at the conclusion of the article, you'll see that it did not say he was totally incompetent but merely too political in his classroom demeanor. Should he soften his actions and stiffen his requirements for the course, the article concluded, there would be no reason to think that he would not have a superior course."

In addition, Clauson said he is at a loss to see the exact basis or purpose of the lawsuit.

"If the article is accurate, and I am told that it is, it is hard for me to see any basis for malicious intent. If a student newspaper writes on an individual's public, rather than private, life, that individual is 'fair game,' so to speak, so long as the statements printed are accurate," said Clauson.

Asked if he believed Cole was merely after an apology, Clauson responded, "If that were the case, I can't believe there would be a need to take this to court. In any case, there is no basis for apology within accurate articles."

The defendants believe another motive may be behind the lawsuit.

"The enormous amount of money that Cole demands may be based more on his desire for personal enrichment than on restoration of his supposedly fractured reputation," suggested former Chairman of the Hanover Review Dinesh D'Souza.

"Cole obviously knows that the resources of any independent student publication are limited. I'm afraid this might just be a ruse to bankrupt the newspaper by means of burying the *Review* in heavy legal debts, regardless of the outcome of the case," said D'Souza.

Cattan, former Editor-in-Chief of the *Review*, stated he personally offered Cole three opportunities to respond to either the accuracy or intent of the *Review*'s initial piece. Cole refused all offers, according to Cattan. Such refusals may originally have been made with the intention of bringing on a lawsuit to damage the financial status of the paper, said Cattan.

The legal technicalities of the *Review*'s defense are obviously not completed, according to Clauson, but the defendants' case is based on two primary points:

1) The article is indisputably accurate.

2) *The Dartmouth Review* has a right to publish the article based on freedom of the press as stated under the First Amendment to the U.S. Constitution.

Should Professor Cole attempt to dispute the first of these contentions, *Review* representatives claim that they will take "all steps necessary" to prove the factual accuracy of the Ingraham article as well as those opinions stated in that article. In short, the following individuals shall be subpoenaed by the defense to testify in support of those opinions expressed in the article.

1) President of the College David McLaughlin to comment on Cole's professionalism.

2) Dean of the Faculty Hans Penner also to comment on Cole's professionalism, or lack of it.

3) Professor of Music John Appleton, who stated that if he were Cole, he would have "busted [Laura] Ingraham's kneecaps."

4) All students enrolled in Cole's Music 2 class, Winter '83.

5) Many students enrolled in Cole's previous Music 2 classes.

6) Many students enrolled in Cole's other classes, Spring '83 and prior.

7) Those professors on the Committee on Advisory to the President for the academic year 1978–1979. That is, those individuals responsible for Cole's tenure. These are Leonard Rieser, Charles Braun, Rogers Elliott, Blanche Gelfant, Hans Penner, William Reiners, and Vincent Starzinger.

8) Those professors on the Humanities Divisional Council of the Faculty of Arts and Sciences for the academic year 1980–1981. That is, those individuals on the council responsible for approving special majors. In particular, those individuals serving with Cole on the board that denied Keeney Jones a special major after Cole was removed for obscene and biased language prior to the hearing. (Mr. Cole later received a reprimand for his actions.) These are Timothy Duggan, Robert McGrath, James Tatum, James Heffernan, Collette Gaudin, Bruce Duncan, Bernard Gert, Steven Katz, Richard Sheldon, and Sara Castro-Klaren.

Pertaining to the second point of defense, the general consensus among the defendants was summed up well by Dinesh D'Souza when he said, "Cole's lawsuit is an obvious attempt to intimidate students and prevent them from exercising their First Amendment rights."

Attorney for the Defense Clausen points out, "I have a hard time understanding a rule that states you can speak so long as you say favorable things. Mr. Cole and others have said things very critical of *The Dartmouth Review* in the past and slander has never even been mentioned by the paper. In fact, Dartmouth students not connected with the *Review* have been much less flattering about professors before this incident."

The defense will also attempt to point out what it sees as errors in the text of the suit. According to Clausen, "I simply cannot see where any damages have been caused. There may be financial damage, although I am not aware of any. However, as I understand it, Mr. Cole is a tenured professor and is in no danger of losing his job. In addition, even if there are damages incurred by Mr. Cole, the defendants are not liable for those damages unless libel or slander has taken place. Based on public knowledge of the case, neither has taken place."

Clauson makes one final comment, "I'm truly sad to see this lawsuit. It's a shame you can't have differing points of view on a campus without a lawsuit coming about as a result. I have always believed the point of a college education is to encourage different points of view—theoretically, over time, the best view will emerge victorious. This lawsuit casts doubts upon that notion."

April 11, 1983

A Motley Crew
The Week in Review

FIFTEEN faculty members have circulated on College stationery an appeal for money to support Professor Cole's lawsuit against the *Review*.

This Gang of Fifteen contains the predictable names. They express "concern" over "the *Review*'s treatment of our colleague, Professor William Cole." They do not challenge any of the facts uncovered by the *Review* regarding Cole's classroom performance, and they are apparently "unconcerned" about his attempts to instigate violence, his racist remarks, and his habitual obscenities.

In short, decent standards of professional behavior count for nothing in the eyes of these "concerned" poltroons.

Might they be worried that some of their own classroom buffoonery will also be revealed?

Dartmouth College
Hanover, New Hampshire 03755

April 5, 1983

Dear Colleague:

The undersigned are concerned about the tactics employed by *The Dartmouth Review* in general and particularly concerned about the *Review*'s treatment of our colleague, Professor William S. Cole.

Professor Cole has initiated a civil action against the *Review* and others in the United States District Court for the District of Vermont.

We would like to lend our encouragement and financial support to Professor Cole. If you are interested in making a contribution to help defray some of the costs associated with the lawsuit, you may send a contribution to:

The William Cole Support Fund
In Care Of:

John J. Long, Jr.
Attorney-at-Law
Johnson & Dunne
Main Street
Norwich, Vermont 05055

Hoyt S. Alverson, Professor of Anthropology
Jon H. Appleton, Geisel Professor in the Humanities
William W. Cook, Professor of English
Robert J. Fogelin, Professor of Philosophy
Nancy K. Frankenberry, Assistant Professor of Religion
Ronald M. Green, John Phillips Professor of Religion
Charles E. Hamm, Arthur R. Virgin Professor of Music
Nelson M. Kasfir, Associate Professor of Government
Helen M. MacLam, Collection Development Librarian, Baker Library
Roger D. Masters, John Sloan Dickey Third Century Professor
Marysa Navarro, Professor of History
Brenda R. Silver, Associate Professor of English
James Tatum, Professor of Classics
P. Esmé Thompson, Assistant Professor of Art
Barbara B. Walsh, Assistant Professor of Art

April 18, 1983

ON THE RIGHT
More on *The Dartmouth Review*
by William F. Buckley Jr.

S TUDENTS OF liberal behavior should be as interested in Dartmouth
College these days as Charles Darwin was in the Galapagos. Whatever one thinks about the political views of the editors of *The Dartmouth
Review*, one should be grateful for the job they have done in examining
what lies on the underside of the granitic liberalism of the Ivy League.

The latest round involves a music professor called William Cole, who
is black. Why is this relevant? Because it is widely assumed that his behavior would not have been tolerated if he were other than black. Years
ago at a criminal trial in New York City one juror gave as his reason for
voting not guilty that he could not bring himself to find a black man guilty.
The difficulty with taking that position, or allied positions, is that one in-
vites precisely the kind of condescension that encourages racism. What
faster way is there to encourage contempt than to say, in effect, that you
cannot reasonably expect black men to live up to the standards of white
men?

A reporter from *The Dartmouth Review*, a girl student, Laura Ingraham,
attended Mr. Cole's music class, along with 150 regularly enrolled students.
It must have been quite a show. He was late. He evidently forgot what his
course's name was, because he needed to consult the school catalog. He
talked pretty much about whatever it was that came to mind. He recited racial slights during his youth. He praised the man who had the week before
attempted to blow up the Washington Monument. Why do so many students
take his course? Because, the article alleges, it is a notorious gut course, i.e.,
you need not study very much to get a high grade.

The response was electric after the story's publication. At 8:30 in the
morning, the story continues, the professor went to the girl's dormitory
and banged repeatedly on the door, using language one still does not print
in a family newspaper and men used not to use in women's dormitories.
That afternoon Mr. Cole, after a few minutes, suspended his class to
celebrate his indignation.

The newspaper offered, and later reiterated the offer, to publish Mr.
Cole's specific complaints, but he declined that offer. Now, three months
later, Professor Cole has filed suit against the newspaper, the girl reporter,
and the staff for several million dollars. He alleges no factual error in the
story, reciting instead a broken heart, and the rest of the legal boilerplate
that stands for injured dignity.

Laughable lawsuits, unhappily, are not always to be laughed at. Cole
has got himself a contingency lawyer, and such money as is required to

pay costs is being raised through a faculty fund. A faculty committee has been formed, and we see such dukes and noblemen as the "Geisel Professor in the Humanities," the "John Phillips Professor of Religion," the "John Sloan Dickey Third Century Professor." The Geisel gentleman above is a solomonic character who is best remembered for his statement quoted last January in the *Review* that if he had been Professor Cole, he'd have "busted Ingraham's kneecaps." I should think that Geisel should rename his chair the "Gordon Liddy Professor in the Humanities."

The prospects? Given recent Supreme Court precedents, the newspaper will almost certainly win on a motion for summary dismissal. Or there could be a jury trial over Miss Ingraham's newspaper story. She might need to summon as many as 150 students who were witness to the kind of thing she wrote about; the president of the university, who is aware of certain difficulties involving Mr. Cole; the faculty members who voted to give him tenure in 1979 not withstanding certain data available to them. A long, windy trial, resulting in her exoneration. Either that, or the repeal of the First Amendment.

But how will all of this be financed? Not by faculty contributions, you bet. Whenever someone does something outrageous at the expense of *The Dartmouth Review*, the Dartmouth faculty becomes incensed at *The Dartmouth Review*.

The objective of this whole business would appear to be to put *The Dartmouth Review* out of business. Then they can give professor Cole another chair.

April 19, 1983; printed in The Dartmouth Review *April 25, 1983*

Any Questions?
The Week in Review

L EST ANYONE doubt the ridiculousness into which the Cole lawsuit has degenerated, here is a sampling of the questions John Long, Cole's attorney, has submitted to defendant Laura Ingraham:

5) Have you ever worked for a newspaper or publication other than your high school newspaper or *The Dartmouth Review*?

6) If the answer to the preceding interrogatory is in the affirmative, with respect to each such newspaper or publication, state the years during which you worked for such newspaper or publications, the full name of each of your immediate supervisors during the years you worked for each such newspaper or publication, and state in detail the nature of each job you held with each such newspaper or publication.

25) List the name of the person who hired you to work for the *Review*.

26) List every reason why you decided to become a member of the staff of the *Review*.

31) In connection with the article, please state the full name and mailing address of the person who told you that the plaintiff looked like a "used Brillo pad."

33) State, in detail, exactly how the plaintiff looks like a used Brillo pad.

51) List all of your objections or concerns, if any, to [*sic*] the athletic program at Dartmouth College.

55) What is *The Dartmouth Review*'s position with respect to the athletic program at Dartmouth College?

69) Describe in detail every asset (including, but not necessarily limited to cars, securities, bank accounts, real estate, jewelry, etc.) in which you own any legal interest, including the location of the asset, the nature of your legal interest in the asset, the value of the asset, and the nature and extent of any encumbrance upon the asset.

June 6, 1983

The *Review* 1, Professor Cole 0
by Peter Arnold

I N MARCH 1983, Chairman of the Music Department William Cole lodged a $2.4 million libel suit against the Hanover Review, Inc., which publishes *The Dartmouth Review*, and three student editors. Cole charged that an assessment of his classroom behavior published in the *Review* and written by Laura Ingraham caused him mental, emotional, physical, and financial distress, yet he specified not a single inaccuracy in the story.

Eighteen months later, in what is the first major development of the case, District Judge of Vermont Franklin S. Billings, Jr. accepted the advice of a federal magistrate and "ordered" that individual defendants Laura Ingraham, E. William Cattan, Jr., and Dinesh D'Souza [be] dismissed from the case."

Thus, *The Dartmouth Review* has now won round one in what has become commonly known as "The Cole Case." Yet the suit against The Hanover Review, Inc. remains.

From the suit's outset, *The Dartmouth Review*'s lawyer, Miss Blair Soyster of the New York law firm Rogers and Wells, drew a distinction between the suit against the corporation and the suits against the three students. Her contention was that the United States District Court for the District of Vermont, which is where Cole and his lawyer initiated the suit, lacked in personal jurisdiction over the three individuals since they all lived, studied, and worked in the state of New Hampshire.

The reasoning behind Cole and his lawyer's decision to litigate in Vermont, as opposed to New Hampshire where every event in question transpired, may seem perplexing. It is easily understood, however, when one considers that half of the $2.4 million suit is for punitive damages— New Hampshire law forbids suing for punitive damages.

On August 16, 1984, the federal magistrate, Jerome J. Niedermeier "recommend[ed] that defendants Ingraham, Cattan, and D'Souza motion to dismiss for lack of personal jurisdiction be granted." According to Vermont law, either party may object to a magistrate's report within ten days after service by filing a written objection with the clerk of the court. Cole's lawyer, John Long, made no objection and refused to discuss the matter with the *Review*: "I can't talk to you. You'll have to talk to your lawyer."

One rather humorous—and telling—part of the Magistrate's report deals with Cole's contention that certain statements made by Cattan and D'Souza to Vermont newspapers were slanderous. There is general agreement in the courts that personal jurisdiction of the court may be asserted over a non-resident due to a single, allegedly defamatory, telephone conversation. Yet it is crucial that the party on the receiving end of the defendant's remarks (the interviewers) be in the court's own state, in this case, Vermont. Cole and his lawyer not only submitted no evidence that the interviewing reporters were in Vermont at the time of the conversations, but one of the memorandums that were filed with the clerk contained a statement that the interviews were given in Hanover.

According to Miss Soyster, Cole and his lawyer are relying on a case just recently decided by the Supreme Court, *Calder v. Jones*, in which the court held that a state may have personal jurisdiction over a writer and editor if "the focal point both of the story and of the harm suffered" is in the forum state of Vermont.

Yet both Dartmouth and the places of residence and work of the three editors are in New Hampshire; ergo, the *Calder* decision cited by Cole and his lawyer was not controlling. Vermont's long-arm statute authorizes a personal jurisdiction over a non-resident only "if it appears that the contact with the state by the party . . . is sufficient to support a personal judgment against him."

Reaction to the ruling was predictably exuberant. Said former Editor-in-Chief Cattan, "Of course I'm very pleased. I think Cole's lawsuit was purely and simply an attempt to harass students who publish *The Dartmouth Review* and to discourage them from exercising their First Amendment rights of criticism and comment. . . . [The case] is flimsy and based on sheer malice." Laura Ingraham said the decision was a "victory not only for the individual litigants, but also for *The Dartmouth Review*."

As for the one final suit against The Hanover Review, Inc., Miss Soyster does not characterize it as part of a "three-down-one-to-go" case, as the suit against the *Review* "turns on issues which were not addressed with the successful motion to dismiss the action against the students."

Summarizing his feelings, Cattan asserted, "I still stand by the facts in the story [and] the right of a student newspaper to criticize questionable professors. I would do it again."

Commented Ingraham, "Half the fight is over. Now it's time to take the gloves off."

October 24, 1984

Professor Cole Drops Lawsuit
by Roland Reynolds

P ROFESSOR William Cole has dropped his lawsuit against *The Dartmouth Review*. Although he asked for $2.4 million from the *Review* and three former editors, Cole gets no monetary reimbursement for two years of effort.

The two parties agreed to issue a joint statement in which Cole repeated his charges about the *Review*'s article about him, and the *Review* stood by every word of its article.

In the joint statement, Cole agrees that the *Review* has the right to report on the classroom activities of professors—a right Cole and numerous Dartmouth faculty contested when the *Review* first wrote its article about Cole.

Cole also concedes that the *Review* has a role in reporting to the Dartmouth community on issues of academic interest and stimulating debate among students, faculty, and alumni. Cole also comes out for the First Amendment, which is sure to dismay some of his allies on the Dartmouth faculty.

The *Review* considers this "an important victory for us and for the free press," as *Review* President Frank Reichel '86 put it. "It should make it clear to our enemies that we never bend to pressure, and there is nothing to be gained by launching frivolous suits." Reichel said the *Review* had not decided whether to counter-sue Professor Cole. "We are looking into the legal issues right now," Reichel said.

The *Review* agreed to a joint statement because it conceded nothing whatsoever to Professor Cole, and it came in the wake of a joint statement between CBS and General Westmoreland which was widely viewed as a victory for CBS and a humiliation for Westmoreland.

The legal contest had been a bit of a comedy, with the *Review* represented by the prestigious New York law firm Rogers and Wells, headed by former U.S. Secretary of State William Rogers, and Cole represented by a local Hanover attorney, John Long.

For the past two years the case has been in "discovery" stage, with both sides collecting information. If Cole had not dropped his case, it would have gone to trial in the fall.

In her investigation, *Review* attorney Blair Soyster was able to subpoena Cole's grades for his Music 2 course that term and also to interview a number of the students in the class. The vast majority of grades handed out by Cole were As, confirming the *Review*'s charge that his course was a "gut." Also the students interviewed in the class substantially confirmed the statements that the *Review* attributed to Cole and the factual assertions made about his class.

Cole may try to interpret the joint statement in a "face saving" manner. Actually, he has very little in which to take solace.

The joint statement repeats Cole's concern that the *Review*'s article was "racially motivated and unfair and inaccurate." But he has maintained that from the beginning. Who cares what he thinks about the story?

Cole was unable to elicit a single admission of error or wrongdoing from the *Review*. Not a comma in the article was retracted. The *Review* presented an accurate picture and stands by it. Cole can continue to maintain whatever he wants for as long as he wants.

In the joint statement the *Review* said that its article "was not intended as a statement on Professor Cole's overall performance as an educator or scholar, but rather was intended to convey information regarding his teaching style and methods in Music 2." This is obvious from reading the initial article; no attempt was made to generalize about Cole's other courses.

The *Review* also "understands that, as a tenured member of the Dartmouth faculty, Professor Cole has the right to conduct his courses in the style and manner he finds most effective." Notice that the *Review* does not condone the tenure system; it merely acknowledges that, while this system is in place, it guarantees professors certain privileges. In fact, the *Review* considers the tenure system a disgrace, because among other things, it often perpetuates complacency both in the classroom and in scholarship.

Cole's effort to expose the *Review* to public humiliation and exorbitant costs failed miserably. It is not known how much money Cole lost by filing the suit—even under contingency, you still have to pay the lawyer's out of pocket expenses. And it cost the *Review* very little—Rogers and Wells graciously took the case pro bono because of the important First Amendment issues involved.

Where Cole's reputation stands now, and whether it is better after this case than before it (and before the national publicity), is a matter of conjecture. But permit us a snicker.

Nemo me impune lacessit.

June 5, 1985

Bill Cole's Last Go-Round
The Week in Review

J UST WHEN YOU thought he was back concentrating on the important music of the African Zumba tribe, professor and unsuccessful libel litigant William Cole is on the verbal rampage again. This time he flexed his didactic abilities in the pages of the *Daily Princetonian*, the official student media organ of Princeton University.

In a feature article on Laura Ingraham '85, the new editor of Concerned Alumni of Princeton's *Prospect* magazine and former *Review* editor, Cole was quoted as saying that she is "a very destructive person." "She will lie and do anything to distort or make distortions," he said. Dauntless Bill even went as far as to call Miss Ingraham "a coward."

Last spring, on the suggestion of his counsel, the case was settled with Cole receiving zero dollars for what his side termed Cole's "emotional anguish."

Further quoted in the *Prince*, Cole claimed that Ingraham's article about him "as much as said I was a buffoon and I was incompetent."

No, Professor, she didn't say that—but you just did. Perhaps our harmonic wonder would be better off confining his hot air to the various effete wind instruments he blows.

November 27, 1985

An Inside Look

Beauty & the Beast
The Week in Review

A GROUP OF students will soon file an application with the Council on Student Organizations (COSO) requesting college recognition and funding for the Bestiality Society.

The logic behind the proposal, according to Bestiality Society President Scott Lamb '84, is that if the College is willing to recognize student groups solely on the basis of sexual affiliation, COSO cannot deny equal opportunity to students who eschew traditional inclinations.

Lamb was referring to the Gay Student Organization, which is recognized by the College, but no longer receives COSO funding. Such funding was discontinued pursuant to an exposé of the organization in this newspaper.

For COSO, the application of the Bestiality Society is a test, a test to determine whether the college is *ad hoc* and whimsical, and whether it is willing to pursue its logic to consistent limits.

Students who would like to be on the B.S. mailing list should send their names to Theodore Crown '84. All correspondence will be treated in the strictest confidence. Meow.

January 25, 1982

An Inside Look at the GSA
by the Editors

T HE FOLLOWING is the first in a series of in-depth reports of activities of campus organizations funded and recognized by the College.

The Gay Students Association (GSA) meeting was supposed to start at 9 a.m. The ten or so students then present just chatted about campus happenings, midterms, the weather. The door was left open so latecomers could straggle in without interrupting the meeting.

Directing the discussion at the GSA meeting was a Dartmouth Medical Student who identified herself only as "Sue" (not her real name).

Within ten minutes or so, different GSA members began talking about a letter to the editor of the *Daily Dartmouth* written by Jay Berkow. Berkow had drafts of two letters he wrote to the *Daily Dartmouth* regarding short news items in the *The Dartmouth Review* about AIDS and a gay funeral parlor. He said that he favored sending the second letter rather than his other, more "standard" one.

After the group discussed both of Berkow's letters, Sue interrupted:

> SUE: I think we could close the door. Is there any other business before we get into what I think this meeting is supposed to be about?
> GSA MEMBER ONE: Oh, has everybody paid their dues?
> SUE: No, I will pay you at the end of this week, May 1.

After this, various GSA members discussed the planning of their upcoming gay/faculty brunch. Ten professors were said to be attending this.

> SUE: I'd like to start this meeting. For those of you who weren't here in the last meeting or so, we decided that there are a number of issues we should try to concentrate on . . . like trying to be more cohesive as a group. One of the ways we can try to do this is to have a rap group about issues that concern all of us . . . because part of the problem in society and at a meeting like this . . . is that everyone is enclosed between glass walls and nobody is willing to trust anybody. . . . The two rules that follow which are standard for any kind of group like this is that anything that gets said here stays here. And that means that you don't tell lovers, friends, or anybody else. . . . The second thing I wanted to say is that nothing derogatory about someone is to be said . . . no one should attack anyone on a personal level.
> DAVID GARLING: There was only one thing that I wanted to ask. Prof. Lynne McFall of the Philosophy Department is teaching this course called "Love, Sex & Ethics" and has asked me to speak to her class on Thursday. I was thinking of doing it in the second half, from 3 p.m. to 4 p.m. Would anyone like to join me?
> JAY BERKOW: What kind of format is it?
> DG: Basically, I'm just going to walk in. I may have something to say ahead of time . . .

In the few minutes following this, the GSA members began giving individual accounts of their sexuality crises. Here is when the GSA finally got down to its business.

SUE: I thought I would start by telling you a little bit about myself. I have been a closet bisexual for the past eight years, which has not been so easy. And there have been times when I wished I wasn't. There have been many times in the hospital where a patient was gay or homosexual and I could not reach out and tell him.

Sue continued to discuss the problems of being a homosexual in the medical establishment.

GSA MEMBER TWO (like Sue, a Dartmouth medical student): I've experienced some of the same things she's talked about . . . at some level I knew I was gay ever since like eighth grade.

REPORTER: How can you know that, though?

GSA MEMBER TWO: It's hard for me to say, you know, for me, like I said, probably since eighth grade I've been wondering "What am I?"

REPORTER: But, I mean I didn't even think about what I was in eighth grade.

GSA MEMBER THREE: I think it has to do with how soon you become aware of sexuality. I knew that I had always been attracted to men. I mean always, as far back as I can remember. But I finally put the word homosexual together with myself when I was about eleven or twelve. I was an early bloomer. [Loud GSA laughter.]

GSA MEMBER TWO: That's not uncommon—that's what you feel like . . . it's sort of a slow process of self-realization. I took a psychology course this winter, Psychology 83, where we lead discussion groups for introductory courses. And that's where I really just started to think about my sexual identity again for the umpteenth time.

Finally, I came out and said to a group of straight people I trusted that "Yes, I guess I am gay." And I didn't feel bad about it.

REPORTER: And you're comfortable with that decision?

GSA MEMBER TWO: Yes, and that's the first time I felt that way because again as far as being sexually experienced, I was a late bloomer. I really didn't have sex with men until about two years ago, but all through that time I knew I enjoyed it, but I just didn't totally say to myself that "Yes, I'm a homosexual." I didn't totally admit it to myself and feel good about it. That's the important point.

GSA MEMBER FOUR: I feel the same way that [TWO] did . . . and what like [THREE] said when you get to that point when you realize what sexuality is—that's the point when you start to label yourself . . . as far back as I can remember I was attracted to men and I would, for instance, look at *Playboy* magazine. And the only pages that I would naturally turn to are the ones where they would be like having *menages* or something with men.

REPORTER: Or you really read the articles, right? [Loud GSA laughter.]

GSA MEMBER FOUR: Yeah, I had no interest in the pictures. When it finally came down to who I was attracted to, I was in a situation where I could have gone to bed with a girl, and I had no desire to at all and it kind of upset her [GSA laughter]. I was dealing with my sexuality in a physical way.

REPORTER: And how old were you at this time?

GSA MEMBER FOUR: I was seventeen. And the next year I had an affair with a friend of mine over the summer. And I was very frightened, but I liked it.

JB: I've made a choice, technically, but I still go back and forth a lot. A lot of people want you to make a decision. "You really must make a decision, Jay!" They want you to label yourself.

REPORTER: You're either straight or you're gay and there's no in between.

JB: Right. Well, I don't label myself a bisexual either.

At this point, several GSA members began to discuss sexual labels and bisexual discrimination. Sue explained her live-in relationship with a man in Philadelphia, who hid from her the fact that he was gay while she hid from him the fact that she was bisexual.

SUE: What do you want to talk about now?

GSA MEMBER ONE: Nothing in particular.

REPORTER: Well, having conversations like this is great, I suppose, but what exactly does the GSA do? [Laughter] I mean you don't just get together each week and rap or anything, do you?

JB: I mean, we've been trying to. We haven't yet.

REPORTER: Do you have functions?

GSA MEMBER ONE: We have parties. Wait 'til you see our parties [loud GSA laughter].

JB: May 12 is the weekend the gay alumni group is coming up, and we're having a brunch and a press conference.

REPORTER: How long has there been a gay alumni group?

JB: I think it was just formed.

DG: A year.

REPORTER: Is it strong? A large membership?

JB: About fifty members.

GSA MEMBER FOUR: As well as social, we're also responsible for political things, responding to different issues on campus.

REPORTER: Do you guys get any College funding of any kind?

JB: Minimal.

REPORTER: Are you trying to do something about that?

JB: Right now we're not a cohesive enough group to know what to do with the money if we had it.

REPORTER: What's your membership now?

JB: Around twenty people.

GSA MEMBER TWO: Not everybody comes to every meeting.

GSA MEMBER FOUR: That in no way reflects the percentage of gay people or homosexual people on campus. They said the GSA was not for every gay on campus.

GSA MEMBER ONE: I think another point too, is that a lot of closet gays are really attracted to all-male frats—for obvious reasons [mumblings of general agreement].

Berkow alleged that one fraternity on campus was 90 percent bisexual.

GSA MEMBER FOUR: I find if very difficult not to be gay. That's why I'm so very blatant about it. . . . I cannot pull off straight any more. I figured a part of my coming out was setting other peoples opinions aside.

May 14, 1984

COS & GSA: An Update
The Week in Review

T ERESA POLENZ '87, our freshman reporter who attended the advertised and open meeting of the Gay Students Association three weeks ago, is being charged with a brand new state statute violation by the College. On Wednesday evening, Miss Polenz received another campus police-delivered letter from Dean Marilyn Baldwin, secretary to the COS (Committee on Standards).

Several days ago, Miss Polenz was charged with violating the New Hampshire privacy statute 644:9, and she was also accused of disorderly conduct. But now the College has realized that the first charge flung at the girl was totally inapplicable, since the New Hampshire law books define a "private place" to be a place which a substantial number of the public does not have reasonable access.

By that definition, the GSA meeting was not a private place. So the College is fishing. Dartmouth's attorneys Gary Clark and Thomas Csatari are fishing to snag Miss Polenz on some charge. It appears that they want to paint over the fact that they did not do their legal homework at the outset of this case. Perhaps they felt that since Miss Polenz is only a freshman, she would silently acquiesce to any charge leveled at her from the halls of mighty Parkhurst. They soon realized that hooking Miss Polenz to mollify the gay community would not be so easy.

She is, as of today, charged with (in addition to the earlier violations) breaking the statutes in Chapter 570A:1 of the New Hampshire state criminal code titled "Wire tapping and Eavesdropping."

This law is more general than the statute previously cited by the College. Usually, this law applies to wiretapping private rooms and telephone bugging, but the College is hoping that this will serve as a sturdy enough noose to wrap around the neck of a *Dartmouth Review* reporter.

With the way Dean Shanahan and the rest of the College bureaucrats are operating—maybe next week Miss Polenz will be additionally charged with having jaywalked on her way to the April 24 meeting.

May 21, 1984

COS Trial Postponed Indefinitely
by Laura Ingraham

I N A TOTALLY unexpected move, on the afternoon of May 25, 1984, Dartmouth College indefinitely postponed the Committee on Standards trial of freshman reporter Teresa Polenz, at least until all legal questions concerning this controversy are settled.

Assistant attorney Thomas Csatari said the postponement was being granted "in the interest of fairness." Earlier Polenz's attorney Laurence Silberman had argued to Dean of the College Edward Shanahan and College Counsel Gary Clark that Dartmouth was guilty of "malicious harassment" of Polenz and *The Dartmouth Review*.

Silberman maintained this because on May 24 he had asked Shanahan to put off the COS hearing scheduled for Friday, May 25, and Shanahan flatly refused him the next morning. This made it necessary for Silberman to fly up immediately from Washington D.C. for the trial. Only after numerous reporters from publications like *The New York Times* had shown up for the COS hearing, and after an editorial that morning in the *Wall Street Journal* compared the trial with the Soviet treatment of Andrei Sakharov, did Dartmouth cancel the planned hearing.

But the ordeal is not over yet for Polenz. At the instigation of either the administration or the Gay Students Organization, a criminal investigator from the state attorney general's office has begun an inquiry to determine whether any statutes have been violated. If he decides they could have been, the state may institute criminal proceedings against Polenz.

Two New Hampshire statutes are in question. The first, Statute 644:9, says that "A person is guilty of a misdemeanor if he unlawfully and without the consent of the person entitled to privacy uses in any private place any device for observing, photographing, recording, amplifying or broadcasting sounds or events in such place." The statute goes on to define "private place" as "a place where one may reasonably expect to be safe from surveillance but does not include a place to which the public or a substantial group thereof has access."

Polenz maintains that since the GSA meeting was publicly advertised, and since not just a portion of the public but anyone in the community was invited to attend the meeting, this statute does not apply.

The second statute, 570A:1, makes a person guilty of a class B felony if he "willfully intercepts . . . any wire or oral communication" where "oral communication" is defined as "any oral communication uttered by a person exhibiting an expectation that such communication is not subject to interception under circumstances justifying such expectation."

Polenz's attorneys are studying this law, but they say that circumstances justify Polenz's taping action within the statute, which was designed to restrain law enforcement officials from intercepting private conversations and is inapplicable, also that the statute may be unconstitutional.

Polenz and *The Dartmouth Review* are being jointly represented by the Hon. Laurence Silberman, former deputy attorney general of the United States and the former U.S. ambassador to Yugoslavia. Silberman is a member of Dartmouth's class of 1957. Polenz also has a local attorney to assist her if criminal charges are filed. The New Hampshire ACLU is also considering whether or not to represent Polenz.

If this legal wrangle keeps up, it could take months, perhaps years, which would render the COS hearing moot. But evidence is mounting that the College is, in ways not fully known yet, connected with the state's investigation into the case.

This would not be surprising, given Dartmouth College's influence with the officials of the small state of New Hampshire. But concrete evidence of this nexus was provided by Thomas Hannigan, an investigator for the state's Attorney General, who came to Hanover to look into charges of criminal wrongdoing, and left the number of Dean Shanahan's office as his daytime phone number.

Dartmouth has officially denied, however, that it contacted the Attorney General's office about the case. Yet Dean Shanahan and several college officials are on record saying that Polenz broke state laws. For example, in a memo to Marilyn Baldwin, secretary of the Committee on Standards, Shanahan wrote, "In my judgment, the recording of conversations during the GSA meeting without the knowledge or acquiescence of the participants was a violation of the criminal code of the State of New Hampshire."

One reason the College may have postponed the COS hearing was fear of national publicity. Prior to the hearing the *Review* contacted newspapers and TV stations, most of which agreed to cover the trial.

The morning of the scheduled hearing, an editorial in the *Wall Steet Journal*, titled "Dartmouth on Trial," castigated the College's arbitrary proceedings.

It began thus: "Consider a trial in which the defendant is accused of a serious crime, one that puts the defendant's future in jeopardy. The defendant has no real right to a lawyer; no right to cross-examine hostile witnesses; no right to compel his own witnesses. What's more, the committee that functions as prosecutor is also the judge and jury. Three in one!"

The issue, as the *Wall Street Journal* saw it, was: "Is the group subsidized to promote homosexuality? Is it merely there to promote discussion on issues of sexual preference? If the latter, what's the harm in reporting it? And is it truly seditious for students to ask why such a group is funded by the College?"

Many observers feel that this editorial had a powerful effect on Dartmouth, particularly on President McLaughlin, who as a former Toro executive is concerned about what the business community thinks of him.

Another reason for the College's trepidation may have been Ambassador Silberman, whose firm is one of the most prestigious in the country. Silberman, who is taking the case pro bono, had six attorneys researching this one case.

When Shanahan turned down Silberman's request for putting off the trial, Silberman and his associate flew up to Hanover. The trial was scheduled for 4 p.m. on May 25. But at 1 p.m. that day Polenz got a campus-police-delivered note saying the trial had been postponed until Monday, May 28.

Silberman was outraged by this late change because it meant his trip to Hanover was in vain. He contacted Gary Clark and Dean Shanahan, who purported to be acting in Teresa Polenz's interest. Shanahan said that the College had learned that Polenz was scheduled to appear before a grand jury at 3 p.m. that day. But that hearing had already been postponed; the College purported not to know this.

But neither did the College contact Polenz or Silberman to ask them if the May 25 hearing would create a conflict. This led many to speculate that the reason for the College's postponement was for its own security.

Not only did vast media coverage and a counter-suit threaten Dartmouth, but also the names of all members present at the GSA meeting were also likely to be revealed. The *Review*, which does not seek to publicize these names, has kept them confidential. But naturally all persons present at the GSA meeting would have to be called as witnesses, because there are disagreements about some of the facts.

GSA members maintain that Polenz took a specific oath of confidentiality before the meeting. "She broke the oath of confidentiality; she lied to us," as Daniel Jay Berkow '85 was quoted in the campus daily. But the tape of the meeting reveals that no such oath exists. The *Review* has petitioned the dean's office to have Berkow tried before the COS for lying and slandering Polenz.

Other GSA members may have to appear before the COS too for alleging falsely that Polenz took an oath of confidentiality. Statements to the COS to this effect were filed by Berkow, Stephen Carter '86, David Garling '86, and Larry Burnett '84.

In his statement, Berkow maintained that "I have personally suffered great emotional and academic damage as a result of Teresa's actions and the subsequent *Dartmouth Review* publication. The GSA has also suffered as a result."

Berkow was, in part, referring to the *Review*'s publication of excerpts of a seemingly racist satire prepared by Berkow for printing in the *Daily Dartmouth* in which Berkow made derogatory remarks about blacks, Indians, and women at Dartmouth, suggesting that they be killed and eaten. In particular, Berkow satirically recommended that blacks be served up in Thayer Dining Hall for chocolate flavoring.

June 11, 1984

Charges Against Polenz Dropped
by Roland Reynolds & Gerald Hughes

THE STATE Attorney General's office has dropped its investigation into Teresa Polenz's taping of an advertised Gay Students Association (GSA) meeting last spring. "As far as the State is concerned, the case is over," said Deputy Attorney General Peter Mosseau.

The New Hampshire A.G.'s office had been investigating whether Polenz '87 could be charged with illegal surveillance under statute 570A:1 of the state criminal code which prohibits "willful interception . . . of any wire or oral communication." After a lengthy period of fact-finding and statute study, Mosseau concluded that no New Hampshire law had been violated.

Upon hearing of the state's decision, Polenz expressed relief saying, "After five months of not knowing where I stood legally, I am glad I won round one. Now I'll be able to put all my energies into studying and reporting." Commenting on the news, Laura Ingraham, Editor-in-Chief of the *Review*, said, "I think the administration owes Teresa an apology. Last spring this ordeal forced her to withdraw for the term, which meant she lost out academically, financially, and emotionally."

Last April, *Review* reporter Teresa Polenz attended and recorded a meeting of the GSA in order to gain information about the organization and its use of College funding. The *Review*, after giving a copy of the article to the GSA and Dean of the College, Edward Shanahan, for their perusal and comments, printed a transcript of the event. It named only the two officers of the organization.

Upon learning of Polenz's affiliation with the *Review*, three GSA members confronted the freshman in her dorm room. Using threats and intimidation, they tried to coerce her to hand over the tape after learning of its existence. She declined.

Failing in this attempt, the members decided to resort to more official means of pursuing their grievances and went to Dean of the College, Edward Shanahan, and the campus police, with whom they filed complaints.

Shanahan followed the lead of the GSA members, summoning Polenz to his office and threatening her with suspension if she did not appear. He then advised her to turn over all tapes and transcripts of the meeting.

The next week Dean Shanahan recommended that Polenz be brought before the Committee on Standards (COS). He flatly chirped, "In my judgment, the recording of conversations during the GSA meeting without the knowledge or acquiescence of the participants was a violation of the criminal code of the State of New Hampshire."

The hearing, however, never convened. After numerous delays, the College finally postponed the trial indefinitely, after an editorial appeared in the *Wall Street Journal* criticizing Dartmouth's handling of the matter. Dean Marilyn Baldwin announced that the College would wait for the State Attorney General's office to investigate the possibility of criminal action before taking COS action.

The state took five months to rule on this case. The delay in the decision was due in part to a pending, relevant New Hampshire Supreme Court ruling, according to Gene Struckhoff, Polenz's attorney. Over the summer, the court heard *State v. Sheedy*, which also involved statute 570A:1, although in a slightly different context.

Since Polenz actually took part in the conversation that she recorded, the word "intercept," which holds together this felony statute, does not apply. The statute is considered by many of New Hampshire's legal authorities to be vague and poorly written.

Four days after the state's decision was announced, College Counsel Gary Clark said, "I don't have any opinion because I don't know what the Attorney General's office said."

The College could, of course, still continue to try Polenz before Dartmouth's COS, and GSA spokesman, David Garling '86, has gone on the record to say that he hopes the College will proceed to discipline Polenz.

"I would be bothered if they pursued it," said Struckhoff. "If they conjure up something else to charge her with, I think that would be unfair."

The Dean's office would not comment on what further action the College would take. Gay Students Association chairperson Steve Carter also refused to comment.

Ingraham said, "I hope the College has more foresight and common sense than to haul her before the COS. But if they insist on a witch trial, they are in for a fight."

If the College does opt to discipline Polenz, under the College rules she could be charged, according to sources in the Dean's office, with disorderly conduct and violating the Principle of Community. Polenz's attorney in the event of a COS hearing is Laurence Silberman of Washington's Morrison & Foerster law firm. Silberman is a Dartmouth graduate and former deputy attorney general of the United States.

"I would have been astounded had the State proceeded against Teresa. It would have taken a torturing of New Hampshire law," Silberman told the *Review*.

Summing up her feelings about the whole affair, Polenz said, "I guess you can say I had quite an interesting freshman spring. But no one ever told me that being an investigative reporter was easy. I'm just disappointed that Dartmouth seems so intolerant of varying opinions and freedom of the press—especially when it concerns *The Dartmouth Review*."

October 17, 1984

Shunning Shanahan

The Week in Review

O N OCTOBER 31, Dean Edward Shanahan sent a letter to all students and faculty members at the College. In it, he announced his decision that no disciplinary action would be taken against *Review* reporter Teresa Polenz '87 for her tape recording an advertised meeting of the College-funded Gay Students Association last spring.

The mild-mannered dean did, however, urge the Dartmouth Community to participate in a public censure of Miss Polenz for her "hurtful behavior." Why doesn't he just have her wear an embroidered "I" (for "insensitive") on her chest for the rest of her time at Dartmouth?

In this profound epistle, Dean Shanahan was very careful to use words such as "alleged" and "perhaps," words that last spring eluded his vocabulary. His expression of personal disgust over the student's actions was his clever way of saying, "Look, liberals, I'm sensitive!" But he ends up scraping face, not saving it.

We commend the administration for pushing aside its pride and consulting outside counsel in this matter. Competent lawyers outside the College arena realize that the Miss Polenz would have legitimate legal recourse if brought before the Committee on Standards.

But a question that comes to mind is: Does a College official have the right to announce to the entire student body the results of what is supposed to be a confidential disciplinary matter, without even consulting the student involved? Many of Miss Polenz's peers knew of the outcome before she, herself, received official word. Certainly, Dean Shanahan is not one to stand on a soapbox about preserving "personal confidences."

So, freedom of the press and the *Review* have won again. But we should all eagerly await the College's new rule that makes the First Amendment a breach of the "Principle of Community."

November 7, 1984

Condemnation
The Week in Review

L AST WEEK, *The Dartmouth Review*'s Board of Trustees and staff voted 35–2 to publicly censure the administration and faculty of the College, due to callous and insensitive comments made by both groups about *Review* reporter Teresa Polenz '87 over the past six months.

Although their uncompassionate acts are non-adjudicable within the context of New Hampshire law and the College disciplinary code, it does not mean their behavior in this community is—or would be—beyond public comment. We therefore urge concerned students and alumni to join in with expressions of public disapprobation about the faculty and administration.

We realize that the faculty, being the rash and overreacting group it is, will probably respond to this by condemning us right back at their next faculty meeting. At least the Dartmouth community will understand their true reasons for doing so.

Shame on you, Dartmouth, for letting such an extended fiasco as the handling of this case take place at our venerable institution.

November 7, 1984

The Indian Wars

The Greatest of Them All
by Laura Ingraham

S AMSON OCCOM was born in the region between the Shetucket and Quinebaug rivers, in the state now known as Connecticut, in 1723. Little did his father Tomockham, a hunter, know that his son would play a historic role in the founding of a small college dedicated to the education of Indians.

Sam Occom got his historic opportunity when he and his mother converted to Christianity. "I was born a Heathen and brought up in Heathenism until I was sixteen," Occom wrote later. One advantage of falling under the influence of the New England missionaries was that the Occoms learned fluent English, and were able to pursue higher studies.

Young Occom was particularly impressed with one Yale pastor, the Reverend Eleazar Wheelock, who was doing missionary work in Lebanon, New Hampshire. For several years Occom lived in Wheelock's home as his resident pupil, where he is said to have mastered the Hebrew Bible and grown in wit and oratorical power.

After his education with Wheelock, Occom opened a small school in Montauk on Long Island. There he shared his time between teaching, preaching, and serving as a judge. An active mind, he also composed devout hymns. One surviving hymn begins: "Awaked by Sinai's awful sound."

In 1751 Samuel Occom married Mary Fowler, another Indian woman who had converted to Christianity. Soon after, he was ordained to the ministry and invited by Wheelock to work in his newly founded Indian Charity School. Occom proved particularly adept in soliciting contributions for the school; in fact, one of his donors was Benedict Arnold. Occom's charisma and devotion appealed to those he asked for money.

When Wheelock was asked by some friends in England to send an Indian missionary who could preach and pray in English, as an inspiration to the British, Wheelock immediately thought of Occom. Although a full-blooded Indian, Occom had picked up all the civilities of Christian civilization, and was fully equipped for his European sojourn.

Accompanied by Nathaniel Whitaker, Occom took off for England in 1765. He had with him sixty letters of recommendation from noted American personalities, including Wheelock. Once in England, his trip was managed by the Earl of Dartmouth, whose generosity would result in the founding of Dartmouth College, whose name would live on in history as the College's first benefactor.

But the reason the good Earl was so inspired was in large part due to the personality of Sam Occom. While in England, Occom met the most important churchmen and dignitaries, including the Archbishop of Canterbury. He even had an audience with the King.

Unfortunately Occom's companion, Whitaker, proved to be a disaster. He got into furious arguments with the British because of the sectarian and dogmatic positions he held. Wisely he was asked to take a secondary stance to Occom, who had already inspired wild praise and attracted many gifts.

Occom returned in triumph to America. But there he discovered that Wheelock had not taken proper care of his wife and children; one of the children was quite ill. This resulted in a bitter falling out between Occom and Wheelock, after which Occom took to drink and dispair, even his Christianity sorely tested.

But the mark of a man of character is not whether he falls, but whether he can pick himself up. Occom did eventually, his faith returning to him. He even went to Wheelock and made up with him, a gallant gesture, because Wheelock was mostly responsible for their falling out.

Occom and Wheelock then shifted the Indian School from Connecticut to Hanover, New Hampshire. Wheelock received a charter from King George III, and Dartmouth College was founded. Initially Occom was upset that Wheelock also planned to admit whites to Dartmouth. "I am very jealous that instead of your institution becoming Alma Mater to my brethren, she will too be Alma Mater to the tawnies," he wrote Wheelock.

Eventually Occom left Dartmouth and lived in the colony of Oneidas in New York, where he lived until his death.

But his spirit lives on at Dartmouth. It is the spirit of honesty, intelligence, faith, self-discipline, courage, and loyalty. That is the spirit of the Indian symbol which honors great Dartmouth graduates who have embodied the same principles as Sam Occom.

If Sam Occom were alive today, he would have chanted loudly our College cry, "Wah-hoo-wah." Sam Occom was an Indian proud of his heritage and confident in his ability. He would have understood what the Dartmouth Indian symbol stood for, because it stood for him.

October 3, 1984

Thank God the Indian Is a Stereotype

by Dinesh D'Souza

T HERE ARE THOSE at Dartmouth who prize the Indian symbol, and sport it proudly in the face of all kinds of contempt. Others despise the symbol, some because it offends their heritage, some in empathy with those it offends, the rest because they feel the entire issue is sort of silly, and the symbol is too divisive to return now anyway.

This is not a war cry for the comeback of the Dartmouth Indian, the College symbol banned by President Kemeny in 1974. It is intended to provoke reflection about the issue, which, contrary to the claims of certain satirists, really amounts to more than much ado about nothing.

Before entering the foray of arguments for and against the symbol, I must ask the antecedent question: Why a symbol? What is its purpose? To me, a symbol is a catchword for an ethos, a simple and appealing emblem of an idea or people or philosophy. And all the richness and complexity of that idea or people can be rallied at the mere utterance of the symbol. In that sense, a symbol is a convenience, somewhat akin to the prisoners who amused each other by reciting the numbers corresponding to jokes in the prison humor anthology.

The Indian symbol has been criticized as a stereotype, and so it is. It has to be. Which symbol is not? A symbol is a stereotype because that is its function—to remind, to stand for, to simply portray. That the symbol is a stereotype does not mean reality is not complex; in fact, it is because reality is complex that it becomes necessary to have symbols. Even the student who whoops the Indian cry oblivious to its meaning is, in this sense, being unconsciously swept into the culture; he has only to use the symbol to set off the reminder.

Of course symbols sometimes estrange themselves from their original meaning, and this is not necessarily bad. In the case of the Indian, it wouldn't be so good if the symbol came to represent rape and saturnalia, and fortunately the only ones who so designate the Indian are those who hate, and do not use, the symbol. But it isn't wrong for the Indian symbol to represent both Dartmouth tradition and Indian culture; in fact, the intent of the symbol is to link the two, because of Dartmouth's historical and cultural committment to the sons of Occom.

It is unfortunate that some Native Americans, as they wish to be called, find the symbol repugnant. I can empathize with this sentiment; in any case, it takes all kinds to make a world. The Native Americans find the symbol offensive partly because they are frustrated at Dartmouth, partly because the fraternity hoopla thing seems vaguely insulting, but mostly because Native Americans before them have told them the Indian symbol is a disgrace.

I find this cultural inculcation—the coralling of Native Americans by extant Dartmouth braves, and their subsequent instruction in how Dartmouth's institutions apply culturally to the Indian race as a whole, rather sad. For one, it denies freshmen Indians a chance to make up their own minds about the symbol. Two, it exploits gullible students for political ends. Yet it is a comment on the Native American Society, and certain professors who will go unnamed, that entering freshmen Indians are carted off to forums, sit-ins, and rap-sessions, at which it is unanimously determined for them that the Indian symbol is a self-evident infliction upon their heritage, of which they would be proud, and they should stand up for their rights, and so on.

What must be faced, in any event, is that the symbol has divided students and alumni these last few years, and it has not lacerated without scars. Some charge that the wounds of the symbol are deep, and it is impossible to return the Indian to Dartmouth because of its forked legacy. Perhaps they are right, I do not know. I, for one, would not want the symbol back if they are.

If it is agreed that the Indian symbol is important to Dartmouth, however, and if it is determined that the unifying power of the symbol that once united is not lost, then I think the old scars of the Indian war can be gotten over. The symbol has divided for five years, but for two hundred it has unified. Much of the division over the symbol has been provoked by administrative diktat over its removal, but now President McLaughlin is committed to allowing students to use the symbol if they want to. Also, the classes most emotional about the armageddon-effects of the Indian symbol are slowly graduating out of Dartmouth, and fresh issues of students come in, who by no means find the Indian *de facto* disgusting.

October 5, 1981

Hovey Grill Murals Covered
The Week in Review

E ARLIER this week, Dartmouth College aborted an attempt to remove the Hovey Grill murals from the basement of Thayer Dining Hall. The murals were to be moved to the Hood Museum of Art for storage. Workmen abandoned attempts to remove the murals after one of the art panels they were trying to remove began to show signs of damage.

The murals are now going to be covered with permanent walls, according to Jaqueline Bass, curator of the Hood Museum. Bass maintains that the walls may be removed at some future time without damaging the Hovey paintings.

The murals were painted in 1938 by Walter Humphrey '14. They were covered by the Kemeny Administration in 1979. Covering the murals, which depict Eleazar Wheelock cavorting with Dartmouth Indians, was widely perceived to be Kemeny's response to an incident that year in which two students dressed as Dartmouth Indians skated on the ice of Thompson Arena between the periods of a Dartmouth hockey game.

Curator Bass said that, before the murals are covered, photographers will make color reproductions of the paintings for the Hood Museum. The reproductions will not be part of the Museum's regular collection. Those wishing to admire the Hood Museum's Hovey Grill mural display will have to make a special appointment to do so, Bass said.

Bass explained that the primary motivation behind covering the murals is that their content is considered to be inappropriate for a dining facility the College would like to use for outside guests.

John Heston, director of College communications, said the murals were "offensive" and "tying up a part of Thayer [Dining Hall]."

April 18, 1983

Art Professors & Critics Blast Hovey Censorship
by Dorn Bishop

S EVERAL art professors and renowned art critics around the country vigorously oppose President David McLaughlin's policy of covering the Hovey Grill murals as a crude form of censorship.

None of the art professors reached expressed approval of the College's decision to cover the murals. The most outspoken opponents of College censorship were Professors Matthew Wiencke of Classics and Robert McGrath of Art, both of whom emphasized that, while the murals were not "distinguished" art, they nonetheless represent an important form of "period art" that should be open to the public for viewing.

Professor Wiencke termed the murals' covering a "blatant visual and graphic demonstration of censorship" on the part of the College. "I truly sympathize with the concerns of the Native Americans here, but to censor art in an adult academic community—I'm against that," said Wiencke.

"Certainly the murals are critical of Native Americans, but a lot of things are offensive to a lot of people. Take the Orozco murals in Baker. There are a lot of people offended by those as well. Yet there would be an extraordinary outcry if they were ever covered. One simply must learn to live with some criticism. Again, I sympathize with the Native Americans, but I frankly think the murals should not be covered."

McGrath took a similar viewpoint to Wiencke but added that he could "tolerate" the covering of the murals.

"I personally see the murals as unfortunate, but the College's action is shortsighted and injudicious. In short, the covering of the murals can be looked upon as a 'band-aid' that merely mutes rather than solves the problem of tolerance in education."

Art Professor Varujan Boghosian compared McLaughlin's covering of the murals with the work of the artist Christo, who is covering with cloth entire islands in Biscayne Bay. There is only one important difference between covering murals and covering the islands, however.

"The islands retain their meaning," said Boghosian.

Professor Perkins Foss had no strong feelings about the matter and called the murals "a dull book." Asked if he would object were the Orozco murals "temporarily" covered twenty years from now because some students were offended by them, Foss said, "Students are here to study for four years. I don't think they should have any say in College policy."

When it was suggested that the Hovey murals were being covered because they offended a group of students, Foss said he was unaware of any such motive for the covering of the murals. Foss acknowledged that he did not keep abreast of the Hovey Grill affair.

Richard Teitz, Professor of Art and Director of the Hood Museum, expressed disapproval of the college's decision.

"What the College is doing is not complete censorship but, by making it so difficult to view the murals, the College is nonetheless exercising a degree of censorship."

Teitz cited the problem of reconciling the right to freedom of expression, as guaranteed under the First Amendment, and a work of art that offends some people. He conceded he would not have counseled President McLaughlin to cover the murals.

Said Teitz, "Dartmouth students are intellectual enough and mature enough to make their own judgments about a work of art. What the College is doing is almost akin to banning a book from a library shelf because it offends some people. We learn by reading and seeing things that might be offensive but nevertheless express a point of view."

The comparison made by Teitz to that of banning a book was a common one among those art critics contacted.

The *Washington Post* art critic Ben Forgey said he would fervently oppose any such censorship. The *New Republic* art critic Jack Beatty said that he would condone a type of "liberal censorship" in some very extreme instances. Although neither of the men were familiar with the Hovey murals, both said, however, that it would be highly unlikely that they were so offensive to Native Americans as to warrant the type of censorship the College has undertaken.

"It sounds like burying your head in the sand to me," said Forgey. "There must be plenty of alternative means available to the College to express interpretations both of art and the period it represents without exercising a type of virtual censorship.

"If the art is offensive to Native Americans, then have an open debate on the matter. Eradication should be replaced by an attempt to learn from others' attitudes. Now there are some practical considerations involved, but it would be far-fetched to imagine that this matter reaches such a level as to warrant censorship, especially at the college level."

Beatty said he could not possibly pass judgment on the murals without having seen them, but stressed that he could not believe that censorship of the murals would necessarily lead to further instances of censorship.

Nevertheless, Beatty said that the proper manner of dealing with the murals certainly is not by covering them up without an open forum for debate.

"If we don't show mutual respect, the melting pot won't have any peace. I wouldn't want to be a young black man in a class studying *Huckleberry Finn*, in which such racist terms as 'nigger' are common. So what the Indian wants in your case stems from a valid feeling arising from social marginality."

Beatty went on to say, however, that the covering of the murals themselves without debate "would seem a little absurd" and pointed out that, based on the action, individuals could not view anything from the past that would be offensive to some people. "I would rather trust viewers to make their own judgments than simply pull a sheet over (the murals)."

Richard Lang, Acting Director of the Wheelright Museum of American Indian Art in Sante Fe, New Mexico, was unfamiliar with the murals but urged that they be open to viewing regardless of whom they offend.

"It is essential that we maintain a perspective on the past if, for no other reason, then simply because it behooves us to retain it so as to formulate a perspective on change and growth."

Lang compared the covering of the murals to destroying the monument erected as a reminder of the Battle of Little Big Horn and stressed that, if the murals have any merit as art, then they are worth preserving.

Wilcomb Washburn, Executive Director of the Indian Bureau at the Smithsonian Institution, was acquainted with the Hovey situation and called McLaughlin's policy towards the murals "a most embarrassing and sad story."

Washburn said that Native Americans are failing to make the distinction between positive and negative stereotypes. The murals, according to Washburn, depict the Native American in a light no worse than that depicted in the leather etchings immediately above the Hovey Grill in the Thayer Dining Hall Lounge.

"By any measure of consistency, these etchings should be covered also."

Washburn stressed that all of the arguments raised thus far have not been relevant to the central issue of the right of freedom of speech and expression. "Just as Earnest Hopkins had the courage to resist covering the Orozco murals when they raised an uproar some fifty years ago, so too David McLaughlin should today resist the pressure to cover the Hovey murals."

May 16, 1983

Freshmen Unravel Indian Controversy
by Laura Ingraham

T HE SECOND QUARTER of last Saturday's football game against Cornell had just ended, the score tied at 10. People in the stands stood up to stretch or to get a snack, while freshmen tore across the field forming their class numerals. The crowd shouted its approval at the rambunctious and spirited 'shmen. And, as expected, the '87s ran up to the top of the Cornell side of the stadium. But then a huge white sheet began to unfurl near the top of the bleachers and a hushed awe fell over the crowd, followed by loud cheers and applause. Freshmen proudly held a colored Indian banner which covered an entire section of the stands below them.

Choruses of "wah-hoo-wah" erupted from the freshmen and were echoed by Dartmouth alumni and students across the field. Even the band members joined the frivolity. Swaying back and forth, arm-in-arm, the beaming '87s portrayed the image of the "united Dartmouth" that campus progressives call for. They ran the banner back down the stands and around the field for alumni to take a closer glance.

Campus police officers stood by, watching this half-time show, and even cleared the way for the banner to be whirled around. A handful of students shouted criticisms at the whooping 'shmen, but these killjoys were drowned out by the ecstatic alumni and undergraduates who bellowed cheers of approval.

Indeed, the class of '87 has shown more resolve toward use of the Indian symbol than any class since the symbol was abolished in 1974 by the Kemeny administration. Two weeks ago in Cambridge, even Harvard students remarked about how spirited and rowdy Dartmouth freshmen were in their yelping support of the Indian.

This incident is not an isolated one. Sales of Indian paraphernalia in Dartmouth's fraternities have risen 25 percent over the last three years. Traditional Indian cheers have been sung at every home game this year, with more and more students unafraid to join in the festivities. And some members of the Dartmouth Rowing Club donned warpaint for last Sunday's "Head of the Charles" regatta.

This is not merely a student backlash to the administration's strident discouragement of the Indian symbol. Undergraduates see the need for a rallying point on campus and see that the Indian symbol has always provided that sense of spirit.

Saturday, the freshmen made Homecoming weekend more memorable than those in years past. They showed that it is possible to have tasteful and clean fun with the traditional symbol. Dartmouth went on to trounce Cornell after half-time. It was a victorious day.

But now Dean of the Freshman Margaret Bonz and President David McLaughlin have expressed "disappointment" over this freshmen lack of "care and sensitivity." Meetings of such organizations as the "Interracial Concerns Committee," the Student Assembly, the Native Americans at Dartmouth, and class councils have been called due to this incident. Ad hoc committees will spend hours in the Collis Center trying to determine how to stop this unusual enthusiasm of the freshmen class. Perhaps "compassionate" and "sensitive" campus crusaders will demand punishment for those hundreds of freshmen involved in toting and painting the banner.

But the sky seems bluer and the sun brighter this week in Hanover, as the wah-hoo-wah's of Saturday's game still echo through Memorial Stadium.

October 31, 1983

Dartmouth: Renew Your Commitment
by Laura Ingraham & Suzanne Schott

T HE EYES of over one hundred Indian leaders from across the nation are fixed on Dartmouth. These men and women have responded in good faith to our questionnaire concerning the Indian symbol.

During the past years, there have been times when the Indian symbol issue has been treated in a frivolous manner. Frustration and anger from both sides have contributed to this, but now these chiefs have voiced concerns which are anything but frivolous.

Throughout the years, the United States has turned its back on the American Indians. So has Dartmouth College. A Sioux spokesman writes to us from Nebraska: "If Dartmouth was founded for the education of Indians, why isn't there more information presented to them?"

Perhaps it is because the College is ashamed at its bungled efforts to make Indians "happy" at Dartmouth. It has segregated them by means of the Native Americans at Dartmouth (NAD) house and the Native American Studies department, and made them so embarrassed of their heritage that they have turned needlessly radical in their confusion.

Ray Burns '86, president of NAD, denounces the symbol as "a racist caricature." He commented recently that it is an "offensive and archaic stereotype" and "looking back . . . ignores the fact that we [American Indians] are a people active today." By logical assumption, Mr. Burns would classify these tribal leaders as "archaic" too, since they do not so readily abandon their past, but use it to give them direction for the future.

At Dartmouth, both the symbol and our Indian students have been neatly removed from the mainstream. The position of both at Dartmouth should be an honorable one. It is anything but that. Indeed, instead of channeling their efforts toward bettering themselves, their people, and the country, Dartmouth's Indians are running with one foot nailed to the ground. The nail—their own opposition to the Indian symbol—is what holds them back from what should be the main benefit from an Ivy League education: learning. Yet the handful of NAD members refuse to acknowledge that a part of their culture can be a unifying and beneficial force here, because they were told before even coming here, that Indian symbol supporters are fanatical bigots. But, one Oklahoma leader writes: "The federal government has been trying to do away with all Indian treaties. But we're here to stay. And we plan to be here for a long time. To me, the Indian symbol is a reminder of our existence and endurance."

These Indian spokesmen and women are not looking for handouts or pity. They're struggling—in many cases against incredible odds—to maintain pride in their culture after years of mistreatment by the government. An Indian governor of New Mexico sees hope for his young people in Dartmouth College. "I believe this school should definitely have an Indian symbol. This school is of the highest kind, elite, and has the best system of education a school can offer to Indians."

Whether or not the College will have the courage to follow a new course of action to welcome American Indians to Dartmouth remains to be seen. Based on what their chiefs have told us, we recommend the following:

> 1) Bring back the symbol. As the secretary of the Crow Tribal Council in Montana believes, the symbol "helps to educate people about Indian culture. . . . Our culture is neglected everywhere else. I hope Dartmouth won't be the same."

> 2) Enforce a "dignified" use of the symbol. If the College can uphold an academic honor principle, it can certainly uphold one concerning the Indian symbol. A Seneca chief admits: "Sometimes the Indian was used badly."

But, he continues: "Those were exceptions. The actual symbol was okay. I was sorry to see the universities do away with it."

3) Foster interest and concern in the real plight of American Indians rather than the contrived oppression of those in the Ivy League. Why not ask young Indians what they think of the symbol before bringing them here and telling them to be offended by it? Expand existing Tucker Foundation projects to aid Indian reservations. Approach reservations to recruit students and offer them a respected—not isolated and forgotten—place at Dartmouth. The possibilities are endless if the commitment to the Indian nation is real rather than token as it has been in the past.

The American Indians do not need another generation of people who shy away from Indian issues. They deserve respect and attention. Soon, the *Review* will begin a campaign to raise money to benefit a national Indian cause. We're doing what we can. After all, if it weren't for the Indian people, there would have been no Dartmouth.

October 3, 1984

Tribal Chiefs: Bring Back the Indian
by the Editors

W HO WOULD HAVE believed it? Indian chiefs across the country are overwhelmingly—repeat, overwhelmingly—in favor of a return of the Indian symbol to Dartmouth.

Don't wrinkle your brow. The chiefs were not misinformed about the situation. They were told about Dartmouth's founding. They were told that the Indian was abolished because some Native Americans and others regarded it as racist and insensitive.

Yet the criticisms of the Indian symbol hardly seemed to affect them. Some had heard the complaints before, and dismissed them as misguided and in some cases radical. But the majority of Indian chiefs found the criticisms of the Indian symbol so absurd as to be incomprehensible.

The Dartmouth Review has for some time had its suspicions about whether people purporting to speak for the vast majority of Indians nationwide were in fact doing so.

We have several examples in our society of labor leaders who don't speak for workers, "civil rights" leaders who misrepresent their minority constituencies, and politicians who don't speak for the people. Now we must add another case to this list.

Our procedure for conducting the following survey was simple. We obtained a list of every single Indian tribe in the country. We decided to conduct in-depth interviews over the phone with some of the Indian chiefs, and sent a mailing (so we could have signed affidavits of their position) to the rest.

The final tallies came in over a period of three months. They were unbelievable to us because, despite our suspicions, even we had begun to buy the Native American Studies professors' claim to speak for the anger of all Indian peoples.

Total Chiefs Favoring the Indian: 125
Total Chiefs Opposing the Indian: 11
Total Chiefs with No Opinion: 15

The chiefs with no opinion said, almost unanimously, that "it is more appropriate to act on the basis of reactions from eastern tribes rather than nationally," as James Hena, the governor of New Mexico's Tesuque Pueblo tribe, put it. Richard Alvarez of Californias Chemehuevi Indian Tribe said that "we must respect the wishes of the tribes in your area."

There were very few chiefs opposed to the Indian symbol, and some of them said they favored a "dignified" Indian symbol. But a handful were adamant. Mike Prescott, president of the Lower Sioux Indian Community Council, argued that "It seems that all college teams in the country are named after either Indians or animals. That suggests that Indians are animals."

Lucy Taylor, secretary of the Prairie Island Community Council in Minnesota, said "we don't need to be put on display like that. I agree with the people who don't want the Indian symbol."

There were a couple of angry letters. Roger Jim, chairman of the Yakima Nation in West Virginia, suggested Dartmouth adopt as its symbol the "Honky." Joseph Russ of the Covelo Indian Council in California called the Indian in "the poorest taste" and noted, "If this is incomprehensible to you, there is nothing we can do to educate you in this matter."

But these comments were in the minority. And some of them were confused reactions. Prescott of the Sioux tribe, for example, attacked the Indian symbol vigorously, and then said he would favor a dignified symbol if Dartmouth provided full scholarships to all Indians who were admitted to the College.

Now that their strongest argument for banning the Indian has been overturned, what will the militants who oppose it fabricate next?

October 3, 1984

Letter from the Editor
by Deborah Stone

Which of the following do you consider unacceptable and boorish behavior?

1) Unfurling a handsome Indian banner at a football game in a celebration of a one-hundred-year-old symbol, or

2) Emptying a bag of unnaturally bloodied tampons at the feet of President McLaughlin and his wife during the Dartmouth Night festivities in front of Dartmouth Hall.

In the unlikely case that you can't decide, here are some additional details: the Indian banner was displayed during halftime by a group of about ten freshmen who acted in accordance with campus police requests; the tampons were deposited by a group of about ten students who were disguised in ski masks and who fled immediately after staging their protest. The tampon tossers were presumably part of a group called "womben to overthrow dartmyth"; in a flyer distributed around campus, this group explained that they were using the "bloodied tampons in protest of both the alma mater 'Men of Dartmouth' and the governing structure of dartmyth college." The protestors concluded, "We force you to acknowledge our presence."

Most would agree that the answer is 2). It seems that President McLaughlin, however, would answer differently. In a letter to the Dartmouth community, McLaughlin criticized two incidents which occurred over Homecoming weekend. One incident was the tackling of some Harvard cheerleaders by freshmen; McLaughlin called this an "institutional embarrassment" for which he sent a letter of apology to Harvard President Bok.

The other incident criticized was the display of the Indian banner, which McLaughlin called "a display of thoughtlessness." He wrote: "To those misguided students who feel compelled to flaunt the 'Indian symbol,' I say unequivocally that such conduct will not return the Indian symbol to the athletic fields of Dartmouth College. . . . Those who persist in offending this community by using the Indian as a symbol are guilty of an insensitivity antithetical to the purposes of Dartmouth."

McLaughlin's only reference to Dartmouth Night, which was disrupted by the masked feminists, was his description of the "outpouring of enthusiasm, loyalty, and good will." Majority support for the Indian symbol, which is orderly and respectful, will never bring it back, but reckless and tasteless protest against the alma mater by a handful of fringe students could soon result in its abolition. Making decisions without consulting students and alumni is one recent tradition which the McLaughlin administration holds dear.

In addition to the unfair psychological intimidation McLaughlin employed in his letter, he falsely outlined the circumstances of the Indian symbol abolition. The president declared that the decision not to use the symbol has been "reaffirmed repeatedly by the Board, the faculty, and the students of the College." This is simply not true; the initial decision was illegitimate—and even it has not been reaffirmed. A majority of students and alumni support the Indian symbol, but alumni are ignored, and students are pressured not to use the symbol.

Members of the Afro-American Society, who tried to rip the Indian banner, were not chastised for their harassment of fellow students. Instead, the administration called an "emergency meeting" of the freshmen class at which the freshmen were ordered not to run on the field at halftime and not to use the Indian symbol. Freshmen were told again at this meeting that the use of the Indian symbol is "not an issue of free speech." Judging from the Administration's reactions to these various campus incidents, one thing is clear: President McLaughlin, Dean Shanahan, and the rest can't distinguish between good and bad behavior.

And people thought Secretary of Education William Bennett was going off the deep end when he charged that leading universities lacked virtue.

October 29, 1986

College Censorship Tactics
by Christopher Baldwin

T HE ANTI-INDIAN MOVEMENT seems to be making little progress at the College. Indeed, the ideational hollowness of Dartmouth officialdom is evident by the most recent scuffle over the symbol—the campus police's confiscation of the Indian banner at the Dartmouth-Cornell football game.

The naiveté of the anti-Indian proponents is demonstrated by the logic of their argument. The symbol should not enjoy official College support, argue Hanover's sophisticates, because it is fierce and unrefined. They will explain that the symbol is not an accurate representation, and more specifically, an anachronism. Therefore, it is offensive. Such specious reasoning shows that the anti-Indian wowsers are trapped in the provinciality of the present, unwilling to recognize the past glories of a dying culture.

But to the dismay of Dartmouth's Indian detractors, 125 Indian tribes support Dartmouth's Indian symbol, while only eleven are opposed. Former Chief of the United Cherokee Council, Jim Gordon, believes that "For Indians to say the Indian symbol is objectionable is to show self-hatred." "Go for it all—Indian dances, Indian cheers, it's something we support," said Mildred Cleghorn, Chairman of the Fort Still Apache Business Committee.

In Hanover, the opinions of America's Indians are unfortunately met by deaf ears. Student supporters are silenced. Administrative pressure. Police intimidation. Censorship. These are the tools of Dartmouth's anti-Indian movement.

While the overwhelming majority of Indian chiefs support the Dartmouth Indian, freshman are subject to lies, misinformation, and vaporous phrases on how the symbol is "not sensitive" and is "racially divisive." Last week's mandatory freshman meeting, or freshman moratorium, is a case in point. The freshman were lectured at by several speakers about the Indian, and ironically, one panelist suggested that the Indian symbol be given the stigma of a Nazi swastika.

Professors and College employees who wish to buy Indian t-shirts from this office do so secretly, either late at night or through the mail. This proves that diversity of opinion is not tolerated by many of their colleagues. At least one campus police officer has been warned by the Administration not to wear his Indian t-shirt while in Hanover.

Campus police confiscate Indian banners, and the freshman caught propagating such heresy are sent to the Commander of Dartmouth Thought Police, Dean Margaret Bonz.

The Hovey murals are covered because Parkhurst (Dartmouth administration), licensed by moral superiority, has decided that Dartmouth students should not view them.

Most recently, the Administration has decided to remove "The Indian Will Never Die" and "Wah-Hoo-Wah" stickers from dormitory doors. (Other stickers are left untouched.) Rooms displaying Indian stickers are reported to the Office of Residential Life, and Buildings and Grounds employees then remove them. Last week, College workers removed stickers from a door in Mid Fayerweather, but a graphic photograph of two lesbians taped directly below was left untouched. You see, at Dartmouth, some forms of speech are more free than others. Lesbian photographs—beautiful. Indian stickers—intolerable.

The College's attempt to censor the Indian is futile—after years of administrative pressure, students still overwhelmingly support Dartmouth's Indian. What Dartmouth's censorship does do, however, is show that Parkhurst is scared. Scared of free ideas. Scared of free thought. Scared of free expression. Why? Because the anti-Indian feelings at Dartmouth are purely visceral, devoid of fact or logic, dependent on the histrionics and bombast of a few intellectual dilettantes.

November 12, 1986

KING FEATURES SYNDICATE
The Savage Side of Parkhurst
by Jeffrey Hart

I JUDGE THE 1974 decision to attempt to abolish the Indian symbol to have been a moral, intellectual, and above all, because we are talking about an educational institution, an educational disaster.

I do not speak from the standpoint of a nostalgic alumnus. I am not nostalgic for the so-called "old Dartmouth" and in fact transferred out of it after two years to Columbia. When I was an undergraduate, at Dartmouth I did not use Indian symbol stationery nor give much attention at all to the symbol.

But the 1974 decision has itself become a symbol much more important than the Indian symbol itself.

First of all, let us address substance. It was essentially asserted by the College that the Indian symbol is insulting to American Indians, or is, in the current jargon, "racist."

This is clearly false. The Indian has appeared on the U.S. coinage, often and prominently, along with Lincoln, Washington, Roosevelt, Kennedy, and other dignitaries. This was not denigration of the Indian. Dartmouth did not evolve its Indian symbol because it looked down upon the American Indian. All of these uses of the Indian symbol did assert a common right to the assorted symbols of America's past—which, I take it, is one thing that is being precisely denied.

Now, if a critic argues that, whatever, the Indian symbol is "perceived"—more current jargon—as "racist," then the only reply that includes respect for the critic is that the "perception" is wrong. If a person tells you that he "perceives" that the moon is made of green cheese, the only reply that respects him is that, sorry, it is not.

There flowed after the 1974 decision a whole train of evil consequences beginning with official misinformation that I must regard as deliberate. That, for example, the Indian symbol was introduced into general usage by "sports writers" during the 1920s. As I write this, I note the nearby presence of my father's Indian-head senior cane, Class of 1921. The sports writers of the "1920s" must have worked rapidly indeed. The Baker Library archives possesses Indian-head canes dating much farther back. Indian figures inhabit the weathervane atop the library and also the College Seal, because they are part of Dartmouth's particular and America's general past. If you enter the lower west entrance of Baker, you will see in a glass case of the wall some memorabilia of a Dartmouth student killed in World War I. It includes a patch of canvas with an Indian head on it. No one can deny him, or us, access to that past.

It was even asserted, at least semi-officially, that the Wah-Hoo-Wah cheer signified an imminent sodomization of rivals taken in war. This turns out to be entirely false. Appropriately enough, the words signify the coming of snow—the snow-job given to the Dartmouth community.

The peace-pipe ceremony in the College field known as the BEMA persists, but perhaps only because the Thought Police have not caught up with it. Which moves us beyond false argument and deliberate misrepresentation to the subject of censorship of art, and other censorships. Yes, deliberate official censorship of art, "book-burning," as President Eisenhower called it in his 1954 commencement address at, yes, Dartmouth. There has been the censorship of our great song "Eleazar Wheelock." There has been the censorship of traditional football cheers. There has been the censorship of the Hovey Grill murals, featuring bare breasted ladies. I certainly would not consider the latter to be great art, but they certainly can be seen as an important period-piece. The same can be said of the much-touted Orozco murals, which are bad art—over-drawn, over-stated, and in bad taste, along with being anti-white and, especially, anti-Protestant; but Dartmouth is not about to cover up work by a Mexican communist, no matter how garish and propagandistic. Dartmouth looks upon the Orozco murals with breathless awe.

Which brings us to the inner, the core meaning of the 1974 decision about the Indian symbol—the symbolism of the decision. What it signaled, and here is the worst educational disaster, was that henceforth minority demands would be specially privileged, even if the demand might be absurd. The same rules of argument and evidence would not apply to minority claims. If a minority—and not just any minority, but henceforth privileged minorities—asserted something, well, then, amen brother, that was it.

And it has been it, from special admissions privileges, to special "programs" in the curriculum, to segregated social arrangements and notable faculty incompetents. It is to Dartmouth's honor that last year twenty-seven Jewish students petitioned against a special minority effort for Jews, asserting that they did not need or want it. Well done.

Of course, Dartmouth will not only survive but prevail. The current auspices of the College are merely leaseholders, not owners. You can, with some effort at selection, get an excellent education here, and, as Adam Smith once said, a "nation has a lot of ruin in it." Indeed, America itself has demonstrated Smith's point.

Dartmouth students are voting with their t-shirts and windbreakers and above all with their brains. It will take ten or twenty years to recover from this issue—but "The Indian Will Never Die."

September 21, 1988

Divestment

Divestiture Campaign Instituted
by William Cattan

A CCORDING TO Alan Berolzheimer of the Upper Valley Committee for Free South Africa, a major push will be made this year to force Dartmouth College to divest from corporations that have significant operations in South Africa.

Berolzheimer added that the Upper Valley Committee for a Free South Africa (UVCFSA) was pleased to have Professor of African Studies Leo Spitzer, "one of our people" and a person "sympathetic to divestiture," placed as the head of Dartmouth's Advisory Committee on Investor Responsibility. "Our practical goal has been to have Dartmouth divest from all corporations that do business in South Africa." "I know him," Berolzheimer said referring to Professor Spitzer. "We're beginning another big push this year."

In our conversation, Berolzheimer referred to Professor Spitzer only as "the new head of the Advisory Committee," not by his name, because he claimed that Professor Spitzer wanted his support of divestment to remain unknown for the moment.

Since Professor Spitzer is head of the College committee, his name and position are considered public information by the College and released on request.

The UVCFSA has targeted several corporations with operations in South Africa whose stock appear in Dartmouth's portfolio. Among those are Amax, Newmont Mining Company, and Englehart Minerals and Chemicals. The Committee hopes to pressure Dartmouth's trustees into selling all stock they hold in those, and several other multi-national corporations. Berolzheimer said he hoped the money saved from South African investments could be channeled into "the regional economy."

UVCFSA is an organization composed primarily of Upper Valley residents, not Dartmouth students. When asked who, in fact, ran UVCFSA, Berolzheimer replied "We're a non-structural organization. We don't believe in hierarchies."

All this would hardly be worth mentioning were it not for two important facts.

One, it is Dartmouth College's stated policy not to invest in any company that has more than 2 percent of its total operations in South Africa. Additionally, of Dartmouth's $500 million investment portfolio, about $80 million of that is tied up in companies that have any operations in South Africa. When one combines both of the above facts, it turns out that only $1.6 million of Dartmouth's monies are actually invested in South Africa; exactly 0.3 percent of Dartmouth's $500 million.

Two, liberals, as well as conservatives, are rejecting divestment as a way of dealing with South Africa. Overall, there remains a universal opposition to the apartheid policy of the South African government— mitigated partially by recognition of moves within South Africa to end discriminatory practices. As Gwendoline Carter, Professor of Political Science at Indiana University, said speaking in Johannesburg in 1979, unless the South African government moves away from apartheid "in a strong and obvious way," it would he difficult for any American government to return to an "open, friendly, give-and-take relationship."

It does not, however, necessarily follow that as a matter of policy American institutions ought to disinvest from South Africa. Consider what some Americans have to say about divestment:

Mr. Vernon Jordan, former President of the National Urban League: "There are many in this country who would discourage and/or legally prohibit U.S. firms from doing business in South Africa and it is easy for them to take this stand because they do not have to witness the devastating unemployment that will accompany massive divestment. . . . After searching my soul, I cannot join those who call for divestment."

Mr. Henry Ford, Ford Motor Company: "U.S companies can do more for blacks by staying in South Africa and giving employment and training. What would happen to our employees if we left? We regard training and education as the key elements in opening the doors to equal opportunity. Equal pay for the same work is a firm policy of ours."

Professor Walter Williams, George Mason University. During a 1980 visit to South Africa, Professor Williams said: "White South Africans could survive very well if foreign industries took their investments out. The people who would bear the burden would be mainly black South Africans."

Mr. William Raspberry, *Washington Post* columnist: "I heard again and again . . . a virtual plea against divestment from (South African) blacks fearing unemployment or mass bloodshed. . . . Whatever their differences on divestment, blacks in South Africa are unanimous on one thing: Americans who are concerned about black South Africans should bring maximum pressure to bear on American-based companies to end their discrimination."

Mr. Derek Bok, President of Harvard: "As an investor, Harvard has declared its opposition to the South African regime and has pledged itself to vote on shareholder resolutions in the manner best calculated to overcome apartheid. I believe that these actions represent the most ethically responsible course for Harvard to take. In contrast, total divestment would almost certainly cause the University to divert millions of dollars in pursuit of a strategy that is legally questionable, widely disputed on its merits, and very likely to prove ineffective in achieving its objectives. Under these circumstances, I find it hard to avoid the conclusion that divestment is an extraordinary proposition that would not receive serious consideration were it not for the passions that are so understandably aroused by apartheid and all its attendant injustices."

Projections of the long term effects of divestment from South Africa indicate that such a program would have the greatest adverse impact on the black labor force by cutting job growth and increasing unemployment. Conversely, foreign investments in South Africa ensure future black labor progress at all levels by increasing the country's overall growth rate, and by expanding the market need for black labor. That also has provided important impetus for upgrading skills within the black labor force.

Divestments, it seems, finally appeal only to those who seek the emotional gratification of witnessing immediate, if bloody, social change.

October 25, 1982

Divestiture Will Cripple Blacks
by the Editors

M RS. LUCY MVUBELO is one of South Africa's most prominent black labor leaders. She is the General Secretary of the 15,000-member National Union of Clothing Workers and Vice President of the Trade Union Council of South Africa.

Born in Johannesburg in 1920, she has been active in the labor movement all of her adult life. Since 1953, she has held prominent positions in the National Union of Clothing Workers, during which time the membership has increased more than tenfold, a significant achievement during a period of great difficulty for organized black labor. Her union is now the largest black trade union in South Africa.

From 1959 to 1964, Mrs. Mvubelo was appointed to the Women's Section of the International Labor Organization to represent black women workers. She was elected to a second five year term, but was prevented from continuing in office when South African participation in the ILO was terminated in 1964. She also serves on the Executive Committee of the multi-racial Women for Peace movement. In April, Mrs. Mvubelo will receive the honorary degree of Doctor of Social Science, honoris causa, from Rhodes University of Grahamstown.

Lucy Mvubelo is convinced that foreign investment offers the best hope of economic progress for South African blacks, both because it increases the demand for workers and because of the influence of foreign-based companies.

THE DARTMOUTH REVIEW: Mrs. Mvubelo, do you think apartheid is beginning to change in South Africa?
LUCY MVUBELO: The apartheid laws have failed dismally. A healthy and growing economy saw to that. The emergence of the Afrikaner businessman has ensured apartheid's permanent demise. Black workers are valued assets, educated and trained black workers even more so. Laborers are no longer in demand for things machines can do. We are not faced with the practical considerations which led to the French Revolution or those which brought the Communists to power in Russia. We are not in the static status situation of peasants or serfs.

TDR: As you see it, what is the most important question facing South Africa at the present time?
LM: The most urgent and pressing problem in South Africa at this time is the political accommodation of the urban blacks.

TDR: What about the "homelands" policy which has created allegedly independent new black states such as Transkei and Bophuthatswana?
LM: For better or worse, the South African government policy of creating independent black republics is or will be an accomplished fact. Nine such republics are planned, and three are already independent—Transkei, Bob-phuthatswana, and Venda. These will soon be followed by Ciskei. Once political independence has been granted, it cannot be taken away. Can you imagine what the world's press would have to say about, for example, the invasion by South African forces of the unrecognized Republic of Transkei? Therefore, as much as we dislike and disapprove of this carving up of South Africa, we have to accept that it is an accomplished fact and cannot be changed. Thus, we are left to consider the key question of the urban blacks, those who are so closely integrated with the whites, coloreds, and Asians in South Africa, that they cannot be separated out and have absolutely no desire to be anything else but South African citizens.

TDR: Do urban blacks consider themselves primarily to be members of particular tribes, such as the Zulu or the Tswana, or do they view themselves as South Africans who desire the equal rights of citizenship with those of other races?

LM: This is an important distinction. To consider the position of the urban blacks is really to consider the situation of Soweto, the apartheid-created black city on the outskirts of Johannesburg, a city with a population of over a million black persons from every black ethnic group in South Africa as well as its neighboring countries. The inhabitants of Soweto are thus anything but a homogeneous society, yet they have much in common. Soweto is urbanized, industrialized, Christianized, and totally dependent on the economic structure controlled by the white man.

TDR: Are you saying that urban blacks, such as those in Soweto, have formed a new community which has replaced the previous tribal identity and loyalties which Soweto residents had when they first came to the area?

LM: Yes, this is certainly now the case. The divergent groups of Soweto have been molded into a society that gives prominence not only to its politicians, but also to a variety of other people. The inhabitants of Soweto have much in common, but theirs is a dependent society. It is dependent for political rights on the white Afrikaner government and for its economic well-being on English-speaking whites.

TDR: What, then, do the urban blacks of South Africa think about their future?

LM: The urban black, whose responsibility it is to decide the future political and economic advancement of blacks in South Africa, is faced with the question of whether equality is to be achieved by evolution or revolution, or by the mythical process of the outside world boycotting South African trade and the disinvestment of foreign capital.

TDR: What is your own opinion concerning these alternative courses of action?

LM: In my view, revolution is totally unacceptable. It is only the far left wing or communist elements which still see revolution as an answer. For any revolution to be successful, it must have the popular support of the people—or at least the majority of the people—and it must have the support of the intellectuals of the society. The concept of communism is alien to Africa and even more so to the well-informed blacks in South Africa.

TDR: Are there any circumstances under which you think that revolution would be an appropriate means for achieving black equality in South Africa?

LM: Revolution as a means of gaining political power can only become a popular concept in a situation which is static and devoid of the future hope of change and the solution of problems. It requires a state of affairs in which a man can have no hopes for himself or for his children. But today's situation in South Africa is neither static nor sterile.

TDR: Many opponents of apartheid in the United States, including many black Americans, have urged a boycott of South African goods as a way to improve race relations in South Africa and push that country to racial equality. What do you think of this approach?

LM: Those in our country who urge a boycott of South African goods and the disinvestment of Western capital are simply a small fringe of desperate revolutionaries. They realize that the basic condition from which revolution can arise does not exist, thus the world must create it. Who will suffer? Clearly the greatest hardships would fall on my people, the black people. They will be the first to lose their jobs. They will be left to die of starvation. They will be the first to be killed in a revolution.

TDR: What do you see as the way to bring black South Africans into a position of equality with whites?

LM: Clearly, there is only one solution, and that is by way of evolution, by negotiation, and utilization of all opportunities which arise, by cooperation when necessary and resistance when necessary.

TDR: Has evolution accomplished much so far?

LM: It has accomplished a great deal. Remember, in 1948, with the election of the present South African Nationalist Government, there was the beginning of a concerted effort to keep the black man in his place. His very slight voting power was destroyed. Wherever possible, he was reduced to the status of laborer. Job reservation measures excluded blacks from most trades and professions. A never-ending list of laws was passed to keep the black man down. But all of these efforts are crumbling, or have already crumbled. South Africa has a new Prime Minister and a definite new direction is being taken. Full trade union rights have been granted to blacks. Training facilities are now available. Job reservation is dead. The Group Areas Act is regarded as applying only to residential areas and neutral business areas will be created in which any businessman can operate.

TDR: But aren't some of these things simply surface changes which keep the underlying inequality of the races basically unchanged?

LM: To say that the changes are "cosmetic" is to misunderstand. It is not plastic surgery any more, but is much nearer to a heart transplant, for a change of heart has taken place. We have really entered a new phase: rights and privileges are being extended to blacks, to coloreds, to Asians. I am convinced that this process will continue provided that South Africa remains economically sound.

TDR: You believe that a boycott or a policy of disinvestment would slow down the pace of change?

LM: There is no doubt about it. Large scale unemployment, although affecting mainly the blacks, can also affect the whites, and the old story of jobs for whites will once again become a major issue. Repressive laws will again be demanded.

TDR: How would South African blacks view a withdrawal by American business?

LM: American culture has had a tremendous influence in South Africa, not only on whites but even more so on blacks. The black man sees in the situation of the American Negroes a comparable situation. We feel a common sympathy for Americans. It is still good business in South Africa for a label to say, "Made In U.S.A." Your withdrawal from the South African scene can only be to your own disadvantage. It will be seen as a surrender to the revolutionary philosophies of the East and a lack of faith in the very democratic capitalistic system which you represent. Remaining in South Africa and increasing your stake will be a boost to the evolutionary process which is now taking place. It will be encouragement that the freedom which is so cherished by the Americans can also be ours.

TDR: Not long ago, Jesse Jackson visited South Africa and called for an end to U.S. investment in the country. Did you meet with Mr. Jackson?

LM: I had an appointment with Jesse Jackson and waited for three hours but he never appeared. He didn't meet the black in the street while he was there. He met only the affluent, and the radicalized intellectuals. I called his hotel many times but was never able to get through to him. We are angry about his call for disinvestment. Before he made such a statement he should have met with black workers—those who would be affected. He called for disinvestment, then he left—he went home. Many blacks said, "Who called on him to speak for us?" Imagine him telling business to withdraw. What will happen to the people who lose their jobs? His only alternative is a war and revolution he will not have to fight.

TDR: Do you think the South African government was mistaken to invite Jesse Jackson to the country?

LM: No, it was good for him to come and for the government to let him. If he really looked at things he would have seen that we blacks in South Africa are often better off than those in so-called "free" black states. Letting Jackson in shows a certain liberalization on the part of the government. They now seem to be taking the view that critics in the United States and elsewhere should be invited in to see things for themselves. We are angry, however, when outsiders tell us that violence is the only way to achieve change. It will be my children's blood which will be shed. We don't want to destroy what we have built.

TDR: Do you believe that outside observers understand the problems which South Africa faces in all of their complexity?
LM: The answer is no. Too many critics are simplistic. They must consider the vastness of our problem: The blacks are divided into nine groups, with thousands more having come in from other states; our whites divided into English- and Afrikaans-speaking, and originating from every conceivable European nation; we also have in our midst considerable numbers of Indians, Pakistanis, Chinese, and Malays from the Far East, and Turks, Syrians, and Lebanese from the Middle East. Just as diverse as our people are, so diverse are their religious beliefs. "How to solve our racial problems?" is the foremost question of every thinking South African, and to all of us one answer has been dismissed: Violence. There are still advocates of violence. As you well know, violence has become a lucrative worldwide phenomenon. So, regrettably, we will have our own IRA, Bader-Meinhof, or Black Panther movement. Whatever it may be, it will remain a minority, even in South Africa.

April 20, 1981

Will the College Act on Shanties?
by Deborah Stone

M UCH HAS CHANGED in Hanover since November, 1985; the last leaves have fallen, two feet of snow have accumulated, and a new year has begun. But one thing that has not changed is the presence of the "shanties," those unsightly structures on the Green which continue to make a mockery of campus protest and the Dartmouth administration.

The Dartmouth Community for Divestment constructed the four shanties to pressure the College Trustees "to immediately commit themselves to divest from all companies that trade with, lend to, or have subsidiaries in South Africa and/or Namibia." The huts sport the slogans "Stop Killing", "Invest in N.H., not in Racist South Africa," and "American Investors Beware"; they are, needless to say, an eyesore to College and town residents. Their prolonged existence represents the latest administrative bungle and the widening of a double standard which threatens the purpose of a liberal arts school. Dean Shanahan said he was on the

Green the first day construction began: "When they were unloading the wood . . . I told them they didn't have permission." Two days later he delivered a formal note asking that the protestors "remove the shanties by the end of the day, or the College will take action." That was fifty days ago. Has the College taken any action? "No, not yet," Shanahan explained.

This administrative indecision sets a precedent it will surely regret. The focus on oppression in South Africa will remain strong only temporarily; it is a wicked problem, but it is not unique. It is another example of a latent inability to deal logically with minority voices on campus. Would the administration have accepted the presence of a teepee on the Green? After all, that's a vigorously debated College issue, just as is divestment. "No," replies Dean Shanahan, "I don't think there should be any kind of construction on the Green."

It is hard to see just how the administration is implementing its policy of objection to the shanties. Indeed, spotlights now shine on the shantytown throughout the dark winter nights, and campus police guard the area at night. At this rate, the Green could become a veritable museum of global strife. Let's hope that if this happens, there will be a toll for crossing the Green which would pay for round the clock police protection.

The Dartmouth Committee for Divestment was making plans this week for activities which continue throughout the term. Ozzie Harris, a member of the DCD who helps guard the shanties, said it was his understanding that "the shanties will stay as long as they serve an educational purpose." He added that the group had received "positive remarks and even donations of wood" from several Hanover residents. A South African who is involved in the protest is dissatisfied with the method of incremental changes the Reagan Administration is pursuing: "The Sullivan Principles will say to the slave that you must postpone your freedom until Sunday," and that while U.S. corporations may "improve the workplace, they don't really do anything to promote freedom." Harris concurred with the warning that "you should be skeptical of any corporation which says their concern is people; their concern is profit. If (their concern) were people, corporations would first be concerned with Americans."

The members of the Dartmouth Committee for Divestment believe "that divestiture offers one of the few opportunities for Americans to hasten the dismantling of apartheid and the achievements of full political rights for all South Africans and Namibians." This prediction has little historic or economic evidence to back it. The very strategy used by the Dartmouth Committee for Divestment contradicts their proposals for dealing with the South African problem. The students in this group are dissatisfied with the policies of their institution; they could drop out of Dartmouth, thereby stopping their support (their tuition money) for South African investment. Instead, they have chosen to remain at Dartmouth, and try to change its policies within. United States corporations are dissatisfied with the conditions in South Africa; but instead of withdrawing from that country, they are trying to make improvements from within.

How long the shanties stay is anybody's guess. The Dartmouth Committee for Divestment intends to coordinate the shanties' continued display with campus petitions to both the McLaughlin and Reagan Administrations. The group claims legitimacy for their demonstration, so the shanties will come down only when the College Administration exercises some logic and decisiveness. This will get harder every day, and soon the College won't be able to draw the lines of acceptable protest. Dean Shanahan left the issue open when he said that the College had "not yet" taken action against the shanties; until that action is taken, Dartmouth will be left wallowing in the skewed logic of an intimidated administration.

January 15, 1986

LETTER
Dartmouth Committee to Beautify the Green Before Winter Carnival
by Teresa Polenz '87, Frank Reichel '86 & Deborah Stone '87

D EAR President McLaughlin,
The Dartmouth Committee to Beautify the Green Before Winter Carnival (DCBGBWC) was formed on Friday, January 17, 1986. Its main purpose is to remove four unsightly "shanties" from the Green before Winter Carnival.

The DCBGBWC was not formed to address the conflict in South Africa, or College policies on investment. Further, the DCBGBWC firmly believes in everyone's right to free speech; it does not believe, however, that the structures on the Green constitute an allowable protest. Indeed, Dean Shanahan himself said that he did not think there should be "any kind of construction on the Green." The "shanties" weaken the College in more ways than just being an eyesore to the entire campus: they exacerbate the bad national press Dartmouth is already receiving, they confuse the student body, they create skepticism among devoted alumni, and they discourage prospectives when they visit the College.

Shanty removal will commence at 3 o'clock in the morning on Tuesday, January 21, 1986. The wood will be donated to Upper Valley charities to help provide fuel for heating stoves. Again, the members of the DCBGBWC are not trying to stifle debate on campus. We are merely picking trash up off the Green, and restoring pride and sparkle to the College we love so much.

January 20, 1986; Printed in The Dartmouth Review *January 29, 1986*

Mission: Shanty Removal

by Jeff Rosenthal

A T APPROXIMATELY 2:45 on the morning of Tuesday, January 21, members of the Dartmouth Committee to Beautify the Green Before Winter Carnival (DCBGBWC) struck the first blows towards the dismantlement of the wooden structures which have defaced the historically charming Green since last autumn. Twelve members of the DCBGBWC, Dartmouth students representing every class presently enrolled at the College and including some staff members of *The Dartmouth Review*, gathered at shortly after midnight on Monday to discuss their course of action.

Over the next two hours, students made several surveillance trips to the Green to determine whether anyone was sleeping in the shanties, and also to survey the relative strengths of the four huts. The DCBGBWC learned that two girls were sleeping in the shanty known as Blackburn Hall. Of prime concern to the DCBGBWC was the safety of both the students sleeping in the largest shanty and the students participating in the campus clean-up effort. The committee members set out to reduce the disgraceful huts to pieces of wood suitable for transport and donation to more worthy charitable causes in the Hanover region.

On the street corner between South Fayerweather and Topliff dormitories, a large flatbed truck picked up the twelve well-prepared students. The vehicle rounded the bend towards Webster Hall while the DCBGBWC members crouched in the back. After the truck stopped next to the Green where the information booth usually stands, emergency lights flashing, the twelve Dartmouth undergraduates walked toward the darkened shanty town.

For less than five minutes the students attempted to purge the Green of these unsightly yet surprisingly sturdy shacks. The dismantlement of the shanties was organized and safely executed as three students hammered inside the structures. One DCBGBWC member noticed the two girls inside the fourth shanty attempting to light a lantern. He warned them to be careful not to start a fire, and asked if they intended to leave. They said that they were not leaving, so the DCBGBWC member gently closed the door to the shanty.

Within minutes the campus and Hanover police appeared at the scene and ordered the students to cease with the destruction of the shanties. All DCBGBWC members complied and then rode together in the truck, escorted by a Hanover police car, to the campus police office, where they freely gave their names, classes, and ID numbers. After the appearance of the College Proctor, the students returned to their dormitories.

At noon on Tuesday, the Dartmouth Committee on Divestment staged a rally on the Green in response to the attempted shanty removal. The rally was attended by approximately 200 students, faculty, administrators, and townspeople, who listened to emotional speeches by members of the DCD which branded the DCBGBWC members "racists." They also witnessed the beginning of construction of a fifth shanty christened M. L. King Jr. Memorial Hall. Later that afternoon, when DCBGBWC members Deborah Stone and Robert Flanigan appeared on the Green to speak with representatives of the press, they were subjected to a barrage of obscenities and insults from DCD members and other equally eloquent protestors.

The next day at approximately 8:00 a.m., some DCD members and their supporters entered Parkhurst Hall and staged a sit-in protest in the office of President McLaughlin. They presented the administration with the list of demands, and declared that they would not move until their demands were met. The number of faculty and student protestors fluctuated throughout the day between fifty and 250 people. At 6:00 p.m. of the same day, the daily hour at which Parkhurst Hall is closed for the night, a group of students were locked inside until morning. The Faculty Executive Committee also met in the morning, and called a moratorium on Friday classes.

January 29, 1986

CAMPUS FLYER
Dartmouth Alliance Against Racism and Oppression

W E, THE MEMBERS of the Dartmouth Alliance Against Racism and Oppression, in response to the deplorable act of violence committed on the night of the first anniversary of the national holiday commemorating Rev. Dr. Martin Luther King Jr., are here in protest. We have undertaken this non-violent action in order to address broad issues of racism and oppression on this campus. These issues have plagued the Dartmouth community for years and the administration has continually failed to deal with them adequately, we will remain here until the following demands are met:

1) That the College officially respond to the deplorable attack on the shanties with a public statement from Dean Shanahan and that the students involved in the destruction of the shanties be suspended immediately pending hearing from the Committee on Standards. That the COS be convened within twenty-four hours.

2) That President McLaughlin recognize the urgency of this crisis by returning to the campus within twenty-four hours; that he convene an emergency meeting of the faculty in order to declare a moratorium on

classes for Friday, the 24th of January, during which day a community forum will be held. The purpose of this forum will be to build an environment more supportive of the needs and goals of a truly diverse community. To this end, we demand formal discussions among students, faculty, administrators, and other members of the community on topics including but not necessarily limited to the following:

a. That the celebration of the birthday of Rev. Dr. Martin Luther King Jr. be commemorated at Dartmouth annually by a teach-in which will review the achievements of Dr. King in overcoming racism and oppression.

b. That the Principles of Community be made adjudicable.

c. That amendments in admissions policy be made so that Hispanics, physically handicapped individuals, and other traditionally oppressed groups other than Blacks and Native Americans be actively recruited.

d. That "Dartmouth" be removed from the title of the *Dartmouth Review.*

January 22, 1986; Printed in The Dartmouth Review *January 29, 1986*

LETTER

Letter from DCBGBWC Members
by Robert Flanigan '87, Teresa Polenz '87 & Deborah Stone '87

S INCE OUR attempted dismantlement of three "shanties" on the Green, utter falsehoods and vicious accusations have been circulating Hanover and the nation. The sole intention of the Dartmouth Committee to Beautify the Green Before Winter Carnival was and is to remove trash from the Green. Our committee was formed after months of administrative inaction, and after about one week of a general abandonment of the "shanties." When the structures were built in November, the administration issued a statement that if they were not removed by the end of the day, College action would result. Since then, the only action the College has taken has been the provision of police protection and spotlights which illuminate the "shanties" at nighttime.

Members of the Dartmouth Committee for Divestment have refused to address the issue raised by the DCBGBWC; instead they have resorted to emotional public displays designed to discredit and slander our actions. So far, they have made the following false accusations: that the attempted dismantlement was planned weeks in advance to coincide with the celebration of Martin Luther King's birthday, that members of our committee are racist, and that our method of shanty removal endangered the lives of two members of the DCD. These assumptions are absolutely incorrect. First of all, our committee was formed four days before the attempted dismantlement, and the actual event took place on January 21, six days after Martin Luther King's birthdate, one day after the celebration of his birthday, and twenty-seven days before the celebration of George Washington's birthday. Second, our committee membership crosses both gender and racial lines. And last, the "shanty" in which two DCD members were sleeping was not touched. The tactics of the DCBGBWC were simply a matter of logistics: the use of four sledgehammers was necessary because the structures were so sturdy, and we chose to operate at three a.m. so as to erase all possibilities of injury, and to ensure at least a partial success in the dismantlement attempt.

Now the College is levying wishy-washy charges, which took 39 hours to concoct, against members of the DCBGBWC. One consideration the administration might keep in mind as it pursues these charges is whom it really needs to reprimand—the students who have pridefully tried to keep their college clean, or the students who scream filthy obscenities and evil lies as they are being filmed by television cameras on their Green?

Printed in The Dartmouth Review *January 29, 1986*

LETTER
Dartmouth College Committee on Standards
by Terrie B. Scott, Secretary Pro Tem

D EAR DEBORAH [STONE]:
I write to inform you that you have been officially charged with violating the College conduct regulations against (i) malicious damage to property, (ii) unlawful and disorderly conduct, and (iii) harassment, abuse, coercion, and violence. Specifically, you have been cited for going onto the College Green with others on the morning of January 21, 1986 and purposely damaging the property of others; namely, the shanties of the so-called Dartmouth Community for Divestment and its members. In so engaging in damaging the shanties, it is also alleged that you engaged in the use or threat of physical violence directed toward the individual students who were in one of the shanties or engaged in other conduct directly toward them that had the purpose or effect of impairing their ability to function successfully in the College environment.

You have been scheduled to appear before the Committee on Standards (COS) at 4:00 p.m. Wednesday, January 29, 1986 in 303 Parkhurst Hall. Before your appearance, I strongly encourage you to familiarize yourself with the green pages of the *Student Handbook*, particularly the section entitled "Rights and Responsibilities of Students Appearing Before the COS" located on pages 112–114. Meanwhile, please complete and return the

"Statement of Understanding of Rights of Students Appearing Before the COS" form to my office no later than *12 Noon* Friday, January 24, 1986.
January 22, 1986; Printed in The Dartmouth Review *February 5, 1986*

Twelve Environmentalists Charged
by Roland Reynolds

T HE COLLEGE has filed disciplinary charges against the twelve students involved in the dismantling of the shanties on the Dartmouth Green. In part, the charges seem to be based on false accusations made by two members of the Dartmouth Community for Divestment, who were in one shanty at the time of the incident. The defendants, who are members of the Dartmouth Committee to Beautify the Green Before Winter Carnival (DCBGBWC), are scheduled to appear before the Committee on Standards at an open hearing on Tuesday, February 4, at 4:00 in 303 Parkhurst. If convicted of the charges against them, the students could receive punishment ranging from expulsion to a letter of reprimand.

The students have been accused of "(1) malicious damage to property, (2) unlawful and disorderly conduct, and (3) harassment, abuse, coercion, and violence," according to the Committee on Standards (COS) Secretary, Terrie Scott. The College has not further defined the charges, other than to accuse the DCBGBWC members of "purposely damaging the property of others."

The vague nature of the charges leaves many questions unanswered. The first charge, "malicious damage to property," is questionable at best. Given the illegal circumstances around which the "shanties" were constructed, the question of ownership is unclear. The Dartmouth Committee for Divestment (DCD) is not recognized by the state of New Hampshire as a corporation; it is not even recognized by the College as an organization. The DCD then is not an entity which can own property.

In fact, one member of the DCD said that "the shanties belong to the oppressed people of South Africa." If this is true, then, in accordance with the Constitution of the United States of America, the first charge should be filed by all of the "oppressed people of South Africa." Also, in accordance with the Constitution, the accused (the DCBGBWC) has the right to face their accusers (the oppressed of South Africa).

The second charge, "unlawful and disorderly conduct," also falls into question. "Unlawful" means, of course, "against the law." Is it against the law to pick up trash from your front yard? The DCBGBWC maintains that the "shanties" were simply trash on the Dartmouth Green. DCD member Kim Porteus admitted that the "shanties" were no longer serving their ostensible purpose, saying "the purpose of the shanties was to open people's minds about the apartheid situation in South Africa. If the shanties are closing their minds against it instead, then it's time to re-evaluate." The third charge, "harassment, abuse, coercion, and violence," was apparently levied because of a complaint filed by two DCD members, Kim Porteus and Lillian Llacer. In a letter to Dean Shanahan, the two students said, "We were victims of personal harassment in the form of violent coercion. We were forced to flee from the scene in panic." The truth of the incident related by DCBGBWC member Robert Flanigan is far different from the girls' statement. "I stood for several minutes outside the shanty with the girls in it," said Flanigan, "After a while, they spoke to me, saying 'We aren't leaving.'" Not exactly panic.

Porteus and Llacer claim that "the attackers acted without self-constraint. . . . There was serious potential for physical injury upon us." In actual fact, the DCBGBWC acted with deference to the shanty-dwellers. When Flanigan noticed that the girls were lighting a small camping stove in their shanty, he warned them to "be careful not to start a fire." The girls' shanty was never touched by the DCBGBWC. According to the Campus Police report, "They (the DCBGBWC) were all very cooperative and stopped (dismantling the shanties) when we asked."

Porteus and Llacer also make a charge of "mental abuse incurred by these acts of violence." Mental abuse is a charge so vague that it is hardly adjudicable. The girls were only spoken to the one time, regarding their fire, and they were never physically touched or threatened with harm. The girls' statements appear to be a malicious attempt to coerce the College into prosecuting the individuals involved in the shanty removal. Indeed, Porteus and Llacer say, "We demand that the students involved . . . be brought before the COS and just disciplinary action be taken against them."

In the past, hearings conducted by the Committee on Standards have been criticized for their disregard of the rights of the defendant. "Consider a trial in which the defendant is accused of a serious crime," ran a *Wall Street Journal* editorial in the spring of 1984, "one that puts the defendant's future in jeopardy. The defendant has no real right to a lawyer; no right to cross-examine hostile witnesses. What's more, the committee that functions as prosecutor is also the judge and jury. Three in one!" The editorial was describing a meeting of the Committee on Standards.

It is certainly questionable whether or not the members of the DCBGBWC will receive a fair hearing before such a body. Members of the administration that is bringing the charges are the same ones who will be sitting in judgment. Also, the members of the Committee on Standards, deans, professors, and students, have, no doubt, been influenced by the hysteria prevalent on the Dartmouth campus in the past week. Without an independent magistrate to hear the complaints, Dartmouth's environmentalists face an uphill battle against an administration that has already judged them guilty, based on the lies of their accusers.

February 5, 1986

College Symposium Serves Up Hysterical Accusations, Confessions
by Jim Sullivan

IN THE EMOTIONAL aftermath of actions taken by Dartmouth's Committee to Beautify the Green, the Faculty Executive Committee voted for a moratorium on classes for Friday, January 24. Instead of attending normal academic classes, the faculty committee asked students to focus on "racism, violence, and disrespect for diversity and opinion, as most recently demonstrated by the act of demolition of the shanties on the Green." The administration chimed in with President McLaughlin calling for "a discussion of the issue of human dignity on this campus."

Three issues have been raised at the College in response to the attempted dismantlement of "shanties." The first focuses on racism, but this is really a non-issue as far as members of the DCBGBWC are concerned: spokesmen for this group have continually made statements on their opposition to apartheid and their abhorrence of racism. The second issue relates to the College's investment policies; in a letter of intent the DCBGBWC stressed that it was not formed to address the debate on divestment. The third and real issue is the one which, unfortunately, has yet to be considered: it raises the question of what constitutes an appropriate and permissible campus protest.

The real issue of campus protest has not only been avoided, it has been twisted to enormous extents. Classes were substituted with what was supposed to be an educational symposium; what ensued was a twentieth-century witch hunt against twelve undergraduates. At the "educational" symposium students, faculty, and administration members openly called for the students' "immediate expulsion," labelling them as "terrorists" and "Klansmen," and demanding that they never be allowed to graduate from the College. "This institution should expel students who participated" in the shanty removal, advised Professor of Spanish Beatriz Pastor. Melinda Lopez '86 warned that "it's time for you (the twelve) to take a Parkhurst vacation." Besides calling for the students' expulsions before a hearing, symposium attenders tossed about vicious lies and offered personal confessions which had nothing to do with the Beautification Committee. Even Professor Gene Garthwaite, who came to the event "not as a teacher, but as a student," admitted his discovery of "how insensitive I really was to racism and sexism."

The College's intellectual leaders also lended some extraordinary perceptions to the moaning audience. Garthwaite, a history professor, after observing that "historians try to make sense of the past," offered this authoritative synopsis: the twelve students "did not attack the flagpoles . . . they did not attack the Senior fence, they did not attack the base of the snow sculpture, they attacked the shanties." Professor of French and Italian, Nancy Vickers, proclaimed that "every quip about the shanties, every prank that destroys, every joke about the Gay Students Association, if carried to its logical extent, is a sledgehammer on the Dartmouth Green."

Margaret Cassidy '87 exclaimed, "I feel pain and I hope you realize that!" Sean O'Hearn '87 asked "are you, my friends, willing to deal with the racism in your hearts, the sexism, the classism, and oops, here's the tough one, homophobia, ok?" The spiritual cleansing which many students and professors undertook perhaps did make the day a personally satisfying one; but by directing this hysteria at twelve undeserving students, the individuals at this symposium launched harassments which far surpass any with which the twelve are charged. Rajiv Menon '86, a member of the Dartmouth Committee for Divestment, made perhaps the most accurate statement of the day when he revealed that "we went around campus trying to discuss these issues with students; the general feeling was that somehow this wasn't even happening at all, that there wasn't really any insensitivity on this campus—and that we as the students bringing up these issues were the ones creating the problem."

But the condemnations continued late into the night; perhaps the only logic found at the entire event was in Phil Burrow's '86 question: "How do you think President McLaughlin felt when he came back and there were people standing on his desk? That is an emotional sort of terrorism and I don't think it's an acceptable form of dissent." Of course, the Parkhurst sit-in violated school rules, but action won't be taken against these students. The administration is too busy aiding and abetting the witch hunt. What this adds up to is reverse discrimination against a conservative environmentalist group, the students who tried to clean their Green.

Dean Shanahan wrote that "it is a sad day at Dartmouth College when a handful of undergraduates take it upon themselves in the middle of the night to remove shanties constructed on our Green for the purpose of demonstrating a deep-felt concern for the injustices suffered by the people of South Africa." But the real sadness becomes clear when it is realized that the College is the party which is acting unfairly. Who is being terrorized up here? Two students who were carefully left untouched in a shanty, minority students who think they're being discriminated against when the College gives them absolute freedom to break its rules, or the twelve students who are now being stigmatized, lied about, and threatened by those who claim moral superiority?

February 5, 1986

ON THE RIGHT
Student Revolutionary Update
by William F. Buckley Jr.

T HE CONTENTIONS at Dartmouth are once again front-page news, for the very good reason that what is going on there is newsworthy. The reason for this is that the students there on the left are highly mobilized, but so also are they on the right, who have their own publication, *The Dartmouth Review*. Since we are engaged in describing an order of battle, one might add that the faculty of Dartmouth is ever so trendy-left, while the president, David McLaughlin, is a centrist. The stage is set for a very long war, the most recent episode of which was The Matter of the Shanties.

A couple of months ago, something calling itself the Dartmouth Community for Divestment suddenly marched into the center of the fabled College Green and erected a number of shanties designed in the mind's eye to imitate living quarters of many blacks in South Africa. Now demonstrations of that order are, in the judgment of reasonable folk, okay as one-night stands. But pretty soon it transpired that the students had in mind a more or less permanent addition to the architecture of Dartmouth, an upsetting development to those with an aesthetic eye, and positively infuriating to those who believe that political demonstrations should be contained within a fairly short leash.

The reaction of the deans was to command the students to remove their shanties. But President McLaughlin, seeking to be as permissive as possible, overruled the deans and said the shanties might stay so long as they served "an educational purpose." One can think, of course, of any number of things that would serve an educational purpose which are inappropriate exhibits in a public park, but nothing was done for weeks until a week ago last Tuesday.

At which point a group calling itself the Dartmouth Committee to Beautify the Green Before Winter Carnival (that is Dartmouth's equivalent of Mardis Gras, the Superbowl, and the Fourth of July, scheduled for this weekend) mobilized at three in the morning. The twelve students, most of them associated with *The Dartmouth Review*, arrived with sledgehammers and, I kid you not, a rented flatbed truck, and before you knew it, Whoosshh!, Divestment City was no more. The Committee left word that it was "merely picking trash up off the Green and restoring pride and sparkle to the College we love so much." There are those who believe that a repristinated campus green is not necessarily a setback for black South Africans.

Mr. McLaughlin had been warned by politically acute observers that he had been mistaken in taking so permissive a stand on the shanties because what the left-students wanted—today as back in the 1960s—was confrontation, and sure enough they got this by staging a thirty-hour sit-in in the office of the president a couple of days after the shanties came down. At that demonstration they were pleading the case against racism, sexism, and the toleration of dissent, which is Newspeak for immunity for whatever left-minded students say or do.

Now President McLaughlin has his own problems, having been denounced a few weeks ago by the faculty for not exercising sufficient "governance," by which is meant docility to faculty edicts which, in Dartmouth, more often than not communicate faculty crotchets, as when the faculty expressed disgust a couple of years ago not with a black dean who physically bit a student editor of *The Dartmouth Review*, but with his victim. Perhaps responding to such pressure, McLaughlin ordered quick trial and execution of the shanty-destroyers, this followed by their hiring an attorney, who has got an extension, etc. etc. etc. One more scene at Dartmouth.

A good thing, in the opinion of some observers, inasmuch as Dartmouth is serving a useful purpose. When in 1968 the campus at Columbia exploded, the students destroyed scholars' papers and defecated into presidential waste baskets and before we knew it it was so in Berkeley, and Iowa State, Cornell and Yale and Harvard and, to be sure, Kent State. The germs of that universal upheaval are not dead and, interestingly enough, not by any means yet diagnosed. (That was the great failure of the American academy, the greatest failure of this century.) The left took effective control of campus life and declared themselves members of a revolutionary movement. Some of those folk are these days tenured professors at places like Dartmouth College.

But this time the right is organizing, if you want to use that word for such as those who believe that if the left asserts the right to build shanties in the middle of the Green, other students inherit the right to tear them down. As New Hampshire goes, so goes the nation.

January 30, 1986; printed in The Dartmouth Review *February 12, 1986*

College Kicks Out Nine Reviewers on Unproved Charges
by the Editors

TWELVE STUDENTS have been suspended from Dartmouth College. Four of them have been suspended indefinitely, that is, without guarantee that they will ever be allowed to return; the other eight have received either one- or two-term suspensions. These punishments were handed down from the College Committee on Standards, a jury of Dartmouth administrators, professors, and students, after nineteen hours of testimony and five hours of deliberation. The defendants are members of the Dartmouth Committee to Beautify the Green; on January 21, they attempted to remove four illegal and abandoned shanties from the College Green. The charges of which the students were found guilty include: malicious damage to property, unlawful and disorderly conduct, harassment, abuse, coercion, and violence.

Unofficially, the twelve students are charged with racism, sexism, homophobia, and terrorism. The level of emotional hysteria which developed on this campus represents a human phenomenon on a par with the Salem witch hunts. Vicious accusations have been launched by members of the faculty, administration, and student body against the twelve undergraduates. At a day long "teach-in" at the College, when all normal classes were cancelled for what President McLaughlin promised would be a discussion on "human dignity on campus," the twelve students were labelled as "Nazis," "would-be Klansmen," "fascists," "brownshirts," and "mother-f*cking, c*ck-s*cking racists." Demands for expulsion were constantly made; requests for a fair hearing were never mentioned.

What has really happened at Dartmouth is that twelve undergraduates have received severe punishments for exercising the precious right of freedom of expression. Unfortunately for the twelve students, the message they expressed was not popular with the faculty and administration. It is ironic that this event took place on a college campus, the citadel of rational examination and exchange of different ideas. And it is hypocritical that the forces responsible for closing the faucets of freedom are the same forces who claim a dire necessity for diversity and tolerance.

The students who belong to the Dartmouth Committee to Beautify the Green attempted to dismantle shanties which, after standing illegally on the campus commonground for two months, had been abandoned by their original supporters. This counter-protest is no different in character than the original erection of the shanties. The plan for this shanty dismantlement was conceived on January 17, 1986. This decision came after formal complaints were made to the town of Hanover, after several articles which called logically for the removal of the shanties appeared in this publication, after a suggestion was made, and subsequently denied, in the Student Assembly to vote on the issue of the shanties, and after a telephone conversation between a *Review* editor and Dean of the College Ed Shanahan confirmed that "structures of any kind should not be allowed on the Green." This decision also came after the original declaration by the College that the shanties had to come down immediately, after the town of Hanover had stated that the shanties violated numerous town building and safety codes, after the administration reneged their initial disallowance of the shanties, claiming they could stand as long as they "served an educational purpose," and after members representing every faction at Dartmouth, including members of the Dartmouth Community for Divestment, acknowledged that the shanties no longer served any educational purpose, and that they existed without consideration for the entire student body. In fact, the cost for campus police protection of the shanties surpassed $21,000. This sum was paid indirectly by every student on this campus; every student on this campus was forced to partake in a political protest against their educational institution.

How was this situation allowed to escalate to one of such hysteria and injustice? Why, when so many opinions have been voiced on this campus recently, were only twelve undergraduates stigmatized? Who really acted irrationally? Who harbored intolerance on this campus? And who, in fact, has been threatened and harassed?

Nearly all of the confusion present at Dartmouth has resulted from submission to political pressures. The administration became paralyzed by political pressure when the shanties were erected; it failed to enforce its own rules. The students who were responsible for this illegal defacement of the Green were never brought before the Committee on Standards. The administration was then trampled on when students twice occupied Parkhurst Hall. One group of occupiers was brought before the COS and found guilty, but were given "no punishment due to their moral conviction." Finally, the twelve students from the Committee to Beautify the Green, after having classes cancelled by the Faculty Executive Committee in their dishonor, were railroaded through a grossly unfair College hearing, and booted out of school.

Proceedings for this hearing began on Tuesday, February 4. The first six hours of the hearing were spent discussing the procedural format. Stephen Davidson '88, whose advisor was Professor Laurence Davies of the English Department, requested a private, closed hearing. Michael Haffner '88, whose adviser was attorney Douglas Moore, also requested a private, closed hearing with his father who had travelled from Texas. Freshmen Christopher Baldwin and Leslie Grant, whose attorneys were William Clausen and Patrick Hayes, together requested a public hearing. The remaining individuals, Robert Flanigan '87, Gerald Hughes '88, Werner Meyer '88, Daryl Polenz '88, Teresa Polenz '87, Frank Reichel '86, Deborah Stone '87, and Marie Trexler '87, requested a postponed public hearing, and a change of location. All of these requests were denied by the COS; they decided to hold a closed hearing for all twelve students that night.

Attorney Clausen proceeded with questions concerning the impartiality of some members of the COS: Professor Bernard Segal previously stated that "all people who work for *The Dartmouth Review* are evil"; Brian

Byfield '86 reportedly boasted to another student that he was looking forward to booting the twelve students out of school; Alice Dragoon's '86 impartiality was questioned, because she has formerly served as an editor at the *Daily Dartmouth*; and Chair of the COS Committee, Dean Margaret Bonz, had already discussed the events with one of the charged students, has previously issued punishments to two of the charged students, and is a well-known critic of *The Dartmouth Review*. Clausen also objected to the Secretary of the COS, and the evidence he had compiled for the hearing: Dean Alex McCormick had publicly chastised the Committee to Beautify the Green, and the evidence he submitted for the hearing was mostly newspaper clippings from the *Daily Dartmouth* and faculty notices soliciting money and support for the shanty-dwellers. However, all members of the COS were declared fit to judge, and further the defendants were denied the right to make their own recordings of the proceedings, both audio and photographic.

Presentation of witnesses finally began around 10:00 p.m. with the testimony of Kim Porteus '88 and Lillian Llacer '88, the two Dartmouth Community for Divestment (DCD) members who were staying in one shanty on the Green, and campus police officer Mark Lancaster, one of the first policemen to appear at the scene of the dismantlement.

Miss Porteus and Miss Llacer attempted initially to take the stand together, apparently unsure of their singular abilities to satisfactorily and similarly recall the events of early Tuesday morning, January 21. All previous statements made by the two girls had been jointly written. Present at their side, an attorney, who had been provided by the College, insisted that his role was merely that of an advisor to the witnesses. He declared that he would not be feeding the girls answers, although he did in fact whisper strategies and exact responses to both of the girls during questioning. Attorney Clausen objected both to the presence of counsel for the witnesses, and their intention to testify jointly. The COS ruled that Miss Porteus and Miss Llacer would be sequestered, and that their lawyer could remain throughout their testimony.

Miss Porteus testified first; she responded to questions from the twelve defendants and the COS members. Miss Porteus stated that she was not physically injured, that she was not verbally threatened, and that "Blackburn Hall," the shanty in which the two girls were sleeping, was not touched. Miss Porteus babbled throughout most of her testimony, continually affirming that she "felt threatened," but could not indicate specifically why she felt "threatened," other than that she heard a lot of noise.

During a recess between the two girls' testimony, they were caught by one of the defendants discussing the content of questions directed at Miss Porteus. When approached, the girls became flustered, and Miss Llacer declared that their conversation about the questions asked was "fair."

Subsequently, when Miss Llacer took the witness stand, she was forced to admit that she had held the discussion with Miss Porteus. Miss Llacer concurred with Porteus's statements that she was not physically injured nor verbally threatened, and she confirmed that no harm came to the shanty in which she was sleeping. Revealing inaccuracies in her written statement of January 22, Miss Llacer admitted that she did not know at the time of the dismantlement that sledgehammers were being used, and she could not cite specifically any forms of "violent coercion" used against her by any of the twelve. The only contact Miss Llacer had with any of the students was a dialogue with Robert Flanigan '87, in which he expressed his concern that she be careful with the lantern she was trying to light. Flanigan then asked Miss Llacer if she intended to stay in the shanty; she answered yes, and he left. Flanigan did not carry his sledgehammer with him when he entered the shanty for this short conversation. While answering questions regarding her loss of a feeling of security at the College, Miss Llacer mumbled vagaries about fears for her minority friends.

The last witness to appear before the COS on February 4 was Officer Lancaster. He reiterated several times the facts of his written report that all of the students were cooperative and orderly, and stopped dismantlement of the shanties immediately when asked.

The hearing continued on Monday, February 10. The twelve students all gave statements and answered questions from each other and the COS members. These proceedings lasted until 1:00 a.m., at which time the defendants left, and COS deliberations went on for two hours. Deliberations continued on Tuesday afternoon, February 11; a witness who at 5:30 p.m. walked past the room in which deliberations were being held, overheard heated argument and shouting. At 6:45 p.m., members of the COS started filtering out of Parkhurst. The first three to leave were Professors Christopher Reed and Albert La Valley, and Tom Funk '87. Each of these three COS members appeared disquieted. Meanwhile, Secretary of the Committee Alex McCormack paced nervously around the building. Chairman of the COS, Dean Margaret Bonz, waited with the College attorney, Sherman Horton, to inform the students of the COS decision. Bonz appeared very nervous and very pleased as she read the fate of the twelve undergraduates.

No explanations were given to the students as to what evidence convinced the COS of their guilt, or as to why they were issued different punishments. Upon careful examination of the charges and the students' actions, it becomes rather obvious that the two do not match up. The legalities surrounding the first charge are still unclear; the question of ownership remains, and if no one owns the shanties, are they property? And even if they are property, was damage done to them maliciously—with evil intent? Certainly not. The intentions of the Committee to

Beautify the Green were outlined in their letter sent to President McLaughlin, Dean Shanahan, and the DCD: its purpose was "to remove four unsightly 'shanties' from the Green . . . not to address the conflict in South Africa, or College policies on investment." The charge of disorderliness was dispelled by all twelve individuals, campus police officer Mark Lancaster, and police reports. The dismantlement was planned in advance, and safety precautions were discussed for several hours prior to the group's actions. The potpourri of accusations listed in the third charge are completely bogus: no one was harassed, no one was abused, no one was coerced, and no violent actions were taken. The attempted dismantlement was no more violent than the ordinary work of a carpenter, or of the DCD members who built and eventually finished dismantling the shanties.

The members of the COS cannot have carefully and fairly heard the testimony offered by the twelve defendants, the two DCD shanty-dwellers, and Officer Lancaster. During the COS hearing, very few questions were raised which applied directly to the rules which were allegedly broken. In fact, Deborah Stone, who never touched a tool or a shanty, has been found guilty of malicious damage to property. To an objective, careful listener, this seems impossible. Miss Stone is, however, managing editor of *The Dartmouth Review*. It cannot have escaped notice that the four individuals who received the most severe punishment are also the highest-ranking, up-and-coming members of this newspaper. The students who received the two-term suspensions are individuals whose involvement at the *Review* range from none to contributing editor. And the student who received the least punishment, was the one who has publicly denounced the paper, and called its style "infantile" during the COS hearing.

It is obvious that the hearing conducted by Dean Margaret Bonz and the College Committee on Standards was not a hearing based on fairness; it was a hearing based on political convenience and personal vendettas. On Tuesday, February 11, several Dartmouth professors and administrative members had their wildest dreams fulfilled: they kicked nine *Dartmouth Review*ers out of school.

Robert Flanigan '87, Teresa Polenz '87, Frank Reichel '86, and Deborah Stone '87 were given the most severe sentence: indefinite suspension from Dartmouth. These four students may apply to return to the College in the winter of 1987; it is unusual, however, for students who receive indefinite suspension to be reinstated within two years. Mr. Reichel was scheduled to graduate this March, while Flanigan, Polenz, and Stone had planned to graduate in the spring of 1987. There are no guarantees that any of these individuals will ever be allowed to return to the College.

Christopher Baldwin '89, Leslie Grant '89 Michael Haffner '89, Gerald Hughes '88, Werner Meyer '88, Daryl Polenz '88, and Marie Trexler '87 were also found guilty of all three charges and suspended for two terms. Stephen Davidson '88, who separated himself from the Committee to Beautify the Green after the attempted dismantlement, and recently resigned from and denounced this newspaper, was found guilty of only two charges and suspended for only one term.

February 19, 1986

Students Stay in School on Appeal
by the Editors

D ARTMOUTH COLLEGE has made specific threats against writers of *The Dartmouth Review*, saying that "there can be another COS hearing" if we publish the story of the twelve students railroaded by the Committee on Standards. Nevertheless, *The Dartmouth Review* believes in freedom of expression, and we are bringing you the complete story of what has happened to these twelve students.

Saying that the "decision was grotesquely unfair," the twelve students who were expelled or suspended by the Committee on Standards have filed an intent to appeal to President McLaughlin, and intend to make a formal appeal within days. Following normal College guidelines on appeals, the College is allowing the students to remain on campus until the president makes a decision on the fate of the twelve students. President McLaughlin has three options in adjudicating the appeal. One, he can lessen the students' punishment or find them not guilty. Two, he can call for another COS hearing. Or, three, he can let the decision stand.

The students charged in a letter to McLaughlin that the "Committee defied all reasonable rules of fair procedure and due process. The Committee's decision was arbitrary and without supporting evidence. The penalties imposed by the Committee were unfairly harsh and grossly inconsistent with the penalties handed down in similar proceedings."

In a letter to the twelve students, President McLaughlin commented that "since the decision on your appeal will be made prior to the end of the winter term, the postponement will not affect your loss of credit for this term unless the suspension for this term is removed as a result of your appeal."

In response to McLaughlin's letter, Frank Reichel commented that, "We shouldn't miss a day of school, because regardless of your opinion on the shanty incident, anybody can recognize that the COS was extremely unfair. That has to be addressed." Gerald Hughes commented, "I'm not going to let five thousand dollars and a term of work go down the toilet."

More evidence of the unfair nature of the hearing has come to light. In the course of the hearing, the two witnesses who were in the shanties contradicted their written statement which was presented to the COS as evidence. In their written statement, the girls stated that they were forced to flee the scene in panic, but Lilian Llacer commented during the hearing that she left the Green in order to inform other DCD members and later the police about the shanty dismantling.

Some of the punished students have also charged that the girls improperly discussed their testimony during the hearing, when they were supposed to be sequestered. Dean Bonz ordered that the girls be forbidden from discussing the nature of the proceedings in between question periods. After Porteus testified, there was a break in the hearing, and Porteus and Llacer were seen talking in the hallway outside the hearing room. When the hearing reconvened Llacer was questioned about the apparent breach of Dean Bonz's order. The conversation went as follows:

HAYS (Defendant's Lawyer): . . . note for the record that contrary to the chairman's order, the witnesses did confer and were talking to each other during the break.

BONZ: Lilian Llacer, I assume you have a statement to make to the committee and the students charged. Would you proceed?

LLACER: First of all, to address that comment . . . Kim and I didn't realize that we weren't supposed to talk to each other at all. We really didn't talk about. . . . I was just talking about the procedure that was going on in here and I don't think we swapped any information that was vital to this hearing.

LONG (Witnesses' Lawyer): We also had a conversation about the procedure that went on. I just explained to Lilian what to expect in terms of how the questions would come and the formalities here.

BONZ: Do you have anything to add to the written statement? Is there any elaboration you would like to make or would you like to move directly into the questions?

LILIAN: Move right into the questions.

BONZ: Deborah, do you have any questions of Lilian Llacer?

STONE: The first question I would like to ask Lilian is whether or not she discussed during the break with Kim Porteus the content of the questions that were addressed in here.

BONZ: Did you discuss during the break with Kim Porteus the contents of the questions addressed to Kim?

LILIAN: Yes, I asked her if they were questions mostly about exactly what happened that night, procedural questions, or if there were other things.

BONZ: Did you hear the answer?

STONE: I heard what Lilian said but that doesn't answer the question.

Did she or did she not discuss the content of the questions that were addressed to Kim? Did you talk with Kim about what Kim talked about in here? The content, not what sentence structure was used.

BONZ: Can you be clear about . . . can you give an example of what you mean by content, Deborah?

STONE: Did Kim say, "They asked me what time I left the shanty." Not how many questions did they ask . . . questions about content.

BONZ: Did you talk about specific kinds of questions that had been asked earlier of Kim?

LILIAN: Yes, I asked her if they were asking specific questions about things that went on that night or if they were asking other types of questions. She said that they were asking questions about the night and some hypothetical questions. And then Debbie was there (nearby in the hallway) and we didn't really talk about anything else.

STONE: I just want to point out to the chairman that that contradicts what Lilian said when she first entered here which was that the conversation was entirely about procedural matters. She now says that it addressed the content of the questions.

BONZ: We'll let the Committee . . . thank you.

Considering the unfair proceedings and the harsh punishments, the students are also considering filing a lawsuit against the College. Frank Reichel, a senior who planned to graduate this winter, said, "I have been damaged by Dartmouth College and I expect the courts will recognize this." Whether the students will actually file suit against the College is unknown.

Despite the campus hysteria induced most notably by the moratorium on classes, the feeling of many students is that the COS hearing was a great injustice to the twelve students and the College. Meanwhile, the COS continues in its role as prosecutor, judge, and jury.

February 26, 1986

Faculty Invests in South Africa
by Christopher Baldwin

A LL DARTMOUTH FACULTY professors invest in a retirement fund which buys stock in companies that operate in South Africa. Furthermore, the retirement fund, Teachers Insurance and Annuity Association, chooses stocks without regard to whether or not they are signatories of the Sullivan Principles. There has been very little discussion, and none public, by faculty about the inconsistency of condemning the College's investment policies, while disregarding what their own money is doing. The ironic truth is that the faculty are supporting a policy of active corporate engagement in South Africa—a policy which they have condemned.

According to the Manager of Employee Benefits' Office, all Dartmouth professors invest with the Teachers Insurance and Annuity Association. The TIAA provides retirement benefits and disability insurance, and upon retirement, investors are eligible to collect $53,910 a year for life, beginning at age sixty-five.

The TIAA is a national organization with over eighteen billion dollars invested in over two thousand stocks. Approximately 190 of these American corporations have direct subsidiaries in the Republic of South Africa, and forty-three of these do not adhere to the Sullivan Principles. The bottom line is that thirty-five percent of TIAA, and consequently of every Dartmouth professor's retirement plan, is invested with blue chip companies that have subsidiary operations in South Africa.

In other words, Dartmouth's faculty crusaders pursue an investment policy which only considers profit. Absolutely no consideration is made for social and moral concerns, according to an investment counselor at TIAA. At a past meeting of the faculty, the professors present voted unanimously for the College to divest and labeled the Sullivan Principles as "a fig leaf for genocide."

Many faculty are members of the Dartmouth Community for Divestment, and vociferously attack the College's investment policies. The DCD has centered its efforts on influencing and galvanizing student opinion, which can in turn put pressure on the Trustees to change their policy. Says the DCD, "Dartmouth College remains a supporter of racism and oppression in South Africa," and "Dartmouth's unconscionable complicity with the apartheid regime" lies in its "investments in companies that do business in South Africa," while faculty DCD members are benefitting from these "blood profits."

According to several faculty members, Dean James Breeden is trying to rectify the moral and intellectual inconsistency of investing in TIAA by pressuring the fund to divest itself from companies directly or indirectly involved in South Africa. Dean Breeden was out of town and unable to comment. Philosophy Professor Walter Sinnott-Armstrong is the faculty representative for Dartmouth College in a national movement to pressure TIAA to divest, but according to Sinott-Armstrong he has only signed a couple of petitions aimed at TIAA.

Superficially, this presents a picture of a Dartmouth faculty that is actively pressuring TIAA's South African investments. In fact, the Dartmouth faculty's pressure on TIAA to divest is virtually nonexistent. Professor Donald Green commented, "I guess I know that there has been some informal conversation about that (TIAA divestment). To my knowledge there is no organized group engaged in talking with TIAA about its investment policy. I think that elsewhere in the country there are though, and I think TIAA has been confronted with requests to consider its investment policy. But I know that only second hand. I don't know of any serious effort by anybody at the College to push TIAA to change its investment policy."

Regardless of the faculty's hypocritical stance, it is readily apparent that divestment is not an effective approach to confront apartheid. American companies are not likely to leave South Africa without selling their holdings to other South African companies (especially to South African insurance groups and pension funds which are not allowed to invest abroad) or to other foreign companies. There is no reason to expect these companies would fight apartheid laws, and they would probably "have a poorer track record than their departed American counterparts," commented economist Daniel McGowan of Hobart College.

In a positive example, General Motors of Port Elizabeth has publicly committed itself to providing "financial and legal support to its employees who defy a law that calls for racial segregation of beaches." This commitment demonstrates the positive impact American companies have in South Africa.

It may be soon that someone calls the Dartmouth faculty's bluff. The faculty is hypocritically, and conveniently, ignoring South African investments that are in their own economic self-interest, and this discredits the faculty's claim to intellectual and moral sincerity. The next protest should be in professors' living rooms.

March 5, 1986

ON THE RIGHT
Hanover Blues
by William F. Buckley Jr.

I T IS NOTHING short of astonishing that events at Dartmouth College continue to crowd the news: ABC, CBS, NBC, three syndicated columnists, countless editorials. One junior wrote elegantly to the student daily, "Having left the Hanover plain for the sunny beaches of Florida last August, I returned in 1986 with a heightened sense of perspective. You see, it was my first term off in over a year, and when one has been here that long, one tends to nonchalantly accept the various campus events and debates as—if you'll excuse my use of a much abused word—normal. It took four months on the "outside" and countless conversations with interested Floridians (who had the benefit of a disinterested and somewhat cosmopolitan view) for me to discover that Dartmouth is the repository of a unique perspective."

Hooray for whoever taught that student how to write English, but the current furor makes the study of English seem, somehow, effete—no, that is a bad word, because, as with their Indian, Dartmouth will come up with a lobby, in this case the gay lobby, to denounce you as a homophobe. The President of Dartmouth, Mr. McLaughlin, reintroduced ROTC, which was one of the totemic victims of the student madness of the Vietnam years, and finds for his pains he is all but asked, by faculty resolution, to resign.

The President leaves town on January 20, and lo, he returns to find his office occupied by protesting students, many of them black. They want to know what in the hell the president was doing off campus on Martin Luther King's birthday. Most people don't remember where they were on Easter Sunday, let alone MLK's birthday, but the poor president had to plead that he was talking in Florida about Dr. King. Not enough: the students wanted, and got, a school holiday so that everyone could chin about race relations and the accomplishments of Dr. King.

Now McLaughlin faces the most severe challenge to his moral authority. A lynch mob, which calls itself the Committee on Standards, met to try twelve students who, after weeks of frustration over an exhibitionistic protest against apartheid—they created on the campus Green, and maintained there, several shanties designed to promote the cause of divestment—organized one night to tear the damned things down. This was done without anybody's being threatened, let alone hurt, never mind the caterwauling of two girls sleeping in the shanties who chose under no provocation to act hysterically. Among the judges of the students was a former editor of the college newspaper which had called for the students' expulsion. Another "judge," a faculty member, had publicly referred to the twelve as evil. An assistant dean had referred to the defendants as "heartless, chicken-s*** people." The *New York Post* editorial writer recalls the disequilibrium of the Dartmouth faculty. "After the 1980 presidential election, the same faculty voted overwhelmingly to condemn Ronald Reagan's landslide victory. It reminded the historians among them of the election of Adolf Hitler."

Four of the students were, in effect, expelled, eight suspended.

I have forever and beyond believed that schools should make and execute their own rules. But if those students are dismissed, notwithstanding that no action was taken against the illegal shanty construction team, none against the students who had occupied the president's office—the record of Dartmouth's permissiveness in dealing with left-oriented protests is massive—then Dartmouth's president forever loses, and should lose, the respect of the millions of non-Hanoverians who have somehow got engaged in what is going on there.

What's going on at Dartmouth is a kind of solipsistic crystallization of ideological interest groups whose cause militant, a few years ago, was the elimination of the Indian, which for generations was Dartmouth College's symbol, implying ethnic prejudice against Indians only to the extent that Yale graduates could be accused of a contempt for bulldogs. Their causes proliferated: gay rights, apartheid, peacenickery, you name it: and there arose, a sign of health, a student newspaper which, although now and again more hot-blooded than the kind of thing you'd have expected from the Founding Fathers meeting in Philadelphia, has nevertheless been a robust and bright attempt to restore balance. The students who tore down the shanties were mostly associated with that paper, the clearly-intended victim of the vindictive petulance of the Committee on Standing. The president is on the spot. He should try amnesty, and a fresh start for Dartmouth College.

February 27, 1986; printed in The Dartmouth Review *March 5, 1986*

And Justice for All?
The Week in Review

INCIDENT: 29 students charged with deliberately obstructing processes of the College in January 9 sit-in.
COS finding: guilty
Punishment: none

Incident: 21 students charged with deliberately obstructing processes of the College in January 22 sit-in.
COS finding: guilty
Punishment: reprimand

Incident: 17 arrested students charged with unlawful and disorderly conduct during the College's shanty removal.
COS finding: guilty
Punishment: none

Incident: 2 students involved in shanty dismantlement who distanced themselves from the *Review* charged with malicious damage to property, disorderly conduct, and violence.
COS finding: one not guilty; one guilty
Punishment: none; reprimand

Incident: 10 students associated with *The Dartmouth Review* involved in shanty dismantlement charged with malicious damage to property, disorderly conduct, and violence.

COS finding: guilty
Punishment: suspensions for all

April 2, 1986

KING FEATURES SYNDICATE

Shanties & Liberal Fascism
by Jeffrey Hart

T HOUGH A PROFESSOR at Dartmouth and therefore naturally in the midst of the shanty mess, I have refrained from writing about it lately for two reasons. First, because it has been so thoroughly covered, and on the whole covered reasonably well, in the national media, with Governor John Sununu and Senator Gordon Humphrey of New Hampshire castigating the College for its handling of the affair. And, second, because I wanted to probe beneath the unfolding events to grasp what is really going on here and on other campuses. A lot is going on.

To recap the surface events. One group of students last fall erected five plywood shanties on the Dartmouth common Green, ostensibly to protest apartheid in South Africa. In doing so, they twice defied direct orders from the Dean of the College. They twice occupied the office of College president and the administration building. In the end, they resisted attempts to dismantle a remaining shanty, and were arrested, one of the students for fighting with a cop.

These students violated any number of college rules, not to mention local laws. Not only was no College action taken against them, the president agreed to their demand to cancel classes in order to discuss "racism" and what have you, also agreed to plant a tree to commemorate the shanties, and raised his baritone with them to the strains of "We Shall Overcome." Much of the Dartmouth faculty expressed "solidarity" with the shanty movement.

Meanwhile, ten students who tried to dismantle the shanties on their own have been hauled before two disciplinary committees and suspended from the College, despite the cogency of their defense: the dismantling was equally a symbolic action, designed to return the Green to the whole student body.

Out at Berkeley, things got characteristically more violent, with shanties leading to 91 arrests, 29 injuries, firebombs, and attempted arson.

The leaders of the campus anti-apartheid movement, however, have let on that it involves much more than South Africa.

Scott Nova, a Dartmouth junior from Greenwich, Connecticut, for example, says that "to limit the movement to one issue is to miss the point." And, what is "the point?" As others have made clear, the issue is U.S. "imperialism," U.S. policy in Central America, nuclear disarmament (ours), "imperialism," and, as always, "racism." That is, the more conscious students in the movement regard themselves as anti-Western revolutionaries allied with revolutionary movements in the Third World. They are also revolutionary in their intent on a whole range of domestic issues. In all of this, they have the backing and often the guidance of a substantial segment of the faculties on campuses across the country.

In domestic terms, of course, they are bitter about racism, sexism, elitism, and homophobia. In practice, all of these terms are hate-filled buzzwords directed at their own society.

Taxonomically, these people are "vulgar Marxists," vulgar because they know nothing of the Dialectic or of the classic texts, but Marxists because of their hatred of everything that actually exists in their own society.

A touch of atmosphere. Not long ago, the official student newspaper at Dartmouth called for a boycott of SDI, and got off this revealing sentence: "But the College's refusal to denounce Star Wars on an ideological basis is even more disturbing," etc. Allowing for editorial sub-literacy, does the writer actually expect the College to take an "ideological" position on SDI?

Of course. That is what the college did on the shanties, after all. The Dartmouth student newspaper routinely censors letters it disagrees with, ignores unwelcome news, and so forth. No wonder an alternative, *The Dartmouth Review*, appeared five years ago. I call the prevailing ethos Liberal Fascism.

Or, as the critic Lionel Trilling once wrote, "Stalinism becomes endemic in the American middle class as soon as that class begins to think."

By "Stalinism," Trilling meant a crude animus against the West, a mindless and aggressive sloganeering, a trampling on others' rights, and a will to suppress opposing points of view.

Call it what you will, "vulgar Marxism," "Liberal Fascism," "Stalinism"—the temper of the campus liberal mind is today increasingly totalitarian.

April 23, 1986

Bill Cole Strikes Back

Bill Cole in His Own Words:
Sound and Fury, Signifying Nothing

by Christopher Baldwin

T HE FOLLOWING is an article on one of Dartmouth's most academically deficient courses, Music 2, "American Music in Oral Tradition," and its instructor—Professor William Cole.

Although Professor Cole is well-liked by many students, and about seventy-five students are enrolled in the class, *The Dartmouth Review* feels that its format does not meet Dartmouth standards and needs to be examined by the community.

This article centers on a transcript of the February 16, 1988 Music 2 class with Professor Cole. The transcript is unaltered and is printed in its entirety.

At least seventy of them wait for the Maestro. They look like your typical crowd—lip-sticked, diet-Coked women, baseball-capped men—basically the blue-jeaned, beer-guzzling, L. L. Beaned types that exude *prepismo*.

Some of the men thumb through the *Sports Illustrated* swimsuit issue, admiring, smirking, wishing.

"Last Saturday my roommate and I bought a bottle of Andre, and we got so ripped," says one girl to another. "People were coming up to us on Sunday and telling us what we did. I really can't believe it . . ."

Then enters the Big Man. Papers ruffle, magazines shut, and glances dart across the room. The Andre woman sits down. Silence.

Class has begun. Well, that's if you could call this a class. Welcome to Music 2, "American Music in the Oral Tradition." Your host is William Cole, University of Pittsburgh graduate, musician, Dartmouth professor, black man. Nobody cares what color Cole is except Cole, and much of the class hinges on this fact. Cole's black, most of the students are white. Get it? This is a Very Important Point in Music 2.

The class is a notorious gut, and Cole is a notable campus figure—"A respected man and a respected scholar," in the words of former Dartmouth President David McLaughlin.

Students are supposed to learn about Alanis Obomsawin, Sarah Clevelend, Jayne Cortez, and the Firespitters. But Bill Cole, the music department's scruffy savant, would rather spend his class preaching what he thinks, or more accurately, what he *feeeels*.

One of the rules of the class is to "read little, think deeply . . . and much," according to a handout. Cole follows this advice, and it shows. He spends class time talking about Very Important Issues—race, poverty, his personal philosophy, and nuclear war. It is apparent that Cole reads little, thinks deeply . . . and too much.

To be fair to students, Music 2 shouldn't be named "American Music in the Oral Tradition." "Subway Grafitti in the Oral Tradition," would be more appropriate. But we're not here to make suggestions. We're here to learn from Cole.

"There's a couple of things I want to talk about in the journals," he says. The journals are the only written work for the course and count toward 15 percent of the grade. The journals are where the "think deeply . . . and much" rule applies. Students are told to meditate for a few minutes to become one with the universe and write Very Important Feelings in notebooks. Cole is returning them today, but students don't expect grades—just Very Important Comments from the Maestro.

"One person indicated that poverty was kind of romantic, that poverty wasn't that bad after all," Cole says. "What's the definition of poverty? Anybody know what poverty is? What's the first thing that comes to your mind when you think of poverty? You. [Cole points to a girl.] What's the first thing that comes to your mind?"

The student looks down at her desk. "I don't know."

Cole smiles, "You don't know? How about you? [Cole points to another student.] Do you know what poverty is? What's poverty? What's your name?"

"Kristie," says the girl. "I don't know."

"You don't know?"

"Nothing to eat?" guesses Kristie.

"Nothing to eat? Yeah, nothing to eat."

"No running water, no electricity," she adds.

"Rats . . . cockroaches . . . poverty of education," Cole stresses. "Poverty of the spirit. I worked on the South Side of Pittsburgh for awhile, a couple of years ago. A long time ago. The South Side is mostly an Eastern European ethnic group, they live there.

"There was this one lady named Murphy, a nice Irish name, and she had—her grandson lived with her. The kid belonged to an Austrian gardener who didn't want to take care of him, so she raised him. She was an old lady in her late seventies. She had this house. In Pittsburgh they had these inspections of houses, and if you had, like, five problems in the house, and you were kind of over the brink, you were in really serious trouble. And this lady had twenty-nine violations. *Twenteeee*-nine.

"She was renting the house from this other lady. So the housing department advised her to put her money in escrow until the house was fixed up. She was paying something like $45 a month. And the landlady, man, she fixed the house up. She raised her rent to $250 a month. And this legal aid society, which they no longer have anymore, helped her because she was poor, and she got her rent raised only to $55. But she couldn't afford that raise, man, she couldn't even afford the $45 that she was paying before. That's what poverty is about," he says with his Bill Cole voice as he does his Bill Cole strut around the room.

"I went one time with this priest to see this lady, and we walked into her house, and I started to sit down on the sofa, and this priest grabbed my arm, and said, 'Don't sit down there, man.' And I checked out this woman's couch, and that thing was saturated with cockroaches. And I mean saturated. There were so many cockroaches in that house, they were vying for the food, they was crawling up the sides of the pot while the pot was on the stove, trying to get that food.

"Poverty is no joke. There is nothing romantic about it at all. It's no joke. And the people who have to live that way, they have to be out there hustling. That's why those people got shot on that subway, 'cause they was out there trying to make a penny. They got shot for it. That's what poverty's about. Poverty drives people onto the subways trying to get some of yours. [Cole points to various students.] Yours . . . yours . . . yours. That's what poverty does. And they just came across the wrong person, 'cause this person had a gun. They got caught.

"I had this guy that worked with me, a guy in Pittsburgh, and he had a friend, and he was seventeen years old, and he and his friends were sticking up this . . . well, they weren't sticking up they were actually burglarizing . . . this merchant's store at two or three in the morning. There were four of them. And these dudes were mean, boy. Really mean. And the guy who owned the store happened to come in, and these dudes grabbed this guy and choked him to death. And they went to jail. One guy was seventeen and one guy was eighteen. They were young. And I talked to this guy. Me and him were driving around. He had been in jail for seven years, and his buddy was still in jail. He had been in for nine years. His buddy had gotten out three years later. And that's what poverty's all about. It makes people mean . . . mean.

"This goes to show how mean some of these people are, and this comes from poverty. You don't ever want to meet this guy—you'd better hope and pray. He'll take you out like that. 'Cause that's their life. Their life is either take out or take off. This guy was seventeen years old and he went to prison, man. This guy was double dangerous. I said, 'What was it like when you went to prison? What went on when you first got there?' He said, 'No, man, I went to prison and I was so bad, people wouldn't touch me.' And his buddy was in prison for nine years. This guy was so dangerous, he was so dangerous, they kept him in solitary confinement for six years and six months. And this guy was so dangerous, and he was walking the streets of Pittsburgh. You don't want to run into him. These two guys, they came from poverty, and none of the institutions ever worked with them—religion, school, government, politics, justice . . . justice? It never worked for these guys. Their thing was survival of the fittest.

"Now there was another comment about the Indian Symbol," says Cole very seriously. You can tell that this is not a laughing matter for him. But you could tell the Reverend Cole was just warming up because he hadn't started to mix up his verb tenses.

"One of the things was that those were rough days," Cole continues. "I've seen year after year after year, and how ridiculed the Native American students are, how insulted and degraded, and they can't deal with it. I see this every year, and this is crazy. But I guess we trample on the rights of all these students, huh? And they're not doing anything. They're saying, 'This is so degrading, and this is how we feel.' They're human beings out there. We can be put here at Dartmouth, but we're not human beings. And they feel it. That symbols have no energy? We think that symbols have no energy.

"I've been thinking about all the holocausts in the past, the holocaust that happened to the black people coming over here, the holocaust that happened to the Armenian people. They killed about a million. The holocaust that happened to the Jewish people, the holocaust that happened to the Natives here. I hope I don't sound like an ongoing dead horse, but these are important things. Sometimes, please, just think about it. It's all in books. There is literally no way to be ignorant about it anymore; you have no excuses. No way—uh uh. Don't tell me you're ignorant. Don't tell me 'I don't know.'

"Now we're going to get to what we're going to do today . . ." Cole smiles to the class, fingers his beard, and continues:

"I don't know, man, I feel, I . . . I've only had a couple experiences on the reservations. And the first time I went, in 1982, maybe it was '81. You know Hafish-Shabaaz, he and I were partners in a thing called Wind and Thunder. It's a little musical group, and he and I did this thing out there. And I remember, it was the first presentation we did out there, it was at this elementary school out on the reservation of the Cochanees. The Cochanee were these people who were drum makers. And I remember that was the first time I ever performed on a reservation. I gave a little talk and he gave a little talk, and we exchanged little talks back and forth, you know, and I couldn't talk. Every time I'd open my mouth, I started crying. You know, I couldn't say a word. You know, I was so embarrassed, man. I just couldn't hold it. Couldn't hold it. I'll never forget that.

"And we did a thing, this time, on a Navajo reservation," Cole added. "We were playing for all these people, and you know, playing for all these people, and you want to, like, get out there and say, 'We're black people!' You know? 'Cause these were our native people. And we're black, and we came here to exchange history with you. I very rarely get a chance to do that. Any questions?"

A rustling silence falls over the class, the only sound being the turning of magazine pages.

After a few comments, one woman asks Cole to explain why there are so few women in jazz.

"It's all sexism," answers Cole. "I guess my immediate reaction to that is that I don't think that the lifestyles that the white people are trying to put out there for themselves is something that the black people are going to embrace. That's not where the black people are coming from. There's no way; they're not coming from there at all. I'm not trying to generalize about the black people, this is my perception.

"I don't really think that's where it's coming from. It is, there's no question about it, an extremely hard lifestyle. But I think that it makes things more hard on women artists, 'cause not only is it hard on them by the people who frequent these places, but they are also hit on by the artists themselves.

"You know, it makes it real difficult, you know, because it gets down to, if you'll excuse the expression, pu**y or no play. But what happens in the situation is that you're talking about an art form that has a very small part of the economic pie. Very small, man. People are gangsterin' to keep people out all the time. But you do have to be super mean to prevail in it. 'Cause a lot of stuff goes down that they never ever write about. People like, physically hurting other people, they don't like them to play. People get fired and they're off someplace in some foreign land somewhere, and they have no way of getting back because they haven't even been paid yet. It's a very hard, a very hard . . . you just get by.

"But I think the predominant thing is sexism. It's the opportunity. People never give people the opportunity. There are only two people in my whole life who ever came down here and asked me to play in their gig: Jayne Cortez and Julius Hemphill. Oh, Warren Smith, that's three. Do they ever call me up and say, 'Come play'? No. And there's a lot of people who can play. Let me tell you, friends, if you play music like Lester Bowie does, you see some incredible things.

"I checked that out when I was about seventeen or eighteen years old, and I said I'm not going that way. I've got to get out of that. I saw all the culture, really, it's amazing. The cultural things. I mean, people are always getting musicians high. A musician can almost go all the way through life without even putting out a penny for anything that gets him high. And those same people wouldn't give you a dime to make a telephone call if your life depended on it. 'Cause it's always that whenever you have creativity happening, you're always going to have male and female happening. 'Cause it takes male and female to make the creative process go down, boom. You're always going to have that happen. That's just the way it is.

"I believe that there is no institution that can maintain creativity without equal male and female input. I'm a strong believer in that . . . very strong. Any institution that doesn't have equal input, to me, there's something wrong with it. Screw it. 'Cause, I mean, how can it be creative? People go through their whole lives, man, and they miss what the Creator has put out there for everyone to see. It's so simple and so pleasant and so something that you can touch and something that you can feel and something that you can check out. You don't have to do nothing, it's all out there. It's all out there . . . it's all out there. I mean, to me, if to procreate takes man and woman, to be creative must also take that. I don't see how it could be any other way. Does that answer your question?"

After his sermon, the Reverend picks up the Good Book, *Native American People* by Marsha Herndon, and reads. Many students stare at their desks, obviously "thinking deep." Cole finishes and plays some American Indian chants. After students are bombarded by drumming and numbed by unintelligible wails, Cole resumes his sermon.

"Why are we willing to put nuclear waste in the ground, and say to ourselves, 'It's cool, because it won't really contaminate things for a thousand years'? Come on, is that cool? 'Cause it won't affect *us*? That makes it cool? And, man, it's going to keep going on. I remember that somebody told me that I was really naive . . . that I had this real thing about nuclear war.

"It scared me. I really thought that with all the lying politicians around that some of them were goin' mess up. And he says, 'Bill, I guarantee you that man could not destroy somethin' that he did not create.'"

"I'll never forget him saying that. We've been creatin' monsters. You know, through what has to survive to make it, but the life force is gonna be here. We've gotta a life force that's so . . . like, like *Aliens*—that we couldn't destroy it. We gotta hang on to what is the only counteractive by its hostilities. Whoa!"

"Cockroaches will still be around," says a heavy-set, t-shirt-clad man.

"I know they will," Cole insists. "All those insects are gonna be around and they're gonna be *dannngerrrous*."

"There's two things he taught me. The other thing he taught me was one of the hardest things for me to get together is that God is good and evil on opposite sides of the same coin. That was the hardest thing for me to get together. Once you understand that, then I think it's a lot easier to understand what's happening on this planet.

"When I was young I used to think that evil would be destroyed by an overwhelming amount of love and kindness, et cetera, et cetera, et cetera. It said, it said, the Bible said that the Creator flung Lucifer from Heaven. He better go back and do it right.

"But the key is how did Lucifer get there in the first place? Will you think about that? Ha, ha, ha. Because the Creator is everything. He doesn't miss anything. Now, what'd you have to insult him? All you guys are honkies . . . I'm serious man. I'm the most serious dude you'll ever see in your life. I'm serious as a panic. I'm serious . . ."

After finishing the sermon, he gives the class his Bill Cole smile and his Bill Cole laugh, turns around, and spins another gut-busting, mind-warping Indian disc.

Yet another class of "American Music in the Oral Tradition" with Professor William Cole comes to an end. A wave of students rises and pours out the door as Cole puts papers into his book bag after a job well done.

In *The Music Man*, Professor Herald Hill of the Sheboygan Conservatory arrives at River City, Iowa and sets up a scam operation taking money from the townspeople to teach children music through "deep thinking." Over time, the people of River City catch on to Hill's deception and try to run him out of town. But at the last minute, to the tune of "76 Trombones," a River City Children's Marching Band parades through town and saves Hill from humiliation. Unfortunately for Professor Cole, the only ones likely to come to his rescue are those for whom tenure is more important than teaching, and racist ranting preferable to competence.

February 24, 1988

Professor Cole Responds
by John Sutter

T HE *REVIEW* solicited Professor Cole's comments prior to completing the article above. The following is a transcription of the ensuing conversation.

FIRST CALL
MRS. COLE: Hello?
THE DARTMOUTH REVIEW: Yes. Professor Cole, please.
MRS. COLE: Who is this please?
TDR: This is John Sutter, I'm calling from *The Dartmouth Review*.

WILLIAM COLE: Yeah.

TDR: Yes, Professor Cole? I'm John Sutter, Executive Editor of *The Dartmouth Review*. We're doing a story on you this week, and on Music 2. We just wanted to ask you a few questions about the class.

SECOND CALL

WC: Yeah?

TDR: Hello, Professor Cole?

WC: Yeah.

TDR: Why did you hang up on me, sir?

WC: Hey, man, you people have known that I don't talk to you, all right? You're racist dogs and you know that's how I think about you, OK? I don't know why you call me, man. I know why you call me, because you people are so disrespectful. So incredibly disrespectful and arrogant. That's why you're calling me. You're going to put your racist b*llsh*t in the paper anyhow, it doesn't make any difference what I say, I saw your man up there taking pictures outside of my window, man, and I knew that you m*th*rf*ck*rs were going to do the same thing you always do. Alright?

TDR: Which is what, sir?

WC: You're racist dogs, man. You're the scum of the m*th*rf*ck*n' earth. All right? I know you're taping this, okay? I know you are. And I'm telling you, man, report you to everybody I possibly can, I know that the people won't do anything about you, alright? But you're gonna be reported to everybody.

TDR: For what, sir?

WC: For lying. For not telling the truth. For putting your sneaky-*ss b*st*rds in my class.

TDR: About what, sir?

WC: Whatever you're writing about!

TDR: Oh, so you already know . . .

WC: You're racist, man! Whatever you're writing about is gonna be a lie! You're a racist! You're bigots! That's all you are! You're racist bigots! You're sexists! You're racists, man! That's all you are! You're bigots! You're racists! That's all you are! You're a bunch of bigots!

TDR: Frankly, sir, I am astounded that . . .

WC: You're a racist, man! You're a bunch of bigots!

TDR: I am astounded that a professor at Dartmouth College, one who is tenured, would use language like that, and I'm sure many other people will be also.

WC: You're all G*dd*mn-f*ck*n'-*ss-white-boy-racists! Is that good enough?

TDR: That was very good, sir. Thank you very much, sir.

February 24, 1988

Profs React to *Review* Accusations

by Sean Nolan

T WO *REVIEW* ARTICLES published last week have met with strikingly different reactions from those involved. The articles, both very controversial, criticized the classes of Professors Richard Corum and William Cole.

The first *Review* article revealed that Professor Corum was not following the guidelines for English 5. Professors teaching the course are required to teach either *Heart of Darkness* or *Paradise Lost*. Corum told his class after the *Review* article appeared that they would now be required to read *Heart of Darkness*.

The article also charged that Corum's classes were too unstructured and did not conform with the spirit of the English 5 guidelines. This situation has also been remedied. One student said that lectures are now more structured and course-oriented. William Spengemann, professor in charge of the guidelines for English 5, said that he was unaware of the changes in Corum's class. The student, however, said that Corum attributed the change to pressure brought as a result of the *Review* article.

Last week's *Review* article on Professor Cole was for the most part a verbatim account of a class during which Cole violated every norm of academic etiquette, referring to "p*ssy" and "honkies." When not cursing, Professor Cole discussed his personal philosophy. The article also contained an account of a heavily censored phone exchange between an editor of the *Review* and the professor, during which Cole slanderously referred to *Review* staffers as "g*dd*mn f*ck*n' *ss white-boy racists."

"The Creator is my only judge," continued Cole, "not *The Dartmouth Review*, not the music faculty, not the faculty, not the administration, not the students . . . I'm a full professor." Despite Cole's statement, it is one of the most important duties of the administration to ensure high quality education for the students.

Professor Cole's reaction has not been as constructive as Corum's. Instead of trying to remedy the faults pointed out in the article, Cole chose to use his Music 2 classroom last Thursday as a personal soapbox. "I heard there was an exposé on me last week," he began.

Cole placed the blame for his embarrassment on the entire Dartmouth Community because they have not stifled the *Review*'s point of view. This provoked dissent among members of the class. "I don't believe in the *Review*, but there are some people who do," remarked one girl. "That rhymes," Cole informed the class, and proceeded to incorporate the phrase into a bluesy tune which he sung repeatedly.

Professor Cole spiced his lecture with slanderous rhetoric such as "they [staffers of the *Review*] are going straight to hell." He let fly accusations of racism. Cole handed down a stinging indictment of the *Review*, saying they want "to maintain the educational system," and adding that "they're saying what most American people believe."

After class, Christopher Baldwin '89, John H. Sutter '88, and John Quilhot '90 entered Faulkner Auditorium and approached Professor Cole, for two reasons. Baldwin presented Cole with a memo offering Cole space in the *Review* to respond, unedited, to the original article. Also, Mr. Sutter wished to procure an apology from Professor Cole, in lieu of legal action, for slanderous comments Cole made February 18 during class and over the phone.

Although the staffers waited until class was dismissed before addressing him, Cole immediately became emotional and violent in manner. He shouted, "You are so disrespectful to come into my classroom . . . and invade my space!" Baldwin, speaking for the group, was both verbally and physically harassed. Cole used terms such as "f*ckin'-*ss" and "racist" and made threatening gestures at Baldwin's face.

This is not the first time Cole has reacted violently towards the *Review*. After hearing of a similar story published in the spring of 1983, Cole rushed to author Laura Ingraham '85's dorm room and pounded on her door for almost twenty minutes. Ingraham was not in the room, but Cole harassed her roommate. Cole also threatened former Editor-in-Chief Deborah Stone '87, saying "I'm going to f*ckin' blow you up." This past history of violence is the reason a photographer was brought.

John Quilhot began taking photographs in order to secure proof of Cole's actions. Professor Cole rushed towards Quilhot, grabbed his arms and broke the flash unit off of the camera. The unit is valued at $230. Sutter pulled Professor Cole off of Quilhot and voiced his request for an apology.

Cole started to shout at Sutter, calling him a "bigot." When Sutter reiterated his request for an apology, Cole would not apologize and demanded that Sutter "take it from me, man."

Chair of the Music Department Melinda O'Neal entered the auditorium. Cole continued to scream, often directly at Mrs. O'Neal. Realizing that any further effort to deal rationally with Professor Cole would be futile, Baldwin gave Mrs. O'Neal his name and asked that any correspondence be sent to his Hinman Box. The group then left.

The *Review* has repeatedly tried to reach members of the Dartmouth Community for comment. Chair of the Music Department Melinda O'Neal refused to speak with the paper, as did Professor of Music Jon Appleton. Dean of Faculty Dwight Lahr and Dean of the College Edward Shanahan both failed to return a series of eight calls made over a four-day period.

One Dartmouth professor commented that in light of Professor Cole's unprofessionalism, "It is unfortunate, especially for the black community at Dartmouth, that Professor Cole is permitted to act in a way that so obviously disparages his reputation and, indirectly, that of others."

March 2, 1988

Lies, Lies & More Lies
by Chris Whitman

O N TUESDAY, March 1, 1988, Native Americans at Dartmouth, the Women's Issues League, the Afro-American Society, and Dartmouth Area Gay and Lesbian Organization issued a campus-wide Hinman Box mailing. One side of the mailing, entitled "The Hanover Review Inc.: A Long History of Illegal Abuse and Harassment," purports to describe some events of *The Dartmouth Review*'s past. The organizations responsible for the mailing, at best, portray our history in a libelous fashion. This is particularly important to note because the College, in recognizing these organizations and providing them with mailing privileges, sanctions such blatant disregard for fact.

Distortion: "1981: A member of the *Review* breaks into the office of the Gay Students Association and steals the mailing list. The paper prints the list of names and sends copies of the *Review* to parents of people on the GSA list."

Fact: This assertion is false on every count. First, the *Review* obtained a list of GSA officers through the Committee on Student Organizations, a member of which approached a *Review* editor with the information. Second, the *Review* named only the four officers in its story and mailed the paper to its regular subscriber list, which included the grandfather of one of the officers. That some or all of the GSA officer's family did not know their young relative is a homosexual is unfortunate, but given that he was an officer for the gay student group, it is hard to charge the *Review* with wrongdoing in this case.

Distortion: "1983: The *Review* illegally tapes Professor Bill Cole's class, and prints an article entitled 'Bill Cole's Song and Dance Routine' attempting to ridicule him."

Fact: "Bill Cole's Song and Dance Routine" did not involve a taping of any class, but mere attendance of Music 2's first meeting of the 1983 winter term. The article, the length of which was about two thirds of a page in the *Review* (including a picture), focused on some of Cole's political rantings—irrelevant to the study of "American Music in Oral Tradition," the course's ostensible subject. What the College-sanctioned mailing neglected to mention is that an enraged Cole went to the dorm room of

Laura Ingraham '85, Saturday, January 15, 1983, at approximately 8:30 a.m. and beat on her door for some twenty minutes. Ingraham was not present, but Cole terrified her roommate and created a dorm-wide scene.

Distortion: "1984: A member of the *Review* illegally tapes a GSA meeting and prints a transcript, including names of people who spoke. The town presses charges but the College does not pursue disciplinary faction."

Fact: Teresa Polenz '87 taped a publicly advertised GSA meeting. Excluding the names of two GSA officers, the *Review* published statements from four GSA members anonymously. The College said it would refrain from action until the state of New Hampshire, which had jurisdiction over any illegality, concluded its investigation. When the state decided that Polenz had not violated New Hampshire statute 570A:1, the College had no grounds to discipline her either.

Distortion: "1986: Nine *Review* members violently sledgehammer the shanties on Dr. Martin Luther King's Birthday, a national holiday. COS suspends the students involved in two separate trials, but President McGlaughlin [sic] calls in an 'objective outsider,' conservative Gov. Sununu [sic], who waives the suspensions, assigning the students service requirements."

Fact: Ten, not nine, Reviewers were among the twelve students on the Dartmouth Committee to Beautify the Green Before Winter Carnival, which attempted to remove the shanties January 21, 1986, one day after Dr. King's holiday. President McLaughlin eventually called upon Walter Peterson, president of Franklin Pierce College, to arbitrate the case. Peterson did not waive the suspensions, but reduced each by one term and added 180 hours of service projects. Four students—Deborah Stone, Teresa Polenz, Robert Flanigan, and Frank Reichel—served one-term suspensions.

Distortion: "1987: *Review* prints a spoof of *Black Praxis* [magazine], calling it *Tan Praxis,* and maligning the civil rights leader Dr. King by calling him 'Dr. Martin Soleil' with the speech 'I have a tan, I have a tan.'"

Fact: The *Review* drew an analogy on the militant *Black Praxis* to satirize people at Dartmouth who categorize others by skin color. The *Tan Praxis* ad lampooned the spring-term *Black Praxis* cover, which showed a group of students saluting with clenched fists. The spoof of the speech read "I have a tan . . . an awesome tan."

The spoof in no way maligned Dr. King. Rather, it poked fun at the notion of reserving ideas that transcend race, culture, or gender for a singular purpose, which the *Black Praxis* had done.

Distortion: "February 25: After Professor Cole's 2A, with students still in the classroom, four *Review* writers come in to 'invite' Professor Cole to 'reply' to their last issue and demand an apology for him [sic] calling them racist. Professor Cole repeatedly asks them to leave, and to stop taking their [sic] picture."

Fact: Although several students were still in the classroom, class had been recessed for some five minutes and only one student was speaking with Cole. When the *Review* writers approached Cole, he had dismissed the student with whom he was speaking. Furthermore, Cole does not own Faulkner Recital Hall. Students of Dartmouth College are not prohibited from entering Dartmouth classrooms when classes are not in session.

Distortion: "February 25 (cont.): After several more vocal requests to stop recording and stop taking his picture, Professor Cole attempted to take the camera and the tape recorder [sic] away. The *Review* does not leave until the police are called."

Fact: When Cole first asked John Sutter, who was displaying the tape recorder from his jeans pocket and who only began taping when Cole started to scream, to stop taping, the request was met immediately. As for the pictures, Cole moved toward John Quilhot, Photography Editor of the *Review*, and, while reaching for the camera, asked for the first time that Quilhot not take his picture. In the same motion Cole jerked the flash bulb from Quilhot's camera.

Distortion: "February 26: The *Review* comes out with another issue maligning Cole. Five years of harassment: for what??? Bill Cole is a full professor and an internationally known and respected musician. ENOUGH IS ENOUGH!!! Students at Dartmouth should be able to make their own decisions about which professors they like; we don't need the *Review* to drive them out of town for us. The *Review* should be allowed to print, but not to personally harass members of the Dartmouth community with libel and illegal means. We, as students, and the College as a whole, must take action."

Fact: The writers of the Hinman mailing that has been reproduced here apparently have a better command of libel than does *The Dartmouth Review*, as virtually their entire letter was founded upon inaccuracy—and some of it contained serious charges that are patently untrue.

March 9, 1988

Facts Do the Talking
by the Editors

I N ITS FEBRUARY 17, 1988 issue, *The Dartmouth Review* published a cultural literacy poll of Dartmouth students which revealed that Dartmouth students are not as culturally literate as should be expected of students in the Ivy League. The average score on the test was less than 50 percent.

The next week, in response to student complaints, *The Dartmouth Review* published two investigative pieces, one on Professor Richard Corum of the English Department and one on William Cole of the Music Department.

Christopher Baldwin, Editor-in-Chief, talked to *Review* Counsel Mr. David Rivkin of Baker and McKenzie in Washington D.C. regarding the Cole story. Mr. Rivkin advised Mr. Baldwin that in light of Prof. Cole's previous unsuccessful attempt to sue the paper for $2.4 million, he should inform Professor Cole via a personally delivered memo and conversation of the editorial policy of the paper and his opportunity to respond. He also advised that Professor Cole should be asked for an apology for his remarks over the phone and in class before the article appeared.

Christopher Baldwin, John Sutter, John Quilhot, and Sean Nolan went to Professor Cole's classroom five minutes after class was dismissed on February 25. Immediately upon seeing Mr. Baldwin, Cole began to yell. As Cole became more violent, poking his fingers at Baldwin's eyes, Sutter turned on a tape recorder. At the same time, Quilhot tried to move into position to take photos of Cole pointing at Baldwin's eyes. Cole, seeing the camera raised, walked to Quilhot, grabbed his right arm and ripped the flash off of the camera. Sutter stepped in between the two men. Cole backed away. Sutter approached Cole, introduced himself, and requested an apology on behalf of himself and the other students on *The Dartmouth Review*. Professor Cole beckoned to Sutter and told him that if he wanted an apology he should "take it from me, come on, take it from me." Professor Cole immediately saw the tape recorder protruding from Sutter's pocket; Cole requested that the tape recorder be turned off. Sutter complied. Soon thereafter, the students left the auditorium.

On Friday, February 26, the four students received notification that they were charged by the Dartmouth Committee on Standards with "harassment," violating the "right to privacy," and "disorderly conduct."

On Friday, February 26, Sutter was threatened by a group of students in the basement of a fraternity.

On Saturday, February 27, a student who is a member of the Afro-American Society at Dartmouth told Christopher Baldwin and John Sutter that on Friday night a student in the class had told the Executive Committee of the AAm that John Sutter told Professor Cole, "We've got to get rid of you incompetent niggers."

On Sunday, February 28, an attempt was made through Professor Douglas Yates to arrange a meeting with the E.C. of the AAm. This attempt failed. A meeting was arranged between Yates, Sutter, and Marcia Jones and Rob Leek, faculty advisors to the AAm.

On Sunday, February 28, John Sutter attempted to contact Dean of the College Edward Shanahan, Dean of the Faculty Dwight Lahr, and Dartmouth President James Freedman. Dean Shanahan was reached. The first time Sutter asked how he would go about making a complaint of harassment against a Professor. Shanahan did nothing beyond telling Sutter to read the relevant section of the Student Handbook. Shanahan told

Sutter that he could consult with the professor involved, the Chairman of the Department, or the Dean of the Faculty. Sutter was unsuccessful in reaching Dean of the Faculty Dwight Lahr despite having left two messages saying that it was extremely urgent that Sutter talk to him before he went to the office on Monday. Sutter then called the home of President Freedman; he talked to Bathsheba Freedman, the wife of President Freedman, about his concomitant problems of harassment by students and the uncooperativeness of an unspecified administrator.

Ten minutes later, Dean Shanahan called Sutter. He asked for the name of the administrator involved. Sutter told Shanahan that he had been referring to Shanahan's uncooperativeness. Dean Shanahan then asked Sutter to get back to him when Sutter found out the name of a student who could confirm the Friday night incident. Sutter called back every ten minutes for an hour, but the phone was not answered. Sutter finally read the relevant section of the Student Handbook, which stated that it was the responsibility of the Dean of the College as well as those mentioned by Shanahan to help students with complaints against professors. Sutter called Shanahan to tell him the name of the student witness and complain about Shanahan's lack of cooperation. Shanahan maintained that he had discharged his responsibility by citing the relevant section of the Student Handbook and then hung up on Sutter.

When the meeting arranged with Marsha Jones and Joe Leek occurred on Monday morning, Jones and Leek refused to set up a meeting with either the AAm or its Executive Committee (E.C.). Sutter informed them that he was aware of the slanderous statement made to the E.C. He said that it was false. Posters advertising the rally went up on Monday. These posters said "We've got to get rid of you incompetent niggers"—John H. Sutter, Exec. Editor of *The Dartmouth Review*. The posters stated that President Freedman would speak. Buildings and Grounds set up the public address system for the rally.

At the rally, President Freedman explicitly said that he could not comment on the specific students' cases, however, he went on to say that instances of harassment, racism, and intolerance have no place at Dartmouth.

After the rally, there was a declared open meeting to plan future actions at Cutter Hall, the black dormitory on campus, and the home of the AAm. Three *Review* contributors, two of whom were black, and one of the two black students in a wheelchair, were told to leave the meeting "for your own safety."

The four students involved in the Cole incident met on Tuesday morning with Kate Burke, Secretary of the COS. She explained the procedures of the COS. John Sutter filed a complaint with Mrs. Burke on Tuesday, requesting a full investigation into the making of the poster and the false racial statement. The four students filed a request for a delay in their hearing date because their advisor, Professor of English Jeffrey Hart, could not be in town for the hearing on that date. The request was denied and the students were offered a choice between having a hearing on Tuesday without Hart or having their hearing on the preceding Saturday, a move forward of three days.

On Tuesday, protestors picketed *Review* advertisers. A tip was phoned into the *Review* that students planned to enter the *Review*'s offices at 37 South Main Street and prevent publication of the next issue. Sutter informed the Hanover police of the call, and they stood on the steps of the building and inside the building for two hours in order to prevent an incident. On Wednesday, *The Boston Globe* quoted President Freedman as saying, "I do not want one minority or woman student to decline to come to Dartmouth because of the perception that this incident is representative of the true Dartmouth. It is not. The timing of this is dreadfully suspicious, coming five weeks before acceptances [of new students] go out."

Students picketed *Review* advertisers again on Wednesday. President Freedman spoke to protestors at approximately 1:45 p.m. Seeing Freedman out the window, John Sutter and Kevin Pritchett left the building to find an opportunity to talk to Freedman. Freedman had left the protestors and was walking back to Parkhurst. Sutter hailed President Freedman and asked if there was any way that Freedman could meet with him or the four students charged before the COS. Freedman said that the only time that any of the students could meet with him was during his office hours on Monday. Sutter asked why he had prejudiced himself in *The Boston Globe*. Freedman denied having done this even when the above quote was made to him. Freedman was informed that Sutter was extremely traumatized by the fact that Freedman had addressed a rally which was advertised with a false racial slur attributed to Sutter.

Wednesday, March 2, local *Review* legal counsel Peter Hutchins of Wiggins and Nourie of Manchester, N.H. sent a letter outlining procedures to ensure a fair hearing to Dean Edward Shanahan, Chairman of the COS and Katherine Burke, Secretary of the COS.

March 9, 1988

Bigotry at the Afro-American Society
by Kevin Pritchett

R ACISM IS ALIVE and kicking at Dartmouth College, but not where you would expect it. The narrow-minded advocates of fear and loathing at Dartmouth are headquartered in Cutter Hall, the building the Afro-American Society calls home.

The current situation on campus has shown the Afro-American Society to be the aggressor through its own use of racial intolerance and deceit. The AAm has started a campaign of racial hysteria and mob rule, destroying the principles of freedom of speech, freedom of the press, and the tolerance of dissenting viewpoints.

As a black student at Dartmouth, I have had the misfortune of experiencing this reprehensible attitude personally. On Monday, February 29, I went to the "open" AAm meeting with three friends of mine, Randall Bloom, Marc Deadrick, and David Smith. The meeting was held at Cutter Hall in the evening, following the "rally" (mob scene) that they held at Parkhurst Hall earlier that day. My friends and I did not go to the meeting to tape-record or take pictures of the participants, but to find out what they felt about the entire situation.

Marc, David, and I were escorted into Cutter Lounge, where the Afro-American Society usually holds its meetings, by a friend of Marc's, Suzanna Dotson '91. We found that there were not just Afro-Am members there, but also members of the Dartmouth Gay and Lesbian Organization, Native Americans at Dartmouth, and the Women's Issues League. Several professors were also there, including Carla Freccero.

Protest, Inc. had assembled in full force.

The atmosphere in the room was that of a war strategy session—the air was thick with hatred, fear, and hysteria. Because the room was packed with people, we crowded in and stood against the door. One woman stared at us and yelled, "We have Reviewers in here." I really didn't pay attention at first, because I was not there on *Review* business. One male in the room said, "You want to leave, don't you?" in a threatening tone of voice.

Somewhat confused by this man purporting to read our minds, we told the group that yes, we were on the staff of the *Review*, but declined his offer to leave. After they had determined that we were associated with the *Review*, they told us to leave in no uncertain terms. I saw Professor Frecerro concur by nodding her head. I was shocked with Freccero's arrogance, because three students in our group are members of the Afro-Am (according to Afro-Am rules, all black students who enter the College are automatically members of the Afro-American Society).

Because of the large number of people in the room supporting these veiled threats of violence, we departed, but this apparently didn't satisfy the crowd—we were followed out of the room by nine men and five women from the room total of about 85 people. We were unfamiliar with most of these people, but we recognized Arthur Edwards, Melvin Hall, and David Bowdon. Another member of this group, Jacqueline Alien '89, demanded to search Marc's backpack for cameras or recording devices. Marc obliged them by removing the backpack from his lap (Marc was sitting in his wheelchair) and placing it on the ground, inviting them to look all they wanted.

Members of the group that followed us out into the hallway asked us why we wrote for the *Review*. Seeing that the situation was potentially explosive, I refused to comment. One of the men in the contingent approached Marc menacingly, cigarette in hand, and began telling him about the supposed *Review* history of "racial injustice."

We decided that nothing would be served by staying in the hostile crowd and tried to leave. Jacqueline Alien, who was questioning us antagonistically, tried to follow us, but finally gave up and let us leave.

Another friend of mine who had entered Cutter Lounge with us, Randall Bloom, was in the room. He was told, "You better leave—for your safety," less than five minutes after Marc, David, and I left the lounge. Naturally, as one person standing against an angry crowd of over eighty people, Randall felt that he had better take their solicitous concern for his health seriously, and left the room.

Yet another incident of intolerance was perpetrated against me during the "Rally For Justice" vigil on Wednesday night. Carla Frecerro was passing out candles for this vigil as I was approaching Cutter Hall at approximately 9:40 p.m. After Carla unknowingly handed me a candle, I lit it and joined the procession. As the vigil was approaching the corner of Webster Avenue and Main Street, a tall black male approached me from the right, and another stepped to my left. Within seconds, I was surrounded by a group of Afro-Am-ers. One of the males who was "guarding" me asked, "Don't you think it's a little dangerous for you to be here?" I asked why. He didn't answer.

Other members of the group around me asked why was I there. I replied, "I am marching against racism and oppression." A woman asked, "Well, don't you think that that is a contradiction, since you work for the *Review*?" Michael Stokes '91 asked me, "Don't you think it's a little dangerous for you to be here?" He didn't let me answer, but went on a long diatribe about how "racist" the *Review* was. Finally, Michael made his feelings clear and said, "I want to kick your *ss." I left, disgusted in the knowledge that these people who purported to be tolerant were so blinded by self-righteousness.

I am sickened that such provincial attitudes rule the actions of students at Dartmouth College, supposedly one of the finest institutions of higher learning in the nation. These people are so caught up with their own selfish demands for attention that they will willingly ruin the lives of four students on this campus who have done nothing to harm them—and the College is a willing participant in this farce. Yes, racists and bigots do exist at Dartmouth, and you can find them at the AAm. The participators in this current farce are making a mockery of the original purpose of the Afro-American Society. It is unfortunate that a potential treasure house of information and a neutral meeting place for blacks on campus that could have been Cutter Hall has instead become a den of lies, deceit, and intolerance.

March 9, 1988

Apartheid at Dartmouth
by Harmeet Dhillon

A PARTHEID: (lit. separateness): separation of the races: racial segregation.

HOMELAND: a state or area set aside to be a state for people of a particular national, cultural, or racial origin.

Do these words call to mind the racist nation of South Africa? Take a look around. They both apply to Dartmouth College. It's not exactly the same thing here, mind you. In South Africa, apartheid is forced on the people; at Dartmouth, it's frequently a matter of choice—I say frequently because students are often pressured or forced into going along with an odious system of self-segregation.

Over the past few years, Dartmouth has witnessed the progressive stratification of the student body, while at the same time, the administration has instituted policies allegedly aimed at increasing integration and "diversity." It all starts before students even get here. Prospective applicants are sent recruitment literature tailored to their racial or ethnic background (Next year, their sex will become an added element of differentiation). Then, if they are admitted and happen to be black, they are invited to Dartmouth for a special orientation weekend at Dartmouth. Previously, Dartmouth avoided telling the students that the weekend was only for blacks; now, it is openly called "Dartmouth from a Black Perspective."

Most have a healthy attitude when they come here. They want to meet all kinds of people, and expand their intellectual and cultural horizons. Yet, if they happen to make more white friends than black ones, they quickly learn the ugly reality of Dartmouth's reverse racism. Normally adjusted blacks are called "incogs" and "oreos," meaning they are "black on the outside, white on the inside." Most frequently, it is blacks themselves who call other blacks these hateful names.

Many black freshmen can't withstand the pressure. 'Shmen often fall prey to herd mentality and insecurity. Add to these factors the extreme peer pressure they receive from black upperclassmen, and you end up with self-enforced segregation. They begin to eat together, live together, and join all-black fraternities or sororities. I knew several well-adjusted blacks when I was a freshman; a few of them were good friends of mine. As time went by, they became more and more separated from their non-black friends and began to associate almost exclusively with blacks. At first, they resisted the pressure to abandon their well-integrated circle of friends, yet were unable to keep up the resistance.

Dartmouth participates in the segregation process by providing Cutter Hall for black housing and the Afro-American Society. Although housing in Cutter is ostensibly available for anyone who wants it, the last time a white student lived there was the winter of 1986. Cutter's militant, in-grown atmosphere ensures that few whites will ever cross the threshold, let alone consider living there.

Blacks are only one example of this problem. Native Americans and international students are under similar pressures to stick together and live together. The College encourages such insular tendencies by providing special housing and funding special programs for these groups to socialize with each other, instead of throwing them in with everyone else and for-cing them to adapt to the general population. Now, even political groups, such as students taking certificates in Women's Studies, are encouraged to live in special areas in order to "enhance the woman's experience."

Why do people who only want to associate with their own kind bother to come to Dartmouth? There are more suitable schools for those who are in-capable of learning to live in the real world. Anyone who has ever lived in a dorm can tell you that the fastest way to learn about someone who is dif-ferent from yourself is by living with them. Dartmouth is supposed to be an institution of higher learning, fostering an open exchange of experiences. Yet students are allowed to segregate themselves and live a cloistered, two-dimensional life here. By encouraging this situation, the College often graduates students whose views are narrower when they leave than when they entered—the very antithesis of a liberal arts education.

Supporters of this quasi-homeland system often say that "racism" makes it imperative for blacks and others to have special places to go where they can be with their own kind, for reassurance and re-enforcement of their own cultural backgrounds. It is astonishing that this view is ac-cepted without a second thought by most Dartmouth students. My family has personally been targeted by the Ku Klux Klan in North Carolina—I know what racism is. Maybe some of these people should take a trip to the Deep South, or go visit South Africa, and see what racism looks like up close. Those who propagate apartheid at Dartmouth degrade the victories of the civil rights movement by comparing today's Dartmouth with times and places where racism is or was a reality. Spurious excuses can no longer be accepted in defense of a destructive system that alienates Dartmouth students from each other.

In his famous speech at the Civil Rights March in Washington, D.C., Martin Luther King said, "I have a dream that one day on the red hills of

Georgia the sons of former slaves and the sons of former slaveowners will be able to sit down together at the table of brotherhood. . . . I have a dream that my four little children will one day live in a nation where they will not be judged by the color of their skin, but by the content of their character." King's dream came true—the America he wanted is here today, but many blacks still choose to sit at different tables and invite judgment based on the color of their skin by asking for special treatment. It's funny how we deify our heroes, yet let their dreams be forgotten.

February 10, 1988

College Bounces Trio, Denies Appeal

by Sean Nolan

A T THE END OF LAST TERM, four students, all associated with *The Dartmouth Review*, were being punished for thoughtcrime—for dissenting from Dartmouth's liberal status quo. Christopher Baldwin, former Editor-in-Chief of the *Review*, and John Sutter, senior editor, have each been suspended from the College for six terms. John Quilhot, photography editor, has been suspended for two terms; this *Review* contributor, Sean Nolan, has been placed on college discipline (i.e., probation) for one year.

In a hearing marked by procedural error and Constitutional violations, Dartmouth's Committee on Standards (COS) found Baldwin, Sutter, and Quilhot guilty of harassment, disorderly conduct, and violation of Cole's right to privacy. Nolan was convicted of disorderly conduct.

The students submitted their twenty-page request for appeal to Dean of the College Edward Shanahan on March 21. The request cited many procedural errors, such as the presence of COS member Chip Telerico, who admitted his bias just before deliberations began. Telerico did not participate in closed-session meetings, but his obvious bias tainted the testimony of many witnesses. The request was promptly and fully rejected.

Under new College regulations, the request for appeal is the only recourse available to convicted students. The four students are now investigating the possibility of legal action. At least three legal firms have offered their services pro bono to the *Review*. Possible suits against the College include: failing to provide a safe environment to pursue an education by not disciplining Cole; violating the *Review*'s First Amendment rights by disciplining the four students; and breaching of contract for failing to comply with the "Freedom of Expression and Dissent" clause in the matriculation contract. A civil suit against Professor Cole for assault, battery, and malicious damage of property is another option, as are defamation of character suits against James Freeman, William Cole, Jon Appleton, Luzmila Johnson, the Afro-American Society at Dartmouth, and Dartmouth College itself.

Dean of the Faculty Dwight Lahr has dropped the students' complaint against Professor Cole. In his public statement concerning the matter, Lahr characterized Music 2 as "a popular course taught by an unusually talented scholar whom Dartmouth is fortunate to have on its faculty." Lahr also commended Cole's lecture following the incident, which included the choice phrase: "they [staffers of the *Review*] are going straight to hell," calling it "thoughtful dialogue."

The March '88 *Alumni Bulletin* featured a cover story on the incident and hearing. Apparently, the administration believes that alumni aren't intelligent enough to make a judgment based upon facts; the bulletin is a piece of propaganda worthy of Orwell's Ministry of Information. The *Bulletin* claims that the hearing was "open to the media," but failed to note that the College allowed in only hand-picked reporters—prohibiting, for example, Jim Finnegan of the Manchester *Union Leader*, New Hampshire's largest daily publication. The College also banned alumni and a representative from the New Hampshire Civil Liberties Union.

The bulletin claims that "the students ignored the professor's repeated requests that they leave the classroom." Testimony at the hearing revealed without a shadow of a doubt that Cole asked the students to leave only once. This occurred at the beginning of the incident, and Cole immediately contradicted himself by engaging the students in "discussion." Although the tape recorder used in the incident was easily visible and most witnesses in the room were aware of its presence, the bulletin labelled it "concealed."

It has become apparent that, encouraged by their successful disinformation blitz, the sensitivity bloodhounds are out for bigger game. The Faculty of the Arts & Sciences held an "emergency" meeting last Monday to discuss the incident and *The Dartmouth Review*. President James O. Freedman, in his speech at the meeting, went further than any other senior College official ever has in denouncing the *Review*. Freedman charged the *Review* with "bullying tactics," "poisoning . . . the intellectual environment of the campus," and "discouraging women and . . . minorities from joining our faculty or enrolling as students." Apparently the Dartmouth community must accept these charges on faith—neither Freedman nor anyone else has been able to substantiate the claims with facts.

Professor of Music Jon Appleton spoke at the meeting as well, claiming that "*The Dartmouth Review* has . . . attempted to persuade white male undergraduates of their racial superiority." Appleton also characterized all staffers of the *Review* as "bitter, angry, insulting, racist, sexist undergraduates."

The outside world has reacted with more sensibility. When the issue first reached national proportions, the media, especially the TV media, latched onto the catch-term "racist," of course—the actions of the Afro-American Society made it difficult for them to do anything else. As the hype dissolves and the facts emerge, however, the tide is changing. In an in-house editorial, the *Wall Street Journal* observes that "a pretext has been found here to rid the school of some conservatives whose opinions are indeed vexatious—nagging, annoying, disturbing, and often irritating." "There seems to be a developing pattern here of administration-condoned, reverse-twist racism," claims the Manchester *Union Leader*'s Jim Finnegan.

Earlier in the month, New Hampshire Governor John Sununu warned Dartmouth to ensure that the "treatment and handling of the students involved be fair." It's a shame that Freedman wasn't listening.

April 6, 1988

Freedman, Faculty Condemn *Review*
by Harmeet Dhillon

A FTER HIDING behind mushy rhetoric for months, President Freedman has finally shown his true colors. Hopeful Dartmouth-watchers said he was a "free-speech" man, a "practiced administrator" who wouldn't become a tool of any campus constituency. They were sadly mistaken.

At the emergency faculty meeting Monday afternoon, Freedman consolidated his popularity campaign with the faculty. His speech condemning *The Dartmouth Review* brought the cheering professors to their feet; he blushed, grinned, and looked like a proud father. He must feel like a clever guy; he's exchanged the faculty-shy posture of the previous administration for a shiny new "user-friendly" attitude.

The speech was carefully crafted to appeal to the soft spots in the hearts (and heads) of the faculty. Freedman began with a series of disclaimers, trying to establish that he has acted with restraint so far towards the *Review*. He certainly has: despite repeated attempts to engage him in meaningful dialogue about various topics of academic and social importance, Freedman has remained virtually catatonic.

The strong opinions expressed in his speech were as surprising as they were inappropriate:

> It is time for me to speak out about the role of the *Review* in our academic community. It is time for me to do so because I now see that the *Review* is

dangerously affecting—in fact, poisoning—the intellectual environment of our campus. . . . I deplore a perversely provocative style of journalism that vulgarizes responsible conservative thought and is, in fact, an affront to it . . . [Dartmouth College] must not stand by silently when a newspaper maliciously engages in bullying tactics that seem virtually designed to have the effect of discouraging women and members of minority groups from joining our faculty or enrolling as students. . . . When the *Review*, year after year, repeatedly attacks women and minority groups, in numbers far in excess of their proportion within the community, it is virtually impossible not to conclude that its true target is diversity.

These statements are all the more astonishing because Freedman, as a lawyer, should know better than to make such gross accusations without substantiating the charges. He denies that the *Review* represents responsible conservative thought, even though many nationally prominent conservatives, including President Reagan, Secretary of Education William Bennett, Congressman Jack Kemp, William F. Buckley Jr., and countless others have acknowledged the *Review*'s contributions to conservatism and, indeed, have praised it as the leading college journal of conservative thought. Freedman's allegation that the *Review* means to scare qualified women and minorities from joining the Dartmouth community is breathtakingly absurd and borders on slander. In fact, if Freedman were as successful as this publication in attracting women and minorities to its staff, his wildest dreams would be realized.

What does Freedman mean by diversity? He doesn't quite know himself: "What do we mean by our insistence upon diversity? We mean, preeminently, differences and otherness, in all of their rich dimensions. We mean a pluralism of persons and points of view. We mean unconventional approaches and unfashionable stances toward enduring and intractable questions. We mean opening up our students' minds and our community's spirit to a richness of different persons, different cultures, different traditions, different languages, different styles of thinking, and different ways of teaching."

This kind of drivel serves only to obscure the charges of *The Dartmouth Review*: that the College has sunk into a marshy bog of feelings and superficial appearances, instead of basing a quality education on the firm ground of academic and intellectual excellence. The *Review* demands equal opportunity for all; the College offers racial and other quotas to satisfy those clamoring for a skin-deep "diversity."

Freedman asserts, "The qualifications and standing of members of this faculty are not decided by ideological provocateurs posing as journalists." He is correct; it is often ideological provocateurs posing as professors and deans who decide the qualifications and standing of members of the faculty.

The *Review* has reported on two cases where Maryssa Navarro, once as head of her department, and again as Associate Dean of the Faculty, kept professors from receiving tenure because their political beliefs were at odds with her own. Sadly enough, most professors have more cause to fear their own colleagues than their students. After all, students come and go, but destructive elements in the faculty can stay around and haunt Dartmouth forever if granted tenure. Again, Freedman chose to turn blind eyes to a grave problem at Dartmouth: students, faculty, and administrators who escape scrutiny and censure solely because of race or sex.

After reading his speech, Freedman left the stage to Jon Appleton, a music professor who has recently defended the quality of Cole's teaching ability. He remarked, "The ideas expressed in [*The Dartmouth Review*] are contrary to our stated purpose. . . . *The Dartmouth Review* has, for the last few years, attempted to persuade white male undergraduates of their racial superiority." If demands for high teaching standards are contrary to the stated purpose of the faculty, then Appleton is correct. His other charge is, again, patently false and can be empirically disproven.

Appleton's baseless accusations continued:

> Professor Cole is an easy target for *The Dartmouth Review*, because he epitomizes those attributes which the publication abhors. He is black, and they are racist. He stands for diversity, and they want the Indian symbol. He is an ethnomusicologist, teaching mostly about non-Western music, and they want to believe that the rest of the world has no cultural significance.

It would be easy to dismiss Appleton's slanderous words as the ravings of a man who has had his earphones turned up too high for too long—were it not for his ominous attack on a colleague and his mutterings about forcing *Review* students to capitulate or get out:

> It is not easy for this faculty to reach these students, especially when one of us is encouraging them, and setting an example for them. I refer to my colleague Professor Jeffrey Hart, who is an advisor to *The Dartmouth Review*. . . . He serves as a model for the racist and sexist behavior of those undergraduates for whom he serves as an advisor . . . if Professor Hart cannot help these students, it is our responsibility to do so. . . . It is now our job to help educate these students . . .

Appleton and others see vocal conservative students as targets for some kind of "re-education," i.e., indoctrination by force. If voices are "contrary to the stated purpose" then they must be eliminated. The "*volk*" will decide what will and will not be accepted.

Professor Navarro was so moved by President Freedman's speech that she rose, burst into tears, and brokenly expressed her appreciation to Freedman:

> It has been very hard to live at Dartmouth throughout the period *The Dartmouth Review* has published, and I want to thank you for being willing to say what no one has been willing or able to say. . . . I was attacked by them, but nobody would defend any of us the way you have defended us today.

If Ms. Navarro has truly been intimidated by the *Review*, one shudders to think what an uninhibited Navarro would be like.

Professor Heffernan rose to inject a voice of reason into the otherwise Kafkaesque proceedings. He stressed that freedom of speech was just as important as a duty to be civil to other members of the community. Heffernan referred to the expulsion of several black *Review* writers from a meeting of the Afro-American Society:

> It has been reported that a certain organization on this campus recently sought to silence dissent within its own ranks, and even to expel from one of its meetings that small minority of its own members who were known to think differently from the rest. . . . I do not know whether the report is accurate, but if we believe in freedom of speech on this campus, then we ought to know. We must investigate the report; we should not have to wait for the American Civil Liberties Union to investigate it for us.

Heffernan received very little applause for his balanced, thoughtful remarks.

The attack on Professor Hart continued. Professor Carla Freccero rose to present a motion containing four parts, one of which resolved that the faculty "Register our disapproval of and dissociate ourselves from the remarks made by Professor Jeffrey Hart at the COS:

> "Professor Cole lives in a sort of mental nightmare populated by cliched demons" and "Professor Cole comes from a background where physical violence is commonplace." These remarks undermine collegiality and encourage racist attitudes among the faculty, students, and alumni of Dartmouth College.

Professor David Becker rose to suggest that Hart's words be stricken from the motion, so that they would not be repeated in the press, and that the faculty condemn him without the supporting quotes. Ultimately, the motion was passed 79–43 with the quotes intact. After Hart got up to defend himself, he was harangued by Navarro and Appleton, who rose from their seats and shouted at him.

The entire meeting was so rich with absurdity that it is difficult to absorb it all. Many motions that were to be considered were simply tabled for action at a later date, including motions to discourage the *Dartmouth Alumni Magazine*'s policy of allowing the Ernest Martin Hopkins Institute to advertise in it, a measure to set up a standing committee of the faculty on *The Dartmouth Review*, and a motion to urge the Trustees to sue *The Dartmouth Review* for its use of the name "Dartmouth." After adopting Freedman's speech and condemning Hart, the faculty decided to call it a day and go home, well satisfied with its afternoon's work. Perhaps Professor Richard Joseph summed it up best; elated by the proceedings, he said: "This is a great day . . . a historic moment for Dartmouth College."

Historic indeed—March 28, 1988, will forever be recorded in Dartmouth memories as the day the president and the faculty took a giant step backwards and made censorship, intellectual parochialism, and moral cowardice the order of the day. The Pied Piper of Dartmouth and his cronies will rue their actions for years to come.

April 6, 1988

ON THE RIGHT
What Happened at Dartmouth?
by William F. Buckley Jr.

A GROUP that actually calls itself the Committee on Standards has recommended that one senior and one junior at Dartmouth (John Sutter and Christopher Baldwin) be suspended from college for a year and a half. Two other students were given lesser penalties. There is (as always) an avenue for appeal. But the judge who decides the question whether to hear an appeal is a pronounced partisan, a hostile critic of *The Dartmouth Review*, of which Baldwin and Sutter are the principle figures.

To grant an appeal, let alone a diminution of the sentence, would require Dean of Students Edward Shanahan to exhibit qualities he has not so far shown in the explosive disruption at Dartmouth involving Professor William Cole. And it seems absolutely clear that the new president of Dartmouth, Mr. James Freedman, wishes above all things in life to appease the college's Afro-American Society, which has engaged in the kind of activity against Sutter and Baldwin that reflects the manners of the Ku Klux Klan, from which the students' forebears may well have suffered.

The Dartmouth Review editors were charged with disorderly conduct, harassment, and violation of privacy at the expense of Mr. Cole, a professor of music. The background of the incident was the publication in *The Dartmouth Review* of an astonishing transcript of the kind of thing that evidently passes for music education at Dartmouth. Professor Cole, the tape recorder revealed, sounded as though he were strung out on dope, reciting a disjointed soliloquy on the subject of poverty, racism, and the kitchen stove, peppered by the language of the streets, as one would most charitably call it. *The Dartmouth Review*'s publication of this specimen of Dartmouth education would be hailed as robust investigative journalism in most circumstances. But Professor Cole is black.

The Dartmouth Review editors reported the furor caused by their publication to the newspaper's lawyer in Washington, who counseled them to go to Professor Cole and to advise him that the *Review* would publish any comments Cole had to make about the exposé. It was the meeting between the four editors and Cole that brought on the formal charges. That meeting lasted just under four minutes. A transcript of what was said exists. It took place in the classroom of Professor Cole just after he had dismissed his students, a dozen of whom, on their way out, saw and overheard the exchange. Baldwin and Sutter a) attempted to press upon Cole a letter communicating the *Review*'s willingness to publish Cole's comments; and b) asked Cole to apologize for references to *The Dartmouth Review* as racist in language that would have embarrassed the late Lenny Bruce. Cole a) declined to read the letter; b) ordered the editors out of the classroom; c) lunged at and broke the flashbulb attachment to the camera of the student photographer, and d) protested violently the machine that recorded the exchange.

A few days later, the Afro-American Society mobilized a rally. This was done by exhibiting a huge poster on which was written, "We've got to get rid of all you incompetent niggers—John Sutter, Executive Editor, *Dartmouth Review*." Sutter denies ever having mouthed (or thought) those words. One black girl student testified that the words were spoken, and a second black girl tentatively affirmed this. But if the statement had been made, a dozen people would have heard it, and none of them testified to having done so. The rally having been organized, it was addressed by President Freedman, who, although he made a pass at neutrality pending the investigation of the Committee on Standards, clearly identified himself with the protesters and helped to whip up a kind of Jacobinical rage against the editors that, a week later, flowered in the extraordinary penalties levied. To tell a college senior to go away for a year and a half is to tell him to interrupt and conceivably even to abort his career.

What is going on at Dartmouth is in embryo form what we saw happening at the early stages of the great debauches of the '60s. And the most direct cause of it is the disorderly fixation of faculty and administration on the notion that if a teacher or student is black, he can pretty well do anything he likes. At the student rally, a demand was even made that Professor Cole be supported. President Freedman proceeded to do everything short of anointing him. There may be obscure aspects of the controversy, but there cannot be two sides to the question of Professor Cole's behavior. His deportment, whether judged academically or socially, was indefensible. To appease Cole by suspending the students who exposed him is a perversion that will do to Dartmouth what that bloodstain did to Lady Macbeth.

March 15, 1988; printed in The Dartmouth Review *April 6, 1988*

EDITORIAL

Dartmouth: The Witch Hunt Goes On

by the Editors of National Review

E VERYONE IS by now familiar with the extraordinary action taken by the disciplinary committee at Dartmouth against four student editors of *The Dartmouth Review*, charging them with various modes of abusive and disorderly conduct. It was much much less than that, and on one matter there simply was no doubt, namely the charge that *The Dartmouth Review* students were racially motivated in their attack on Dr. William Cole was preposterous on the face of it.

Notwithstanding, the President of Dartmouth, Mr. Freedman, pursued the case, student editors, and *The Dartmouth Review* as if it were plain that Dartmouth was being threatened by the Ku Klux Klan. The most plausible inference is the newly installed President is afraid that the Afro-American Society was going to occupy his office. This is a routine activity by the black student lobby at Dartmouth, and nobody has figured out how to reprimand students for doing so. It isn't as easy as dealing with two white editors, whom you kick out of Dartmouth for eighteen months, the two others receiving lesser penalties. But the latest aggression is mounted by a member of the faculty, a professor Carla Freccero. She sent out a summons for a meeting of the Faculty of Arts and Sciences for the purpose of: "Register(ing) our disapproval of and dissociating ourselves from the remarks made by Professor Jeffrey Hart at the COS (Committee on Standards) hearings: 'Professor Cole lives in a sort of mental nightmare populated by cliche demons' and 'Professor Cole comes from a background where physical violence is commonplace.' These remarks undermine the collegiality and encourage racist attitudes among the faculty, students, and alumni of Dartmouth College."

Now the two sentences quoted by Professor Freccero were a part of the brief for the defense offered by Mr. Hart, a senior editor of *National Review*. As to the first, it is simply not possible to read the the transcript of Professor Cole's lecture and to come to a different conclusion. Except that this transcript teems with obscenities, it might be reprinted to make the point manifest. But even a bowdlerized version of his lecture would prove the point. Mr. Hart was, the context of his statement clearly establishes, suggesting that Professor Cole's truculent behavior when approached by the young editors (he swore at them and lunged at a camera) could perhaps be, if not explained, mitigated by Cole's own account of the violence that surrounded him during his early years, such violence as is graphically described in Claude Henry's classic, *Man-Child in the Promised Land*. It is a further irony that the same context shows that Professor Hart reprimanded the young students for physically presenting themselves to Mr. Cole with the document their lawyer advised them to hand to him. Given Cole's notorious volatility, Mr. Hart said, it would have been better to mail the recommended letter to Cole rather than to appear in his classroom (after his class had disbanded) to hand it to him.

To suggest what amounts to a vote of censure against a respected colleague for making the two points above suggests that Dartmouth is at the point of hysteria. Better—would have suggested this if the motion had been carried. It was not. But this was owing to the absence of a quorum. One hopes that the majority of the faculty, for reasons intellectual and moral, wished to dissociate themselves from Professor Freccero's unbridled passion, and simply stayed home to avoid direct confrontation. We shall see: the meeting has been postponed for two weeks.

Concerning the general appetite to dramatize the case of the four young editors, on April 27 the *New York Post* ran a six-column headline: "Buckley hires axed Dartmouth editor." The lead sentences: "Chris Baldwin, the Dartmouth junior who was suspended for humiliating one of the college's music professors, has found an ally in William Buckley. The conservative columnist—convinced that Baldwin was railroaded because the professor happens to be black—has given the student, who is white, a full-time job at the *National Review*, the magazine which Buckley edits."

The story goes on, failing only to mention that Christopher Baldwin was hired as a *National Review* intern four months earlier, in recognition of his journalistic abilities and his high academic record. It would have been more correct but less dramatic to say, "Buckley declines to fire Dartmouth editor, persecuted by Dartmouth College."

May 27, 1988

THE WALL STREET JOURNAL

Intolerance & *The Dartmouth Review*

by L. Gordon Crovitz

TOP EDITORS OF *The Dartmouth Review* were suspended from Dartmouth College in March for a year and half for engaging in "vexatious oral exchange" with a professor. A group of twenty-nine students who occupied and refused to leave the college president's office in 1986 were found in violation of college rules, but not punished. These students received no penalty, a college committee explained, "in light of how your actions were motivated by strongly held convictions about the educational goals and responsibilities of this College, how the issues to which you are committed are vital for Dartmouth and the larger society, and how you took care to minimize the obstruction while respecting the rights of others."

The *Dartmouth Review* editors suspect their real crime was what their newspaper prints. It pushes conservative causes, as in its editorial campaign for a common core curriculum, and opposition to racially based preferences. The twenty-nine who escaped penalties belonged to an anti-apartheid group defending the presence of shanties. The contrast in the two cases was only one of the disclosures of double standards in discipline brought out in a New Hampshire courtroom last week.

The students are seeking a preliminary injunction, before a full-scale jury trial, to re-admit them for the term beginning next week. They argue that the college violated its contractual promises; the student guidebook includes pledges of free expression and the implicit assurances of fair and equal treatment and due process in any disciplinary hearing. Harvey Myerson of Myerson & Kuhn, one of New York's hardest-nosed litigators, agreed to handle the case at reduced rates.

Mr. Myerson also introduced evidence that at Dartmouth, even rape is punishable by a lesser punishment that the six terms *Review* students received. A student "charged with engaging in sexual abuse, in that you engaged in sexual relations with X without her consent" was suspended for just one term. The offense came under the heading of "Harassment, Abuse, Coercion and Violence."

It is probably foolish for private colleges to allow courts to intervene in their internal affairs, but Dartmouth lawyers willingly admit that the student handbook is legally enforceable. Whatever ruling Judge Bruce Mohl makes in the case later this week, the evidence already introduced raises the stark question of whether college campuses tolerate conservatives.

The off-campus *Review* has been the obsession of liberal Hanover since its founding in 1980. The *Review* uses a sharp writing style—that too often tilts to the sophomoric—to argue against special-interest curricula, racial quotas, and what it views as silly pieties such as dropping the Indian as the school symbol. In February, as part of its campaign for a common core curriculum and higher teaching standards, it ran articles criticizing an English professor who failed to teach the required books and music professor William Cole. The English teacher changed his class, but Mr. Cole's reaction led to a confrontation.

The article, headlined "Bill Cole in His Own Words—Sound and Fury, Signifying Nothing," was based on a tape of one of Mr. Cole's classes that a discontented student gave to the *Review*. His rambling lecture included profanity that can't be published here, racial epithets, and discourses on political subjects. Mr. Cole unsuccessfully sued the *Review* for libel in 1983, so a *Review* lawyer advised that Mr. Cole get a chance to respond. Christopher Baldwin, the editor, and three other staffers hand-delivered a letter to Mr. Cole after class asking for a response, with tape recorder and camera to document any reaction.

Accounts of the details differ, but words were exchanged, including obscenities from Mr. Cole, who broke off the camera flash. The four students were tried and convicted in a disciplinary hearing of "vexatious oral exchange" amounting to harassment of Mr. Cole and violating his privacy right. Mr. Cole is black, the four students are white, and the college treated this as a racial incident.

The *Review* punishment was perhaps predictable given a peremptory official declaration that the students were guilty as charged. Soon after the Cole incident, students from the Afro-American Society met with Dartmouth President James Freedman, who agreed to address their rally later in the day. Although he hadn't discussed the incident with any of the accused—he didn't meet with any *Review* students until after their hearing—he referred to his "deep personal concern" about "acts of disrespect, insensitivity and personal attack" and "racism, sexism, and other forms of ignorance." Before the *Review* hearing, President Freedman told the *Boston Globe*, "I feel dreadful about the attack on Professor Cole."

Mr. Baldwin testified that he was surprised to learn in President Freedman's speech of the date of the disciplinary hearing against him and the other *Review* staffers. He said the Freedman speech, "whipped the kids up into an even greater frenzy by giving the charges an official stamp of approval." He testified, "I couldn't believe President Freeman could attribute racial hatred on my part without even talking to me, and on the eve of my disciplinary hearing."

Mr. Myerson asked President Freedman, a former law school dean, if he worried he might have prejudiced the hearing. He replied, "Not for a minute." After the hearing, President Freedman told a faculty meeting that "the qualifications and standing of members of this faculty are not decided by ideological provocateurs posing as journalists" and called the *Review* "irresponsible, mean-spirited, cruel, and ugly."

Freedman testified that he made his public comments because "I had a responsibility to keep the peace and calm of the campus." He said he had been "worried about racial incidents of the kind we have had at campuses all over the country." There is some merit to this argument, but at the cost of what Mr. Myerson in his courtroom questioning called a "classic example of prejudgment of the facts by a president of a university."

Indeed, the administration helped agitate the issue. An assistant dean helped organize some of the demonstrations. A letter was introduced at the trial from him addressed to the presidents of Dartmouth fraternities, "Re: Vigil Supporting Professor Cole." The letter said it was "important that people show their support or concern" and asked the fraternities to "encourage member attendance."

Also introduced last week was a confidential letter from the dean of the college, Edward Shanahan, to Mr. Cole saying he had temporarily stepped down as chairman of the disciplinary committee to become "personally involved in the attempt to develop the case" against the student who had taped the Cole class, and apologizing for failing to make a case. In testimony, he admitted it was rare for the dean, who usually also passes ultimate sentence, to act as prosecutor, and that he had also stepped down from the committee two years ago to investigate a shanty case involving Mr. Baldwin.

Perhaps the most extraordinary document *Review* lawyers uncovered was a handwritten note Mr. Shanahan wrote to himself after the *Review* hearing. The top line read, "Sanctions—incident only?" This and testimony from members of the disciplinary committee might tend to undermine the college's position that the case has noting to do with the *Review* or its politics, and concerns only the Cole incident. The next line read, "Destroy notes today (normal procedure)." This could be trouble at the planned full-scale state and federal trials. A jury might wonder about destruction of documents and why someone would indicate in a note to himself that this was normal procedure. Mr. Shanahan explained that he was "fastidious."

Mr. Baldwin also testified that contrary to the college guidelines, he did not get a list of the committee members within seventy-two hours of the hearing. This safeguard was supposed to give the accused a chance to establish the bias of any committee members. This turned out to be a kangaroo jury.

Mr. Baldwin testified that only after the hearing did he learn that several members on the committee had previously made hostile comments about the *Review*. One faculty member had written President Freedman two letters criticizing the *Review* for "distorted and slanderous articles" that "have reached the point where they seriously threaten the principle of academic freedom on this campus." Mr. Baldwin said another criticized a college employee for reading the *Review*, which he testified she called a "fascist rag." A student participated in the hearing but resigned because he had written a work of fiction blasting the *Review*.

There was also evidence that the administration was able to inform the *Dartmouth Alumni Magazine* that Mr. Shanahan had denied the students' request for a reconsideration of their punishment—even before they had filed their appeal. As Alice learned from the Queen in Wonderland, "No! No! Sentence first—verdict afterwards."

Judge Mohl of Grafton County Superior Court plans to rule this week on whether Mr. Baldwin, a junior, and John Sutter, a senior, can go back to classes pending a full trial on the contract-breach claim. No one can know if the judge will conclude that any amount of evidence is enough to rule for the students in a preliminary hearing, but Dartmouth is already getting outside pressure. President Freedman testified he told the Trustees the "hardest questions to answer from alumni" were how Mr. Cole remains on the faculty and how he got tenure in the first place.

Yet in Hanover the *Review* remains heresy. So much so that Mr. Cole's wife, an Italian professor, thought it was appropriate to ask for an exam essay on the *Review*. Few students could have felt free to propose a Pulitzer.

The great irony is that this persecution of *Review* students has accomplished one of the newspaper's goals in urging educational reform at Dartmouth: Remind everyone that a higher education must include the basic texts of Western civilization or we risk developments as outrageous as political creeds for colleges—Suffer in silence, conservatives, or leave. A series of required classes in the Great Books including Mill on free speech, Aristotle on justice, and Blackstone on the common law might be just the remedy.

December 28, 1988; printed in The Dartmouth Review *January 11, 1989*

THE WALL STREET JOURNAL
Blacks on the *Review*
by L. Gordon Crovitz

P ROBABLY NO ONE objects to the accusations that *The Dartmouth Review* is racist, sexist, and anti-Semitic more than its black, women, and Jewish staffers. The current editor, Harmeet Dhillon, is a Sikh and the *Review*'s third woman editor. An earlier editor, Dinesh D'Souza, was born in India. The newspaper has had a Jewish president and many Jewish writers.

Blacks on the newspaper bore a special burden during the Cole affair. One is sophomore K. Christopher Pritchett, who has spent the past several months as an intern on the *Journal*'s editorial page staff. Mr. Pritchett is a studious and quiet-spoken young man whose description of being black, conservative, and at Dartmouth is worth some attention.

Mr. Pritchett, who testified on behalf of his *Dartmouth Review* colleagues last week, says he was physically threatened twice by other black students after the Cole incident. When he and two other black *Review* members were seen in the black dormitory, someone announced, "We have *Review*ers in here." A crowd gathered and accused them of being "Uncle Toms." Mr. Pritchett says one black *Review* student confined to a wheelchair, Marc Deadrick, had smoke blown in his face by a menacing black football player. A few days later at a public candlelight vigil against racism, Mr. Pritchett was again cornered. One black student said, "I want to kick your ass." Mr. Pritchett had a friend, a burly Canadian shot-putter, escort him around campus for several days.

Mr. Pritchett told Dartmouth President James Freedman about these incidents and what he called a "lynch mob atmosphere" that intimidated at least one black off the *Review* staff. Mr. Pritchett reports that Mr. Freedman listened to him, then said, "Well there are some complex social dynamisms at Dartmouth, aren't there?"

Mr. Freedman testified that he didn't recall the details of the meeting, but denies the quote. Dartmouth announced five months after receiving Mr. Pritchett's complaints that it would not press any charges arising from the dorm incident. The other complaint is officially pending. College spokesman Alex Huppe said Mr. Pritchett's report of the threats is "in waving distance of the truth," and that "how grievous it was in my mind is not perfectly clear."

December 28, 1988; printed in The Dartmouth Review *January 11, 1989*

A Choice for Dartmouth
by Harmeet Dhillon

I N CASE you haven't heard, *The Dartmouth Review* won. On January 3, 1989, Judge Bruce Mohl of the Superior Court of New Hampshire ordered the Dartmouth administration to "forthwith reinstate the plaintiffs Christopher Baldwin and John Sutter as full-time students at Dartmouth College."

The judge's ruling is "a tremendous victory for free speech and fair play not just at Dartmouth, but at campuses across the country," according to Arthur Ruegger of Myerson and Kuhn, the New York law firm representing the *Review*.

When the students on the *Review* first filed suit, Dartmouth spokesmen pooh-poohed it. "A frivolous lawsuit," we heard from a number of College officials, especially College counsellor Sean German, speaking at a Washington press conference. "A waste of the court's time." "The annual lawsuit filed by *The Dartmouth Review*."

That was before Judge Mohl found that the *Review* students, despite the odds, met the heavy burden of showing both a "clear probability of success" on the merits of the case, as well as "irreparable harm" to the students.

Judge Mohl states clearly that when the case goes to a full trial later this year, the *Review* will probably win. "It is the Court's view that the plaintiffs will likely prevail in their claim to set aside the Committee on Standards' finding against them." Myerson says the students are proceeding full speed ahead with both their state and federal claims, seeking vindication and damages before a jury. A defeat for the administration on racial discrimination grounds could mean not only liability for trustees and the administration but also endangerment of Dartmouth's federal funding.

Despite this, College spokesman Alex Huppe reacted to the trial by— declaring victory! "We welcome the court's findings that the College has safeguarded the students' First Amendment rights and that the College's disciplinary procedures are fair."

That this is a massive distortion of reality should be evident to anyone who reads carefully what the judge wrote.

Judge Mohl seems to identify three central issues in the trial. First, was the COS prejudiced and were its findings tainted by bias? Second, did the College's penalty fit the crime? Third, was the penalty equitable when matched against COS penalties for comparable offenses?

Judge Mohl divided the first issue into two parts. Is the COS structurally or intrinsically biased, or was there COS bias incidental to this case? Mohl concludes that "the court cannot find that the COS hearing failed in any material respect to afford the plaintiffs their procedural rights." His reason is that a private college need not follow constitutional standards. Thus the facts that the COS does not permit attorneys, does not provide adequate time to prepare for a hearing, does not allow direct cross-examination, etc. do not, by themselves, prove structural bias. "Informal" procedures are allowed.

Then Judge Mohl says that even though Dartmouth is not held to courtroom standards, even though its procedures are informal and self-imposed, despite this lower standard, the COS failed in this case to ensure that it was substantially free of bias and prejudice against the students.

"There is little doubt that Section 12 of the COS guidelines is intended to assure that the COS panel members who hear disciplinary matters against Dartmouth students shall be free from any bias or prejudice," the judge says. The judge then focuses on the flagrant bias displayed by one member of the panel, Professor Albert La Valley.

Shortly before the hearing La Valley denounced the *Review* for racism and sexism and "scandalous articles" which "seriously threaten the principle of academic freedom." Dean Edward Shanahan had the La Valley letter but did not show it to other members of the COS. La Valley was not asked to step down from the panel; in fact, he played an active part in it.

After the COS verdict, La Valley wrote a second letter, this time to President Freedman. Here La Valley confirmed that, at least in his mind, the trial was not about the conduct of a few students, but rather was about stifling conservative views on campus.

"As a gay faculty member," La Valley wrote, "I already feel a sense of intimidation has been lessened, a threat blunted." La Valley deplored the "already somewhat conservative student body" and expressed enormous relief. "I feel as though a cloud has been lifted."

Judge Mohl finds "substantial animosity toward *The Dartmouth Review*" in La Valley which undermined the "indispensable requisite of integrity and objectivity." La Valley's bias alone, Judge Mohl says, settles this case. It is outrageous enough, by itself, to warrant an injunction. "Given the court's ruling with respect to the bias of the COS, it is not necessary to reach the further issue of whether the COS decision is supported by the evidence, or the plaintiff's additional claim that the penalties were unduly harsh or discriminatory."

College spokesman Huppe has distorted the clear meaning of the judge's words, claiming that they vindicate the administration on the issues of fairness and discrimination. Even a student columnist for the campus daily, Doug Anderson '89, saw through Huppe's transparent attempt to turn the defeat into a victory. Anderson commented, "The decision was narrowly focused because it was unnecessary to investigate further when the improprieties necessitating an injunction were discovered."

As Anderson shrewdly pointed out, President Freedman has denounced the *Review* for alleged distortions—"poisoning the intellectual atmosphere on campus." But why aren't students and alumni getting the truth from the administration? "Someone should tell the president that people in glass houses shouldn't throw stones."

In the media, the College has stressed Mohl's contention that "The court finds no persuasive evidence that Dartmouth College . . . has pursued disciplinary action against the plaintiffs on account of their association with *The Dartmouth Review*." But his statement did not address the issue of whether the severity of sanctions resulted from the students' positions as *Review* editors; it merely opined that the decisions to hold hearings were not. Judge Mohl's finding that "Contrary to the College's position, the charges against the four students did arise directly out of their activities on the *Review*" is a powerful repudiation of the administration's position throughout the dispute.

For the past several months, the Dartmouth administration has been spreading half-truths and selective accounts of the facts through the *Dartmouth Alumni Magazine* and other official publications. It has persuaded Freedman apologists like Allan Gold of *The New York Times* and administration lackeys like Morton Kondracke of *The New Republic* to seed their publications with official Dartmouth propaganda. Now the truth has begun to emerge in an impartial judicial setting—a fact that is bound to be slightly discomforting for many alumni. Perhaps this decision will finally convince loyal alumni that they can no longer afford to approach the College with an attitude of blissful ignorance.

President Freedman now faces a crisis of enormous proportions. He has invested the reputation of his presidency in a scuffle with an under-graduate newspaper. He is spending hundreds of thousands of dollars of alumni and parent contributions to prosecute this struggle. Justice, how-ever, does not appear to be on his side.

The dilemma for the trustees is even greater. When President Freedman was first introduced to the Dartmouth community, chairman of the Board of Trustees Norman "Sandy" McCullough promised boldly, "I'll stake my reputation on this man!" But are the trustees willing to gamble Dartmouth's reputation on a president who has led them to their current predicament?

"All that is necessary for evil to triumph is for good men to do nothing," Edmund Burke once said. Dartmouth has come to a fork in the road to its future. Now is the time for those who love Dartmouth to choose a path.

It is time to help place our small College back on the path to standards of all-around excellence, respect for free speech, and equitable standards. Examine the evidence in this issue and coming issues and make your choice for the future of Dartmouth College.

January 11, 1989

THE WALL STREET JOURNAL
Fundamental Fairness
by the Editors of the Wall Street Journal

THE MEN AND WOMEN who run America's universities should do some deep thinking about a decision just rendered in a superior court in New Hampshire. It strongly suggests that the circle many of their faculty have drawn around what constitutes acceptable political opinion is too small.

Judge Mohl has ordered Dartmouth College to reinstate immediately as full-time students two members of the conservative *Dartmouth Review*, who'd been suspended from school last March by the college's discipli-nary committee. The students and the *Review* for which they wrote had become embroiled in a dispute with a black, liberal music professor. Though narrowly reasoned, Judge Mohl's decision granting the students injunctive relief against Dartmouth focused precisely on the kind of think-ing that now stands as a high wall between conservatives and liberals on many campuses. It is a kind of thinking that looks upon itself as fair and reasonable. It is not.

Months before the disputed incident, faculty members on the Steering Committee of the Women's Studies Program sent Dartmouth President James O. Freedman a letter, written in the earnestly sensitive language of wronged academics, saying the *Review* had subjected their colleagues to "slanders" and "sexist and racist" characterizations. A co-signer, Albert La Valley, sat on the committee that suspended the *Review* staffers, and Judge Mohl said the Women's Studies letter clearly reflected bias and prejudice against *Review* staffers. Mr. La Valley, he said, shouldn't have been on the disciplinary committee.

We suspect that Mr. La Valley, his co-signers, and faculty at schools all over the country are shocked to discover that a New Hampshire judge finds his views expressed in that letter reflect prejudice. Indeed, in another letter that Mr. La Valley sent to President Freedman three days after he participated in the students' suspension, he speaks of "a threat blunted." He says the *Review*'s "attacks on women, minorities and gays subtly feed into an already somewhat conservative student body—and thus stops the flow of needful dialogue." The phrase "flow of needful dialogue" will serve well enough to describe the larger issue at stake in *The Dartmouth Review* decision.

The flow has been narrowed. It has been narrowed because so many college presidents, trustees, and deans haven't had the courage to blow the whistle on the radicalization of their faculties. Many college administrators call themselves and indeed are liberals, but only through the most extraordinary acts of self-delusion or timidity could they believe that the intellectual atmosphere these faculties have fostered has much to do with anyone's definition of liberalism.

It is an atmosphere that is not liberal. It is sneering, condescending, and intolerant of uncongenial views. Conservatives and liberals, for instance, should have little problem at this point in our history absorbing into a huge college curriculum courses called Women's Studies or Black Studies. In practice, much of this turns out to be the most intolerantly argued propaganda. (Judge Mohl's decision, for instance, notes that "several black students who worked for *The Dartmouth Review* were harassed or threatened by other Dartmouth black students.") Surly administrators know this. And knowing this, how can they claim to be offended when bright eighteen- and nineteen-year-old conservatives muster what resources they have developed to counterattack? The kids at *The Dartmouth Review* aren't unique, and anyone paying serious attention to college life knows it.

In his decision this week, Judge Mohl noted the court's reluctance to enter a controversy involving "private educational institutions such as Dartmouth." He further defended the informal nature of the school's disciplinary proceedings. We share the view that colleges be left to manage their affairs free of the sort of Miranda-like proceduralism that plagues and stifles the world beyond their walls.

These schools should understand, however, that they will become in-

creasingly less free (and ultimately less relevant) if they ignore the conditions that cause students to create a *Dartmouth Review* or an Allan Bloom
to write *The Closing of the American Mind.* We suspect the Albert La Val-
leys of the nation's faculties will continue to believe that in every respect
they've been more than fair to their conservative students and colleagues.
The job then falls to the people running the country's colleges and universities to relearn and restore the fading standard of fundamental fairness.

January 5, 1989; printed in The Dartmouth Review *January 11, 1989*

KING FEATURES SYNDICATE
Junk Thought Hits *TNR*
by Jeffrey Hart

I HAVE TO CONFESS that previously I had not thought of Morton
Kondracke, talk-show personality and *New Republic* editor, as a recep-
tacle for junk thought. Of course I knew that he is much less impressive
intellectually than he deems himself, but that is a common enough afflic-
tion. I thought, however, that he was an honest man. I was wrong.

In the December 12, 1988 *New Republic,* Kondracke perpetrates an article called "The Dartmouth Wars," caricaturing some extremely serious
and important disputes that are taking place at that institution. These disputes involve the nature of the curriculum, the national phenomenon of
reverse discrimination in the academy, and the assault Dartmouth has been
conducting against civilized norms, such as making available to all incoming freshmen equipment for male-to-male oral-anal sex. That's right.
Passing out the equipment.

Many students are outraged by all of this, and some of them, brilliant
student journalists, write for the independent conservative weekly *The
Dartmouth Review.* This newspaper is now in its ninth year of publication.
Former editors and staffers have gone on to posts in journalism, the
academy, the foundations, legal practice, and the White House.

But the puffed-up Kondracke is sore at them. He actually, and in broad
daylight, calls them, and I quote, "pre-fascist brats."

What in the world can "pre-fascist" mean here? I suppose Kondracke
wanted to call them "fascists," but was warned off by the *New Republic*'s
libel lawyer.

These student journalists, whom I have known over the years, and
whom Kondracke has never bothered to know, are anything but fascists.
They are for limited government, for example. They abhor the centralized
fascist conception of the state. But that doesn't matter to Kondracke.

And what might "pre-fascist" mean anyway? That they are not quite
fascists this year, but will be fascists next year? Is it a chronological term?

No, it's not. It is just old Kondracke vomiting in print in *The New Republic*.

Kondracke also, and I suppose deliberately, leads *New Republic* readers to think bad thoughts about the funding of this student enterprise, representing it as supported by conservative fat cats. Wrong. The newspaper does get some minor funding. But its budget is sustained by some 6,000 subscribers, mostly Dartmouth alumni, who pay $25 a head. Some send in $50, for fun. *New Republic* readers won't learn this from Kondracke.

I've got a piece of news for Mr. Kondracke. On November 17, 1988 Judge Lawrence Silberman of the District of Columbia Court of Appeals declined a Daniel Webster Award, given under Dartmouth auspices. Why? I quote from Judge Silberman's letter declining the award. He cites the "undisguised hostility" on the part of Dartmouth officials to "the political views expressed in *The Dartmouth Review*." The judge observes that "At Dartmouth, last fall, I gained the strong impression that in the official opinion of the College there is a morally right and wrong answer to 'disputed' questions. Therefore, those alumni who advocated the 'wrong' answer were not entitled to be represented—at least in any significant numbers—on the governing organs of the College, and those students who advocated the 'wrong' answer to those questions were to be discouraged from expressing their views in too assertive a fashion."

Judge Silberman's letter represents extreme understatement.

And there were a lot of things that Kondracke does not tell his *New Republic* readers. For example, that he is, for all practical purposes, an official of Dartmouth College, sitting on the board of the *Dartmouth Alumni Magazine*. Is that honest or even principled journalism? I think not, myself.

Michael Kinsley is the editor of the *New Republic*. Martin Peretz is chairman and editor-in-chief. I suggest that they change Kondracke's title to Editor in Charge of Junk Thought.

Printed in The Dartmouth Review *January 11, 1989*

ON THE RIGHT

The Wild Indians at Dartmouth: Stopped by the Court

by William F. Buckley Jr.

T HE RULING by Judge Bruce Mohl in the Dartmouth College case is a stunning blow to the pretensions of Dartmouth Justice. Judge Mohl was ever so careful not to speak broadly about the case of the Dartmouth administration vs. two students involved in student conservative journalism. He elected to rule on a narrow point, and gave a gentlemanly dismissal to the broader charges against Dartmouth's disciplinary committee. But the fact remains that the whole Dartmouth Establishment has been discredited. It boils down to this: Dartmouth College ordered two students, Christopher Baldwin and John Sutter, to stay away from the premises of the College until September, 1989, and the court has issued an injunction requiring Dartmouth to reinstitute the two students effective immediately. That is the nut of what has happened.

Details:

The conflict arose when *The Dartmouth Review*, the dissident, conservative student paper, published a transcript of the classroom meanderings of a wild black music professor, raising the question whether he was qualified to teach American Music, when what he spoke primarily about was white racism, exploring the frontiers of abusive and profane language. After the publication of the transcript, four students approached the professor after his class, intending to advise him that he was free to answer in his own language the article published about him. This encounter resulted in the exchange of vivid language, primarily that of the professor who instantly fled to the authorities demanding that the students be prosecuted, which they were by Dartmouth's Committee on Standards (COS) which, after a hearing, found the students guilty of harassment, disorderly conduct, and invasion of privacy. The penalty: six terms' suspension. Judge Mohl restricted himself to documenting that one of the jurors on the disciplinary committee, Professor Albert La Valley, was clearly disqualified from rendering a disinterested vote given that four months before the affair he had written a private letter categorically denouncing *The Dartmouth Review* and all its works.

Judge Mohl having found for the plaintiffs, tossed a posy at the bloodied Administration by saying that he found "no persuasive evidence that Dartmouth College has retaliated against or otherwise pursued disciplinary action against the plaintiffs on account of their association with *The Dartmouth Review*." Ho ho.

—Twenty-nine students occupied the President's office in 1986, to protest investments in South Africa. The penalty? Nothing. The reason given by the Dartmouth Administration? That their "actions were motivated by strongly held convictions."

—A student (it transpired during the trial) found guilty of rape was suspended for one term.

—It transpired that the Dean's office had surreptitiously egged on a public demonstration against "racism" immediately before the disciplinary committee met.

—A memo from Chairman of the COS, Dean Edward Shanahan, intended to be read and then destroyed, suggested that the disciplinary hearings were not confined to the incident in question involving the mad, black professor.

—It transpired that evidence of gross bias by more than one member of the disciplinary committee had been concealed by the Administration.

—And it transpired that the moment the COS ruled that the defendants were guilty, the Dean rushed out to give the good news to—the AP? UP? *New York Times*? No: to the Afro-American Society, the Black Caucus, the Native American Society, the Women's Issues League, and the Dartmouth Area Gay and Lesbian Organization. The longtime targets of, and adversaries of, *The Dartmouth Review*.

Theoretically, the College could send the case back to the Committee on Standards, minus Professor La Valley, and try the whole thing again. But this time, it would need to make a case in the teeth of all the information that came out during the heavy depositions that preceded the trial before Judge Mohl. That is Dartmouth's alternative.

The students' alternative, it would appear to this layman, in the absence of counsel, is to file a damage suit against Dartmouth. The case was won under the brilliant leadership of a major New York trial lawyer, Harvey Myerson of Myerson & Kuhn, and New York lawyers do not give away lightly two or three hundred hours of their time. The careers of the two students have been set back by one year and they will not graduate with their classes. How much is that worth, in a society that sets dollar figures to calibrate the value of everything from a bloody nose to palimony?

What yells out at the U.S. public, alerted to the Dartmouth Case by columnists, editorial writers, feature writers, and *60 Minutes*, is the incandescent hypocrisy of so many people who, in the name of free speech, persecute its practitioners—if their opinions are conservative.

January 5, 1989; printed in The Dartmouth Review *January 11, 1989*

And There Was Much Rejoicing . . .
by Kevin Pritchett

B LACK MUSIC PROFESSOR William Shadrack Cole has left Dartmouth. "The end of my association with Dartmouth is liberating," said Cole in a prepared statement last month. Contrary to what the College and the *Boston Globe* contend, the *Review*'s coverage of Cole's classroom performance had nothing to do with Cole's race. If race has ever entered the picture, it is because Cole has done a disservice to his own race by his actions.

Cole's classes were extremely easy, so much so that if one had vital signs, one could get an A. The language he used in the classroom and to express his feelings ("p*ssy," "m*th*rf*ck**r," "b*llsh*t) would make even *2 Live Crew* blush. Cole frequently called the white students in his classes "honkies." Cole should have gotten the boot for good years ago. (Especially after he yelled "I'm gonna f*ck*n' blow you up" to a student across the Green several years back, and after he assaulted a student two years ago.) But, he fits perfectly into the three-ring circus that is Dartmouth: "Step right up folks, come see the Amazing, Stupendous Black Professor Spewing Racial Epithets and Profanity—But He's Diverse, Though!"

We at the *Review* give Cole no flowery valedictions, and we do not mourn because of his departure. All we have to say is "Au revoir, Adios, Aloha, and Get the Heck Outta Town."

September 19, 1990

Sex Ed

Administration & Health Service Condone Bizarre Sexual Activities

by Christopher Baldwin, Mark Behnam & Harmeet Dhillon

THIS MONTH BEGINS a stepped-up "sexual-awareness" campaign at the College. The Dartmouth College Health Service, known as "Dick's House," has become far more aggressive in its approach to student sexuality this term. This is evidenced by the introduction of free brochures and sex kits at Winter Term registration.

In the past, Dick's House has offered brochures along with a "Conception-Control Roadshow," free or heavily subsidized birth control, and individual counseling.

Currently, the College distributes *Partners in Health*, written by Beverly Conant Sloane, Director of Health Education at the College. This publication was copyright in 1986 by the Trustees of Dartmouth College. *Partners in Health* is a sixty-four-page handbook which is offered to students at no charge. It covers sexual choices and preferences, methods of contraception, the condition of pregnancy, the mechanics of male and female reproductive systems, and details on various sexually transmitted diseases.

There are more than ten methods of contraception outlined in *Partners in Health*. Two of these, condoms and "Morning After Pills," are offered at no cost to students. According to Dean of the College Ed Shanahan, the condoms are "donated" to the College. Condoms can be picked up at Dick's House by either male or female students. The cost of a condom at a Hanover drug store is approximately $1.70.

The "Morning After Pill" is given only to female students who must sign a release form prior to consumption of the controversial pill. The purpose of this pill, as described in *Partners in Health*, is to "prevent survival of a fertilized egg." It is also pointed out to students, in the handbook, that this pill is not approved by the U.S. Food and Drug Administration."

Actual student phone conversation with Dick's House official:

STUDENT: Hello. Um . . . I was having sex with a girl and my condom broke. A friend of mine told me you had these Day After Pills. . . .

DICK'S HOUSE: Well, when did this happen?

STUDENT: It happened last night.

DICK'S HOUSE: Well, rush her down right now and we can give her the pills.

STUDENT: I actually haven't talked to her yet about this. Are they safe?

DICK'S HOUSE: Yeah, they're safe. But you don't have a lot of time to think it over. If you bring her down soon we can do it, but we're closing soon.

STUDENT: Well, I'm kind of worried about it.

DICK'S HOUSE: Well, it's a hell of a lot better than pregnancy, isn't it?

STUDENT: Well, yeah, well, I'm going to just go talk with her about it.

The birth control pill is available to female students for $1.00 to $1.25 per month; it is one of the most popular forms of contraception at the College. Students must undergo a complete physical examination in order to receive a prescription for one of three brands of "the pill" offered at Dick's House. The quoted cost of birth control pills at the local drugstore is $13.00 per month.

Diaphragms are available to female students for $4.50 after a free fitting for size. The quoted cost for this type of contraception at the local drugstore is $15.00. Spermicides and jellies, often used in conjunction with the diaphragm, are available at Dick's House for $1.00 per tube. The local drugstore's quoted cost on this product is $9.00.

"Fertility Awareness," or the "Rhythm Method," is also described in *Partners in Health*. The handbook explains that "there are no medical risks associated with the fertility awareness method . . . (but) the failure rate for fertility awareness is higher than with other methods."

Several types of abortion are outlined in *Partners in Health*: "Menstrual Extraction," "Dilation and curettage," "Vacuum Aspiration," "Dilation And Evacuation," "Hysteronomy," and "Induced Labor With Intra-Amniotic Infusion: Saline Abortion and Prostaglandin Abortion." Beverly Conant Sloane, Health Education Director, would not comment on the types or costs of abortions. Mrs. Sloane also declined to explain the extensive subsidy programs which exist for all forms of contraception and abortion.

In fact, Mrs. Sloane would comment on nothing regarding this article; she said she did not "trust the *Review*," and she asked the editor to "call off the dogs." She would not even consent to a taped interview concerning her own health program when promised an immediate copy of the tape.

Dr. John Turco, Director of College Health Service, was finally reached for a brief interview in which he stated that birth-control pills, diaphragms, and spermicides are sold "at cost to students." He confirmed that condoms have been donated to the College in the past, but added that funds currently used to buy them are taken from the Health Service budget.

Abstinence is the last topic mentioned in *Partners in Health* under the category of contraception: "Abstinence means not having intercourse with the penis in or near the vagina. It does not mean abstaining from sex. Many couples substitute oral sex, mutual masturbation, or other erotic activities for intercourse." One listed problem of abstinence is that "many people find it difficult to abstain from intercourse. It is easy to underestimate the desire to have intercourse."

The "Conception-Control Roadshow," or "C. C. Roadshow," has been offered at the College for several years now. The "Roadshow" is a less serious version of the information sessions held weekly at Dick's House; it is given several times each term in various dormitory clusters. The purpose of the "Roadshow" is to inform students and make them comfortable with sex and contraception. Somehow, it also manages to turn what should be an intimate, adult experience into an informal, raucous game. In the past, the "Roadshow" has advertised: "Come dressed as your favorite contraceptive."

At the "C. C. Roadshows" and at the Dick's House information sessions, students meet "Eve," a plastic vagina. Members of the student audience are invited to experiment with various contraceptives on "Eve." An atmosphere of levity is fostered by the casual strewing about of condoms accompanied by the catchy jingle: "You say condoms, I say jelly." Students often make balloons out of the condoms, and, in at least one instance, students were strongly encouraged to taste some contraceptive foam so they would be "more comfortable with it during oral sex."

The "Roadshow" method of sex education has been compared to the Rassias language method because it is extremely lively and there is a lot of audience participation. Indeed, Undergraduate Advisors often recommend the "Roadshow" to freshmen as an evening of entertainment, and most students admittedly attend the "Roadshow" "just for laughs."

The most recent piece of sex education literature to hit the campus is a color brochure entitled "Safe Sex." This brochure is published by the Charlottesville AIDS Resource Network. Over 500 of these brochures were distributed with small "sex kits" at Dartmouth's Winter Term Registration.

This brochure classifies many different physical activities as either "safe," "risky," or "dangerous," and the kit (which is assembled at Dick's House) consists of devices which are supposed to contribute to "safe sex": two condoms, a "rubber dam," and a small package of "Probe" lubricant. The "rubber dam" is a device used to guard against the transmission of sexual diseases during oral/anal and oral/vaginal sex. Both the brochure and the "sex kit" are given to students at no charge.

Sex Ed

Activities listed as "safe" in the brochure are: "dry kissing," "masturbation on healthy skin," "oral sex with a condom," "external water sports," "touching," and "fantasy." "Water sports," it turns out, consist of urinating on your partner(s). The brochure warns that while "urinating on skin without open cuts or sores is safe . . . urine that enters the mouth, vagina, or rectum can spread viruses such as AIDS or hepatitis-B."

"Protected vaginal intercourse" and "protected anal intercourse" are described as "possibly safe." The risk of AIDS and hepatitis-B viruses is listed as extremely high if condoms are not used during anal intercourse, and possible if condoms are not used during vaginal intercourse. Further, "the rectal lining is often injured during anal intercourse and germs can easily enter the bloodstream through bruised tissue."

Activities listed as "risky" include: "wet kissing," "masturbation on open/broken skin," "oral sex on a woman," amphetamines, amyl nitrite, alcohol, and marijuana. Oral sex on a male using a condom is described as "safe," and "as long as ejaculation doesn't take place in the mouth, unprotected oral sex probably does not transfer AIDS or hepatitis-B virus."

Activities listed as dangerous include: "oral sex without a condom," "unprotected vaginal intercourse," "unprotected anal intercourse," "internal water sports," "intravenous drugs," "sharing a needle," "fisting," and "rimming." For those who are unfamiliar with "fisting" and "rimming," the brochure supplies ample definitions: "fisting" is described as "putting a hand or fist into someone's rectum or vagina," and "rimming" as "oral/anal contact."

The brochure provides other tidbits of caution and advice: "The bruising that occurs during anal intercourse can be greatly decreased by the use of lubricants . . . oil-based lubricants such as Crisco or Vaseline are unsafe . . ."; "Using poppers during anal intercourse can expand the blood vessels of the rectum and as a result increase the risk of receiving the AIDS virus"; "Most sexually transmitted diseases are spread by germs moving from one person to another . . . you can limit this spread by enjoying sex that shares love, tenderness, and passion, but doesn't share germ-carrying fluids."

While initial investigations into this story were being conducted, it was unclear whether this was an Administration-backed project, or the brainchild of a renegade College health official. A conversation with Dean Shanahan revealed that he had thoroughly read the "Safe Sex" brochure and approved its campus distribution. Shanahan added that his office had not approved the free distribution of condoms, and that this "sexual-awareness" campaign was not sparked by any single incident, but rather by growing concerns about sexually transmitted diseases and unwanted pregnancies.

Actual student phone conversation with Dartmouth Health Administrator:

169

STUDENT: I'm curious to know how dangerous anal sex is. I've never done that before . . . it seems kind of dangerous to me.

ADMINISTRATOR: Well, anything at this point is risky. You're really not sure who your partner has had sex with. . . . It is risky; you need to have condoms. There is a rubber dam included in the kit, as well as the condoms. But even using the condoms, you have to be careful that no semen escapes.

STUDENT: I was more worried about muscle bruises. My boyfriend and I have been going out for several years, so I'm not so much worried about sexually transmitted diseases as I am about possible muscle strain.

ADMINISTRATOR: Well, at first you never know; he may have a blood transfusion or anything like this. That is also a source of AIDS, and could then be transmitted sexually. If you have received—or he has received—a blood transfusion by someone who is an AIDS carrier or victim, then you are exposed to it.

Anal intercourse is something you could talk to more in depth with a physician, but that would be done certainly slowly and with lubrication, and with gentleness and with caring for each other it would probably not be painful. It's just whatever is mutually satisfying for both of you. Certainly, to be started very carefully and done over a period of time, and of course your body would adjust appropriately to accommodate more comfortably, let's say.

It's the same as if, you know, you were doing it in what you would call, i.e., the regular position. Very definitely with care, until you feel your body has adjusted. If it's uncomfortable then certainly you would not want to continue. You know, your tissues are rather delicate—in either area. Just to take care and be concerned about the other person.

STUDENT: So, would you suggest also the rubber dam for this?

ADMINISTRATOR: I think probably the condom would be easier. Some people would use both. It's just to be extra careful that no semen escapes, which can be easy with either technique. . . . I personally would think the condom would be easier to use. You'll know best when you try them which is more comfortable. And you can use both at the same time—some people do.

STUDENT: The other thing I was going to ask was about fisting. It seems that any muscle bruising would only be compounded by that.

ADMINISTRATOR: Yes, uh-huh.

STUDENT: So I guess that's something you can try after you get used to anal sex?

ADMINISTRATOR: Yes, mm-hmm, and it's an individual preference of course. Whatever's comfortable and feels natural to you. I mean, your body's going to tell you whether it's painful and whether to stop. I mean you're getting signals from your body as much as from your mind. So you can go by those indications—if it's uncomfortable, then you would not want to continue.

Excluded from the decision to implement this "sexual-awareness" campaign were spiritual leaders from the College community. The Dean of the Tucker Foundation, James Breeden, was not consulted prior to the commencement of this term's activities, and at the time of this writing he had not yet seen the "Safe Sex" brochure.

When a reporter described the contents of the brochure to Breeden, he commented that it seemed to contain a "truncated discussion" of sexual activities. "It sounds like sex is treated medically," he said, noting that there is a "huge dimension missing." Breeden felt that an analogy to this situation would be a discussion of the use of alcohol just as a poison. Without mentioning the social aspects, this too would be a "truncated discussion."

Msgr. William Nolan, head of the Catholic Aquinas House, and Rabbi Michael Paley, head of Dartmouth Hillel, also had not been consulted prior to distribution of the "sex kits" and "Safe Sex." Father Nolan explained that while it is not his duty to instruct the administration on moral matters, he believes that the sex brochure "ignores completely the ethical, moral, and spiritual issues that are involved." He also warned that he was sure "there was something like this before the fall of the Roman Empire. Morals and ethics hold things together."

At this writing, Dick's House's supply of the "sex kit" is exhausted. More material has been ordered, however, and new kits are scheduled to be ready on January 23. Although a female associate of Dr. John Turco said that he was worried about the controversial nature of "Safe Sex," he stated in an interview that he did not believe that this brochure would have any detrimental effects on any student's moral education.

Turco denied that the brochure "promotes promiscuity," and he used the analogy that putting seat belts in cars will not induce more people to become drivers, but will only serve to "protect those who already drive." For many, however, this recent "sexual-awareness" campaign seems excessive and misdirected; it also seems to have been implemented hastily by a small group of people who did not fully consider the possible repercussions.

January 21, 1987

Dr. Sloane, Dartmouth's AIDS Messiah

by William Grace

L AST WEEK I was tempted to write a venomous attack . . . but have decided to resist it.

What got my goat was a rhubarb between our Health Educator, Beverlie Conant Sloane, and *Review* photographer, John Quilhot.

Mrs. Sloane ordered Mr. Quilhot to stop photographing her student group RAID (Responsible AIDS Information at Dartmouth). She stated that photographing RAID, which was performing publicly in Quilhot's dormitory lounge, was prohibited by the honor code. Without going into Mrs. Sloane's general ignorance of the law and Dartmouth regulations, it is easy to understand why she didn't want photos for the family album.

During this "responsible" exhibition of safe sex, a male student puts a plunger between his legs and a female student slides a condom down the handle. Later, RAID passes around a fake penis and condoms. The students have time trials to see who can place the condom on the dildo the fastest.

The most frightening thing about the whole safe sex show is not the moral and aesthetic implications; it's that Dartmouth bureaucrats old enough to be your parents are championing it. Try to fathom Mom and Dad organizing condom-on-the-penis races like Beverlie does.

Sloane is the latest Dartmouth AIDS Messiah—one of the anointed ones who have been divinely guided to save our lives by handing out condoms and safe sex kits.

But why does a student who achieved a 750 on his math SAT need a contraceptive "Sesame Street" to explain something that is less difficult than pulling on a sock?

February 17, 1988

Sex, Lies & Rubber Dams
by William Grace

O N A BITTER COLD TUESDAY, a fortnight ago, about thirty undergraduates and a handful of Dartmouth administrators traipsed down to the Choates dormitories. They converged on the Cohen-Bissell Lounge, an ultra-modern den that usually services undergraduate food and TV cravings. But that night was different. That night the lounge-goers would get something with a social conscience. Something progressively entertaining. They settled into the hard foam rubber couches and waited for the featured presentation. And finally, the music started . . .

Four undergraduates stood on a makeshift stage and gyrated for the lounge audience. The performers' purpose that night, as their appellation "RAID" suggested, was to educate undergraduates on how not to contract AIDS. The performers danced to Tina Turner music pounding from a ghetto blaster operated by AIDS mentor Beverlie Conant Sloane, the Assistant Director of College Health Services. While the other three dancers performed a perfunctory two-step, one lanky male member of the chorus line vigorously thrust his pelvis backward and forward and grinned ecstatically, looking to the audience for approval.

Alternately, Mrs. Conant Sloane stopped the disco tape and the AIDS dancers froze. After a moment, a dancer would step forward and deliver a prepared line:

"You know I really don't want to have sex with anyone tonight," and with a concerned look, "but I've been drinking a little and I don't know if I can stick with it," or, "I had sex last night; we didn't use a condom," and with womanly delicacy, "I hope I didn't catch anything."

After this sexual vaudeville, the AIDS troupe put on a series of didactic skits. The first skit demonstrated the proper way to tell your significant other, before fornicating, that you want to use a condom. (RAID recommended using humor.) The second skit presented a dramatic confrontation between two old lovers. Over "orgasmic orange" and "jism jasmine" teas at Collis dining hall, the woman suggested they begin to use prophylactics for their mutual "protection."

The final skit was prefaced by an apology for the two previous skits' overly "heterosexual orientation." So in an act of sensitive balancing, the third skit featured a sob-soaked confession of lesbian infidelity. As the scene opened, the offending lesbian (Laura) walks into her room and greets her faithful lover (Dawn) . . .

LAURA: Dawn!

DAWN: Hello Laura.

LAURA: So what have you been doing tonight? Studying?

DAWN: Yeah. How was the party?

LAURA: Oh, fine. Really good. What are you watching on TV?

DAWN: Oh, yeah, an AIDS special, which is really very interesting and everything. I guess I'm learning a lot and everything, but I'm so glad we don't have to worry about that. Because as lesbians, we are in the lowest risk group anyway. And being monogamous and everything, I guess we don't need to worry.

LAURA: (In a grave tone) Dawn, we have got to talk.

DAWN: (Perceiving something is dreadfully wrong) What's wrong?

LAURA: I slept with a man.

DAWN: Oh. Well, do you love him?

LAURA: (With a protracted nasal whine, next to tears) Noooo.

DAWN: Well, then why?

LAURA: Well, it just happened! We were at this party and we were drinking and dancing and it just happened.

DAWN: (Growing angry) Has this happened before?

LAURA: Yes.

DAWN: A lot?

LAURA: Not really.

DAWN: (With the first strident tones of hysteria) Laura! You know I thought we had something! I thought that you loved me! I thought that we really had some thing here! (Gagging on tearful histrionics) I . . . mean . . . Sh*t! . . . did you even use a condom!

LAURA: (Meekly) Usually.

DAWN: (Mimicking Laura softly) Usually. (With full feminine rage) Laura! Christ! Besides our relationship, have you thought of your health? (Now really weeping) Did you know for Christ's sake that you could have gotten AIDS! And that you could have given me AIDS!

LAURA: No. I'm sorry. I just knew I had to tell you. (Now the two lesbians embrace in a long and all-forgiving hug.)

After these first-rate, Sarah Bernhardt theatrics, the audience couldn't help but to put their hands together and give these fine actresses a round of applause. But no accolades from the audience could match the enthusiastic participation of Dartmouth's Christian Chaplain Gwendolyn King. Reverend King liked the AIDS show so much she could hardly stay in her seat.

In ten-second intervals, the priestess leaped from her seat and, standing on her toes, attempted to get a clear view of the RAID actors re-creating a romantic interlude. Then, King would return to her seat, twitching with nervous energy like a hyperactive four-year-old. Then, like a gymnast on the parallel bars, Reverend King would push off the armrests and swing her feet underneath her denim swathed buttocks, crouching on the chair. Then, King would stand straight up on the chair, her head near the ceiling, taking in a giraffe's-eye view of the actors writhing on the couch.

When Reverend King wasn't performing calisthenics on her chair, she was doubled over in hysterics, repeating the punchlines to the blue jokes and dirty double entendres that laced RAID's skits. At other times, she sat back in her chair, slowly stroking the packing fluid of a wrapped condom from one end to the other.

After the skits, RAID offered a condom and rubber dam workshop. A little, well-built fellow stepped forward: "The rubber dam was originally designed for dentists, but now it is highly recommended for all anal/oral/vaginal contact. What you need to do with the rubber dam is place it over the orifice of interest, before any exchange of bodily fluids. Make sure to hold it in place while contact is being made. . . . We also suggest, if a rubber dam is not available, using microwavable plastic wrap," and here the small fellow paused and with a smile, added, "Saran Wrap: It's not just for breakfast anymore." At this Reverend King, jiggling perilously with laughter, fell off her seat and onto her knees repeating between gasps for breath, "Not just for breakfast anymore, Saran Wrap—oh Lord!—it's not just for breakfast anymore!"

As the hilarity subsided and Reverend King resumed her normal chair calisthenics, the RAID actress who had played the lesbian stepped forward and announced: "What we'd like to do now is show you how to use a condom! First of all you get your condom." She unwrapped a fresh one. "Then, you find your erect penis." She slid the condom over the fingers of her male assistant. "Make sure the condom is right side up and then apply the spermicide to the tip."

After the RAID professionals had demonstrated the finer art of condom application, it was time for the audience to join in the rubbery, slippery fun. The actress from the lesbian skit perked up again: "Now we are going to play 'Time That Condom.' Because we always have the complaint that, 'God, putting on the condom just takes too long.' Well, we are going to show you that that's just not true. With one of our cosmopolitan audiences, a football player took only seven seconds to put on a condom. Let me ask you, is foreplay any shorter than that guys? Now we are going to need two volunteers from our audience."

For one long minute, no one volunteered for the condom race, despite the impassioned pleas from the RAID troupe. So one RAID performer announced it was OK with him if one member of the audience volunteered another member of the audience. Finally, the audience turned on two student dorm representatives and cajoled them into racing.

To the theme song from the movie "Chariots of Fire," the two dorm reps raced to slide the condoms onto the fingers of a RAID actress. The other RAID members huddled around the contestants and cheered them on like ringside coaches: "Go!—go!—go!—spermicide!—spermicide!— spermicide!—spread it all over the tip!—pull it down!—pull it down!— pull it down!—go!—go!—go!" Finally, one of the dorm reps threw her arms up and bobbed joyously up and down, victorious. The RAID show had come to a thrilling end.

The audience pulled on their jackets and gathered up their knapsacks, canvas bags, and piles of textbooks. They exited down the cement and steel hand-railed stairwell through the metal fire door and walked up the dirt path toward Baker Library.

We sit by and watch the Barbarian, we tolerate him; in the long stretches of peace we are not afraid. We are tickled by his irreverence, his comic inversion of our old certitudes and our fixed creeds refreshes us; we laugh. But as we laugh we are watched by large and awful faces from beyond; and on these faces there is no smile.—Hilaire Belloc

November 15, 1989

The First Stone

Alumni Magazine Embroiled in Hitler Letters Dispute
by Christopher Baldwin & John Sutter

ENGLISH PROFESSOR Jeffrey Hart is planning to file suit against the *Dartmouth Alumni Magazine* and its editor Jay Heinrichs for printing what he feels are libelous letters in its summer issue. Negotiations between the *Alumni Magazine* and Professor Hart are underway in an attempt to avoid what would no doubt be a nasty public court battle.

The letters in question focus on Professor Hart's involvement with the embattled Hopkins Institute, a conservative alumni group which publishes a Dartmouth news bulletin sent to all alumni. The disputed letters, submitted by Charles Fryer '51 and M. H. Cohen '80, are in response to the first Hopkins bulletin. The bulletin, which contains several articles by Professor Hart, was called "a children's story-telling book edition of *Mein Kampf*" by Cohen. Fryer's letter refers to Professor Hart and the Hopkins Institute as reminiscent of "John Birch, Joe McCarthy and Adolf What's-His-Name."

Professor Hart contends that the letters printed are injurious to his reputation as a nationally syndicated columnist and as a public figure. Hart, who is also a Senior Editor at William F. Buckley's *National Review*, said "that sort of gutter stuff never should have been printed in the magazine."

Many national figures have rallied to Professor Hart's defense. Letters by Secretary of Education William J. Bennett and Dinesh D'Souza '83, a White House domestic policy advisor, appeared in the October issue of the *Alumni Magazine*. "Nothing in his [Hart's] professional or personal life could possibly justify comparing him with Adolf Hitler, as did two of your correspondents," writes Bennett. "Such language diminishes the level of discourse in the Dartmouth community and debases your journal."

D'Souza comments, "I think we can all unite in condemning statements which trivialize the indescribable suffering of six million Jews. . . . It is not too much to ask that Fryer and Cohen apologize in public for the consequences of their loose language on a good man's reputation."

When contacted by *The Dartmouth Review* regarding his letter and the uproar it has caused, Mr. Fryer admitted his letter was a "wee bit of hyperbole." He said he was compelled to write the letter because he "felt the references to homosexuals [in the bulletin] were frankly racist."

Fryer added that he thought that he "got carried away in drawing the parallel between Hart and Hitler. . . . Good Lord, I certainly would never call a guy Adolf Hitler. That is not only libelous, it's stupid."

Fryer was upset that some people might construe his letter as trivializing the Holocaust. "That really hit me," he said referring to D'Souza's charge. "If I am guilty of that sin, that is horrible. You'd have to be a monster or a fool to do that."

"I am very sorry that this whole issue has raised such overstated and exaggerated emotions," Fryer said. "I greatly regret that I had played any role in this affair. I guess that I let my emotions run away with me."

Alumni Magazine editor Jay Heinrichs asserts that he did not "act maliciously" by printing the letters, but feels that both are "a hell of a lot of hyperbole. I think they were silly." "We print virtually every letter to the editor except those that are factually inaccurate or clearly libelous. . . . I am ethically and personally responsible for every letter that is printed," he added.

In keeping with his policy of printing both sides of controversial issues, Mr. Heinrichs claims that he sent both letters to Hopkins board member Avery Raube '30 and invited a reply. Mr. Raube's rebuttal appeared in the summer issue along with both letters, but Raube asserts that "I don't think I saw either of those letters. The letter he sent me was from some cluck that I knew." Raube's response was not directed specifically at Fryer or Cohen.

Professor Hart has been in contact with his lawyers at Wiggin and Nourie, a prestigious law firm based in Concord, New Hampshire. Hart is determined to resolve this issue because he feels that Heinrichs's printing of the letters was "unacceptable journalistic practice and, in fact, illegal." While no suit has as yet been filed against the magazine, Professor Hart stated that research into precedents for the case is continuing. Hart plans to continue preparations for the suit "until some possible settlement has been reached with the College."

College legal counsel Sean Gorman would not make any comment on Hart's prospective lawsuit. "I'm not going to discuss confidential matters of a legal nature," said Gorman. However, Mr. Gorman asserts that "the *Alumni Magazine* was well within its rights to print those letters."

While the College remains silent on this issue, the editorial board of the *Alumni Magazine* has asked Regan Professor of Policy Studies Douglas

Yates to investigate the incident and prepare a report. According to Jay Heinrichs, Yates was asked to do so by Susan Dentzer '77, a senior writer for *Newsweek* magazine and Chairman of the *Alumni Magazine*'s editorial board. A copy of Yates's report was sent to Ms. Dentzer, according to Jay Heinrichs. Ms. Dentzer says the report is "in a preliminary form" and presently a collection of recommendations; no one has gone out and actually compiled a "fact finding" report.

Many people connected with the magazine and in the community are trying to work out a settlement which will satisfy all concerned. According to one mediator between Hart and the *Alumni Magazine*, who requested anonymity, "there have been a number of discussions [regarding a settlement], and there are very high hopes." Another member of the community who also wished to remain anonymous said "any settlement will be based on the report Doug Yates makes to the editorial board."

Professor Yates believes that any lawsuit would be harmful to both Professor Hart and the College. Said Yates, "I am indeed a negotiator [of an agreement] and that's because I am on the editorial board of the magazine and also a friend of Jeff's. We're trying to find an agreement, and we're working hard on it."

Ort Hicks '21 agrees with Yates that a settlement is necessary. "I'm naturally on the College's side," he said, "but I am also on Jeffrey Hart's side because he is my friend." Hicks believes that "Jeff is due an apology. Now, it's only a question of who gives that apology. . . . There should be an apology from the magazine for using that exact phraseology."

The hopes for an agreement between both groups were dimmed by Susan Dentzer. "I know that Mr. Hicks and Professor Yates have been involved in discussions which they think will lead to some kind of settlement." She does not, however, believe that a settlement is necessary, or even desirable. Yates's report calls on the *Alumni Magazine* to make an apology to Professor Hart, said Dentzer, but "it is extremely unlikely that the magazine will print an apology . . . I doubt that it will go any further than that [the discussion stage]." While Ms. Dentzer feels that Fryer and Cohen's letters "are very strong and extremely hyperbolic," she dismisses Professor Hart's claims. "We don't think he [Hart] was in fact injured. If he chooses to feel injured, that is entirely his prerogative."

When told of Ms. Dentzer's position that the *Alumni Magazine* would probably not print an apology, an enraged Hart said, "The law suit is definitely on the tracks . . . it's going to cost Dartmouth ten million bucks."

All sides agree, however, that the editorial board of the *Alumni Magazine* will have to review its "letters" policy at its next meeting at the end of October. Heinrichs says, "I think that Professor Hart clearly is upset about this. I think that his being this upset warrants a look at our editorial policy vis a vis letters. The editorial board will probably discuss it at our next meeting." Despite Heinrichs's willingness to consider needed changes, Dentzer has already reached her conclusions: "Frankly, my feeling is that after airing some thoughts about it, we'll probably decide we have a pretty good policy, and we'll stick with things the way they are."

October 21, 1987

Alumni Magazine Apologizes
The Week in Review

T HE *DARTMOUTH ALUMNI MAGAZINE* decided at its fall editorial board meeting to extend an apology to Professor Jeffrey Hart for publishing letters that compared him to Adolf Hitler. Printed below is a draft of the apology under consideration by the *Alumni Magazine*:

> The publication of letters in the summer *Alumni Magazine* comparing Professor Jeffrey Hart with Adolf Hitler, and his written work with *Mein Kampf*, was a serious error. Equally so was the comparison published between Professor Hart and the late Senator Joseph McCarthy, as well as the comparison with "John Birch." The publication of such patently scurrilous material was simply an editorial mistake. Professor Hart has taught at Dartmouth since 1963 and is widely known as a scholar, editor, author, and journalist. For the mistake made I offer apologies both to Professor Hart and the wider Dartmouth community.

The *Alumni Magazine* will publish the letter to avoid a libel lawsuit. The magazine will not, for legal reasons, admit to libel, but it will admit having made a mistake in printing the letters.

Pressure from Dartmouth's highest administrators was necessary to make some editorial board members agree to print the apology.

November 18, 1987

Liberal Fascism

Ein Reich, Ein Volk, Ein Freedmann
by James Garrett

I T BEGAN as a twisted dream . . .
In the last years of the twentieth century, an itinerant lawyer rose to be
absolute dictator of one of the most cultured and beloved colleges on the
face of the earth. He called himself *Der Freedmann,* "The Sensitive One."
In the only book he ever wrote, *Mein Krise und Administrationen* (My
Crisis), *Der Freedmann* describes how he came to the realization that he
and he alone was capable of saving Dartmouth. In its pages, he dismissed
Dartmouth's perceived inferiority to Harvard and Yale by claiming that
Dartmouth had been betrayed by conservative alumni and *Review* staffers.
He promised to establish a New Order for Dartmouth (*Ein Reich, Ein Volk,
Ein Freedmann*).

Der Freedmann rose to power rapidly in a Dartmouth demoralized and
divided by defeat. An orator of brilliance, his speeches could whip professors into frenzies of hysterical joy or paroxysms of fanatical hatred. At
vast torchlight gatherings, like the enormous party rallies held each year,
Der Freedmann told the massed ranks of scholars and academics that they
were the master faculty, that it was their destiny to rule the Ivy League
("*Heute Dartmouth, und Morgen die Welt*").

He gathered about him a collection of thugs and misfits as savage as
any that ever darkened the face of a college campus. There was Al Goebbels, the cynical Minister for Propaganda, who taught that Dartmouth
alumni would swallow any lie, if only it were big enough. There was Bill
Goering, a jazz musician and drug addict, who rose to command
Dartmouth's hysterical Blackshirts. There was Scan Himmler, the petty
bureaucrat who oversaw "Special Treatment" for conservative undergraduates, and Carla Koch, called "the Mule" for her tendency to kick
Review staffers in the groin. Worst of all, there was Ed Bormann, the
shadowy and sinister party secretary, who persuaded *Der Freedmann* of
the necessity for a "Final Solution" to the Conservative Problem.

Der Freedmann balked at nothing to achieve his ends. When the Campus Police had outlived their usefulness, he ruthlessly eliminated them, to replace them with a private army absolutely subject to his will, the legendarily brutal SS (*Der Saftiche und Sekuritat*). The twin lightning bolts of the SS insignia struck terror into dorm parties and fraternity basements all over Dartmouth, and came to be a symbol of random oppression and the mindless abuse of power. He went further, reorganizing the COS (*Commitat Obersturm-bahnfilhrer Schtandart*), and giving them sweeping powers of surveillance, arrest, and punishment. *Der Freedmann* would need such a weapon to carry out his most precious dream—the "Final Solution" to the Conservative Problem at Dartmouth. With a COS capable of unilateral action against Indian symbol supporters and "Men of Dartmouth" singers, a COS immune to judicial review or reprimand, *Der Freedmann* had paved the way for a holocaust.

I asked Hewlett Astor, a survivor, how such a thing could happen at Dartmouth. "It is the curse of men that we forget: When we saw the tampons thrown upon the lawns of Zete and Beta (*Tamponnacht*), we told ourselves that the madness would pass, that such things could not long persist in the land of Wheelock and Webster. Even when we saw the careers of students ruined and blighted, when friends and colleagues were deported in cattle cars in the night, we could not allow ourselves to believe that it would end as it did. We made the mistake of believing that the good professors and administrators at Dartmouth would save us. But they closed their eyes and did nothing, as the trains left the station every night bound for oblivion."

Kiki Harris, another survivor, tells this story: "I had a friend named Rutherford Pierpoint. He did not look conservative, never spoke publicly about his conservatism, and did not associate openly with his conservative friends. One night, for a joke at a hockey game, he skated out onto the ice in Indian war paint. The SS knocked on his door that very night, and the COS condemned him to "Special Treatment."

"I never saw him again."

What all the survivors share is their outrage at what was done to them, and their bewilderment and confusion that they were unable to recognize the danger signals as they appeared. "We failed to realize," says Merriweather Blake, "that the cataclysm never begins at the gate of the concentration camp or the door of the gas chamber. It only ends there.

"Like most of the tragedies in life, the Holocaust begins when a single individual is denied a right to speak because of the content of his words, or is punished as a criminal for the ideas and beliefs he holds. And each time we allowed *Der Freedmann* and his followers to get away with their injustices, we made it easier for them to perpetrate ever greater outrages. By our cowardice, we eventually placed ourselves in a position where not even courage could save us."

Perhaps the most poignant comment on the era was written by an anonymous *Review* staffer, one of the multitude caught up in the maelstrom that engulfed a generation of dedicated Conservative Dartmouth Students. It can stand as an epitaph for us all:

"When they took away the Indian symbol, I did not speak up, because I was not an athlete. When they took away the Hovey Murals, I did not speak up, because I was not an art lover. When they took away the alma mater, I did not speak up, because I was not a singer. And when they came for the fraternity system, I did not speak up, because I was not in a fraternity.

"When at last they came for me, there was no one left to speak up."

October 19, 1988

Nemo Me Impune Lacessit
by Harmeet Dhillon

O N OCTOBER 19, 1988, *The Dartmouth Review* published a column by James Garrett entitled *"Ein Reich, Ein Volk, Ein Freedmann."* The column drew an analogy between President James Freedman and Adolf Hitler, and compared his administration to The Third Reich.

The column, written in the tradition of "shock" journalism started by Jonathan Swift's *A Modest Proposal*, was hyperbolic. Given the intentionally strong, admittedly excessive nature of the comparison, the Editors of *The Dartmouth Review* can understand how members of the Jewish faith might be offended by the column.

What we cannot understand, however, is the professed outrage over the column by several prominent members of the Dartmouth community. *The Dartmouth Review* has, several times in its history, gone too far in its criticism of College policies so that other people will feel compelled to go far enough. But to characterize young student journalists attempting to provoke debate and intellectual discussion on this campus as "pre-fascist thugs" and "anti-Semites" (as several top faculty members and administrators have, in their public letters), is nothing short of an attempt to crush dissent and stigmatize critics of the College with a pernicious label.

This episode of public breast-beating is yet another example of the liberal hypocrisy that has been practiced and institutionalized at Dartmouth over the past generation. Unfortunately for them, however, Dartmouth's *soi-disant* arbiters of public sensitivity have chosen the wrong issue upon which to challenge *The Dartmouth Review*, because the charge that the *Review* is anti-Semitic is patently absurd. I will not give credence to the allegations of these hate-mongers by naming the dozens of

Jews who have written for and occupied top positions in *The Dartmouth Review* over the years.

No publication on this campus can claim to be a stronger supporter of Israel's right to exist than *The Dartmouth Review*. In fact, James Garrett, the columnist who is being currently excoriated, wrote a column published in the *Review* on February 10 abhorring the College's recognition and funding of a pro-PLO student organization, the "Committee for Palestinian Rights." Referring to recent acts of terrorism against Jews, he commented, "The actions perpetrated in the name of Palestinian rights should fill every civilized man and woman with bottomless revulsion and disgust. The sanctioning of those terroristic acts by an organ of the Dartmouth administration should shock all of us no less deeply."

Let us examine Dartmouth College's record of support for Jews and Israel over the past few years. The College has recognized and funded the abovementioned "Committee For Palestinian Rights" since 1987. Last year, when the World Affairs Council invited an ambassador of Israel to speak at the College, members of the CPR heckled the speaker and disrupted the event; their disorderly conduct was ignored by the College.

Dartmouth has, for several years, funded and granted office space and privileges to *Stet*, a leftist journal that regularly supports the PLO in its pages. In fact, *Stet*'s latest issue is entirely devoted to the condemnation of Israel and the denial of Israel's very right to exist.

Just a few weeks ago, Dartmouth paid an honorarium estimated at $10,000 to Angela Davis, Communist and *emerita* of the FBI's Ten Most Wanted Criminals list (she was wanted for the murder of a judge). When a Jewish student stood up after her keynote address and challenged her to condemn the anti-Semitism of Louis Farrakhan, she actually laughed at him and said that Farrakhan's beliefs were laudable compared to those of "fascist" George Bush.

Ironically, among those who stood and cheered after Davis's meandering diatribe against men, whites, Jews, and anyone else she could think of were Deans Richard Sheldon, Gregory Prince, Maryssa Navarro, and Dwight Lahr, all of whom have publicly expressed their "outrage" at *The Dartmouth Review*'s "incredible insensitivity" for printing Garrett's column.

Where were these deeply caring individuals when black *Dartmouth Review* staffers were threatened with physical violence by members of the Afro-American Society (in full view of many witnesses)? They and faculty members who have signed similar letters to the community "deplore" the language used by the *Review* to criticize President Freedman, but where were they when similar language was used, in letters printed in the *Alumni Magazine*, to criticize Professor Jeffrey Hart, a conservative whose feelings are apparently not protected by the blanket sensitivity insurance the College promises to others?

Where were Dartmouth's outraged historians when Professor Thomas Roos called one *Review* action "brownshirt bullying on the order of Kristallnacht"? Where were the defenders of "fair play" when Professor Deborah King, in front of over a thousand Dartmouth students, faculty, and administrators, called *Review* staffers "on par with the Ku Klux Klan?"

Growing up in North Carolina, I and my family have been the victims of explicit and implicit harassment by the Ku Klux Klan; several other minority staffers have faced similar bigotry and hatred; yet Freedman and his cronies have encouraged an atmosphere where Dartmouth faculty and students feel free to make casual comparisons between the *Review* and a group that lynched a black man as recently as 1981. It is shocking that charges of racism and anti-Semitism are thrown around so freely by mature "intellectuals" whose only information about intolerance comes from books, movies, and their own self-righteous fantasies.

As if this hypocrisy weren't nauseating enough, the fact that the entire "groundswell of outrage" is a public relations ploy for the College should make every self-respecting son and daughter of Dartmouth sick.

That's right, this entire ugly escalation of name-calling has been engineered by the College's PR puppeteers for the express purpose of discrediting the *Review* in the weeks before its lawsuit against the College for the reinstatment of students in the Cole case (*The State of New Hampshire Superior Court, Grafton County, SS; The Dartmouth Review, et al., v. Dartmouth College*). Consider the facts:

—The College is already losing the case; so far, every challenge Dartmouth's lawyers have brought to limit the scope of the Review's suit has been rejected by the courts.

—The College, with a losing case, has over $30 million at stake as well as its credibility as an intellectually tolerant institution; it simply can't afford to lose, even if winning means spreading vile lies about its opponents.

—The "outrage" over the allegedly inexcusable column took nearly three weeks to materialize.

—The College's propaganda officer, Alex Huppe, contacted the *Review* for the addresses of members of our Advisory Board two days before the first "letter to the community" ever appeared in the *Daily Dartmouth*; this, despite the fact that the faculty and administrators writing the letters claim to be acting independently, out of their own moral indignation.

—The so-called "personal" letters of indignation were in the hands of top reporters at the *Boston Globe* and *The New York Times* days before they were sent to their addressees.

—November 4's article in the *Times* is its third in two weeks to criticize *The Dartmouth Review* and praise President Freedman—surely no one will claim that such adoring coverage of Dartmouth's position is a coincidence. The *Times* is even planning to write an editorial on the issue—unprecedented attention to the contents of a student publication. Dartmouth's Chairman of the Board of Trustees, George Munroe, is also a member of the Board of Directors of the New York Times Corporation, and can be expected to use his influence at the *Times*, considering the fact that he is one of the defendants in the *Review*'s lawsuit.

If the editors of the *Daily Dartmouth* expect anyone in this community to believe that it took them three weeks to convert their "visceral repulsion" at Garrett's column into an editorial, they are only kidding themselves.

Professor Arthur Hertzberg, a member of Dartmouth's current cabal of moralists, called the *Review*'s editor a "pre-fascist thug . . . [a] dog" in virtually the same breath with which he deplored Garrett's comparison of Freedman to Hitler. If he expects us to believe that he has been reining in his seething outrage for three weeks, then he, too, insults the intelligence of this community. Other professors and administrators who signed on to this ill-conceived hate campaign have already shown us that their intellectual integrity is nonexistent.

The significance of the three-week lapse between column and reaction is exactly this: three weeks is how long it takes to get Dartmouth College's various far-flung resources assembled, organized, choreographed, and set into motion. No other explanation can account for the remarkable escalation of this incident into a crisis.

If the stakes weren't so high and the charges so serious, this transparent effort by Dartmouth's masters of distortion might almost be comical. But the lowball tactics of the administration force the *Review* to treat the accusations of anti-Semitism, racism, sexism, and any other -ism the press office chooses to try (what will they think of next?) with the utmost gravity.

In fact, this entire episode has served to point out the frightening accuracy of the *Review*'s warnings to the Dartmouth community about President Freedman and his cohorts. Which intellectual community in this, the freest nation on earth, would seek to bludgeon to death the only independent, provocative, and nationally significant journal on this campus? Does any other college have a small army of lawyers, administrators, and public relations officers who trip over one another in their bumbling attempts to eradicate an independent group of twenty-year-olds?

Over the past two decades, several ominous events have come to pass at Dartmouth. A vigorous effort to erase Dartmouth's history has been largely successful. Songs have been banned. Historical artwork has been plastered over. Religious icons have been boarded up. Students who sport certain symbols have been punished. Those daring to espouse certain beliefs have been exiled.

President Freedman's personal contribution to Dartmouth College has been the elevation of the popular community ethos above the personal rights of the individual; he has legitimized this dictum by making it the preeminent judicial principle of Dartmouth. Webster's Dictionary defines as a fascist a person who rules a community based on the above principles. You be the judge.

November 9, 1988

LETTER TO THE EDITOR

Beyond Hyperbole
by Rabbi Daniel Siegel & Seth Rosenthal '89

Y OUR COLUMNIST, James Garrett, tried to make the deaths of one third of the Jewish people, countless other incidents, and all those who died in the fight against the most monstrous evil the world has known into the stuff of comedy. It was not funny. President Freedman is not Adolf Hitler. Professor Bill Cole is not Hermann Goering. Sean German is not Heinrich Himmler. Not by any stretch of the imagination. *Kristallnacht*— when synagogues were burned, hundreds of Jewish businesses were looted and destroyed, and thousands were taken to concentration camps—and what you called "Tamponnacht" are not analogous, not even slightly. Students dismissed from this college for disciplinary reasons have not come close to experiencing the trauma of being "deported in cattle cars in the night." In fact, Mr. Rutherford Pierpoint is alive and well and working (as of 1986) at Princeton University in the hockey team office.

You see, Mr. Garrett, we understand that hyperbole can be a useful journalistic device. But when you make the comparisons you did in your column, you severely abused that device. You have made light of the Holocaust, poked fun at genocide, trivialized mass murder and insulted, not liberals like us, but the intelligence of your own conservative constituency.

Printed in The Dartmouth Review *November 9, 1988*

LETTER TO THE EDITOR

An Ignorance of History
by Harvey N. Mandell, MD, '46; D.M.S. '48

A S A DARTMOUTH alumnus, I am disappointed by your ignorance of modern European history.

As a Jewish Dartmouth Medical School alumnus, I am appalled at your mockery of the Holocaust. Among my patients I have had many survivors of that time, and you should talk to them before you compare the Dartmouth scene with that event.

As an American citizen, I am concerned that you are giving conservative thought a bad name.

Printed in The Dartmouth Review *November 16, 1988*

LETTER TO THE EDITOR

Give Me the *Review* Any Day

by Robert Peter Held

A S A JEW and a survivor of the Holocaust, I have far more to fear from the associates of Mr. Freedman and his ilk, because the Freedmans of this country are blind to a great many facts which can be the downfall of everybody, among them—or perhaps first of all—the Jews.

Any political group which accepts the dunghill ideas of a Jesse "Hymietown" Jackson, and defers to it without examination, is a group which indeed can be described by your phrase as carriers of "liberal fascism."

The incident with the black music professor, Mr. Freedman's speech to the faculty in the aftermath, and the shabby and totally unjustified treatment of the suspended students mark Mr. Freedman as a scoundrel whose last refuge is to cry the harmed Jew. I, as a Jew who barely survived and lost two thirds of my relatives, am not insulted by a satire. I am not insulted by the liberals expropriating the Holocaust for their malignant purposes (such as equating South Africa with Nazi Germany). A satire—questions of taste aside—never pretends to be anything but a satire. The hypocrisy of the Freedmans, on the other hand, pretends to be all-knowing and leaves no room for dissent.

If I have to choose between the *Review* and the Freedmans—give me the *Review* any day!

Printed in The Dartmouth Review *November 16, 1988*

LETTER

Phony & Outrageous

T HE UNDERSIGNED, who are Jewish, deny emphatically that *The Dartmouth Review* is anti-Semitic. We regard the charge as scurrilous. We also regard it as a short-run and opportunistic use of the charge of anti-Semitism for political purposes. Anti-Semitism is a serious matter, and to use the charge frivolously is dangerous.

The Dartmouth Review has been a staunch supporter of Israel, an opponent of the PLO, and very firm on issues of intense concern to the Jewish people. The record of *The Dartmouth Review* could well stand comparison on these points with the record of Dartmouth's president, James O. Freedman.

It is clear that the Dartmouth administration is using, opportunistically, an article that was in questionable taste, as part of its ongoing effort to crush an independent newspaper. And this effort is being made by a Dartmouth College which recently honored Angela Davis, an anti-Semite who is a public supporter of Louis Farrakhan. In today's world, serious anti-Semitism is coming from the Left. It is real and it is dangerous. For the Dartmouth administration to attempt to smear student journalists with anti-Semitism is phony and outrageous.

David Brudnoy, TV commentator and journalist
Chris Ehrlich, Dartmouth student
Don Feder, columnist
David Horowitz, author
Steve Kaplitt, Dartmouth student
Adam Meyerson, editor, *Policy Review*
David Klinghoffer, *National Review*
Burt Pines, author of *Back to Basics*
Sidney Zion, author and journalist
Diana West, *Washington Times*

Printed in The Dartmouth Review *November 9, 1988*

LETTER

To Professor Hoyt Alverson, et al.
by William F. Buckley Jr.

A copy of the following letter was sent to signatories, including Anthropology professor Hoyt Alverson, of a College-sponsored declamation of The Dartmouth Review. *It is in response to a letter Mr. Buckley received asking him to disassociate himself from the* Review.

I HAVE READ the article (*"Ein Reich, Ein Volk, Ein Freedmann"*) published in *The Dartmouth Review*. And of course I have read your covering letter. Here are my thoughts on the subjects you raise:

1) The article is callow, the product of immature humor plus innocence. On the latter point, it came to mind that the students at Hunter College, twenty years ago, invited to speak George Lincoln Rockwell, the founder and head of the American Nazi Party. The President of Hunter thought it

an appropriate gesture to suggest to the faculty that they convene, while Rockwell spoke at their college, at a synagogue in a memorial ceremony honoring the victims of Hitler. He observed, in his open letter to the students, that clearly they were too far removed from the Nazi era to understand its special hideousness.

The editors of *The Dartmouth Review* did not commit that kind of an error. They published a caricature, designed to make their point, which is that the Administration of Dartmouth is tyrannical. The metaphor was noisome; the students' motives understandable.

2) The actors in *The Dartmouth Review* are nineteen and twenty years old and one therefore assumes they will make errors in judgment. But you are not minors, and your letter tends to confirm what the student dissenters at *The Dartmouth Review* are complaining about. As an outsider looking in from time to time on the Dartmouth scene, I worry much more about the activities of such as President Freedman and you than about *The Dartmouth Review*. You jump to the conclusion that anti-Semitism is the students' motive, even though it is preposterous to assume any such thing about young people who are merely resisting the attempt to encourage a trendy liberal uniformity at Dartmouth that ordains that criticism of the deportment of a music professor has got to be because he is black, and that of a college President because he is Jewish.

3) I have been fighting anti-Semitism in the conservative movement for thirty-five years. This is well-known, and has been documented in academic and biographical studies. I am an enemy of anti-Semitism, and also an enemy of the use of anti-Semitism as a weapon designed to discredit and to silence opposition. I am not, as it happens, on the advisory board of *The Dartmouth Review*. For reasons that have never been explained to me, the editors list me below their masthead as someone to whom the *Review* owes "special thanks." I take the opportunity to reciprocate those thanks to the editors of *The Dartmouth Review* who, for all that they occasionally betray their age and inexperience, persevere in their struggle, risking the heaviest penalties an academic institution can level against challengers to radical chic.

Printed in The Dartmouth Review *November 9, 1988*

Caveat Emptor

Harmeet Dhillon

ONCE AGAIN, *The Dartmouth Review* would like to extend its apologies to any readers who were offended by the comparison of Dartmouth's administration to the Third Reich in James Garrett's "*Ein*

Reich, Ein Volk, Ein Freedmann." At the time of its publication, the editors of the *Review* examined the column and honestly believed the comparison to be harsh but appropriate. We regret that many of our readers found the analogy to be in poor taste.

It is essential that readers evaluate several elements of the entire controversy surrounding the column and recognize them for what they are.

First, it is important to note that the overwhelming majority of the protest was sponsored by administrators attempting to take advantage of the situation. If there is still any doubt in anyone's mind about this, the fact that the College alerted the national media to its "condemn the *Review*" campaign should clinch the matter.

The phony outrage professed by the main actors in the administration's public melodrama and the casual abuse of the epithet "anti-Semitic" have ultimately had an effect exactly opposite to that intended by the *Review*'s antagonists. Many of the *Review*'s perennial critics have themselves been exposed as supporters of anti-Semitism.

In fact, Dartmouth College may be the only school in the Ivy League to subsidize anti-Semitism. While administrators continue to fabricate excuses as to why the College has no kosher dining program, they remarkably come up with the funds to support such intellectually bankrupt publications as the anti-Israel *Stet* and the blatantly anti-Zionist *Committee For Palestinian Rights*.

They plead "other priorities" when Jews on campus call for a synagogue, yet they magically produce huge speaking fees for societal ciphers like the anti-Semitic Angela Davis. They make empty gestures and statements about the need to recruit more Jewish students, yet seem oblivious to the fact that few will come when the facilities for spiritual and social fulfillment are nonexistent. What has Dartmouth done lately to increase its attractiveness and hospitableness to Jews? The silence is deafening.

One of the most disturbing aspects of the last few days has been the full-blown campaign to silence the administration's most vocal opposition. The writers of the letters and editorials condemning the *Review* and its supporters sought nothing short of the eventual drowning of an independent voice in a sea of distortion.

This ignoble attempt would not be surprising if it came from a community of illiterates or intellectual retrogrades; the fact that it came from the leaders of this community makes one shudder at the potential implications if their sortie had succeeded. While those who vilify this publication take care to preface their attacks with the remark that they have no desire to stifle freedom of speech, they nearly always set out to define what is and what is not acceptable expression of opinion on this campus; in terms of a newspaper's content, this sentiment translates directly into censorship.

Do faculty, administrators, and trustees have a right to voice their opinions as private individuals who dislike the politics and practices of the *Review*? Certainly.

Do faculty, administrators, and trustees have a right to exploit their positions of power at Dartmouth and turn them into pulpits from which to fulminate against the *Review*? Certainly not.

The fact that so many have openly abused their positions in the current controversy is proof positive of the progressive disintegration of integrity among Dartmouth's ruling classes. The rampant lack of accountability and increasingly brazen displays of censorship are succeeding in their goal: students are beginning to question whether or not they can afford public censure, academic harassment, or even suspension for simply expressing their beliefs in print.

When the trustees, several deans, and top faculty members produce a "sensitivity" commandment, how many students will have the courage to ignore it, when in their hearts they know it is wrong? When association with the *Review* can mean the immediate censure of a professor by his colleagues, how many will take the chance that they will be treated with the professional respect they deserve as scholars? When support for this or any other conservative group on campus can cause an alumnus to be labeled an uncaring or even sinister reactionary, how many will bother to put up with the abuse?

On the emotional level, campaigns of censorship and hatred couched in the language of "sensitivity" can be seductive. On the civic level, appeals to base majoritarianism phrased in the language of "diversity" can be compelling. On the spiritual level, the goal of moral relativism disguised as a desire for tolerance can seem attractive. But on the intellectual level, there can be no mistake: these phantasms of "liberal" learning dissolve when exposed to the cold but beautiful light of reason.

November 9, 1988

Sabotage

Hate Upon Hate
by Kevin Pritchett

I T IS IMPOSSIBLE to face what has happened to the Dartmouth community in the last week without being saddened for all parties involved, and Dartmouth College most of all.

The ugliness began when an unknown perpetrator—whether staff member or outsider is as yet unknown—slipped into the *Review* credo an anti-Semitic quote from Adolf Hitler. The issue was distributed with this defect unknown, escaping the notice of all until the following Sunday. Raising the hateful words to yet another level of cruelty, the sabotage was cunningly planned to coincide with the holiest day of the Jewish calendar.

The Dartmouth Review threw itself into frantic action the same night the sabotage was discovered, retrieving the offending issues, issuing an apology, and immediately beginning to question staff about how this could have happened. Everyone did their utmost to ameliorate the harm, and everyone behaved in a thoroughly admirable manner. For this, *The Dartmouth Review* thanks its staff.

The incident, however, was immediately taken up by the *Daily Dartmouth* as proof of the *Review*'s latent views, without any effort to see and understand our sorrow and rage at the mistake. Our apology, expressing the strength of these emotions, was torn apart by campus pundits because they considered its style, no different from the *Review* editor-in-chief's usual style, "offensive." President Freedman issued a statement saying that the quotation was indicative of the *Review*'s attitudes, that the *Review* attacks minority groups solely on the basis of their skin color, gender, or sexual persuasion. Alex Huppe, College spokesman, suggested to the *Washington Post* that the *Review* not even try to identify the person responsible, but just "look in the mirror."

Review staff have received threats against their lives, and have been harrassed by prominent members of the Dartmouth community, including an obscene call to a Jewish staffer from the cartoonist for the *Daily*

Dartmouth. Another *Review* staffer, whose family lost more than thirty loved ones to the Nazi Holocaust, found a swastika affixed to his door.

A rally was held on Thursday, October 4, on the Green, "against hate." This rally, however, was a hate rally in every sense of the word.

The irony of this rally was that many of the radical members of the organizations present regularly spit on the right of Israel to exist as a sovereign nation, and are supporters of the PLO. One only has to read the campus newspaper *Stet* to view real advocacy of violence against the Jewish people. The height of the irony was reached when a speaker for the Afro-American society closed her speech commiserating with the offended Jews with a quote from Malcolm X.

In contrast to these hypocritical speakers, *The Dartmouth Review* has consistently defended America's strong support for Israel, and her right to exist. There have always been Jewish members on the *Review* staff, as there have been members of many different races and creeds. The *Review* could not conceive of attacking these friends or our allies in the Middle East.

When crises have struck this paper in the past, we could always rely on the strength of the ideas we were defending to answer our critics. But there is no idea behind this incident—it is devoid of any intellectual message. This awful message has not been, is not, and never will be the policy of *The Dartmouth Review*. This quote by Adolf Hitler is the product of a sick mind. This was done *to* us, not by us.

Already the cry has gone out that once again the College's reputation has been tarnished. To the extent that this incident would have garnered attention anyway, it is unfortunately a result of this mistake. But the majority of the blame must rest with those who seized upon this incident as a political weapon, and brandished it against us. Without James Freedman and others, this College would not be seen as a scene of racial conflict. But, unfortunately, now it is, and if minority applicants increasingly shun Dartmouth in the future, we will see the sad effects of blithely using such a potent political weapon to try to discredit an undergraduate journal. Creating a mob atmosphere is never constructive.

We again express our deepest regret. *The Dartmouth Review* did not do this vile act. It was done to us. We have asked the Anti-Defamation League of B'nai B'rith and the College to aid us by conducting an impartial, external investigation. We hope that, with joint action, we will find the culprit.

October 10, 1990

NOTICE

Statement of *The Dartmouth Review*
by the Editors

W E SHARE the deep shock and distress of the Dartmouth community over this vicious anti-Semitic slur. It got into the newspaper
through an act of sabotage, a subterfuge, a dirty trick that we are determined to track down and expose.

For the past ten years *The Dartmouth Review* has espoused strongly
pro-Israel policies. We have consistently denounced anti-Semitism. We are
not the perpetrators of this anti-Semitic slur. We are the victims of criminal
sabotage. Since it appeared without our knowledge in our newspaper,
however, we convey our deepest apologies to the Jewish community for
the pain caused by this incident.

In order to find out who committed this reprehensible deed, we have
launched an immediate investigation. We will be contacting the Anti-
Defamation League of B'nai B'rith to help us locate the culprit. We call
upon President Freedman and Dartmouth to work with us to uncover the
perpetrator of this vile act we all deplore.

Unfortunately, Dartmouth officials to date have shown no interest in
uncovering what happened, and indeed convened a lynch-mob to make
scapegoats of innocent students. In effect, this is Dartmouth's Tawana
Brawley case: a sabotage and hoax is cynically exploited by demagogues
to stir up hatred and polarization. In a total abdication of their leadership
responsibility, College officials are manipulating the grave issue of anti-
Semitism for ends of self-aggrandizement and expediency. President
Freedman's willingness to convert a serious issue into a political weapon,
aimed at ruining the lives of many innocents, makes him the Al Sharpton
of academia.

October 4, 1990; printed in The Dartmouth Review *October 10, 1990*

THE FORWARD

Dartmouth's Test
by the Editors of The Forward

W HEN THE HISTORY of student activism in the 1980s is written, it
is likely that a sizeable chapter will be devoted to one undergraduate newspaper, *The Dartmouth Review*. Independent of the College
administration, it has published for the past ten years a weekly stew of
news, commentary, and satire—designed to puncture what it sees as the
liberal biases of most students and faculty, and, indeed, the Dartmouth ad-

ministration. It has been one of Israel's defenders in a campus debate that has grown increasingly receptive to anti-Israel agitation. The newspaper's detractors have accused it of being racist, sexist, and homophobic, although the paper's top editors have included women, blacks, and Jews. The paper's defenders insist that what the *Review*'s critics really dislike about the paper is its conservative politics. At one point the college tried to suspend two members of *The Dartmouth Review*—only to receive a humiliating rebuke from a Granite State judge who ordered the college to reinstate the students.

All these passions are now coming out in a new brouhaha that erupted on the eve of Yom Kippur. It seems that someone inserted into the masthead of *The Dartmouth Review*'s latest number a quote from Adolf Hitler. The paper's editors say they discovered this to their horror after the paper was distributed. They posted and published an apology and have launched an investigation. The president of Dartmouth, James O. Freedman, is being quoted by *The New York Times* as saying the incident continues the publication's "reprehensible pattern" of discriminatory attacks. We invited the paper's editor, a young African-American named Kevin Pritchett, to give his account. He says the paper was sabotaged. A few years ago, one of Dartmouth's highest ranking graduates, Judge Silberman of the Federal Court of Appeals in Washington, likened the Dartmouth administration's treatment of the *Review* to McCarthyism. Its fair-mindedness will be well-tested as it sorts out the facts of the latest affair.

October 5, 1990; printed in The Dartmouth Review *October 10, 1990*

THE FORWARD
Storm Over Dartmouth: Image & Reality
by Kevin Pritchett

A S I LOOK OUT the window in the offices of *The Dartmouth Review*, I see the winds whipping the autumn-tinged trees and dark clouds scudding by. It is about to storm. But it will probably be a minor squall compared to the tempest that has already begun around the paper I edit here.

Last week *The Dartmouth Review* was distributed on campus, as it is every week. But this week was different from every other week. In our October 3 issue, our paper's credo, a quote from Theodore Roosevelt, which has been the same for the *Review*'s ten-year history, was changed. Usually, the credo reads: "Far better it is to dare mighty things, to win great triumphs, even though checkered by failure, than to rank with those poor spirits who neither enjoy much nor suffer much, because they live in the gray twilight that knows neither victory nor defeat."

In this issue, embedded in the original credo, is a quote—from Adolf Hitler. "Therefore I believe today that I am acting in the sense of the Almighty Creator: By warding off the Jews, I am fighting for the Lord's work."

There was an act of sick sabotage perpetrated against *The Dartmouth Review*. It carried a double sting, for it came on the eve of the holiest day in the Jewish calendar, Yom Kippur. Someone either outside or—more likely—inside the paper's staff maliciously put this reprehensible statement into the masthead of the *Review*. Realizing only later—after the issue was distributed—that this act of sabotage had occurred, we at the *Review* wrote up an explanation, apology, and disavowal of the quote. We distributed this to everyone on the campus. It was posted on every campus building. We also took out a full-page ad in the campus daily, the *Daily Dartmouth*, which disavowed, apologized for, and explained the situation.

Unfortunately, some on the campus have used this mistake to bash *The Dartmouth Review*. *Review*-bashing is the fashionable thing in some liberal circles at the College. One case that has made the national newspapers before is that of Professor William S. Cole. The professor, who spewed profanity in class and called his white students "honkies," was written about in the *Review*. To the more enlightened, though, the *Review*'s articles were seen as racist. I, as a black person, read the articles in question, and felt they were not racist.

We have never hesitated to use satire. The College and radicals on campus have tried to pin every "ism" on the *Review*—isms that turn out, upon reading of the *Review* and meeting its staff members, to be untrue.

In the current case, the *Review* has promised to seek out the person who inserted the Hitler quote in the paper. If the person is found to be a member of the *Review* staff, that person will be exposed and kicked off the staff of the *Review*.

Despite this promise, despite our efforts to set a dialogue between campus leaders and the *Review*, despite the disavowals and apologies, there are those on campus—including President James O. Freedman—who feel that the *Review*, the only independent voice in Hanover, should be eradicated. He has accused us of bigotry that has no place at the College.

Review students "are scum," a professor of French and Italian here, Carla Freccero, told the *Washington Post*. The *Review*'s former and present Jewish staffers, editors, and presidents would not be and are not amused by this assertion. The *Review* has been a staunch supporter of Israel. We berate Dartmouth for inviting speakers such as Angela Davis, who is an acknowledged anti-Semite. We castigate the College for financially supporting campus groups such as the Committee for Palestinian Rights. The CPR a couple of years back heckled the Israeli ambassador when he visited campus. We exposed the fact that Dartmouth funds a newspaper called *Stet*, which has called for the destruction of Israel. When the *Review* addresses the foreign policy aspect of the Israeli debate, we have always come out squarely in favor of Israel.

We have no guilt concerning anti-Semitism. We feel outraged—at the person who committed this act against the *Review* and the Dartmouth community. We also feel outrage, though, at the feigned rage that many students are showing on campus and in the press. I personally talked with several such persons. One was Brian Ellner, president of Dartmouth's Student Assembly. We talked about ways to defuse this situation before it exploded. We had a positive chat. But the next day, what did Mr. Ellner do? He was a main cheerleader of the anti-*Review* brigade.

Review staffers have been harassed since this affair exploded, a message scrawled on one student's door, a message left on the telephone answering machine of another. Rallies are being planned. False petitions are being distributed. The *Review* did not want this situation to happen. We have apologized. We have disavowed. We will do all we can.

There has been a lot of agonizing, even before this incident, over the image of Dartmouth in the national press. We at the *Review*, though we have exposed a lot of bad things at Dartmouth, have also been distressed over Dartmouth's image. We feel that if this college does away with the radical chic that has tarnished its image, then the institution's reputation will get better. Yet the chic amongst the students, faculty, and administration at Dartmouth have used the false charge of anti-Semitism to bash the *Review*. The only detriment will be to Dartmouth College.

October 5, 1990; printed in The Dartmouth Review *October 10, 1990*

Campus Blowhards Raise Cain, Excoriate Review for Quote
by the Editors & Staff

T HE POWERS THAT BE at Dartmouth College have finally shown how hypocritical they really are. Last week, much of the campus gathered on the Green for what was advertised as a "Rally Against Hate." The resulting product, however, was a hate rally against *The Dartmouth Review*. No sooner had the first speaker stepped up to the podium than the diatribes began, with each successive speaker increasing the degree of animosity towards the newspaper. As recently as minutes before the rally, Student Assembly representatives guaranteed that the purpose of the rally was to oppose hate and that the day would not degenerate into a massive offensive against the *Review*.

This sentiment soon dissolved, as participants were offered t-shirts emblazoned with a drawing by Jake Tapper, cartoonist for the *Daily Dartmouth*, reproducing an image he ran in that newspaper last spring depicting a lawn jockey that many have taken to be an allusion to the black editor-in-chief of *The Dartmouth Review*. On the t-shirts with this offending image was written, "I do not support the *Review*."

When the speaking began, the rally became a vehicle for many of the "special interest" groups at Dartmouth to polemicize about how much the *Review* (and Dartmouth as a whole) have hurt them not only in the past decade, but also in the history of the College. The end result was a competition of sorts, with each speaker trying to prove that he or she represented the most oppressed minority on the Dartmouth campus. What was advertised as "Dartmouth United Against Hate" was neither united nor against hate.

Student Assembly vice-president Tara McBennet opened the rally by announcing that the "immediate impetus for the event was the insertion of the quote from Adolf Hitler into the credo of the October 4 [sic] issue of the *Review* and the *Review*'s subsequent apology." A minute into the rally the mud-slinging began. It is absurd that an apology should spark outrage of any kind, let alone enough animosity to call for a rally. The very principle on which the rally was founded was abandoned in failing to accept the spirit, if not the exact wording, of the apology.

President Freedman followed with a speech accusing the *Review* of advocating exclusion of minorities from Dartmouth, further stating that, "Dartmouth is a commonwealth of liberal learning, united in celebrating the dignity of the individual . . . the organizing principal of this commonwealth is inclusion, not exclusion." No one noticed much celebration of the dignity of *Review*ers, nor the inclusion of *Review* members in the Dartmouth community. In fact, when one *Dartmouth Review* staffer went to visit his friend in the Choates dormitory, he was accosted by a student who asked, "Don't you have to be a student to come in here?" The implication was that Dartmouth is for all—except *Review* staffers. President Freedman repeatedly asked, "What kind of people did they think we were?" Perhaps the *Review* mistakenly thought they were rational people, those who would not hold innocent staff members culpable for an act of sabotage, something that was not their fault.

In contrast, Freedman hardly seemed to notice this past spring the disgusting antics of the participants in the International Students Association rally for additional financial aid. When an "oppressed" minority group defaced Parkhurst Hall with hammers and sickles, anarchy symbols, and, yes, even swastikas, they received a slap on the wrist. When someone defaces the credo of the *Review* with a disgusting quote, the entire staff is impugned.

The President of the Dartmouth Alumni Council, William Montgomery '52, was next in line to malign the *Review*. Montgomery also chose, as many members of the Dartmouth community have, to ignore the *Review*'s denial of having placed the quote in the credo or subscribing to its message. The mobocracy had brainwashed yet another responsible individual to abandon rational thought.

History Professor Bruce Nelson continued the program along its radical course, referring to *Review* staffers as "self-important harpies who have created this atmospheric pollution." His speech promoted a liberal agenda for the College and an attack on the *Review*. He asserted that the *Review* is attempting to build a wall around Dartmouth which must be torn down and in turn be replaced by a wide pathway that says, "Welcome, to those whose gifts will help to create a diverse community in which many cultures and many angles of vision will enrich our quest for truth and understanding, and a more humane and just world." Apparently, in Professor Nelson's opinion, the *Review*'s "angle of vision" is too far off their "path" to be appropriately diverse. Who is preaching exclusion?

It is ironic that this is not the first time Professor Nelson has taken exception to something printed in the *Review*. It is ironic because one such article reported that the keynote speaker at a civil rights conference, Vincent Harding, had expressed anti-Semitic views and had subsequently intimidated Jewish students. Professor Nelson staunchly defended Harding, a notorious anti-Semite, even going so far as to verbally assault the *Review* editor who authored the article. Somehow, by Nelson's twisted definition of justice, it is acceptable to hold the *Review* accountable as "bigots" and anti-Semites by ascribing to it a quote it has denounced. Nelson does not, however, deem it equally acceptable for Harding to be criticized for blatant, admitted anti-Semitism.

Next, Professor Arthur Hertzberg of the Religion Department railed against the *Review* and its supporters, calling the *Review* "an ongoing and continuing act of hooliganism." Hertzberg does not, however, object to the views of the *Review* staffers, allowing that "they are here to engage in the dialogue of our various views." But then he departed from the realm of reason. He proceeded to barrage the eminent and well-respected individuals and organizations that support the paper in a financial or an advisory capacity, saying that they should be ashamed of themselves. Among these he mentioned the Olin Foundation and the Hopkins Foundation chairman, "John [sic] Champion, Class of 1920." He continued his attack by targeting William F. Buckley Jr., referring to him as "a man who would like to be considered a respectable conservative and have dinner with decent people."

Hertzberg found fit to bring into his discourse the opinions of a member of the *Review* advisory board. "Peter [sic] Buchanan." Mr. Buchanan made a controversial comment about the U.S. presence in the Persian Gulf on his CNN talk show, *Crossfire*. Had Professor Hertzberg read the September 26 issue of the *Review*, he would have found an editorial distancing the *Review* from Mr. Buchanan's view of the situation—arguing against it, in fact. It would be a sad state of affairs if Dartmouth students, *Review* staffers or not, are not able to reach their own conclusions but instead are willingly spoon fed perspectives.

It is difficult to resolve the animosity Hertzberg displayed towards these prominent men with a rally against hate, although his comments regarding the *Review*ers themselves kept with the purported objective of the rally. Unfortunately, his denouncement of driving out members of the *Review* from the Dartmouth community was overshadowed by his venomous closing remarks aimed at, among others, a member of the Dartmouth community, English Professor Jeffrey Hart. Music Professor Jon Appleton took special pleasure in the condemnation, exclaiming "Wooooo!" with glee.

The first speech by a student was given by the president of the African-American Society, Trecia Canty '91. In addition to finding fault with the *Review*, Canty upbraided students, professors, and administrators alike for not attending the various rallies held at Dartmouth in the past. Canty concluded by reminding the crowd that "we are not fighting for censorship or integration, nor are we fighting for separation." While this comment was in keeping with the theme of the rally, Canty attributed the sentiment to Malcolm X, hardly a proponent of peaceful conflict resolution, or a prominent defender of Jewish rights.

Following Canty, Amanda Roth '93 addressed the crowd as the president of the Dartmouth Hillel. On behalf of the Jewish community of Dartmouth, Roth advocated the uniting of all parts of the campus in a straightforward, concise statement regarding the detrimental effects of acts of hatred, without blatantly condemning the *Review*. This sort of rationality would have served the rest of the speakers well.

Representing Native Americans at Dartmouth, the group's president Jodi Archambault then spoke. She immediately condemned the *Review*, completely ignoring the *Review*'s denial of having inserted the quote in question and apologizing for it. Archambault charges the *Review* with having "sought to incite racial unrest . . . and . . . to hinder Native Americans and other groups from gaining the education which we have earned the right to." Interestingly, she claimed that the *Review* has been the proponent of such actions since 1769. As the *Review* has only existed for ten years, it is doubtful that this journal could have been seeking these goals for more than two hundred years. In an effort to further her own personal agenda, Archambault used her time to attack the Indian symbol and equate its use to anti-Semitism.

Speaking as Dartmouth Area Gay and Lesbian Organization chairman, Allen Drexel succeeded in cheapening the proceedings even more. As emcee of the rally he had been giving it a game show atmosphere and now took the opportunity to reveal what the game was. The rally had become a contest of one-upsmanship in victimization. As Drexel rattled off his list of complaints regarding the *Review*'s stance on homosexuality, it must not have occurred to him to peruse an issue of *In Your Face* and consider the heterosexual bashing which regularly graces its pages. Said Drexel, "I am heartened by the sight of so great a mass of Dartmouth students standing tall and strong against hatred. . . . I believe in you Dartmouth! Let's come together!" Ahem. Recall that *In Your Face*'s slogan is, "Homo-A-Go-Go, Het-Het-A-No-No!" Does that promote unity?

In light of the fact that homosexuals are especially oppressed, the Dartmouth Gay and Lesbian Organization (DAGLO) felt that it deserved two speakers at the rally. So, following Drexel's pitiful display, Elyse Wolland stepped up to the podium and reiterated the complaints of homosexuals. Again stressing the lack of unity, despite this being one of the underlying purposes of the rally, Wolland stated that she "cannot feel a part of such community," because there hasn't been as great a show of support solely for homosexuals as there was against hate as a whole. Wolland went on to remind the crowd of the non-Jews who died during the Holocaust, seeming to imply that the *Review* harbored hatred against these groups.

In a stranger twist, members of the International Students Association spoke next. At rallies in the past, leaders of the ISA had used their speaking time to condemn the state of Israel and its right to exist. This time the speakers tried to mask their blatant anti-Semitism, proclaiming, "We would especially like to take this opportunity to clarify that the fight for anti-Arab discrimination and for Palestinian rights, which the ISA has consistently tried to highlight, is not anti-Jewish, as it is often portrayed by writers of the *Review* and others." Well, if calling for the destruction of the state of Israel isn't anti-Jewish, we don't know what is.

The first speaker noted: "We are, however, disappointed, although not particularly surprised, that attempts were made to exclude the Dartmouth Gay and Lesbian Organization, the Native Americans at Dartmouth, and the International Students . . . maybe they thought that we would not toe the party line." In a refreshing display of rationality, this speaker pointed out, "It is much easier for all of us to isolate the *Review* and blame it for all the hate attacks on campus. Maybe this is the time to point out that even without the *Review*, some members of the Jewish community and some members of other so-called minority religious groups do not feel a part of the Dartmouth community. Even without the *Review*, some women do not feel a part of the Dartmouth community. Even without the *Review*, some African-Americans, Asian Americans, Hispanic Americans, Native

Americans, and other people of color do not feel a part of the Dartmouth community. That even without the *Review*, some members of the gay and lesbian community and international students do not feel a part of the Dartmouth community. Maybe this is the time to point out that if Dartmouth is to be really united, it must be united at all times, or risk the total alienation of these so-called minority groups." So-called minority groups? Are they not minority groups? Do they not seek to be recognized as such? She continued, "If seven years ago the Dartmouth community had come out with similar anger and disgust at the *Review*'s constant and unjustifiable harassment of Professor Cole, then maybe he might still be teaching at Dartmouth today." Perish the thought!

The other ISA speaker read a statement from the Dartmouth Alliance Against Racism. Although the preceding speaker questioned the authenticity of minority status of "so-called minority groups," this speaker repeated one of the former's gripes while referring to minorities: "The very organization of today's rally bears testimony to the subjugation of minority voices. Originally, the International Students Association, the Dartmouth Gay and Lesbian Organization, the Native Americans at Dartmouth, Milan, the Dartmouth Asian Organization, Al-Nur, La Alianza Latina, and the African-Caribbean Students Organization were not invited to speak at this rally. These are precisely the groups most trodden over not only by the *Review* but by the campus at large." Is it feasible to have a representative from every organization on campus participate in a rally and expect to maintain a crowd on the Green for the entire time?

The next speaker, Nicole Hager '91, participated because she was in no way a politically active student and thus represents those who have remained silent during their time at Dartmouth. Hager couldn't seem to decide whether or not she is a victim. She first asserted that she had been hurt by alleged "sexist remarks and oppressive attitudes." Then she went on to say that she has been "outside the issue" for her first three years at Dartmouth by choice, because she had "bought into the fallacy that only those who have been the target of social and moral ignorance are the ones being victimized . . . racism is not only an issue for people of color. Sexism is not only an issue for women." Now, is she a woman and if so, according to her logic, isn't sexism an issue for her? But, then, how does it come to be that she remained silent as one who had not been "victimized"? Whatever.

Jake Tapper had the audacity to speak out "against hate." That's quite hypocritical for someone who calls a fellow member of the Jewish and Dartmouth communities "a f*ck*ng disgrace," and who drew numerous anti-*Review* cartoons, before this issue even arose.

As painful as reminders of the Holocaust are for Jews, reminders of slavery and discrimination are for blacks. Tapper must find a way of differentiating the two, however, since he not only saw fit to portray what appears to be the black editor of the *Review*, Kevin Pritchett, as a lawn jockey but also referred to the same editor as an "Uncle Tom." The t-shirts displaying his character weren't precisely promoting unity on campus. Tapper's lack of judgment and good taste, as well as his fostering of racial enmity, made him a poor choice as a speaker, considering the tone that was supposed to have been set for the day.

The final speaker was Brian Ellner '92, president of the Student Assembly. Calling for "a new Dartmouth," Ellner defines this as being "a place where persons can dare to be themselves and proceed without any threat of persecution" and "celebrate our differences and learn from one another." Of course, this freedom from persecution depends on whether or not one's differences are sufficiently diverse to be socially acceptable to the powers that be.

A member of the Board of Trustees of the *Review* and Dartmouth '83, Dinesh D'Souza, had asked to speak at the rally, but he was denied permission to do so. Denied, despite the fact that it was a rally to unite Dartmouth against hate and despite the possibility that allowing D'Souza to talk to the campus might dissipate some of the ill-will toward the *Review*, which had escalated during the rally.

Although some of the speaker's remarks were not particularly unifying, the crowd at the Dartmouth United Against Hate Rally was for the most part unified—in hate for the *Review*. Any guesses as to the true purpose of the rally? Perhaps some people can vindicate retaliating against the members of the *Review* by intentionally directing hateful barbs at them for an act they did not commit. But perhaps it would be prudent to think twice about giving a forum for that type of demagoguery under the guise of speaking out against hate.

October 17, 1990

THE WALL STREET JOURNAL
Moral Cowardice at Dartmouth
by L. Gordon Crovitz

H ANOVER, N.H.—Another school year, another controversy at Dartmouth College. This time, however, *The Dartmouth Review* is vilified not for what it said, but for what it vehemently denies it said. After years of attacking the independent conservative student newspaper for its views, the Dartmouth administration is taking full advantage of the appearance in the *Review* of an outrageous item that the editors say was sabotage.

Since it was founded a decade ago, the *Review* has published on its masthead as its credo a line from Teddy Roosevelt, "Far better it is to dare mighty things . . . than to rank with those poor spirits who neither enjoy much nor suffer much." In last week's issue, however, the credo was altered. Appended to part of the credo was a quote from Adolf Hitler that included, "By warding off the jews I am lighting for the Lord's work." That the paper was published on the eve of Yom Kippur, Judaism's holiest day, made the Hitler quote even more horrifying.

Since then, culminating in a huge rally on the Dartmouth Green yesterday, the campus has been inflamed by anger at the anti-Semitism, which has become a potent force attacking the integrity of the *Review*. Dartmouth President James Freedman blamed the review for "an act of moral cowardice" and "vicious hatred," which he called part of a "reprehensible pattern" of "appalling bigotry." Eighty congressmen took time off from the budget to denounce the *Review*. A campus petition gathered more than 1,000 names.

The problem is that top *Review* editors say they were as shocked as everyone else to see the substitute credo. Editor-in-Chief Kevin Pritchett and other top staffers say they did not learn of it until Sunday, two days after the newspaper was published. They immediately distributed an apology and retrieved and destroyed 10,000 of the 13,000 copies. Mr. Pritchett says he immediately called student leaders and the college rabbi to say that the faked credo was a disgusting slur that was also an attack on the *Review*.

This message got lost in the official denunciations. Indeed, college leaders fanned the incident by treating the substitute credo as *Review* policy. Mr. Freedman has not spoken with any *Review* staffers about the incident. Still, his spokesman announced that "No one on campus believes it was an accident."

Mr. Pritchett says it was "sabotage" and held an emergency staff meeting on Monday. Some staffers were confronted, but all denied inserting the Hitler quote. Mr. Pritchett says evidence pointing to an inside job includes earlier cases of lewd remarks prepared for publication that were caught by editors at the last minute.

Yet even the phrasing of Mr. Pritchett's apology has been analyzed as reminiscent of Nazi propaganda. He pledged that "This cancer amongst our ranks, we assure you, will be sought out and thoroughly punished." A Dartmouth professor of German, Wemer Hoffmeister, told *The New York Times* that he found this wording "troublesome." (The professor might want to analyze George Bush for latent Nazism; this week the president referred to the budget deficit as a "cancer gnawing away at our nation's health.") Another professor described *Review* staffers to the *Washington Post*. "They are scum," she said. "It's as simple as that."

The Hitler quote was sure to cause an uproar, so if the perpetrator wasn't just an extraordinarily stupid prankster, this could have been calculated to harm the *Review*. Circumstantial evidence that it was either a low-level staffer or even an outsider includes a typographical error; the apostrophe in "Lord's" appeared in an incorrect style; whoever inserted the false credo made a key-stroke mistake on the computerized layout program. The *Review* announced yesterday that it hopes to hire a lawyer to investigate the matter, asked for help from the Anti-Defamation League of B'nai Brith, and may press charges if the guilty party is found.

This is not the first time a newspaper has suffered such an embarrassment. An anonymous *Boston Globe* staffer in 1980 changed the headline on a report about a Jimmy Carter anti-inflation program to "Mush From the Wimp." As newspapers become increasingly computerized, opportunities for mischief increase.

How to explain the Dartmouth insistence that the substitute credo was an intentional act reflecting the views of the newspaper? It may simply be that critics of the *Review* saw their chance and took it without worrying about the details, such as whether the *Review* might also be a victim. Asked before yesterday's rally if his attitude would be any different if it turns out that the substitute credo was the work of some prankster or saboteur, Mr. Freedman said, "I just haven't thought about that." He has not been in contact with *Review* staffers to hear their suspicions.

Former *Review* editor and current trustee Dinesh D'Souza came to Hanover to investigate. Mr. D'Souza, now a scholar at the American Enterprise Institute, says that "Dartmouth officials to date have shown no interest in uncovering what happened, and indeed convened a lynch mob to make scapegoats of innocent students." Mr. D'Souza said this might turn out to be "Dartmouth's Tawana Brawley case," making Mr. Freedman "the Al Sharpton of academia."

Andrew Baer, a sophomore and staff writer for the *Review*, published a letter in the official Dartmouth student newspaper that also criticized anti-*Review* demagoguery. Mr. Baer, many of whose Jewish ancestors were killed in the Holocaust, wrote that he was glad to see the campus united against anti-Semitism.

"I am sickened, however, to see the Third Reich," he wrote, "used as a campaign commercial for certain anti-*Review* demagogues." Because of his affiliation with the *Review*, "I have been the target of ugly stares, have been called 'fascist' by people whom to my knowledge I have never met, and have cowered behind the locked door of my room at night, listening to the people on my floor bellow 'Sieg Heil!' at the top of their lungs." He wrote that "with a few strokes of a Macintosh keyboard, a bigoted and probably unstable individual ruined my world."

A swastika was later drawn on the door to Mr. Baer's room. "Any crusade that considers a swastika either a 'joke' or a fitting take for a person like myself is no crusade but an ugly, opportunistic mob action," he said. Similar campus pressures drove several *Review* staffers to resign.

It's also true that this is only the latest skirmish in Hanover. In 1988, Dartmouth tried to suspend top editors of the *Review* for "vexatious oral exchange" with a black music professor whose teaching style had been criticized in the *Review* and who has since resigned. In this case, too, Mr. Freedman, a former law professor, refused to discuss the issue with the accused students. He publicly declared them guilty before their disciplinary hearing of "acts of disrespect, insensitivity and personal attack" and "racism, sexism, and other forms of ignorance."

A New Hampshire judge declared that "Dartmouth is to be held to the standard of fundamental fairness" and forced the college to reinstate the students. Among the problems was that one of the faculty members of the discipline committee was already on record attacking the *Review* for "slanders" and "sexist and racist" articles.

The judge also noted that "several black students who worked for *The Dartmouth Review* were harassed or threatened by other Dartmouth black students." One of those threatened was Mr. Pritchett, then a freshman. A judge could see what was happening, but the administration never punished those who assaulted the black *Review* students.

Which brings us to perhaps the likeliest explanation for why Mr. Freedman chose not to defuse the horror of the Hitler quote by joining with the *Review* to search out the culprit, but instead fanned the notion that the *Review* stood for Nazism. Mr. Pritchett is a black conservative, who became editor of the newspaper that Mr. Freedman has for several years labeled "racist." A black editor of *The Dartmouth Review* is an idea so off the academic plantation that this incident may have been the best way to smear him. Like William Lucas and Clarence Thomas, Mr. Pritchett is paying the liberals' high price of apostasy.

This page has special reason to sympathize with Mr. Pritchett. He was recommended to the editors of the *Journal* by a Dartmouth professor as the brightest student he had seen in a generation. Mr. Pritchett, now twenty-one, worked during the past three summers on the editorial page staff of this newspaper in New York and Brussels, writing editorials and book and art reviews.

One sad irony is that as editor in chief of the *Review*, Mr. Pritchett set out to smooth some of its rougher edges. The tone is still arch, the satire sometimes still overboard, but increasingly the newspaper is more journalistic than sophomoric. The *Review* continues its campaign for a common-core curriculum and higher teaching standards.

Mr. Pritchett published an article this week in the *Forward*, a national Jewish weekly, under the headline "Storm Over Dartmouth: Image and Reality." He called the switched credo "an act of sick sabotage perpetrated against" the *Review*. *Forward* editor Seth Lipsky, formerly *Journal* foreign editor and editorial page editor of the *Journal*'s European edition, says he invited Mr. Pritchett to write the article because "I thought our readers would want to know what he had to say."

An accompanying *Forward* editorial noted that the *Review* "has been one of Israel's defenders in a campus debate that has grown increasingly receptive to anti-Israel agitation." It concluded that Dartmouth's "fair-mindedness will be well-tested as it sorts out the facts of the latest affair."

So far, official Dartmouth seems much more interested in taking advantage of this terrible slur to attack the *Review* than in finding out exactly what happened. Mr. Freedman has stoked the same fears and hatreds that he says justify his attacks against a student newspaper. The truth about this incident will not be easy to establish, especially if the college does not care to discover the facts.

October 1, 1990; printed in The Dartmouth Review *October 17, 1990*

KING FEATURES SYNDICATE

Dartmouth: The Nazis are Coming
by Jeffrey Hart

A HUGE AND ESSENTIALLY ABSURD FUROR has blown up like a tropical typhoon at Dartmouth, convulsing the campus and causing people from whom one expects dignified behavior to say stupid, indefensible things. The whole affair is of general interest only as an illustration of the feverish atmosphere that afflicts so many campuses today.

A bizarre incident, which I will describe, moved the president of the college, James Freedman, to say things that will surely embarrass him. His target was the independent newspaper, *The Dartmouth Review*.

"For ten years," said President Freedman, "*The Dartmouth Review* has consistently attacked blacks because they are black, women because they are women, homosexuals because they are homosexuals, and Jews because they are Jews."

That statement has no truth in it whatsoever. The *Review* indeed has opposed racial quotas. But not attacked skin color. It has a black editor-in-chief. It has had three women editors, and two from India. It has not attacked homosexuals as such, but opposed Dartmouth's funding of gay groups. President Freedman needs a tranquilizer. Unfortunately, he is a leading figure in this silly season.

A graduate of Yale Law School, he plunged ahead without any attempt to ascertain the facts in the incident, and offered a public denunciation of the *Review* that is without foundation in reality.

What happened in this incident is indeed zany.

As the October 3 issue was going to press, it was the victim of sabotage. Someone clandestinely gained access to the newspaper's word-processing equipment. On its masthead, the newspaper always runs a statement by Theodore Roosevelt about the man "in the arena" of active life.

The saboteur wove into the middle of this statement two sentences from Hitler's *Mein Kampf* declaring his enmity to Jews.

The paper was distributed on campus, containing the error, but distribution to subscribers was halted. A corrected edition will be distributed. The paper's editors immediately disavowed the Hitler sentences. There is no reason to believe that any student writing for the paper admires Hitler or is anti-Semitic. The paper has had a Jewish president and has had many Jewish and black staffers.

Since no one can possibly believe that anti-Jewish sentences from Hitler represent *Review* editorial policy, the furor surrounding the episode is manufactured, utterly bogus. College officials and College spokesmen issued statements they should be ashamed of.

The true scandal here lies in the fact that such college personnel are eager—and obviously delighted—to exploit this bizarre incident in a calculated effort to damage an important conservative newspaper. It does not matter to them that they could also damage their own students' lives. As the famous lawyer Joseph Welch asked of Joe McCarthy at the Army-McCarthy hearing, "Have you no shame, Senator?"

My guess is that this feverish rhetoric will backfire, damaging, perhaps irreparably, those who use it.

It is a peculiar phenomenon of our time now, when racial animus is at a historic low, opportunity widening, and anti-Semitism practically invisible, our "educators" keep screaming about "racism" and "bigotry." Their own credibility is at stake.

Printed in The Dartmouth Review *October 17, 1990*

ON THE RIGHT
Hating Hatred at Dartmouth
by William F. Buckley Jr.

I WAS PRACTICING MY SCALES in North Carolina a couple of days ago, called into my office and received word that AP, the *Boston Globe*, *The New York Times*, *The Washington Post*, ABC, CBS, and NEC wished to talk to me. It flashed through my mind that my wife had defected to the Khmer Rouge, or that my magazine in my temporary absence had come out for Teddy Kennedy for president. No, no, I was reassured, it was the Dartmouth situation they all wanted to talk to me about. What was the Dartmouth situation?

As everybody now knows, the latest issue of *The Dartmouth Review* appeared not with the traditional logo from Theodore Roosevelt giving "The Review Credo," but with a supplanted stretch of text that no one happened to notice for two whole days. (How often do you pause to read, "All the News That's Fit to Print" when you pick up *The New York Times*?) What the sick computer hacker had done was to insert, so to speak in the mouth of Theodore Roosevelt, a couple of lines from Adolf Hitler's *Mein Kampf*, calling for the persecution of the Jews.

What was the reaction of the editor of *The Dartmouth Review* when he discovered the editorial vandalism? He recalled every issue that hadn't already been distributed, publicly apologized for what had happened, and promised to conduct an investigation in an effort to discover who had been the malefactor.

You would not think that that episode would become a national story, but wait.

Official Dartmouth, whose sense of public relations makes New York gubernatorial candidate Pierre Rinfret sound like Perry Como, decided to explode. There is nothing Dartmouth President James Freedman is better at doing than calling the attention of the whole world to the putative delinquencies of his own college. After all, *The Dartmouth Review* is made up of Dartmouth students, it has been around for ten years, its alumni have distinguished themselves in various lines of activity, and it is wonderfully popular with an alumni body, much of which reels with embarrassment at Dartmouth's dogged, humorless liberal trendiness.

Now the question is reasonably asked: Is it possible that the editor-in-chief of *The Dartmouth Review* himself injected those lines from Hitler, was frightened by what he had done, and pretended it was the work of someone else? Well, that is a hypothesis worth a moment's attention. It does struggle, however, against the odds.

Kevin Pritchett is a black student, rather sensitive to race prejudice. For three summers he has worked with the *Wall Street Journal*, distinguishing himself as an intern. Nobody has ever heard him utter an anti-Semitic word. Nor, for that matter, has the *Review*, which revels in controversy, ever been charged with anti-Semitism. It is, instead, charged with sexism, homophobia, and (non-anti-Semitic) racism, the latter primarily because of its defiant defense of a continuation of the use of the Indian symbol, plus one column using black doggerel to make fun of extremes of affirmative action. Homophobia is of course defined as a belief that homosexuality is aberrational, and sexism means that you didn't come out for a woman for president, or for coeducational fraternities.

But so anxious was President Freedman to give the impression that the Hitler quote was the collective responsibility of all the editors of the *Review* that he called an anti-hate rally, in which a thousand or so

Dartmouth students convened to prove that they hated hate more than anybody since St. Matthew.

But the hate-haters are going to have to practice a little, as witnessed by the treatment of one writer for *The Dartmouth Review*. Outside his dormitory, students gathered to chant "Sieg Heil!" And outside his door a large swastika was placed, decorated with the phrase, "Nazi Pig."

The New York Times never caught the hacker who would certainly have lost his job for inserting the single comma in the headline on the social page, "Jacqueline Screws,/ Becomes Affianced."

Mr. Pritchett thinks he knows who his malefactor is. If he will just identify himself, he is guaranteed to receive an honorary degree from President Freedman.

October 5, 1990; printed in The Dartmouth Review *October 17, 1990*

ON THE RIGHT
Prove You're You
by William F. Buckley Jr.

E VERYWHERE I GO, all that journalistic brethren wish to talk about is: *The Dartmouth Review*. How can I "associate" with a journal that is anti-feminist, homophobic, and racist?

It is a very frustrating business. The Internal Revenue Division of New York recently asked me to "prove" that I had spent the months of February and March, 1985, in Switzerland. That was the—let me see—twenty-fourth consecutive winter I had spent in Switzerland; I stayed in the same house I had been renting for fifteen years; I entertained guests, wrote a book, kept a diary. . . . But my passport hadn't been stamped in & out by Swiss immigration (they usually don't bother) and suddenly it became, well, an epistemological challenge to prove to Internal Revenue that I had spent those two months in Switzerland.

It is so with *The Dartmouth Review*, which suddenly has to "prove" that it is not anti-Semitic, having been charged publicly by Dartmouth president James Freedman with being so because someone stole into its computer one night a few weeks ago and inserted into its logo a couple of let's-all-hate-the-Jews sentences from *Mein Kampf*. The (black, by the way) editor of the *Review*, upon discovering the mischief, recalled the issue, launched an investigation designed to establish the identity of the mischief-maker, and invited the State Attorney General to investigate what is a felony under New Hampshire law. All of this is substantially ignored by the President of Dartmouth and his epigone in the press, who simply assume that *The Dartmouth Review* is anti-Semitic.

"Dear Fox," I wrote to *The New York Times*'s Fox Butterfield on October 7, "You know how highly I rate your work." (The reference is to his classic book on Mao's China, *China: Alive in the Bitter Sen*). "For that reason I was especially alarmed by the lead sentence in this morning's *New York Times* piece on *The Dartmouth Review*, to wit, "For a decade, many students and professors at Dartmouth College have watched with quiet dismay—and occasional anger—as a handful of writers at a conservative weekly shaped a public perception of Dartmouth as hostile toward blacks, women, and Jews."

"I take the liberty," I went on, "of enclosing a column on the most recent incident published today in the *New York Daily News*. I record in it that there has never been a charge of anti-Semitism made against the *Review*. Racking my mind since reading your piece I do recall something at the expense of President Freedman that used Third Reich formalisms of some kind or another, but it was clearly miscast drollery rather than anti-Semitism. I see only three or four issues of the *Review* every year. But I am highly sensitive to anti-Semitism and yours is the very first article I have ever seen in which it is matter-of-factly set down that the *Review* has that reputation. I am quite sure that you are wrong. If I am wrong, I do wish you would let me know of it, and I will, I assure you, take strenuous and public measures to disengage." Result? One phone call from Mr. Butterfield. (I was out). I returned the call twice, but nothing from Mr. Butterfield, no subsequent phone call, no letter. He is out there in the field, perhaps trying to prove that he actually spent time in China.

Alan Lupo, a correspondent for the *Boston Globe*, writes about John MacGovern, running hard and successfully against the incumbent head of the Democratic Party of Massachusetts. MacGovern was one of the founders of *The Dartmouth Review* and refuses to disavow it for the best of reasons, namely that other than occasional sophomoric excesses, the paper—which has had three women editors, Jewish editors, Third World editors, and has been consistently pro-Israel in foreign affairs—is none of the things popularly suggested. Lupo reveals that MacGovern's father was a Jew-hating Feenyite. (Father Feeny was excommunicated by Pope Pius XII.) That's true. And he died when MacGovern was four years old. Lupo concludes, "MacGovern may not have a bigoted bone in his body, but his history and associations raise serious questions about his judgment and his qualifications for Congress." Meanwhile, his opponent, the incumbent Atkins, has a radio ad. "'By warding off the Jews, I am doing the Lord's work.' Adolf Hitler wrote those words back in 1924, words of hate and intolerance. But those words are back to haunt us. *The Dartmouth Review* printed those words on its masthead on Yom Kippur, and John MacGovern, candidate for Congress and founder of the *Review*, refuses to separate himself from those words of hate."

It is a mad world, but those who have a capacity to experience indignation should direct it against the Freedmans of this world, not the young editors of *The Dartmouth Review*.

October 25, 1990; printed in The Dartmouth Review *October 31, 1990*

LETTER

To Mr. E. John Rosenwald, Trustee of Dartmouth College

by William E. Simon

A former Secretary of the Treasury, William E. Simon was president of the John M. Olin Foundation at the time of this writing. This letter follows an op-ed by Mr. Simon that appeared in The New York Times *on October 20, 1990.*

I AM WRITING, as you might guess, about the recent conduct of Dartmouth's president James Freedman, which has been irresponsible in the extreme with regard to the latest controversy between Dartmouth College and *The Dartmouth Review*.

When we spoke two years ago about the troubled relations between the College and the *Review*, we agreed it was time to call a truce in this long-running battle, and that it would be best for all concerned if both parties could carry on their work in a spirit of peaceful co-existence. Since that time, I have done my utmost to keep the peace, and have succeeded in cooling some of the extreme passions surrounding *The Dartmouth Review*. I would not have become involved at all in the current controversy except for the recent attacks by Mr. Freedman not only against the *Review*, but also against national supporters of the paper including Bill Buckley, George Gilder, the John M. Olin Foundation, and myself.

I was most distressed to learn that the *Review* had published a hateful quotation from Hitler's *Mein Kampf* in its credo. When we learned more about the episode, however, we were satisfied that this was probably an act of sabotage, and that the quotation appeared without the knowledge of the editors. In response to calls from the press, I issued a measured statement condemning the words, expressing regret that the incident had occurred, and despite my private suspicion of sabotage—withholding any comment about sabotage or culpability until more was known. At the same time, I was encouraged to see that the editors of the *Review* moved quickly to denounce the words and to apologize for the distress caused by the appearance of this quotation in the paper. They also called immediately for an impartial investigation to identify the perpetrators.

I expected that the College would also respond in measured terms to learn the facts behind the incident and then to take appropriate action when these facts were in hand. Instead, the Dartmouth administration, led by James Freedman, took the opposite approach, fanning the flames of hysteria on campus and in the national press, and disregarding elementary rules of fair play in levelling hateful accusations at innocent individuals. Mr. Freedman even took his campaign to the editorial pages of *The New York Times*, where he said that any consideration of the facts of this case "misses the point," and where he attacked me by name, criticizing the John M. Olin Foundation too for providing support for *The Dartmouth Review*.

John, I did not wish to re-open the issue of *The Dartmouth Review*. I had no choice but to respond, however, when Mr. Freedman launched his despicable attacks on the *Review* and everyone associated with it. It is plain to all that he has used this incident as a pretext to settle old scores with the newspaper. In this process, sadly, he has dragged Dartmouth's name through the mud in the national press, and has fatally compromised any reputation the college might have had for good sense and fair play. In addition to the damage he has done to Dartmouth, he has done great harm to his own name, since anyone who says facts don't matter in a situation like this, and who is prepared to smear innocent individuals in complete disregard of the facts, has thoroughly destroyed his credibility as a man of principle and good judgment.

I cannot be expected to remain silent when I am called "irresponsible." I have been called many things in my life, but never irresponsible. Is Bill Buckley "irresponsible"? Is George Gilder "irresponsible"? This is what Mr. Freedman says in his *Times* article. If anyone is irresponsible, I am afraid it is James Freedman and those who have encouraged him to engage in character assassination.

Mr. Freedman says that the *Review* is "bigoted." But the facts say otherwise. The current editor, Kevin Pritchett, is a black student. The year before last the editor was a young woman from India. The paper's staff has always included several Jewish writers and editors. Indeed, the staff is probably more diverse than the Dartmouth student body. What is Freedman talking about? Has he turned logic on its head just because the *Review* is a relentless critic of his policies?

Mr. Freedman makes a great deal of the support the John M. Olin Foundation has provided to the *Review* and to its student editors. As you know full well, nearly all of these funds went to help the students defend themselves in court after the College unfairly suspended them in proceedings resembling a kangaroo court. This case was reviewed in detail by a state judge who ordered the students readmitted to school and who made some stinging statements about Dartmouth's disciplinary proceedings. I'm sure Mr. Freedman is still smarting from this, and is now trying to exact his revenge on the current editors of the paper.

His complaints about our support boil down to just this: that he should have free rein to violate the rights of *Review* editors in suspending them from school, and in addition, to deny them the resources to petition the courts to defend these rights. This is one of the most contemptible and arrogant claims I have ever heard, especially coming from a lawyer and a man who claims to be a student of the law. Has Daniel Webster's college finally come to this?

The fact of the matter is that *The Dartmouth Review* does not require our support to publish its weekly editions, because it is funded through subscriptions and small contributions from alumni and friends. Mr. Freedman is therefore deluding himself if he believes he can exploit this incident to destroy the financial underpinnings of the paper. I suspect that his conduct will have the opposite effect of redoubling the efforts of supporters to make sure the paper survives. Indeed, this has been the result to date.

I have also heard the charge that the supporters of the *Review* are not even Dartmouth alumni, as if this is anything other than a smokescreen to divert attention from the real issues. This is in fact a matter of ideological bullying by a group in the Dartmouth administration and faculty against conservative students who happen to think differently than they do. I know prejudice when I see it, and this is a clear case of bigotry against these students. One does not have to be a Dartmouth alumnus to speak out against it; I am entitled as a concerned American to call attention to this bullying by intolerant liberals and to come to the defense of these students.

For reasons known only to themselves, Dartmouth officials have invested all of the power and prestige of their institution in silencing a small, student-edited newspaper that happens to take a conservative position on the major issues of the day. Instead of debating the issues, they have tried over a period of nine years to destroy and to intimidate the paper. They will have no more success now than they have in the past in suspending the First Amendment in Hanover.

What is required to rectify this sorry state of affairs? Sadly, Mr. Freedman has already done irreparable damage, and it is doubtful that he retains sufficient credibility to set things straight. The college could help by joining in an investigation to learn the facts behind this episode, so that those who are guilty can be punished and the innocent exonerated. The college should also consider how it will make amends to the innocent students who were smeared by Mr. Freedman's reckless charges issued in his official capacity.

I did not start this fight, John, but I assure you that I am fully capable of seeing it through, determined to see justice done, and to resist Mr. Freedman's public misrepresentations and bullying of students. If he is spoiling for a fight, he has pushed the wrong guy in attacking Bill Simon.

I'm very sad about all this, John. I'm sure it's even more sad for you because you love Dartmouth College, and the institution has suffered immeasurable damage as a result of the reckless actions taken in the past three weeks by Mr. Freedman. It goes without saying that if you'd like to discuss this matter, I'd be happy to do so any time.

Printed in The Dartmouth Review *November 14, 1990*

All the News That's Fit to Pimp
by William Sushon

A LL THE NEWS that's fit to print. That's the motto of *The New York Times*, one of the nation's most widely read and respected newspapers. The problem is that in the recent *Review* sabotage case, *The New York Times* saw fit to print some "news" that was not news at all. It printed bald-faced untruths. It is indeed shocking that a journal of such stature would be willing to risk its reputation as an unbiased source of news in order to create a story against *The Dartmouth Review*. Is it thus the policy of *The New York Times* to distort the facts? Or was there some special pressure brought to bear on the publication by outside forces?

George Munroe '43, Chairman of the Board of Trustees of Dartmouth College, is also a member of the board of *The New York Times*. It is not usually considered proper etiquette for the trustees of a publication to conduct editorial policy, but it seems that *The New York Times* may be allowing that line to be crossed. What Mr. Munroe may not understand is that the public lends a lot of credence to *The New York Times*, and they also tend to listen to people with the stature of Mr. Munroe, the retired Chairman of Phelps Dodge corporation.

In his October 7, 1990 article entitled "The Uproar at Dartmouth: How a Conservative Weekly Inflamed a Campus," Fox Butterfield claimed in *The New York Times*, "The *Review* sponsored a free lobster and champagne feast to coincide with the campus fast for the world's hungry." The *Review* did not sponsor a free feast; instead, it organized a charity event— to show how poverty could be addressed through private means—which raised $300. The proceeds from this event went to Sisters of Chanty, Mother Theresa's Calcutta group. The point of the event was to raise money for the hungry, not to prove that Dartmouth students could withstand hunger themselves. Mr. Butterfield, however, did not acknowledge this fact.

One need look no further than one line down the page to see Mr. Butterfield's next inaccuracy. He claims that "In 1981 [the *Review*] published a list of the members of the school's Gay Students Association." Again, Mr. Butterfield seemed to ignore facts that did not support his thesis. The

Review, in that issue, published the names of the officers of the GSA (now DAGLO), names which were a matter of public record. But the *Review* did not print their names for the purpose of exposing them; their names appeared in an article discussing the financing of the GSA, and as officers, they are responsible for this facet of their organization.

Two lines later, Mr. Butterfield wrongly attributed to Dinesh D'Souza a quote which read, "It is not a question of whether women should be educated at Dartmouth, it is a question of whether they should be educated at all." Mr. D'Souza never said this. It is a quote from another former *Review* staffer who intended it as a joke. Yet Mr. Butterfield chose to ignore this fact as well. The individual responsible for the quote was not involved in the recent controversy. Mr. D'Souza was, as he came to Hanover as a representative of the Board of Trustees of the Hanover Review, Inc. to deal with the press and get to the bottom of the sabotage that occured.

In his reporting on the incident at Dartmouth, Mr. Butterfield completely ignored the *Review*'s claim that the quote appeared in the newspaper as the result of an act of sabotage. Again, this fact did not support Mr. Butterfield's apparent preconceived notions of *The Dartmouth Review*: namely, that it is a racist, sexist, homophobic rag sheet given to excesses of journalistic zeal that often propel it into the realm of the offensive. The facts just didn't fit Mr. Butterfield's equation, so he simply ignored them.

Finally, Mr. Butterfield claimed that the *Review* receives funding from the John M. Olin Foundation in the amount of hundreds of thousands of dollars. Tacitly, he claimed that this money went toward the *Review*'s operating expenses, which tally in excess of $150,000 per year. In fact, the money that came from that group was used to defray the legal costs incurred by Christopher Baldwin and John Sutter as a result of the Cole incident in 1988. Mr. Butterfield well knew this fact, as it had already been pointed out several times in other publications. Yet again, he chose to ignore the facts and write what was convenient.

Why would any journalist risk his credibility by printing what were obviously untrue statements about *The Dartmouth Review*? Well, that is a difficult question. Mr. Butterfield is an eminent reporter; the work he did in China is widely respected by his colleagues. It is doubtful that someone of his stature would take it upon himself to do anything of the sort.

When contacted about the inaccuracies in his recent works on the *Review*, all that Mr. Butterfield would say was that he distilled his information from back issues of *The Dartmouth Review*. When asked where he got those issues, he replied, "Look, I prepared a memo outlining my facts and where they came from. . . . I gave it to my national editors." He claimed that the national editors discussed that memo with a representative of *The Dartmouth Review*, Dinesh D'Souza. D'Souza, however, never received any phone calls or faxes from representatives of *The New York Times*. The explanations that Mr. Butterfield mentioned must have taken place in the same reality where *The Dartmouth Review* throws free champagne parties—the reality inside his own head.

Several attempts were made to contact the national news editors of the *Times*, all to no avail. They were constantly in meetings for two straight days and unavailable for comment. They were left with phone numbers where this reporter could be reached on a twenty-four hour basis, yet they made no attempts to return several phone calls. One employee at the national news desk recommended that the *Review* send a letter if it wanted this topic to get any attention. However, several letters and faxes from Mr. D'Souza made no headway whatsoever, and there was no reason to assume that official communications from *The Dartmouth Review* would be treated any differently.

Mr. Butterfield was quite defensive about the half-truths contained in his article. He felt that his distortions were merely "a different interpretation of the facts." When he was asked if he could detail exactly what back issues of the *Review* were used to supplement his article, he muttered something about an important deadline and rushed this reporter off the phone. It seems that Mr. Butterfield's "interpretations" are difficult to support. The difference between claiming that a lobster and champagne dinner was given for free and given as a fundraiser can hardly be called a disagreement over interpretation of the facts. The difference between printing a list of dozens of students' names and merely the names of the officers of a student organization is not a disagreement over the interpretation of the facts. The difference between attributing a quote to Dinesh D'Souza and attributing it to another former *Review* staffer is not a disagreement over the interpretation of the facts.

When asked if he had ever been approached by George Munroe about anything to write in the stories about the *Review*, Mr. Butterfield replied that he did not even know who Mr. Munroe was. This fact may not seem especially interesting on its face, but does when one examines it more closely. Mr. Munroe is a board member of *The New York Times*, Inc. He is also the Chairman of the Board of Trustees at Dartmouth College, an important entity in the two pieces that Mr. Butterfield wrote. It seems somewhat strange that Mr. Butterfield would not know such an important and prominent figure. But then, Mr. Butterfield did not realize that he was distorting the facts, either.

Attempts to contact Mr. Munroe met with no success, but it is doubtful that he would admit to having tried to exert any influence over Mr. Butterfield, Ms. Soma Golden (National News Editor), or anyone else on the *New York Times* staff. But the fact remains that Mr. Munroe is on the board of the corporation.

The fact is that Mr. Butterfield did have some preconceptions of *The Dartmouth Review*. In an interview with the *Daily Dartmouth*, he made several comments which exposed his feelings toward this journal, "the *Review* has dominated the College for a decade. It takes up the headlines and that is how the world sees Dartmouth."

He added that, "Twenty years ago [the anti-Semitic quote in the *Review*] would have been unthinkable. Now it raises the question of whether students are more intolerant of blacks, Jews, and women." The articles Mr. Butterfield wrote have a very carefully calculated spin; they paint the *Review* as a bastion of intolerance without ever actually making that claim outright. By shading meanings, misunderstanding past events, and omitting key details, Mr. Butterfield did quite a hatchet job on *The Dartmouth Review*.

November 14, 1990

Human Rights Chief, ADL Exonerate *Review*

by Kenneth Weissman

T WO INDEPENDENT REPORTS issued in the past week have served to vindicate *The Dartmouth Review* against reckless attacks by the administration of Dartmouth President James Oliver Freedman. Barry J. Palmer, Chairman of the New Hampshire Human Rights Commission, studied two years of the *Review*, and "didn't find any hint of bigotry or prejudice," a statement which blatantly contradicts numerous statements of Freedman's.

In a separate study, the Anti-Defamation League of B'nai B'rith confirmed that *The Dartmouth Review* is not anti-Semitic and that the anti-Semitic quote inserted into the *Review*'s masthead was neither perpetrated nor approved by the editors of the *Review*. This statement directly contradicts statements made by both Freedman and Dartmouth College spokesman Alex Huppe, who said *The Dartmouth Review* "should look in the mirror" to find the party guilty of inserting the quote.

In Palmer's study, released December 31, Palmer says he read the issues of the *Review* written over the past two years and found no evidence of bigotry or prejudice in the publication. After concluding his research, Palmer, in a strong blow to the credibility of Freedman, "began wondering what all the fuss was about" concerning Freedman's notoriously wild attacks on the *Review*.

Palmer's interest in *The Dartmouth Review* stems from the Freedman administration's attacks on the *Review* during the Professor Cole incident. Said Palmer, "[The Dartmouth administration] was charging racism, discrimination, and that sort of thing. Since that's within the domain of the Human Rights Commission, I felt it necessary to take a look at the publication and see if these charges were justified. We're the first ones to blow the whistle on that sort of thing." In the winter of 1988, the *Review* printed a transcript of one of Cole's classes, revealing Cole's repeated use of obscenity and street talk. The *Review* was charged with being racist for its report on Cole, who is black.

When Palmer requested evidence of the *Review*'s discrimination from Freedman, he was told to obtain copies of the paper, which he did. In two full years' worth of the publication, Palmer "read every single thing they wrote about teachers. I reviewed editorials and editorial cartoons. And I didn't find any hint of bigotry or prejudice."

Freedman has made a career out of recklessly attacking the *Review*, which often exposes the severe inadequacies of his policies. Yet never has Freedman attempted to substantiate his claims of the *Review*'s so-called bigotry and hatred. Now, the Chairman of New Hampshire's Human Rights Commission has come in and planted Freedman's feet firmly in his mouth.

Since he took over Dartmouth's presidency in 1987, Freedman has consistently accused the *Review* of racism, sexism, and many other politically incorrect "isms." For Freedman, attacking the *Review*, and thereby attempting to destroy its credibility, has been his only defense against the *Review*'s questioning of his competence.

In his latest display of public verbal recklessness, at the so-called "Rally Against Hate" in October, Freedman accused the *Review* of "attacking blacks because they are black, women because they are women, homosexuals because they are homosexuals, and Jews because they are Jews."

Not so, according to the Human Rights Commission. Palmer said that the *Review*, in questioning the actions of people who happened to be minorities, displayed no prejudice. "It's all right to criticize people who are black or female or Jewish, providing that the criticism is levelled at their performance. Those have always been the guidelines."

Palmer called the roots of numerous anti-*Review* tirades by Freedman part of an "ideological debate" between the two. When Palmer was asked about the lynch-mob atmosphere that Freedman's rhetoric encouraged, he said, "I would think that a college president should be able to accept criticism, and argue with his opponents logically."

It would seem that if any independent organization is qualified to judge fairly Freedman's statements, it would be the New Hampshire Human Rights Commission. In the words of Palmer, who was unfamiliar with the *Review* before he initiated his study, "The Human Rights Commission is sensitive to anything which takes away from a human being's self-worth and is always seeking evidence of such bias, whether in print or verbal form."

As of yet, Mr. Palmer had received no response from Freedman concerning the study. Freedman also could not be reached for comment by the *Review*.

But that is not to say that Mr. Palmer has not gotten any reaction to his study. The usual suspects have been up in arms, claiming that the findings of Palmer, who is a copy editor of the *Union Leader* of Manchester, New Hampshire, are not valid, since Palmer's position at the *Union Leader* supposedly constitutes a conflict of interest. The *Union Leader* has in the past supported the *Review* against Freedman's vicious attacks, but this is irrelevant, says Mr. Palmer, who has never edited any of the stories run in the *Union Leader* concerning the *Review*. "I was quite surprised at the amount of reaction this study got. I guess I was a little naive in that respect."

Roland Adams, of the College News Service, was quick to point out that the administration "obviously" disagrees with Palmer's conclusion.

Then, in an attempt to discredit Palmer's study, Adams continued, "There was no proper study conducted here. Unfortunately, a lot of the news that has come out about this has presented this as being a study by the New Hampshire Commission for Human Rights. That's not the case. [Palmer] conducted this study in his private capacity."

But when Palmer was asked about this, his answer was quite clear and quite the reverse of what Mr. Adams said. "I am the Chairman of the New Hampshire Human Rights Commission, and this study was done in my capacity as Chairman of the Commission."

On October 7, approximately one week after an issue of the *Review* appeared with a quote from Hitler inserted in its masthead, Dinesh D'Souza, a trustee of the *Review*, wrote to the ADL to ask them to help find the saboteur.

The ADL sent six investigators to Dartmouth on a fact-finding mission. The group conducted interviews with, amongst others, *Review* editors, Dartmouth administrators, and various Jewish students on campus.

While the ADL did not focus its attention on trying to find who inserted the anti-Semitic quote, the findings of the group strike another sharp blow against the Dartmouth administration's anti-*Review* propaganda campaign.

In response to the ADL's report, which was released January 9, the *Review* issued the following statement:

1) *The Dartmouth Review* asked the ADL to come in and help us with our investigation of this obviously anti-Semitic incident. At our request, investigators came to Hanover to look into the insertion of the Hitler quote.

2) The ADL's primary concern was not to find a perpetrator of the insertion, but to look at the situation at Dartmouth and *The Dartmouth Review*.

3) We are grateful to the Anti-Defamation League for investing time and effort into compiling its report. While we regret that the ADL investigation did not lead to the apprehension of the culprit responsible for inserting an unauthorized anti-Semitic slur into the *Review*'s masthead, we

note that, pursuant to its investigation, the Hanover Police have arrested a disgruntled former staffer, Pang-Chung Chen, and charged him with harassing Dartmouth Professor Jeffrey Hart in the wake of Hart's efforts to uncover the saboteur. The police also administered polygraph tests to top editors, and the police found no evidence to link them to the sabotage. The Hanover Police Investigation has uncovered important items of information that the *Review* intends to report in the near future.

4) The ADL "does not believe the students of the *Review* are intent on a campaign of unrelenting malevolence."

5) The ADL confirmed that *The Dartmouth Review* is not anti-Semitic. Though the ADL points to past incidents (such as the article "Ein Reich, Ein Volk, Ein Freedmann") that were "insensitive," the ADL did not report any anti-Semitism that might have been perpetrated by the *Review* during the past ten years. Prominent Jews, including David Brudnoy, David Horowitz, Sidney Zion, and Dennis Praeger have also said as much—that the *Review* might be insensitive on some occasions or sometimes runs items that are in poor taste, but it is not anti-Semitic. Quite the contrary, the *Review* has been a consistent supporter of Israel and Judaism, and condemns anti-Semitism.

6) The ADL confirmed that the anti-Semitic quote inserted into the *Review*'s masthead was neither perpetrated nor approved by the editors of *The Dartmouth Review*. This is in direct contradiction to the statements made by Dartmouth College spokesman Alex Huppe, who contended that if *The Dartmouth Review* wanted to find the perpetrator of the insertion, the paper "should look in the mirror."

7) The ADL makes the important point—a point aimed at the College and meant to castigate the Dartmouth College administration—that free speech is inherent in the American way of thinking. "Any society that ensures freedom of speech and of the press must be prepared to live with the occasionally frustrating consequences of its guarantees," said the ADL. The College has, since the *Review*'s founding, tried to inhibit the *Review*'s right of free speech, by suspending its top editors, blocking donations to the *Review*, lawsuits, and other intimidations.

8) *The Dartmouth Review*'s primary regret is that the ADL chose to highlight a few items published in the newspaper as far back as 1982, when the current editors were in elementary school. Some of these items have nothing to do with anti-Semitism or Jewish issues. The ADL gives no importance to the Dartmouth administration's recognition and subsidy of *Stet*, which has published blatantly anti-Semitic material, nor does the ADL address Dartmouth's speaking invitations to avowed anti-Semites like Vincent Harding.

9) The ADL report serves to cause Dartmouth President James Oliver Freedman a great deal of embarrassment, as Freedman has contended

through this past "Hitler Quote Controversy" that the *Review* is "anti-Semitic." After this ADL report, Freedman is going to have to answer for his falsehoods.

January 16, 1991

Former *Review* Staffer Arrested
by Kevin Pritchett

T HE ARREST of Pang-Chun Chen '92 on January 9 was caused by a prank phone call made by Chen two months ago to Dartmouth English Professor Jeffrey Hart's home, in response to a *New York Times* letter written by Hart. Chen, a former disgruntled *Dartmouth Review* staffer, has been a main suspect in the sabotage of the *Review*'s masthead quotation in its October 5 issue.

On Friday, November 2, a letter about the Hitler quote controversy by Professor Jeffrey Hart was published in *The New York Times*. Hart wrote that the sabotage might have been perpetrated by "a disgruntled or perverted junior staffer on the newspaper" who "invaded the word processor circuit." Hart, as well as the editors of the *Review*, had at the time of the letter's publication some ideas on who might have inserted the quotation, and whether the saboteur was an insider or outsider. Evidence pointed to an inside job, but the possibility of outside sabotage was still seriously looked at, because of factors like a hole in the door to the offices of the *Review* which was present before the sabotage.

On Sunday night, November 4, Nancy Hart, Hart's wife, received a call at home from someone who identified himself as "a student." The "student" asked for Professor Hart, who took the call. The caller, after Professor Hart had picked up the phone, made a lewd remark and hung up.

The Harts, after receiving the lewd phone call, called *Review* Editor-in-Chief Kevin Pritchett, who told them to find a way to trace the call. They also informed Pritchett that the voice of the "student" sounded like the voice of Pang-Chun Chen. The Harts had recognized Chen's voice from a videotape of the "Geraldo Show," on which Pang had appeared with friend David Budd '92 on a "campus controversy" segment.

The next day, Professor Hart called Hanover Police Detective Nick Giaccone, who is heading the *Review* investigation. "I informed the police about the phone call, and I told Detective Giaccone about my suspicion that the caller was Pang," said Hart.

Giaccone questioned Chen about the call. Chen denied that he made the call. Giaccone then sought court authorization to have the phone call that was made to the Harts traced.

After receiving court authorization, the phone call was traced to David Budd '92's room. Giaccone along with an assistant went to Budd's room after the phone call was traced. Leaving his assistant at Budd's door, Giaccone went to a lower floor of the dormitory and called Budd's room. Budd answered, and Giaccone said that there was "some interesting new information" about the prank phone call and that he wanted to talk to Budd.

After Giaccone's phone call, his assistant heard Budd, Chen, and friend Matt Henken '92 discussing what they were going to say to the detective. Giaccone a few minutes later came up to Budd's room, separated Budd and Chen, and questioned them. First, the two denied having anything to do with the prank phone call; but when faced with the fact that the call had been traced, it was confessed by the two that Chen had made the call.

The Hanover Police on January 9 arrested Chen, and charged him with harassment. Chen will be arraigned on January 22.

Pang-Chun Chen '92 has been one of the main suspects in the sabotage against *The Dartmouth Review*. The editors of the *Review* since the beginning of the "Hitler Quote" controversy have suspected that Chen inserted the quotation into the *Review*'s masthead; this suspicion is based on Chen's actions going back as far as last summer. It must be stressed that no formal charges of computer tampering have been lodged against Chen.

Chen was a contributor to *The Dartmouth Review*, and had been since January of 1990. Staffers and editors of the *Review* say that Chen had not been a troublemaker and had not done anything suspicious until the summer of 1990.

The *Review* publishes one issue during the summer term every year. This past summer, the summer of 1990, Chen, along with *Review* contributor Deborah Spaeder '92, was assigned an article for the summer issue (dated July 25, 1990) on the reform of the National Endowment for the Arts. Chen felt as the article neared completion that he should get the sole byline for the story.

"He demanded that he get the byline for the entire thing," says *Review* Managing Editor William J. Sushon '92, who was head of production for the July 25, 1990 issue. Sushon disagreed with Chen, saying that both Chen and Spaeder had worked on the article. Sushon referred the matter to *Review* Executive Editor Hugo Restall '92, and Restall concurred with Sushon. "[Chen] was still angry about the whole thing long after the article was published," says Sushon.

Last fall term's issue of the *Review*, dated September 19, 1990, was partially put together on the *Review*'s Macintosh computer layout system by Chen. Chen, according to Sushon, who also ran production for the September 19 issue, was the last one to use the layout system, as Chen laid out his own article—a review of Kevin Phillips's book *The Politics of Rich and Poor*—which was the last thing to be added to the computer files.

On the day when the issue galleys for the September 19 issue were to be taken to press, *Review* staffmembers noticed a quotation in the "Last Word" section of the *Review* which said, "I am an *ssh*l*, really." The quote was attributed to "William J. Sushon '92."

The quotation was quickly replaced by the layout staff of the *Review*. After the issue went to press, editors questioned staffers about the quotation. It was found out by the editors that Chen had been in charge of the "Last Word" section that week, and that Chen was the last to use the computer. Chen denied placing the quote in the newspaper. The staff was warned by the editors that the insertion of lewd quotations would not be tolerated.

Chen was given complete responsibility of the "Last Word" section again for the next issue, dated September 26, 1990. Chen was to look up quotations in the dozen or so books of quotations that the *Review* has in its offices, type the quotations into the *Review*'s computer system, and lay them out in the *Review*'s computer layout system.

In the September 26th issue, a questionable quote by Anatole France ran that said: "A woman without breasts is like a bed without pillows." The "Last Word" section that week was the responsibility of Chen. When asked, Chen admitted to putting the quotation into the newspaper. *Review* editors in a private talk made it clear to Chen that lewd comments were detrimental to the *Review*'s mission, and would not be tolerated.

To give Chen another chance, *Review* editors allowed him to edit the "Last Word" section for the next issue, dated October 3, 1990. Before the issue was printed from the *Review*'s computer system, Managing Editor William J. Sushon found a quote concerning masturbation by Truman Capote, which said "The good thing about masturbation is that you don't have to dress up for it." Sushon removed the quote, informed the other editors, and replaced the quote. Chen again was castigated by the editors. When Chen was asked why he selected the Capote quotation, he told the editors that he "thought it was funny."

The October 3 issue was also the issue that contained the quotation from Adolf Hitler. The three people known to have used the *Review*'s layout system are Pang-Chun Chen, *Review* Editor-in-Chief Kevin Pritchett, and Managing Editor William J. Sushon. Both Pritchett and Sushon consented to lie-detector tests; both were cleared as suspects. Chen, according to Detective Giaccone, refused to consent to a lie-detector test.

After the Hitler quotation was published, the *Review* mounted an internal investigation. Staffers were questioned about the insertion of the quote. There were no definite suspects, but a couple of factors contributed to the possibility of Chen being the saboteur. First, Chen had been in complete charge of the "Last Word" section; thus he had access to the *Review*'s quotation books, from which he might have gleaned the Hitler quote.

Staffers on the *Review* after the publication of the quote found the exact Hitler quotation in an edition of *The Great Quotations*, compiled by George Seldes, a common reference for the "Last Word" section of the *Review*. Second, Chen had in the past tried to or succeeded in placing obscene quotations into the newspaper. Third, according to many *Review* staffers, Chen still held a grudge against members of the *Review* because of the summer issue byline incident.

Though the *Review*'s internal investigation pointed to no specific culprit, Chen and his friend and fellow *Review* staffmember David Budd '92 felt that Chen was being "scapegoated." No reason was given by the two. Chen and Budd refused to take part in the *Review*'s internal investigation even before it got underway.

On October 1, 1990, Budd and Chen submitted their resignations from the *Review* to the Student Assembly, The resignations were distributed at dinnertime in Thayer Dining Hall. The *Review* knew nothing of the resignations until a freshman brought copies of the resignations to the *Review* offices.

On October 4, 1990, the *Review* called in Anti-Defamation League of B'nai B'rith and the Hanover Police to help investigate. Detective Giaccone headed the Hanover Police team. Along with administering lie-detector tests, Giaccone questioned staffers and collected statements. One piece of evidence he gleaned from the tampered-with masthead was a misplaced colon in the inserted Hitler quote. Giaccone found that Pang Chun-Chen's written statement also had misplaced colons. This does not, of course, prove a definitive connection.

On January 9, 1991, the Anti-Defamation League of B'nai B'rith issued a report on the controversy. The ADL concurred with one of the two views the *Review* has maintained on who might have put the Hitler quote into the newspaper—the view of an inside job. "Given the presence of the offensive Hitler quote in a frequently used book of quotes located in the offices of the *Review* . . . the conclusion seems inescapable that the Hitler quote was inserted in the masthead by a member of the *Review*," the ADL report said.

Also on January 9, Pang-Chun Chen was arrested for phone harassment, at the same time the ADL report was released. According to Detective Giaccone, who heads the *Review* investigation, the formal charge was harassment. But the *Review* case is not shut yet.

January 16, 1991

It has never been officially established who inserted the Hitler quote in the credo of The Dartmouth Review.

For more on this episode and its aftermath, see In Search of Anti-Semitism, *by William F. Buckley Jr. (Continuum, 1992; pages 45–59).*

The Freedman Legacy

The sabotage of The Dartmouth Review *and the College's response to this event through its "Rally Against Hate," outlined in the previous chapter of this book, damaged the reputations of both Dartmouth College and* The Dartmouth Review. *In the national consciousness, both institutions became equated with anti-Semitism, both unjustly so. Yet, while an anti-Semitic act was carried out through subterfuge against* The Dartmouth Review, *Dartmouth College actively positioned itself as the victim and ergo perpetrator of this heinous crime—Freedman both vanquisher and president of a purportedly anti-Semitic student body.*

In 1990, President Freedman sacrificed his children to Moloch for the opportunity to eliminate The Dartmouth Review. *Freedman's "Rally Against Hate" became merely the second act of sabotoge perpetrated against* The Dartmouth Review *that year.*

The events of 1990 nearly fulfilled Freedman's wish. Several staffers of The Dartmouth Review *quit under pressure over the "Hitler Quote" controversy. It would be several years before staff recruitment and alumni fundraising at the* Review *fully recovered. At the same time, Dartmouth College set about altering its strategy of engagement with the newspaper. Up through his rally, President Freedman attacked the* Review *head on; after, he adopted a policy of passive-aggressiveness: ignore the* Review *one day, coordinate attacks through College publicity and his connections in the national press the next.*

The following chapter documents President Freedman's continued efforts to silence The Dartmouth Review *after 1990.*

David & Goliath

by James Panero

W E OFTEN HEAR DARTMOUTH ACADEMICS call for "greater intellectualism among students." President Freedman paid lip service to these sentiments in his inaugural address of 1987—the famous "creative loner" speech:

> We must strengthen our attraction for those singular students whose greatest pleasures may come not from the camaraderie of classmates, but from the lonely acts of writing poetry or mastering the cello or solving mathematical riddles or translating Catullus. We must make Dartmouth a hospitable environment for students who march to a different drummer—for those creative loners and daring dreamers whose commitment to the intellectual and artistic life is so compelling that they appreciate, as Prospero reminded Shakespeare's audiences, that for certain persons a library is kingdom large enough.

At Freedman's Dartmouth, students are welcome to talk about classwork with peers. T. S. Eliot and computer science—okay. Move away from the classroom to politics and it better be pre-approved. Talk about curriculum and shoddy professors and *watch out*! Publish a newspaper about it and you're DOA. Freedman's creative loners are conformists— students who care about classroom work at the expense of the life around them. "Expand your horizons, but do it within the course syllabus" sums up their mentality.

The Dartmouth Review has been attacked from day one of publication. Editors have been called names, even bitten, by reputedly educated intellectuals. And I know what scares these academics and administrators: they will never have control of this newspaper. Independent journalism can be a scary thought when your job is on the line.

The crime of *The Dartmouth Review* is that it *exists*. It speaks to students and alumni free of administrative control. Over the years, the College has used every opportunity to destroy us—quoting out of context and distorting the truth beyond recognition.

There have been rebuttals, but the voice of New Dartmouth is powerful. Such was the case over Christmas 1996, when President Freedman took part in a combined and most likely coordinated attack on *The Dartmouth Review* through articles in *The New York Times* and the *Dartmouth Alumni Magazine*.

In an article that began, "What ever happened to *The Dartmouth Review*?," the *Alumni Magazine* published an editorial masquerading as news. It included no specifics from recent *Review* issues, and called the newspaper "boilerplate." In the past six months, the *Review* has run a series of articles calling for a core curriculum at the College. We have examined the direction of college expansion, and put in doubt this administration's commitment to undergraduate education. We have interviewed such scholars as Donald Kagan and Roger Kimball. Is that "boilerplate"?

Perhaps we should expect this response from the *Alumni Magazine*. They want to put the best spin on the College. In their opinion, Dartmouth would be best without *The Dartmouth Review*.

A January 4 story in *The New York Times*, titled "A Shy Scholar Transforms Dartmouth Into a Haven for Intellectuals," came as a greater surprise. A good third of this piece was dedicated to *The Dartmouth Review*. Here is what it said, in part:

> While he defended [the *Review*'s] right to publish and to be provocative, Mr. Freedman insisted on civility. In two speeches before the faculty and the students in 1988, he declared that "racism, sexism, and other forms of ignorance and disrespect have no place at Dartmouth." As president, he said, he had a responsibility for protecting the college's "moral endowment no less than its intellectual and financial endowment."
>
> Once Mr. Freedman spoke up, the *Review*'s influence began to decline dramatically. Now it has a much lower profile.
>
> Donald Pease, an English professor, recalled: "That was a moment of great moral courage. Everything turned on that moment."
>
> Looking back, Mr. Freedman said he had felt compelled to act after meeting with a group of black students. "Those kids just felt vulnerable," he said. There were some who said, "Who is going to defend us? Who is going to speak up for us?"
>
> Defending them, Mr. Freedman said, was a personal liberation of sorts.

No mention of black *Review* editor Kevin Pritchett, harassed by the "vulnerable" black students' organization; no questioning of the mass hysteria behind the "Rally Against Hate"; no alternative perspective. I wrote the following letter to *The New York Times* a few days after its article appeared:

> I am a junior at Dartmouth College and Editor-in-Chief of *The Dartmouth Review*. Winter classes began here on Monday, January 6. By chance, I arrived a few days earlier than that. So on Saturday, January 4, I was enjoying my first Hanover breakfast of 1997: waffles, coffee, and *The New York Times*.
>
> I was born and raised on the Upper West Side of Manhattan, and I've come to have respect for the *Times*. So I must confess, the cover story of the January 4 National Section left me disappointed. In her half-page article about Dartmouth President James Freedman, Sara

Rimer takes president Freedman's statements at face value. When Mr. Freedman proceeds to malign the history of my own newspaper, Ms. Rimer fails to print any of the quote-unquote other side of the story.

It was only the following week, when I first opened *The Dartmouth Review* offices after Christmas break, that I found a phone message from the *Times* about the Saturday article—dated January 2. A simple call to the registrar would have revealed that students were on break in early January. In no way was the Freedman article time-sensitive. Ms. Rimer should have waited for a second opinion before publication. While I may be new to the newspaper business, I believe this would have been the professional thing to do.

Isn't it odd that *The New York Times* printed a story almost identical in substance to an article in the *Dartmouth Alumni Magazine*? Since when does the *Times* coordinate its attacks with the college publicity office? Was the newspaper an unwitting accomplice to James Freedman and Dartmouth publicity?

President Freedman can sound quite convincing. He plays the underdog beautifully. In Freedman's account of the Hitler Quote incident, the *Times* quoted him as saying, "The *Review* incident forced me to display a side of myself I had never displayed before. I had to face someone down. I had to attack someone. It is just not who I am fundamentally."

So Freedman is the David who stood up to the great Goliath of *The Dartmouth Review*. I didn't know David had the undivided attention of *The New York Times*.

Freedman is now entering his tenth year as president. The *New York Times* article may be his first attempt to put some "positive closure" on his career. I find it a bit strange that a man—a scholar of the First Amendment—takes so much pride in attacking a paper edited by his own students.

Much of the national press, aside from *The New York Times*, found that Freedman's response to the Hitler Quote incident was a serious blunder. Rather than call for an investigation (as the *Review* did), he organized the famous "Rally Against Hate." This was his chance to get the *Review* while it was down. The tactic backfired.

The *Review* still exists. It is a blemish on the illiberal resume of Mr. Freedman. Many observers believe Freedman's handling of the Hitler Quote incident cost him the presidency of Harvard. You can bet he'll never forgive the *Review* for that.

January 22, 1997

Alumni Mag & NY Times Attack

by *Arthur Monoco*

B ACK IN THE SUMMER OF 1996, a source close to the *Dartmouth Alumni Magazine* confided private information to the editors of *The Dartmouth Review*—myself included. The magazine was planning to run a major story about the *Review* in December. While vague about specifics, the source did admit the magazine sought to show that the *Review*'s prominence on campus has drastically declined over the past few years.

The source also identified Bill Kartalopoulos '97 as a contributor to the magazine's story. Kartalopoulos had worked on *The Dartmouth Review* since his freshman year. Late in his sophomore year, he rose to the position of Graphics Editor. Then, a year ago, in Winter Term 1996, Kartalopoulos applied for the position of Editor-in-Chief. He was one of many candidates, and ended up losing.

He stayed on the *Review* staff as Senior Editor until mid Spring, when he resigned under good terms, citing editorial differences. Kartalopoulos went on to pursue his interests in campus politics, running for positions on the Committee on Standards and the Student Assembly. He bleached his hair, and pierced his ears in a few different places. I remember that Kartalopoulos had always been an admirer of the political writer Hunter S. Thompson, author of *Fear and Loathing in Las Vegas* and *Better than Sex: Confessions of a Political Junkie*. Late in the spring of 1996, Kartalopoulos published his own mini-magazine—something he believed followed Thompson's model of "gonzo journalism." Entitled *Screed*, it was distributed at his own expense throughout campus.

Although wary of Kartalopoulos's motives, the *Review* extended full cooperation to the *Alumni Magazine* in the August 21 issue: "No one has called our offices yet, but we extend an open invitation to the *Alumni Magazine* to contact us. We're ready to help out however we can." The invitation was accepted in mid-October, when Jay Heinrichs, editor of the magazine, contacted *Review* Editor James Panero for an interview.

On a Monday in late November, Heinrichs came to the *Review*'s Main Street office. I remember it well, since I was there with Panero. He asked Heinrichs if he had seen any of the recent issues. Heinrichs said yes, and with the exception of the two issues devoted to College expansion, he spoke favorably of the newspaper during Panero's tenure.

Mehling took pictures of Panero in front of an American flag, and Heinrichs conducted the interview—a copy of which Panero approved.

This was the last we heard until late December. With the campus on Christmas Break, the January issue of the *Alumni Magazine* was published and mailed to every Dartmouth alumnus. The eight-page article, written by

Michael Cannell, began on page thirty. It was entitled "Whatever Happened to *The Dartmouth Review*?" and its slant was as expected: "Seventeen years after it first roiled Dartmouth, the *Review* itself is no longer the juggernaut it used to be." Cannell opens with a discussion of the heyday of the Reagan Revolution in Washington, when "bright young Republicans—the so-called 'mini-cons'—swarmed town like a conquering cadre." According to Cannell, "None arrived with greater stature than the erstwhile editors of *The Dartmouth Review*, the obstreperous student weekly that, for many, symbolized the conservative youth surge of the Reagan era." However, "The *Review*'s precocious progeny came to Washington swathed in promise, but, with a few exceptions, notably that of the prolific author Dinesh D'Souza '83, they are no longer credential players in the capital's neo-conservative circles."

Canell summarizes the paper's history, stating, "This is no epitaph—the paper's budget still appears to be healthy, and its staff continues to show up at its office. Consider this, instead, a stock taking." Cannell's "stock taking" focused on the various controversies and confrontations peppered throughout the *Review*'s first seven years. However: "By most accounts, a turning point came when President Freedman delivered a special address to the faculty on March 28, 1988. He defended the paper's right to publish, but warned that 'the *Review* is dangerously affecting—in fact poisoning—the intellectual environment of our campus.'"

According to Cannell, "Observers credit Freedman with shoring up Dartmouth's self-image as a community of scholars unruffled by innuendo. From then on, Dartmouth diminished the *Review*'s impact by responding to its taunts with moderation."

Cannell further praised Freedman for his handling of the Hitler Quote incident. "It was one provocation more than Dartmouth could abide, and the campus erupted. Led by President Freedman, 2,500 students, faculty, and administrators massed on the Green for an open-mic discussion of racism." Although the Anti-Defamation League of B'nai B'rith found the event to be an act of sabotage by a disgruntled staffer—the magazine states this fact—Cannell asks the question, "If so, then who?"

Panero's interview was run separately as a short transcript. Discussion of the newspaper's present content was decidedly sparse in the main article—aside from a few quotes at the start: "Piles of the newspaper still land in dormitory hallways. But most are left untouched." "The *Review* thrived for a decade as a notorious bomb-thrower, but it has recently dwindled into a punchless version of its former self." "Some students read it, but it no longer arouses much heat." "'They try to be inflamatory,' said Professor Wood, 'but you get the impression they're just not as bright. The outrageous idea just isn't there. They haven't come up with any new issues. It's just unimaginative political boilerplate.'"

Cannell links the demise of the *Review* to the decline in influence of many of its past editors. He also states: "The one-time flagship of the conservative student movement has been eclipsed by an expanding breed of papers engaged in less adversarial debate over political correctness and other university issues." The *Alumni Magazine* printed a list of these "rival" publications. Among the seventeen listed, BLD, *World Outlook, Disquisitions, Aporia,* SANDpaper, *Freehand Publications, Easterly Winds,* and *Rice* have rarely—if ever—been printed.

Also included in the spread was a short, separate column writen by Kartalopoulos entitled, "Why I Left the *Review.*" He concluded that, "As much as Reviewers mock the campus for its intellectual immaturity, they suffer from the same stupid disease."

While we expected the negative article in the *Alumni Magazine,* the January 4 issue of *The New York Times* came as a surprise—and indeed felt more damaging. On the front page of the "National Section" was an article by Sara Rimer entitled, "A Shy Scholar Transforms Dartmouth into a Haven For Intellectuals." The "shy scholar" was President Freedman, and the article gave him credit for single-handedly transforming "Dartmouth in the past decade from a college known for its fraternities and athletes into one that also embraces those students whom he calls the creative loners."

President Freedman has a long history of connection with *The New York Times*—a history which began with the aforementioned Hitler Quote controversy. At that time Freedman wrote an op-ed piece about the incident which appeared in the *Times.*

Chester F. Cotter, a Dartmouth alumnus, wrote unfavorably of Freedman's changes in a letter published January 10: "As a senior alum, I can't think of a single thing wrong with old Dartmouth, except possibly the spring mud requiring duckboards across the Common. It was truly Camelot. . . . Perhaps Mr. Freedman should have founded Freedman's College with a huge orchestra and left Dartmouth men to howl at the moon."

After some delay, *The New York Times* finally published a letter by William F. Buckley on January 16, seriously questioning the journalistic credibility of the original article. Buckley calls Rimer's accusations "baseless" and states, "Her perspectives on the Dartmouth scene are her own, but should not be confused with reality."

January 22, 1988

LETTER
To the Editor of *The New York Times*
by William F. Buckley Jr.

"WITH AN ADVISORY BOARD that included William F. Buckley Jr. and Patrick J. Buchanan, the paper [*The Dartmouth Review*] described a black music professor as a 'used brillo,' published a confidential roster of a gay students group, and ran a front page cartoon that showed Mr. Freedman [Dartmouth's president], who is Jewish, in a Nazi uniform and Hitler mustache."

That's a hell of a paragraph, brought off by Sara Rimer in her encomium (January 4, "A Shy Scholar Transforms Dartmouth Into a Haven for Intellectuals") on Mr. Freedman, and her diatribe against *The Dartmouth Review*. Her perspectives on the Dartmouth scene are her own, but should not be confused with reality. Just for one instance, I have never served on the advisory board of the *Review*. I did write a book ("In Search of Anti-Semitism," 1993) which was warmly received in the *New York Times Book Review*, one chapter of which examined and found baseless the inferences now excreted by Ms. Rimer. My single contact with Mr. Freedman was when we were both speakers at a 100th anniversary celebration of Temple Emanuel.

January 16, 1997; printed in The Dartmouth Review *January 22, 1997*

President Freedman Rambles On
by Steven Menashi & Alexander Wilson

IN THE PAST WEEK, two incidents have focused campus attention on the issue of anti-Semitism. On February 11, President Freedman gave an interview to *The Los Angeles Times* discussing his speech on anti-Semitism at Dartmouth, delivered at the dedication of the Roth Center for Jewish Life. Six days later, the Dartmouth community experienced an act of anti-Semitic vandalism.

A female Jewish student returned to her room that night to find her door defaced with a Star of David and the words, "Death to you." The student, who wished to remain anonymous, resides in the River apartments.

In a statement issued on Thursday, February 19, Dean of the College Lee Pelton wrote, "Dartmouth College deplores these acts of racism and hate. This behavior is contrary to the College's educational values and its Principle of Community."

President Freedman, however, has yet to comment on the issue. He did, however, address the issue of anti-Semitism at Dartmouth in *The Los Angeles Times* interview. According to Freedman, there is a pattern of anti-Semitism on the campus.

"In my time at Dartmouth," he said, "we've had enough evidences of anti-Semitism from *The [Dartmouth] Review*." Freedman thus reiterated his long-standing belief in the *Review*'s anti-Semitism. This comes in spite of the fact that its staff is currently 25 percent Jewish, and that three out of its four top positions are held by Jews.

Unlike Freedman, the victim of Dartmouth's recent bias crime sees no atmosphere of anti-Semitism at the College. "I don't think [the incident] is a mirror of my experience here," she said. "I've always felt very comfortable here."

Jewish leaders concur with her statement. David Levi, President of Hillel, reports that he has never seen any evidence of anti-Semitism in his years here.

In a joint statement, the Jewish student group wrote, "We wish to assert our belief that the Dartmouth community is a welcoming and supportive place for Jewish students. . . . [The incident] is not in any way a reflection of the attitudes of the Dartmouth community."

"I have felt very at home on the Dartmouth campus," says Hillel Vice-President Douglas Newton, "I have actually never felt uncomfortable or been treated differently because I'm a Jew here." President Freedman, Newton continued, "feels a sharp disdain for the *Review*. . . . It seems to be a personal vendetta."

The harassment of Jewish *Review* staffer Andrew Baer following the "Rally Against Hate" so frightened his parents that they made him resign from the *Review*, and considered withdrawing him from Dartmouth. Freedman never commented on this incident.

In his *Los Angeles Times* interview, Freedman says "the *Review* surely misled people in giving the impression to many that there was an anti-Semitic tone [at Dartmouth]." It would seem, however, that this "impression" stems far more from Freedman's rhetoric than from any of the *Review*'s actions.

Dinesh D'Souza once dubbed Freedman the "Al Sharpton of Academia." He still merits the title.

February 18, 1998

President Freedman: Using His Religion

By Steven Menashi

I N THE FEBRUARY 11 *Los Angeles Times*, James O. Freedman observed: "It's fascinating that there was not a Jewish president of a major university—with one or two exceptions—until about fifteen years ago. And then all of a sudden—without notice—there are Jewish presidents now at dozens of major institutions."

Among all those presidents, however, Freedman remains among the most outspoken on Jewish issues in higher education. Through a series of public comments, notably his 1990 attack on *The Dartmouth Review*, Freedman has repeatedly used his ethnicity to make a name for himself in academic circles.

The *Los Angeles Times* interview concerned his comments at the opening of the Roth Center for Jewish Life, in which he "exposed" Dartmouth's history of anti-Semitism. Since the Roth Center dedication, Freedman has returned to the Roth Center only once—for his annual visit to Hillel at Friday night services.

At last year's visit, Freedman mentioned that Dartmouth tries to recruit both Jewish faculty and students because, the *Daily Dartmouth* reported, "It is important to have diverse faculty because it is important to give minority students more role models."

It is curious that President Freedman, supposedly a Jewish role model himself, has such a weak connection to Judaism that he attends religious services only once per year.

In 1989, the College scheduled Freshman Parents Weekend for the beginning of Passover. Freedman expressed "regret," but took no action to change the date. Evidently, he wasn't planning on being busy.

Freedman explained his Judaism in a column in the December 4, 1994 *New York Times*. "Being Jewish means many things to me," Freedman wrote, "but none more important to my identity than being part of a tradition of scholarship and learning." His "house abounded with books and conversation about ideas" and he "gradually came to understand that serious learning was a core Jewish value connecting us with the wisdom of the past."

He even goes so far as to say that "By pursuing scholarship and learning, American Jews have preserved their identity . . . and fortified the covenant between themselves and God." In Freedman's formulation, his own identity as a Jew and, indeed, the character of American Jewry itself, is a bookish and academic nature.

Studying may, in fact, be a noble pursuit, but the simple fact remains that one need not be Jewish to pursue it. Stereotypes aside, the truth is that gentiles are equally capable of "scholarship and learning."

In any case, Freedman's conception of Judaism is one that can be expressed in a purely secular way. In fact, his own list of "Books that influenced my development," available on the Harvard bookstore's website, contains no texts on Jewish subjects. A Judaism centered on scholasticism can hardly preserve Jewish identity, much less fulfill a holy covenant.

Jewish faith and practice have sustained the Jewish community throughout history by conveying a set of shared values and beliefs and distinguishing it from non-Jews. To replace that spirit with nondenominational pursuits is to erode the core of Jewish identity.

It is to supplant Judaism with a faint "Jewishness" that can hardly attract the passion of succeeding generations. The failure of the Jewish civil religion can be seen in the fact that one-third of Americans of Jewish ancestry no longer report Judaism as their religion; twelve percent are now practicing Christians. Being a Jewish role model ought to entail some commitment to Jewish faith.

Were ethnicity the sole determinant of Jewish identity, Freedman would not even be Dartmouth's first Jewish president. That would be John Kemeny, who was also of Jewish origin.

Yet, whereas Kemeny did not identify himself as Jewish, Freedman uses his religion to gain political mileage—even to the point of perpetuating myths about Dartmouth. In 1990, he fought nonexistent anti-Semites and race-baiters in the student body. In his Roth Center speech, Freedman used information from a senior thesis by Alexandra Sheppard '92 about the role of Jewish students at the College from the 1920s to 1940s.

Freedman left out her conclusion that despite quotas and masked anti-Semitism, Dartmouth was at the time a "good place to be Jewish."

Sheppard also noted that during the 1930s, the percentage of Jewish enrollment at the College was higher than it is presently. The class of 1935, for example, was about 15 to 20 percent Jewish, while Jewish enrollment today remains around 10 percent.

This is not to trivialize the anti-Semitism that did exist at the time, but merely to note that President Freedman failed to paint an accurate portrait of Dartmouth past.

Freedman likes to see himself as having opened Dartmouth up to Jewish students. He called the Roth Center an important step in "the legitimization of the authentication of Judaism" at Dartmouth.

Whatever that means, the truth is that Dartmouth opened its doors to Jewish students and Judaism by the late 1950s and put the study of Judaism in its curriculum in 1964.

Today's Dartmouth is still a "good place to be Jewish," but Freedman's political grandstanding does not contribute to that environment and has, in fact, harmed it.

April 8, 1998

Sara Rimer: Then & Now

by J. Lawrence Scholer

O N NOVEMBER 12, 2002, *The New York Times* ran a front page
story on Dartmouth's struggle to achieve diversity on campus. The
article described how the administration has worked to change the image
of Dartmouth, particularly during freshman orientation: "It used to be that
freshman orientation here at Dartmouth College revolved around hiking
up mountains and sleeping in huts along the Appalachian Trail. But this
year one of the highlights was a talk by Karim Marshall, a senior, who told
the 1,100 new students about his arrival on campus from a predominantly
black high school in Washington." (I gather this refers to the District of
Columbia, not the state, although the author leaves this unclear.)
Presumably, most students, regardless of whether they are inclined to the
outdoors, would prefer hiking to listening to a fellow student share his
touching personal story, but apparently not. Marshall's words moved students. Matthew Oppenheimer '05 told the *Times*, "I couldn't imagine what
it was like to come from his community to Dartmouth. I have such respect
for him being so open."

So students have fallen for the ploy. Most striking, however, is
Dartmouth's efforts to promote this diversity. The *Times* reported that
Dartmouth spends "millions" to achieve diversity and also offers diversity
training courses to students and faculty. The College even forces staff
members to take the course.

The article reads like a diversity pep talk—no surprise there—but the
most disturbing aspect of the article is not in the text, but in the byline.
The author of the article is Sara Rimer, no stranger to diversity or to
Dartmouth. Rimer has reported on Dartmouth news for a number of years,
and with each report she produces a pro-diversity, pro-administration
editorial in the guise of news. And Rimer is no stranger to the *Review*—
she hates us.

On January 4, 1997, Rimer penned a gushing piece on James Freedman
and his "creative loners." Freedman preceded James Wright as president
of Dartmouth College and served a rocky term, frequently challenging the
Review. Rimer's piece on Freedman, "a shy, self-effacing scholar," sounds
eerily familiar to her latest opus: "[Freedman] has transformed Dartmouth
in the past decade from a college known for its fraternities and athletes
into one into one that embraces those students whom he calls creative
loners." So from creative loners, Dartmouth now turns to diversity.
Moreover, Rimer describes Freedman's attacks on the *Review* in a very
sympathetic light. "While he defended their right to publish and to be
provocative, Mr. Freedman insisted on civility," she writes, failing to note

that his definition of "civility" left the door open for repressive speech codes. And, when Rimer attacks the *Review*, she conveniently neglects to mention the *Review* by name: "The 61-year-old Mr. Freedman, who counts among his heroes the late Justice Thurgood Marshall, for whom he was a law clerk, has also restored tolerance and civility by standing up to a group of right-wing students—and their prominent, adult benefactors—whose harassment of blacks, homosexuals, women, and Jews had deeply wounded many on campus." When Rimer wants to attack the *Review* for lack of tolerance she refers to it as "right-wing," but, when she wishes to praise Freedman for his false tolerance of ideas, she refers to the *Review* as "neo-conservatives."

That was not all the praise that Rimer showered upon Freedman. On June 15, 1998, Rimer wrote "Dedicated Intellectual Ends Chapter as Dartmouth President," which bade Freedman farewell from Hanover. According to Rimer, Freedman changed the face of Dartmouth. He had achieved parity among males and females and had changed the nature of the Dartmouth student from the rugged outdoorsman chugging kegfuls of beer to the "self-effacing idealist." Rimer also quoted notoriously liberal professors. Susan Ackerman, now co-chair of the Department of Women's and Gender Studies and Professor of Religion, said that Freedman had "upped the intellectual ante." And to appease any doubts that Ackerman exhibits a liberal bias, she recently told students and faculty regarding the recent elections, "I'm always surprised every election, and especially this election, when things that are so obvious to me are not obvious to 50 to 60 percent of the American public."

In Rimer's most recent article, the bias exhibited is not striking when compared to the bias inherent in the questions she asked the students whom she interviewed.

One student, John Stevenson '05, posted excerpts from his conversation with Rimer—they never appeared in Rimer's story—on a weblog, dartobserver.blogspot.com, to which he frequently contributes. After receiving some leading questions about his race, Stevenson wrote Rimer by e-mail, "I do not regularly think of myself as African-American primarily. In the back of my mind, the identification is there. However, I think primarily of myself as John Stevenson."

Rimer was not pleased with Stevenson's statement, so she pressed on for one that would fit the tone of her report. She responded to Stevenson, "But it is important that I underscore that you are proud to be African-American and have African-American friends. So can you tell me anything along those lines—do you drop in regularly at the African-American Affinity house? Is Booker T. Washington a hero of yours, or someone else? Can you name one or two of your close African-American friends? I just don't want people to get the mistaken idea that you are putting aside your blackness."

Rimer's leading questions expose the problems with her article and the administration's push for diversity. Rimer writes that Dartmouth and other colleges are spending millions in an attempt to get students to "connect across racial and ethnic lines." But when Rimer meets a student who had crossed those lines, without the College's provocation, she urges him to cross back and seek refuge with students and scholars of his own race.

Rimer's article and reporting inadvertently expose the shallowness of the College's efforts to promote diversity. The administrators no doubt felt that this article exposed all the good things it is doing to increase diversity on campus—it was a front page *Times* story. But, in the end, the story exposed all that is wrong with the College's efforts, and the journalism of Sara Rimer.

November 27, 2002

The Freedom of Assembly

Fighting Frats & the First Amendment
by Keeney Jones

G EORGE ORWELL, call your office. Just when you'd think the administration had gone about as far as they could go, the miscreants were able to find a new plateau.

Last week, the new administration decided to pursue this newspaper for using the name "Dartmouth." It's an old tactic—getting a bit stale, to say the least—but they added a new twist. College officials were ordered not to talk to, play with, or sign autographs for anyone from the *Review*.

This week there is a fresh target. The bureaucrats are after our friends in the fraternities—men who ask for nothing more than a place to be merry. This time the do-gooders are holding out the carrot of financial help. But watch out for the stick.

It seems that the mess started because Beta fraternity is more than $100,000 in arrears. Beta's corporation president, heavily influenced by administrators, suggested the wonderfully wacky idea of turning over fraternities to the College in order to give tax-exempt dollars back to the fraternities.

Now that all sounds peaches and cream. But the question remains, will fraternity donations significantly increase to the point where this singular, questionable advantage counters the stick?

And the stick is this. The College can wipe out the fraternity system as we know it. Frats with extra beds may find those beds filled with outsiders—even women. Basements and living rooms may be assigned by the Events Office. Just think—the Dartmouth Women's Association could meet in Theta Delt on Tuesday nights. Double or even single rooms may become triples. Television rooms might be reconstructed to become bedrooms or women's bathrooms.

In short, frats would become dorms—and thus the College would solve its housing crunch and maybe even its parking crunch. When the Rockefeller Center is finished there will be a huge parking problem. Brothers will probably be ordered to park at the College's remote A-lot, and the grassy knolls behind the frats will have a new color—blacktop.

You probably think I am overdoing it—but remember I should know. This newspaper is used to dealing with the College. Two weeks ago Professor of English Jeffrey Hart had a pleasant meeting with David McLaughlin. But McLaughlin was deceitful enough to forget to mention the College's new policy concerning the *Review*, even at the moment it was being implemented by legal genius Gary Clark.

Last week, sports information director Art Petrosemelo was ordered to revoke the sideline photo passes of our photographers. Hanover Inn manager Robert Merrow was ordered to remove newspapers from the Inn. A couple of administrators who happen to be personal friends of staff members were ordered not to talk to those students on threat of their jobs. The Council on Student Organizations (COSO) secretary Dee Johnson told a freshman, "Because you're affiliated with *The Dartmouth Review*, that is reason enough not to give you any information."

My friends in the frats, take it for what it's worth. There's something rotten in the state of affairs at Dartmouth—something rotten in an administration that only two weeks ago promised that nothing would be handed down from Parkhurst *ex cathedra*. Cross your fingers and hope it's not true. Remember there's been a change of administration at Dartmouth this past summer. Or has there?

In the end, the College doesn't care about our use of the name Dartmouth or the financial condition of some bankrupt frats. In the end it is freedom that they oppose and control that they want. "My God," as Gary Clark told a group of us last year, "what if the alumni get two opinions?" And what if the fraternities want to restrict their memberships, play beer pong, slip in their mud bowls, and have a little fun?

But this is Dartmouth. Whether it's the fraternity system or a renegade newspaper, this Ivy League institution continues to find itself on the wrong side of the fence. Thank God that on the other side stands and stares the First Amendment. Fight them boys.

October 12, 1981

Wright, Trustees to Close Down Greeks

by Andrew Grossman & Alexander Wilson

T WO RELATED INCIDENTS at Dartmouth have put the future of the College's treasured Greek system in severe jeopardy. On February 9, 1999, the Trustees of the College released a letter to the student body, and President James Wright gave an interview with the *Daily Dartmouth*. Taken together, these announcements constitute a new administrative policy. Dartmouth, it seems, in a new "spirit of inclusion," has threatened its fraternities and sororities to become coeducational by policy. President Wright says he expects the changes to take place in time for next fall's rush.

The forced coeducation of fraternities and sororities has uncorked a firestorm of student and alumni protest.

Though the fraternities and sororities are ostensibly independent entities, Dartmouth will likely outlaw those houses which choose not to accept the changes, and prohibit their members from registering at the College.

Recently, Bowdoin, Colby, and Middlebury Colleges have all outlawed single-sex fraternities by these means. Though lawsuits are still pending, to this date the courts have consistently upheld the right of colleges to outlaw private student associations, among them fraternities and sororities.

The Board's decision was phrased as an attempt to revitalize the College's "residential life," to make it more "inclusionary." Several student groups, then, have argued that those Greek houses which own their own physical plant might not freely comply, since they are not strictly College residences. The legal grounds for this argument are murky.

President Wright, however, announced that the Board of Trustees was willing to put up "tens of millions of dollars" to purchase the physical plant of those houses—twelve in all—that the College does not own.

The last time the College had a serious confrontation with the independent fraternities they compelled cooperation by convincing the Hanover Police Department and the Hanover Fire Department to raid the houses routinely for underage drinking and fire violations. The fraternities, under serious legal threat, capitulated.

This latest hubbub started when the student body received a seemingly innocuous set of letters from both the president and the Board of Trustees. Masked by their conciliatory tone, the letters critique Dartmouth's current out-of-classroom experience and announce a new policy that, if enacted, would alter the lives of Dartmouth students forever through the elimination of the current Greek system.

Implying that the current residential system doesn't "contribute significantly to each student's intellectual and personal growth and well-being," the Board criticizes the system that has been central to campus life for 158 years. Stating that their goals are incompatible with the current system, the Trustees presented a list of principles that they say will "characterize the [future] residential and social system at Dartmouth."

While few have opposed calls for "greater choice in residential living," "additional and improved social spaces," and a reduction in the number of students living off-campus, the mandates for a "substantially coeducational" environment and the elimination of the "abuse and unsafe use of alcohol" seem to many to be direct assaults on our way of life. While everyone is against the abuse of alcohol, such a vaguely worded and sweeping statement could bring forth many repercussions. In an interview with the *Daily Dartmouth*, President James Wright explained that the Trustees' decision would, in fact, put an end to the Greek system "as we know it." He asserted that a new social system, one "not built on single-sex fraternities and sororities," will be created.

Said Wright, "This is not a referendum. We are committed to doing this." The strength of Wright's words have left many students wondering if their opinions will be ignored. Interestingly, Wright encourages these same disenfranchised students "to participate in the process of identifying specific ways to meet [the Trustees'] objectives."

Although the (as yet) unformalized changes will not be enacted immediately, it seems unlikely that there will be traditional rush next year. Wright suggested that the system may well be dissolved by the time this year's pledges are seniors.

Although Wright has stated that the Trustees are "prepared to invest money to meet [their] aspirations," it is unclear how this decision will affect the financial standing of the school, which relies heavily on the donations of alumni, many of whom were members of fraternal organizations.

On special weekends such as Homecoming and Winter Carnival, many alumni return to campus to visit their houses, strengthening their continuing bond with the College. Some have threatened to withhold donations in coming years as a protest against the elimination of the system that made Dartmouth a challenging and unique environment during their time here.

In his interview with the *Daily Dartmouth*, President Wright was asked if Dartmouth's four traditionally black fraternities and sororities (Alpha Phi Alpha, Alpha Kappa Alpha, Kappa Alpha Psi, and Delta Sigma Theta) would be included in the new plans to go coed—if, in effect, Wright's new "spirit of inclusion" would extend to houses which are vocally exclusive.

"I think that most of the historically black fraternities and sororities are not residential," Wright told the *Daily Dartmouth*, "so they are not playing the same sort of role in the social life of the community that the residential houses are." In other words, they'll be spared the ax.

Several alumni have raised the question of whether this is part of a long-term ploy for dormitory expansion. Wright has long talked about bringing more students on campus, and about creating an in-house dining system on the Harvard model. That would mean building more dorms.

The only geographically feasible place that the College hasn't yet built on is that land owned by the fraternities—particularly Webster Avenue. This announcement by the Trustees, some alumni have speculated, may be the first step in a long-term strategy to displace the fraternities and build more dorms on their land.

February 3, 1999

Carnival Canceled in Response

By Christian Hummel & M. Ryan Clark

I F PRESIDENT WRIGHT'S announcement was intended to shake things up and create a debate on social and residential options at the College, it certainly worked. Students awoke to headlines in *The New York Times* and the *Boston Globe*: the Greek system as it had existed at Dartmouth was over. Fraternities and sororities would be coed.

Reaction was swift and decisive. In a survey taken by *The Dartmouth Review* on Wednesday afternoon, an overwhelming majority of students opposed the trustees' proposals. Of 373 students surveyed, 331 were against the plan, twenty-two supported it, and twenty were undecided.

Flyers were posted announcing a rally on the Green to be followed by a march to the President's house on Webster Avenue. That rally, however, was canceled when the Coed Fraternity Sororities Council decided to hold a meeting to discuss the situation and plan an organized response. CFSC voted, 24–12, to cancel all Winter Carnival parties. The vote is binding.

Naturally, current members of Greek houses have found themselves in a bit of confusion. Several house presidents were reported to have been getting in touch with their corporations or national representatives seeking advice and help in this crisis.

Locally, members expressed their displeasure in several ways. A few fraternities and sororities played Bob Marley's "Get Up/Stand Up (For Your Rights)" over outdoor loudspeakers. Brothers at Psi Upsilon constructed and hung a banner that read, "JUDAS, BRUTUS, ARNOLD, WRIGHT" from the side of their house, facing Collis and Thayer Hall. An American flag flew upside-down.

On Wednesday night, over a thousand protestors gathered on the lawn of President Wright's official Webster Avenue residence, sang the Alma Mater, and left peaceably.

"I think the protest tonight showed how united the campus is on this issue, and how seriously Dartmouth students take the Greek system," said one sorority sister who participated in the protest.

Though CFSC had already canceled the Greek system's participation in Carnival (leaving it little more than a ski race and a poorly realized snow sculpture of a barely recognizable dog on the Green), President Wright spoke at the official inauguration of the Winter Carnival weekend on Thursday evening. Protestors, many of them wearing their Greek letter shirts, chanted pro-fraternity and sorority slogans and cheered, threatening to drown out Wright.

Reactions from individual members were predictably blunt.

"I have my rifle ready," one fraternity brother said.

"I want my money back. All $120,000. I didn't pay to go to a school with a particular reputation and then have it change and have to justify it for the rest of my life," said a senior member of another house. "We will never sell this house back to the College."

Chi Gamma Epsilon President Yale Dieckmann said, "The Greek system is and long has been an integral part of the Dartmouth experience, and that is what attracts many applicants from all over the country and the world. Should they take it away, the identity of the students who attend the College and that of the College itself will be irrevocably sacrificed."

The ambiguity of the announcement has prompted speculation. An optimistic few hope that little change will occur; others are concerned that Greek houses will be completely banned within the next few years.

One sophomore was "pissed that the students had no input, that it was just sprung on everyone."

Many were confused as to what the proposal is supposed to accomplish.

Roham Rafat '01 said, "If it's [the proposal] to increase on-campus housing, it won't. It's not like we would be able to fit any more people into the house if it were made co-ed or if it were abolished. If it's to curb drinking, it will do the exact opposite.

"Abolishing the Greek system will not stop drinking; people will instead drink in smaller groups, to a greater extent, and sometimes even get into their cars to go somewhere instead of just walking to the next frat or back home.

"At a frat, there will always be a few sober people who can take care of a drunk person, whereas on a small, underground level, there is less likelihood that this will happen."

Comparisons have been made to other schools which have threatened or banned fraternities within recent decades. For example, Amherst College used to have a vibrant Greek life until the system was eliminated in the early 1980s.

Whether the College will be able to force the Greek houses off-campus is unclear. Bills have been introduced in both Congress and in the New Hampshire State Legislature which could have an impact on the ability of the College to limit or restrict a student's right to live on- or off-campus.

The tactic used by the administration in the case of Beta fraternity in 1997 was to de-recognize the organization's ability to allow members to live in its house. The fraternity was destroyed, although the fraternity still owns the building, now inhabited by Alpha Xi Delta sorority.

Some fraternities and sororities are already owned by the College and face the most immediate threat. Chi Heorot and Alpha Chi Alpha are both College owned as are all the sororities with the exception of Alpha Xi Delta. In the case of Amherst College, the houses owned by Greek organizations were purchased by the College and transformed into residential houses. That seems to be what Wright has in mind.

Many alumni are expected to be in Hanover this weekend during the Winter Carnival festivities. Some houses are already planning meetings with the alumni to discuss what the future may hold. Alumni response has been as strident as student response.

Todd Zywicki '88, a Professor at George Mason University Law School, wrote an open letter to the Board of Trustees.

"I would say that the Trustees don't understand the role of fraternities as an intermediary institution in the educational life of Dartmouth, as Tocqueville would have recognized," wrote Zywicki.

"I would say that the Trustees fail to appreciate the role of fraternities in providing the 'little platoons' that link atomized students to the history and legacy of Dartmouth's greatness, as Burke would have recognized.

"I would remind the Trustees that members of the Greek system provide the backbone of Dartmouth's spirit and traditions."

Parents, too, have noted their displeasure with the decision.

John Leo, parent of an '02, said "I certainly think it's a waste of money as well as intrusive social engineering and the feminization of male life. . . . Soviet Russia would have loved it: control everything and push people around after you and your elite clique have decided what's best for them."

Dartmouth, dependent upon the giving of the alumni and parents for its endowment, might be forced to accept some compromise on the issue.

Local businesses have also weighed in to support the Greek system. Hanover restaurant Everything But Anchovies has announced that it will contribute 5 percent of all this weekend's receipts to the Greek system.

The next few months could represent the end of the Greek system as it has been experienced by generations of Dartmouth students. Whether Wright's proposed move runs counter to the notions of tradition held so dear by so many in the Dartmouth community remains to be seen.

February 3, 1999

A History of Lies
by the Editors

DARTMOUTH'S PROPAGANDA MACHINE wants you to think that there are no concrete plans for a "new social system," that "nothing has been decided," and that any changes will be "up to the students." This, of course, is not the case.

The set of recommendations that constitute the Trustees' plan to end Dartmouth's Greek system "as we know it" is the culmination of a two-decade long anti-Greek initiative. To pretend that this sort of initiative does not know where it is going, and will need to rely on student direction (as the Trustees claim) is a ridiculous assumption.

In 1987, President Freedman formed an ad hoc College Committee on Residential Life at the College—chaired by James Wright. The Wright Report (as the committee's findings quickly became known) was strikingly similar to the precepts outlined by the Trustees last week. The Wright Report called for the long-term conversion of fraternities and sororities into College-owned residential halls: In their place, Wright's committee proposed the creation of coeducational residential clusters, with substantial programming budgets and "common academic interests"—along the model of the East Wheelock cluster. (The purpose was to increase the intellectual and social interaction of Dartmouth's students.) The Wright report ignores the fact that more than twenty such groups, residential units built around common interests, already exist at Dartmouth—they are called fraternities and sororities.

Wright's committee, of course, wasn't really concerned with the intellectual progress of Dartmouth's student body; if it was, it would recognize the positive role Greek houses can play. What it was explicitly concerned with was the elimination of Dartmouth's reputation as a drinking school.

Both that report and the current plan ignore an important and fundamental reality: national statistics consistently confirm that binge drinking and deaths from drinking are equally likely to occur at schools that have fraternities as at those that do not have fraternities. Even the administration admits as much.

The Wright Report also recommended that rush be delayed so that students could not join Greek houses until their sophomore spring, and that fraternities be closed during sophomore summer. There is no cohesive rationale behind these proposals; their sole aim was further to disable the Greek system.

The Wright Report was followed by a 1994 report from the College Committee on Diversity and Community, which further condemned the fraternity system as encouraging "anti-intellectualism, sexism, racism, and homophobia"—the standard charges the College uses to attack any group it opposes, most notably *The Dartmouth Review*.

The Trustees have convinced themselves that there is a fantastically simple dynamic at work here: an intellectual campus and a social campus are two irreconcilable concepts. An intellectual campus is responsible for academic esteem, serious thinking, diversity, and good things like that. A social campus mainly promotes drinking and intolerance and death. The Trustees, then, taking their advice from parochial academics like James Freedman and James Wright, have resolved to destroy the Greek system.

Unfortunately for President Wright, things simply aren't that simple.

Since President Freedman took office, the average SAT score and class rank of Dartmouth's entering freshman class has increased markedly. Karl Furstenberg, the current Dean of Admissions, was hired with the explicit charge to admit more "intellectual" students—students who wouldn't join fraternities. Despite all of this, and the implementation of sophomore rush, membership in fraternities and sororities has also increased substantially in the same time frame—and fraternity and sorority members do better in school than their non-Greek counterparts. It seems that intellectualism and the Greek system are not antagonistic; they are complementary.

What the Trustees are hoping is that the flurry of media attention surrounding the recent hazing-related deaths at MIT and at Louisiana State University and the health community's myths about binge drinking will help nudge Dartmouth's alumni into agreement. They hope to convince the alumni that fraternities today are an entirely different animal than they have been in the past: dangerous, anti-intellectual, bestial, and abusive places where nothing happens but hazing and unhealthy drinking.

Protests like the literate and intelligent rally staged at Psi Upsilon over Winter Carnival, then, are useful, because they make an important point. They show alumni that the Greek system is highly popular, that its members are smart and thoughtful, and, most importantly, that Dartmouth's fraternities and sororities will not go down without a fight.

Hundreds of alumni have already pledged not to contribute to the College so long as it continues to try to dismantle the Greek system. Many more have already withdrawn their contributions.

The administration's twenty-year effort to dismantle the Greek system shows that President Wright and his cronies are in it for the long haul. The powerful response the student body has offered gives evidence that the system will not go quietly. The final decision, though, will be made by the alumni, who will say with their wallets whether or not they feel passionately about traditional Dartmouth. Let us hope that they do.

February 17, 1999

ON THE RIGHT
Dartmouth's Fraternity Row
by William F. Buckley Jr.

D ARTMOUTH COLLEGE has for a dozen years attracted national attention not alone for its fine academic work and the achievements of its graduates but because it is a groundhog of sorts, a kind of P.C. super-vane, which tends to advise us seasons ahead of anybody else what it is we're to do in order to be upright.

Most conspicuous, at the beginning, was Dartmouth's idea that it was unconscionable to continue to use an American Indian as its mascot. That argument went on and on for years and still simmers, but for all intents and purposes the Indian is gone. There followed a long series of offenses, synthetic offenses, neo-synthetic offenses against race, color, creed, and sex; out of which rose a student weekly, *The Dartmouth Review*, remarkable in America for signalling the desire of a body of students to voice a conservative position in the clamor of liberal trendiness.

With the election of a new president, there were those who thought that the ideological offensive had ended, or at least slowed down. But last week Dartmouth announced that from now on single-sex fraternities would cease to exist. An announcement that categorical in character caught the attention of what in academic terminology they call the "Greeks."

One learns from the ongoing commotion that notwithstanding the tidal wave of coeducation, all-male fraternities continue gradually to expand. At Dartmouth one-half of the upperclassmen are members and there are all-female sororities which, too, are to end. In substitution for what? The usual things, expressed in the usual vacuities ("improved social spaces").

The single concretely phrased objective is to eliminate "the abuse and unsafe use of alcohol."

In a longer statement, the president of Dartmouth announced that it was not his "fantasy" to make Dartmouth dry. You might as well fantasize making it empty. Both would happen at the same time.

The social routine at Dartmouth (we learn) is that the fraternities are always open, sponsoring two or three special parties per month.

Everyone who wants to come in, does so—with the single exception of first-semester freshmen, fresh ladies, fresh braves, you take it from here.

After that, they come in and if they desire to drink some beer, they go to the cellar of the building (there are about twenty) where the springs of malt run headily.

Enter the term "binge drinking." It has only recently become a household term, and means drinking too much. But pollsters require definitions. Accordingly, it crystallized that a binge drunk was a man who had consumed five drinks at a single occasion or a woman who had consumed four. It was not, in the study, specified that these drinks should have been imbibed within a time of one hour or five hours.

Many Dartmouth students, male and female, emerge from fraternities as binge drunks though their coordination is such as to permit them to walk over a tightrope while conjugating irregular Latin verbs.

Which does not mean that there aren't just plain drunks coming out of fraternities at Hanover, but does raise the question, can you remove the drunks by removing the fraternities?

Manifestly, the answer is no. At Dartmouth a student caught wobbly on campus at night is given draconian treatment, much more severe than if picked up by local police. It can include a five-hundred-dollar fine and commitment to spend time at alcoholic abuse centers.

There was considerable student protest when the ukase was announced. It is an interesting stylistic touch that it was given without embellishment: This is not a call to a plebiscite on the question, the president announced. There is a tradition for this in academic idiom. The president of Yale, seventy-five years ago, miffed that the student body had overextended the pew-holiday associated with the Junior Ball, announced after prayers at the morning assembly: "As for the Ball, there will be no Ball."

The settled thought of alert Dartmouth-watchers is that what we have here is not really a serious attempt to alleviate the pangs of lonely fresh-women, nor to hit back hard at demon rum. It seems one further venture in the ideologization of life. Don't countenance situations where men and women are formally separated. We won with the coed bathrooms, now let's go for the fraternities. And the whole thing on the binge-drinkers— blame it on them.

Dangerous stuff, because by such reasoning one might end by blaming binge-drinking on Dartmouth.

February 16, 1999; printed in The Dartmouth Review *February 17, 1999*

A House of One's Own
by Catherine Muscat

M OST OF THE PRESS about Dartmouth's Greek crisis has focused almost exclusively on fraternities and their soundbite-friendly *Animal House* antics. Unfortunately, the fate of almost half the Greeks— the sororities—has been ignored. In the name of "improving gender rela-tions," sororities have been caught in the crossfire of the administration's long-standing animosity towards fraternities, inflicting potentially ir-revocable damage to women's progress at Dartmouth.

Sororities burst onto the Dartmouth campus as soon as the College went coed in 1971, and today there are six of them, some boasting mem-berships exceeding 120 women. Although the newest sorority, Alpha Xi Delta, has helped ease the crowding a bit, it too has quickly built a large membership. The Greek system has come a long way since coeducation caused fraternities to sing boorish songs about the new "cohogs."

Indeed, this year Jaimie Paul '00 was elected president of the Coed Fraternity Sorority Council, becoming the first woman to head the or-ganization in its thirty-year history. "I have a serious problem with the idea that you can force coeducation in order to 'civilize the men,'" Paul told the *Review* in a recent interview. "It disturbs me that I am the first woman to head the CFSC in its history," she added, highlighting the disparity between the number of men and women who pursue and attain leadership positions at the College. According to Paul, some of the most compelling arguments for keeping sororities single-sex are the "incredible opportunities" afforded to women who may not otherwise have a chance to become campus leaders.

Caroline Fayard '00, president of Delta Delta Delta, also defended the integral role of sororities at the College.

In response to trustee Kate Stith-Cabranes's assertion that women do not need sororities to secure campus leadership, Fayard told the *Review* that, "saying women do not need sororities to attain leadership positions at Dartmouth misses the point . . . women don't need an Ivy education to succeed in life, either, but does that mean we should get rid of elitist, expensive Northeastern schools?"

Fayard also cited the existence of single-sex schools like Wellesley and Bryn Mawr as a valid examples of single-sex environments that prepare women for the real world. "Obviously their educational and leadership opportunities must somehow be inferior to ours because they aren't 'substantially coeducational,'" said Fayard dryly. While Stith-Cabranes dismisses the leadership opportunities offered by sororities as a crutch that fails to prepare women adequately for the "real world," the fact remains that Dartmouth and Hanover, New Hampshire are about as close to the real world as a Norman Rockwell painting.

Lisa Bradford, chairwoman of the National Panhellenic Conference, denounced the annulment of single-sex sororities in an angry statement to the Associated Press soon after news of the Trustees' announcement broke. According to Bradford, "improving the education and social lives of female undergraduates should be Dartmouth's constant guiding star . . . eliminating single-sex fraternities will do little if anything by itself—either to end alcohol abuse and its consequences or to prepare young people for their future careers."

The local Panhellenic Conference is currently drafting a proposal to the task force on the trustees' initiatives to highlight the ways that the sorority system currently fits into the controversial five principles. "When the initiatives say that 'student life should . . . engender a strong sense of involvement in and responsibility to our very special community of learning,' my reply is 'welcome to Tri-Delt,'" said Fayard. Sororities provide a large portion of anti-sexual abuse and assault programming through Sexual Awareness through Greek Education (SAGE).

Despite the sororities' compelling arguments for remaining single-sex, they have resisted the temptation to distance themselves from their male counterparts. If the Dartmouth administration had hoped to secure a virtual plea-bargain with the sororities, it was grossly mistaken. All of the CFSC houses, both coed and single-sex, are unified in their opposition to the trustees' initiative.

If anything, the trustees have only managed to strengthen the bond between brothers and sisters in the Greek system. Rather than dissolving into a melee of bickering and infighting, the Greeks have unanimously passed new resolutions with the goal of improving non-alcoholic programming within the Greek system. The CFSC now requires that two houses offer nonalcoholic social options on a rotating basis every week. Epsilon Kappa Theta's recent water pong tournament—the proceeds of which benefited the winner's favorite charity—was very popular, and was a good example of the non-alcoholic programming that should proliferate in the future.

Debate over the current controversy painfully highlights how the plight of the sororities is virtually ignored. By eliminating single-sex sororities, Dartmouth is essentially reneging on its promise to provide a safe social space for all women—a covenant into which the College willingly entered when it agreed to admit them.

April 7, 1999

Hula No More: Lu'au Called Racist
by Steven Menashi

A LPHA CHI ALPHA Fraternity and Delta Delta Delta Sorority are racist and ignorant, some students are saying, because of a social event they planned for last weekend.

"It has come to our attention that Alpha Chi Alpha Fraternity is having a Lu'au party where people are encouraged to dress up like Hawaiians," wrote Omar Rashid '00, president of Lambda Upsilon Lambda, Dartmouth's Hispanic fraternity, in a message to the Coed Fraternity Sorority Council. "Perhaps the rest of the members of the CFSC will tolerate bigotry, however, we Los Hermanos Imprecendibles [sic] de La Unidad Latina, Lambda Upsilon Lambda Fraternity Incorporated will not be a part of any organization that does not reprimand its members who engage in RACISM."

Rashid informed the CFSC that, if the council did not penalize Alpha Chi Alpha for "this vile act of incivility," LUL would renounce its membership in the CFSC. Aaron Akamu, President of Hokupa'a, the Hawaii Club at Dartmouth, also sent an e-mail message to the CFSC. "As a native Hawaiian," he wrote, "I am deeply offended and hurt when I heard of the party that is being planned for Friday Night." He urged "all of your organizations to take action on this issue."

The Lu'au event that was to be held Friday was neither registered with the College nor publicized on campus. Rashid and Akamu learned of the party through an e-mail message that Kimberly Lenox '01, Social Chair of Delta Delta Delta, sent to members of her sorority. "[T]omorrow night sounds like a lot of fun," she wrote. "[W]e are having a luau at alpha chi."

She asked party attendees to dress up "hawaiian style" and promised "authentic hawaiian music." The message included plans for activities and drinks—"we're thinking vodka in watermelons and pineapples and stuff"—and a request that members invite several guests.

The complaints from Rashid and Akamu were sent to the CFSC at 11:28 p.m. and 11:48 p.m., respectively. At 5:02 a.m., an e-mail message was sent to the campus from Eric Kelley, Summer President of Alpha Chi Alpha, and Alexandra Sophocles, Summer President of Delta Delta Delta.

"Recently the members of AXA and DDD planned a joint social event incorporating Lu'au as a theme," they wrote. "It has come to our attention that this theme has offended members of the Dartmouth community. On behalf of AXA and DDD, we would like to apologize for any disrespect and harm our actions caused." With "hope that change will take place," the two Greek societies and Hokupa'a "will host a forum about the misuse of culture and ethnicity on campus."

The apology was swift and surprised many students, who believed that the Lu'au was not racist or offensive.

"I am a native German," said Philipp Saumweber '01, Summer President of Alpha Delta Fraternity. "Since coming to Dartmouth, I have attended several events that have mimicked German cultural customs, such as the German Night at Westside [Buffet] or the Oktoberfest party at Sig Ep. These events were extremely fun. I felt that people were actually making an effort to try and show others the fun aspects of German culture. I was in no way offended. I believe that the people here at Dartmouth that are complaining about intolerance should be a bit more tolerant themselves and try out new experiences."

"The Lu'au was not offensive," said Matthew Wilkens '01. "It cannot be defined as offensive because it does not make fun of, put down, [or] belittle any part of the Hawaiian culture." LUL's "call for disciplinary action is incredible. Being offensive is not illegal and if the College shelters its students like this, we are going to have a rude awakening in the real world.

"AXA and DDD had no right to apologize. I have talked with members from both houses and none of them actually are sorry for organizing this party—and right they are. No wrong was done that they could be sorry for." In fact, the apology by Kelley and Sophocles appears to have been motivated by fear of demonization or punishment rather than by genuine remorse. "Unfortunately, on this campus, when accused, it seems you have to roll over—otherwise, you're implicated even more," said Kelley, explaining his apology.

Many students perceive an oppressive environment on campus, where non-minority students must avoid any mention of ethnic or cultural issues, and especially expression of unpopular opinions, lest they be condemned as racists. Indeed, since her e-mail message was made public, Lenox has received several hostile messages accusing her of bigotry.

"I have read the supposedly offensive e-mail that was sent out," said John Phinney '00, former Vice-President of the Class of 2000. "The most ethnically charged phrase that I saw was 'Hawaiian style.' This is supposed to be offensive?"

Still, students and student organizations apologize almost reflexively for speech and expressive conduct deemed offensive to minority groups— regardless of the merit of the charges.

Last November, when some students objected to a party with a "ghetto" theme, Andrew Cohen and Jill Carey, presidents of Chi Gamma Epsilon Fraternity and Alpha Xi Delta Sorority, published a public apology on behalf of their organizations: "We realize why the theme is offensive and find the campus reaction justified." They sponsored a community forum "to address this and other recent issues of insensitivity on campus."

Writing in the *Daily Dartmouth* January 11, Rashid condemned Sigma Phi Epsilon for sponsoring a party with a "Miami, Will Smith theme," in which participants were encouraged to dress up "like Cubans." Rashid, a member of Dartmouth's Committee on Civil Discourse, wrote that "bigots in our community have conspired to commit yet another hate crime in order to discourage potential Hispanic students from applying to our great institution and to intimidate Hispanic students already attending" the College.

As if by formula, Sig Ep officers published a letter, stating that "diversity and understanding are cornerstones of any successful community," and explaining that their comments had been taken out of context.

AXA and Tri-Delt's apology followed a familiar formula: apologize, then host a community forum—never mind the merit of the accusation.

"Let's not argue about whether Hawaiians should be raising hell about this," wrote the CFSC President in a message to Greek presidents. "The fact of the matter is they are upset at what almost happened, and we have to deal with it."

Early Friday morning, CFSC Secretary Eric Etu '01 sent a message to the Greek presidents instructing them not to make any public comments about the Lu'au controversy, and especially not to respond to a series of questions from *The Dartmouth Review*. That afternoon, Etu sent another message, which included a response to the *Review*'s questions that Etu had written and Adofo-Mensah approved. "If you would like to respond [to the Review]," Etu wrote, "we encourage you to use this as it captures the ideals of the CFSC (and hopefully of your house as well)."

But, "if you want to use it," Etu cautioned, "leave mine and JoJo's

names off of it, AND leave the CFSC out of it. The CFSC, as an organization, will not be making a public statement."

Etu's response affirmed students' charges of racism and took a strong
stand against Alpha Chi Alpha and Tri-Delta: "A Lu'au is a religious
ceremony, and the fact that organizations wished to use it as the theme of
an alcoholic party is unacceptable. If this party were to happen, it would
have made a mockery of both Hawaiian religion and history." Etu said that
the call for disciplinary action against Alpha Chi Alpha "was completely
appropriate and action will be taken." Alpha Chi Alpha and Tri-Delta "did
not act in accordance with [Dartmouth's Principle of Community], and
therefore there is no question that they must and will be punished."

In addition to the punishment to be meted out by the CFSC, Etu wel-
comed further sanction by the College administration against Alpha Chi
Alpha and Tri-Delta: "We expect that Dean Redman and Dean Larimore
will also issue comments and may wish to heighten the punishment issued
by the CFSC, and we support this possible intervention by the College."

Etu's comments ostensibly represented "the ideals of the CFSC." Yet,
the response was extreme and failed to evaluate the initial claim that holding a Lu'au is a racist act. Many Greek presidents voiced dissatisfaction
with Etu's position.

The CFSC, however, adopted the position not out of actual offense that
the Lu'au party was planned, but out of cowardice in the face of charges
of bigotry and a potential public relations disaster. Etu's statement wasn't
what the CFSC believed, but what Etu thought the College wanted to hear.

In fact, after a meeting with Dean of the College James Larimore and
Dean of Residential Life Martin Redman, at which it was established that the
College did not find the Lu'au objectionable, the CFSC dropped its contention that any wrong had been done. The CFSC canceled its emergency
meeting, which had been scheduled for Sunday night. Instead, the Council
released a statement—the first public comment by the CFSC about the Lu'au:

> The Coed Fraternity Sorority Council deeply regrets this unfortunate inci-
> dent. However, we believe that the way in which it was resolved demon-
> strates the type of relationship that needs to be formed among the CFSC sys-
> tem and other students and student groups.

The CFSC, apparently, applauds Alpha Chi Alpha for canceling the Lu'au
and for apologizing to the Dartmouth community. The Council, however,
expressed no opinion on the Lu'au itself, except to say that it hopes to
"prevent incidents such as this from arising in the first place." The CFSC
no longer plans to penalize Alpha Chi Alpha.

The Council's statement, however, fails to address what many students
see as the real issue.

Students at Dartmouth "can never really be sure anymore if their actions will fall within the range of the continually expanding range of offensiveness," said Phinney. "It would seem that the answer now is simply to never act in a way that could be construed as even the tiniest bit outside the range of 'your culture.'"

On campus, many find an environment of fear and intimidation, where students are afraid to express an opinion, or sponsor an event, that addresses issues of cultural diversity, race relations, or minority politics—especially when their opinion is an unpopular one. That perception was reinforced by the CFSC this weekend, when the Council instinctively supported the protesters, and failed to defend Alpha Chi Alpha.

April 7, 1999

The Real Racism

by Dave Pan

ONE OF THE FIRST friends I made at Dartmouth was "John." We had been on the same DOC trip section and soon became good friends. Both of us were Asian, but he had grown up in California, where most of his good friends were Asian as well. I had gone to school in suburban New Jersey where most of my friends were white. It was in a conversation during Freshman Orientation that I learned how different we really were.

"Dave, man, I hate it here at Dartmouth. I wish I was going to Stanford or UCLA or something. There are no Asian people here. White people are okay, but I just don't want to talk with them, you know?"

I was shocked. "Well, it really doesn't bother me all that much."

"Yeah, but you went to prep school in Jersey. You didn't have any Asians in your school anyhow," pointed out John.

"That's true, but I didn't spend that much time with the kids in the Asian community at home. We definitely had AP there." (For those not familiar with Asian separatist vernacular, AP stands for Asian Power or Asian Posse. KP refers to Korean Power or Korean Posse.)

"Why didn't you?"

"Well, the kids that were big on AP wanted everyone to be all or nothing. If you were Asian, you couldn't occasionally hang out with Asians and spend the rest of your time with white people. You had to spend all of it with Asians. It's as if you're a member of a club that dictates who your friends are."

"Yeah, but that's not so bad. At least you would've been friends with Asians. It's not like we should talk to other people all that much. You were making connections with your own people, which is what you should be doing—I can't believe you weren't big into AP."

I was stunned. "Did you hang out with anyone except for other Asian people in high school?"

"No. Things don't work like that back in L.A. You have the twinkies, or sellouts, and you have pure Asian. Pure Asian believes in AP4: Asian Power, Asian Posse, Asian Property, and Asian P***y. You're lucky you aren't from L.A. You probably wouldn't get along with people there if you didn't hang out with Asians."

"Wait . . . what are twinkies?"

"You know, man. yellow on the outside, white on the inside. Just like you." He laughed.

Before I arrived in Hanover, I envisioned a blue-blazered sea of Anglo-Saxon prep-school boys. Even though I had spent high school at a largely white prep-school, my experiences there had done little to mitigate my fears.

After my first year here, I've learned that it's not Dartmouth's white population that's racist or exclusionary, but rather it's the organized minority groups themselves. At the beginning of this year, I was given a Big Brother by the Dartmouth Asian Organization (DAO) to help me get settled, was put on the Asian Christian Fellowship (ACF) mailing list, and invited to numerous exclusively Asian functions. In the abstract, these seem to be ideal ways to help freshman adjust to a new school. In reality, however, such practices have quite a different effect.

I met with my Big Brother once. I quickly got to know my tripmates and hallmates, so I ignored DAO, the ACF, and all the other Asian organizations that had tried to enlist me. I didn't want to associate myself with any group yet—I wanted to make friends on my own terms. The last thing I wanted was to be force-fed friends because they had similar skin pigment.

I soon discovered that I had effectively blacklisted myself from Dartmouth's Asian community by ignoring these groups. One evening, I decided to stop by a predominantly Asian fraternity on campus to visit a friend there. Arriving at the door, I was greeted by a drunken brother.

"What's your name?" he asked.

"Dave Pan. I'm supposed to meet someone here."

"Oh, you're Dave Pan. Sorry dude, we don't allow sellouts in the house."

"What do you mean, sellout? I just want to talk to my friend for a few seconds."

"You're Asian. You're supposed to hang out with Asians. From what I understand, you don't like Asians. You embarrassed of your race? Look, you're either with us or against us, and it seems that you're not with us."

Distraught, confused, and upset by my rejection, I walked away to the slurs of "whitebread" and "sellout." I wandered home in a daze, my mind full of questions.

What does it mean to me to be Asian? I was born in Taiwan, keep in good contact with my relatives back there, and visit every few years. I am fluent in Mandarin, possess a thorough knowledge of Chinese history, observe my ancestors' traditions, celebrate Chinese holidays, and love my heritage. But am I somehow relegated to being a "twinkie" because I'm not an Asian groupie?

You aren't an Asian because you hang out with other Asians. Such illogical, superficial segregation has split the United States, and indeed Dartmouth as well, into a turbulent sea of minority groups all clamoring for their own vaguely self-defined rights. Earlier this year the *Daily Dartmouth* published a cartoon poking fun at the stereotypical nerdy Asian studynut. DAO and Korean American Student Association (KASA) immediately demanded retribution for the racist attack. Their clamor soon escalated into a call for an Asian-American dean.

I wonder what an Asian-American dean would do. The College already provides an extensive selection of Asian Studies courses and supports DAO and KASA. Are there special Asian academic or social needs that I didn't know about that a special Asian-American dean could provide? DAO and KASA claimed that a full-time dean would lend credibility to being "Asian."

DAO, together with many other minority groups, perpetuates a segregated campus. No longer is there a society of whites that attempts to exclude minorities, but it is the minorities themselves that are divorcing themselves from society. In twenty or thirty years, these will be the same people that complain that people don't accept them. How is society supposed to absorb people that refuse to even associate with anyone outside their own narrowly defined cliques?

To those who say that assimilation into society means abandoning your cultural identity, you've got it all wrong. Assimilation is not conformity. Rather, it is accepting others as the people they are, rather than basing friendships on skin color. No more hyphenated Americans. No deans for individual ethnic groups. No exclusion. No barriers between the races.

May 28, 1997

Dartmouth's Racial Separatism

by Alexander Talcott & Darren Thomas

In April 1999, following widely publicized announcements by President Wright on changes to Dartmouth's "social system," College trustees established a "Committee on the Student Life Initiative," co-chaired by Trustees Susan A. Dentzer '77 and Peter M. Fahey '68; this committee released a document, known as the SLI Report, detailing its aims in January 2000.

I N APRIL 2000, Dean of the College James Larimore distributed a memo to the entire campus detailing changes to be expected in the next phase of the Student Life Initiative. "Now that President Wright and the Board of Trustees have provided a guiding framework for the future of student social and residential life at Dartmouth," he began, "I am writing to share with you some of my initial thoughts on the exciting opportunities before us." Among the changes, Larimore explained that "The advisory positions for African-American students, Latino/Hispanic students, Asian Pacific American students, and Gay, Lesbian, Bisexual and Transgendered students will be expanded from half-time to full-time." Apparently, the advice provided by class deans is inadequate, or culturally indecipherable, for students with minority backgrounds (or alternate sexual orientations). As such, Dartmouth is providing special advisors just for them.

Despite Dartmouth's stated faith in multicultural integration—the College's "Principle of Community" states that diversity provides "an opportunity for learning and moral growth"—the administration continually creates group distinctions among students, and separates them along racial and sexual lines.

According to Michele Hernandez, a former Assistant Director of Admissions at Dartmouth and author of the 1997 book, *A is for Admission: The Insider's Guide to Getting into the Ivy League and Other Top Colleges*, applications from minority students are literally flagged early on. "At Dartmouth," she writes, "minority-student status is designated by blue tags for black students, red tags for Hispanic students, and black tags for Native American students." Admissions officers apply different criteria to these applicants. Hernandez says that officers are willing to trade off test scores for class rank, or vice versa—and will generally "give less weight to test scores and class rank than would be accorded to nonminority applicants"— when weighing a decision about a non-Asian minority candidate. "For white students without tags, modest test scores are not offset by superior class rank." According to 1992 data, the average SAT score of black students at Dartmouth is 218 points below that of whites.

Hernandez notes the cost of hosting minority students for special recruiting weekends—"Dartmouth in a typical year spends in excess of fifty thousand dollars to fly or bus accepted minority students to the campus"—and finds that the real difficulty is that "many of the highly selective colleges end up fighting over a small number of qualified minority students, such that it becomes a Sisyphean task to enroll even a low number of minority students at each individual college."

The College actively recruits minority students through a series of mailings, meetings, and weekends targeted at black, Hispanic, and Native American students. Before his acceptance, Taylor Keitt '04 attended one such weekend. "The trip up was fully paid for, and we were set up with hosts for the three-day stay in Hanover," Keitt recalls. "We were given information packets that detailed campus events, classes, financial aid workshops, and other assorted social goodies across campus. I got assorted mailings detailing perspectives from minority viewpoints, the website for Shabazz House, etc."

Kieron Bryan '04 says that his "personal experiences have reflected that Dartmouth definitely does a lot as far as minority recruitment is concerned." He received mailings as well as invitations to various minority-only events. "I know that I was receiving mailings from Dartmouth during my entire application process starting junior year," says Bryan. "I think the efforts that Dartmouth made at those particular meetings outdid those that other universities made."

Minority students who read the mailings and participate in the weekends are introduced to a number of minority-specific programs. There's the Mellon Minority Academic Careers Fellowship Program, which encourages undergraduate African-American, Native American, and Latino students to pursue academic careers, and is thus designed to increase the number of minority professors in the academic world. The program does not include Asian-Americans, who are already "over-represented" in academe—that is, they exceed their proportion of the population.

Dartmouth also participates in the Doctoral and Dissertation Scholars program, which was inaugurated in 1994 by the New England Board of Higher Education under its Equity and Pluralism Action Program. Dartmouth's math department participates actively in the program, which "aims to increase the number of Black, Hispanic, and Native American graduate students who complete doctorates and become professors." Through the program, NEBHE engages in "community building with students and faculty mentors," brings researchers to meet with the students, and provides "professional development seminars" for minority students. "Different perspectives ought to be brought into academia and we're doing our part," says NEBHE Vice-President JoAnne Moody. She further explains that the program is open to only African-Americans, Hispanics, and Native Americans because those groups are "most underrepresented in academia."

Initiated in 1992, the Ernest Everett Just Program for Students in the Sciences at Dartmouth funds forums, workshops, discussion groups, visiting scientists, and research internships to reverse the under-representation of minorities in science by supporting Ph.D. candidates. Dartmouth also hands out three different fellowships every year: the Thurgood Marshall Dissertation Fellowship for African-American Scholars, the Caesar Chavez Dissertation Fellowship for Latina/o Scholars, and the Charles A. Eastman Dissertation Fellowship for Native American Scholars. The three programs are identical except for the racial identity of those invited to apply. Fellows receive a $25,000 stipend, office space, library privileges, and a $2,500 research assistance fund in order to complete a Ph.D. dissertation.

These programs, and others, along with Dartmouth's minority admissions and recruitment policies, mean to broaden the representation of different cultures within the university community. Yet, while the College maintains that contact with a diverse student body enriches and facilitates the learning experience, Dartmouth also encourages self-segregation among the student body. Aside from special academic programs and advisors, Dartmouth also maintains four "cultural affinity" houses, where students of particular ethnic backgrounds live and interact with their cultural advisor and members of the faculty.

The houses include the El-Hajj Malik El-Shabazz Center, focused on African-American culture; the Native American House; and the Asian Studies Center House. Next term, the College will complete construction of a new Latino Academic Affinity House, located on the former site of Pike House on North Main Street. The house will accommodate about thirteen students and an in-house advisor. Dean Larimore called the house "a wonderful opportunity for integrating, in significant and meaningful ways, [student's] academic, residential and social lives."

It remains unclear, however, whether minority housing strengthens the educational experience. "By treating minority students as surrogates for their communities rather than as individuals, ethnic dorms foster racial group thinking and defeat a university's mission to broaden all students' horizons," argues Michael Meyers, Executive Director of the New York Civil Rights Coalition. Meyers, who became the youngest Assistant Director of the NAACP in 1975, urged the Education Department to examine Cornell University's ethnic dormitories as a violation of the 1964 Civil Rights Act.

The investigation found that students are not required to identify their race on applications to live in the residences, and so they do not constitute racially segregated housing. Still, no one can accurately label the system of ethnic dormitories "integrated." Noting that only one of the 122 residents of Cornell's African-American House was white, Meyers denounced university-sanctioned de facto segregation. "Aside from the university's and the regents' collective failure to correct the pattern of racial segregation, they have ratified this segregation with the double-talk of 'freedom of choice,'" he said. "If Cornell were a Southern university standing behind white students who chose to live in segregated dorms, the feds would demand immediate desegregation."

Dartmouth also ostensibly allows students of different backgrounds to live in the Native American House or in Shabazz Hall (typically, none do), so it's unlikely that Dartmouth will encounter legal difficulties. Yet, if personal interaction is the key to fighting ignorance and reducing racial tension, then Dartmouth maintains a self-destructive policy. With minority students sequestered in separate dormitories, it remains possible for white students to graduate without having substantial contact with minority students, and—especially—vice versa. The ethnic residence halls are part of a larger institutional separatism, which includes special academic support programs for certain minority groups, whole academic departments, and extracurricular programs which range from professional groups such as the Society of Black Engineers to clubs based solely on ethnic and racial affiliations.

Minority students drop out of school at a higher rate than do whites or Asians, and so many race-specific programs are employed to retain minority students and to ameliorate criticisms that affirmative action admits under-qualified applicants. Dartmouth's Native American Program, for example, has succeeded in raising the graduation rate of Native American students at the College to 72 percent—far above the graduation rate of Native Americans nationally, but below the College's overall rate of 94 percent.

While such programs sustain preferential admissions policies, they tend to exacerbate racial tensions on campus. Special programs and awards tend to reinforce stereotypes and promote the belief that it is through the assertion of group power rather than the pursuit of individual achievement that one succeeds, enforcing the perception that, as Shelby Steele has put it, "somehow color, not our hard work, can bring us advancements." As such, the isolation created through separate housing and activities fosters racial consciousness, encouraging students to define themselves not as individuals, but as part of a racial group. Campus debates take the form of group conflict, and students increasingly see themselves as victims of a bigoted society—and college.

A 1993 study by Alexander Astin of the UCLA School of Education found a correlation between an institution's "diversity emphasis" and the perception that the institution suffered from racial conflict. When students are categorized and divided according to race, it's not hard to see what lesson the College is teaching.

February 12, 2001

Revel in Structured Options
by Matthew Tokson

A S MANY OF Dartmouth's prospective and incoming students already know, Dartmouth has been undergoing something known as the Student Life Initiative (or SLI) for the past few years. The initiative is designed to promote new social/residential options and to discourage use of Dartmouth's dominant social option, its fraternity and sorority system. The College has invested a great deal of time and effort towards changing these student lives, towards shaping students' social behaviors into different forms.

Until now, most student attention has understandably been focused on the College's efforts to curtail the current system; the removal of all beer taps and permanent bars, the prohibition of the formation of new fraternities or sororities, the reduction of house income and membership by altering new-member policies, and, most recently, mandatory weekly house inspections by Safety and Security officers. As a member of a fraternity, these SLI measures have certainly had an impact on my social life, as they have on nearly all students, whether "affiliated" or "independent."

But for incoming students, the most relevant part of the SLI will be the social options built to replace the current system. After all, as incoming Dartmouth students, you probably value life outside of the classroom a great deal. A vital social life and the overall quality of student life are two of Dartmouth's biggest selling points, complementing its well-known academic excellence. Indeed, when you were looking at colleges last year, the Princeton Review's popular college guidebook *The Best 331 Colleges* ranked Dartmouth first in the nation in its "quality of life" category. The Class of 2005 will be faced with an unprecedented degree of both social choice and uncertainty, as Dartmouth's fraternity and sorority culture is increasingly hobbled. So let's consider your 150 or so future weekends at Dartmouth and ask ourselves, what now?

Surprisingly, not much. That there have been fewer open fraternity and sorority parties in recent terms doesn't help, but the problem is still broader.

Dartmouth has always had a vibrant weekend culture in and out of its Greek houses. Dorm parties are generally the most popular option for freshmen, at least until the spring when many start to feel more comfortable in Greek houses. Off-campus social life is generally a popular option for College seniors, especially in the last few years as fraternities have been increasingly restricted.

But the College is taking steps to curtail these unregulated options just as it has the Greek system. Off-campus housing especially has been targeted by the administration. President Wright said in a February 1999 interview about the SLI, "I'd love to get back on campus what we think to be around two hundred students who live currently off campus," and recently the College has taken steps to do just that. Several popular houses that once rented to students have been purchased by the College, which also built a luxury housing complex for faculty on what had been privately owned land adjacent to the Kresge Fitness Center. Indeed, the house where my friends and I had planned to live during our senior year was purchased by the College, and we have been forced out by a planned renovation—or demolition, communication hasn't been clear which—to take place in the winter.

The town of Hanover has also begun taking steps to limit off-campus student housing, threatening some owners who rent to students with punishment for violating zoning laws that limit the number of unrelated residents per house. The result is that off-campus housing is increasingly expensive and hard to find (especially considering this year's on-campus housing crunch), and will probably become less of a social option as the College purchases more houses. If a fraternity or sorority tries to operate independently of the College, the College may respond by requiring its members to live in approved housing. Slowly but surely, the College is working to eliminate off-campus housing altogether.

Dorm parties, already a fairly limited option, are also likely to be further restricted. No alcohol is allowed in the common areas of student housing, limiting the party to the confines of a single room or two. This especially affects freshmen, who tend to live in dorms with tiny rooms, like in the Choate and River clusters. Multi-room parties are likely to generate a great deal of attention from the Safety and Security officers who patrol the dorms at night. As upperclassmen generally realize, room parties are seldom worth the expense, the mess, and the risk of College discipline. The College is also considering a recommendation in the SLI report calling for mandatory registration of gatherings of seven people or more; hosts would be required to employ a specially licensed bartender to dispense drinks.

By reducing on- and near-campus options, the College seeks to exercise greater control over Dartmouth students' social life, which is generally perceived as beer- and party-intensive. Thanks in large part to the popular movie *Animal House*, Dartmouth's party scene, especially its fraternity scene, often gets more attention than its excellent academics, to the perpetual chagrin of professors and administrators. President Wright has justified the SLI by arguing that "part of education is to provide an appropriate environment."

If Dartmouth's students are to behave more appropriately, to imbibe less alcohol and spend their free time more productively, they need other options. Some students spend their weekends hiking, biking, or mountain climbing, often under the oversight of the excellent student-run Dartmouth Outing Club. Others avoid the party scene by spending their weekend evenings watching movies, pursuing hobbies, or just hanging out in their dorms; these would be the once-ballyhooed "creative loners," the former administration's poster students. But under the SLI the current administration has moved beyond promoting solo activities to providing social options for the majority of students looking for a party, or at least to be social, on their Friday and Saturday nights.

The plans for a new student-run social space like the old Webster Hall (now Rauner Library), where students threw unregulated parties, have now been shelved indefinitely. Potential legal liability for alcohol-related injuries (another of the College's reasons for cracking down on Greek houses) would be exponentially greater in a College building, making the realization of such a space far-off at best.

Similarly, plans for new residential halls or social spaces have been forgotten or delayed by funding and space problems. Dartmouth is extremely unlikely to construct any significant new social spaces in the foreseeable future; it struggles now just to house its students. Providing students with dance floors, cafes, and lounges has become a secondary concern.

What Dartmouth does plan to provide for incoming classes is a great deal of what it calls social programming. The salaries of Undergraduate Advisors (UGAs) have been tripled, and the UGA training process has intensified considerably in an effort to generate more dorm-specific programming events. The "First Year" orientation program has been greatly expanded to introduce incoming students to new programming social options on campus. And, most directly, funding for the Office of Student Life, the Programming Board, and the "Bigger, Better, and Later" social programming initiative has been increased and a permanent head for the latter hired. Dartmouth is planning even more support for its programming initiatives and for Collis Student Center this year.

Unfortunately, perhaps inevitably, Dartmouth's programmed events have fared as well as one would expect a "programmed" social event to fare. As one of Collis's student managers, I've seen a tremendous increase in programed events over the past year and a tremendous drop in student satisfaction. Collis is generally used for non-social campus events (like meetings and lectures in the Commonground room), for studying, for playing pool, and for snacking at the cafe or the Lone Pine Tavern. Sadly, in the last year Collis removed its billiards room, the most popular social space in the building, and replaced it with Poison Ivy, the Dartmouth version of a dance club, complete with a very expensive lighting system and thumping speakers.

In the year since Poison Ivy's opening, hundreds of events (most straight out of summer camp nightmares) have taken place in the refurbished room. The events were nearly always failures, with attendance below expected levels and, fortunately for me and other Collis staff, piles of free food and other goodies left over at the end of the night. It has become a joke among managers at our weekly meetings to second-guess proposed events to be held in Poison Ivy: "Um, are you sure you want to have it there?" Meanwhile, the pool tables were scattered between a smaller room in Collis and a room in the basement of Food Court, cutting their accessibility considerably, and bass from Poison Ivy regularly disturbs students from studying, eating, talking, or really doing anything at all on the second floor.

Poison Ivy is not Dartmouth's only recent programming failure. Collis's Commonground has hosted a great number of social events over the past year, again promoted by "Bigger, Better, and Later." The events are uniformly amateurish and attendance tends to be dismally low, especially on weekends (with the single exception of Sheba's hip-hop dance concerts).

Yes, there's a pattern here. Social events for Dartmouth students, whether in a basement dungeon or a brochure-friendly "student activities space," tend to be more popular and successful when students themselves conceive, organize, and control them.

Go down this route, though, and a familiar problem presents itself: letting students control their own social lives means that not everything students do will be to Dartmouth's liking. From the outside campus, some student events may appear beer-soaked, offensive, or worse. So the administration steps in, disables student events, and creates its own bland alternative.

Tubestock, the summer's biggest party, really the only school-wide party not recognized by the College, is the perfect example. The mid-day event consists of students and some locals drinking and carousing on inner tubes and student-built rafts that float along the Connecticut River while bands play from the Vermont shore.

The combination of intoxication and water can be dangerous. Some may consider the party—with its floating kegs, rampant nudity, and chaotic atmosphere—loud, obnoxious, and inappropriate. But it is also the kind of party that students love; they flock to it, and many remember Tubestock as the most thrilling, strange, enjoyable party they have attended.

Last year, Dartmouth tried to foist on students a less-rowdy alternative to Tubestock. Summer Carnival offered students free grilled foods, carnival rides, a "foam party" enclosure, and a DJ blasting tunes across the Green. The event was very popular among Hanover's families, especially those with younger children, who mobbed the rides. For college students, though, Summer Carnival just wasn't exciting.

Dartmouth's administration promises to provide yours and future incoming classes with bigger and better social programming events, as they reduce independent social options, in an effort to improve Dartmouth's image and students' social lives. Indications are that their efforts are backfiring. The newest edition of *The Best 331 Colleges*, released just weeks ago, reports that despite much higher per-student funding for programed social activities, Dartmouth's quality of life ranking has fallen from first to fourth.

I'll see you at Poison Ivy to celebrate.

September 17, 2001

The Student Life Initiative has brought significant changes to Dartmouth's Greek system, including a more stringent set of standards governing Greek behavior. Many observers believe these rules have been designed to legislate fraternities out of existence, without banning them outright.

Due to significant alumni pressure, much of it brought to bear through articles in The Dartmouth Review, *the Wright administration has yet to enact fully the policies of SLI.*

Deviance on Tap

Assignment X: The Drag Ball

by Benjamin Wallace-Wells

T HE DARTMOUTH RAINBOW Coalition's "Damsels in Dis-Dress"
drag ball was billed as a lavish, Wigstock-esque gala celebration of
Gay Pride. But the event held the Friday night of Winter Carnival 1997 at
the dark, dank, and dirty Webster Hall was more a fearful, apologetic
statement of resignation to Gay Gloom.

There were no RuPauls at the drag ball, no outlandish, colorfully clad
collossi of cross-dressing acuity. In fact there were very few cross-dressers
at all. The "girls" that did grace the Webster Hall dance-floor were clad in
the sort of drag that purports to raise the fashion sensibility of middle-aged
tract home housewives to an art form. They mainly cowered in the corners, in groups of two or three, and complained about the lighting.

The costumes first. One word: lame. The staple of the drag costume—
the wig—was conspicuous by its complete absence. I thought I caught a
glimpse of a wig at a distance, but it turned out to be only remarkably ratty
hair. The only skirts visible were ankle-length floral patterns usually worn
by overweight women named Irma while slouching around a trailer park.
There were no dresses and the tops were nothing adventurous—the "girls"
generally wore tops that would not have looked out of place on Stormin'
Norman Schwartzkopf.

When I was informed by a superior at the *Review* that I, Benjamin C.
Wallace-Wells, heterosexual, would be the *Review* representative at the
Winter Carnival Drag Ball, he could not mask his glee. I suspected it was
because I was the most junior staffer present. I had two immediate reactions. The first was pure, 100 percent, unadulterated dread. The second,
after a quick consultation with my laundry pile and my ironically symbolic
closet, was that I hadn't a thing to wear!

I expected this drag ball to be an orgy of homosexuality. I pictured
having to strut on a runway, through a wild pigsty of men, dressed mainly
in whips and chains, shrieking "You go, girl!" I expected to see millions of

watts of lighting screaming in my eyes and "YMCA" blaring at unprecedented volume. It was not a pleasant picture. My greatest fear was that all of the homosexuals would immediately identify me as heterosexual, and chase me out of the place. I therefore resolved (despite the fact that all my clothes were made for men) to dress as fully in drag as I could, so that I could attend the gala incognito. I did, however, need to procure women's clothing. When I mentioned my problem to my friend, an enormous smile slowly spread across her face, and she had only one word for me: "Leopardskin!"

As I was pondering the previously inconceivable topic of leopardskin, my friend rushed back out of her room with not one but three leopardskin patterned sleek tops. Though I wondered where people could get such things, I tried on all three. I finally found that the largest one was actually big enough to cover most of my top half, although when I leaned back it had an annoying tendancy to reveal significantly more of my midriff than I would have liked.

Another problem was my chest. Although I do have a bit of flab about my pecs, I have nothing that would really qualify as breasts. I tried stuffing a leopardskin bra with tissue paper, but it simply looked too ridiculous. I would have to attend sans bosom.

By now my little project had begun to attract a budding crowd. Almost all of the girls on my floor were swarming about my room, lipstick and mascara readily at hand, while my roommate shook his head and peered at me with wary disdain. At this point I retained little decision-making control over the state of my own wardrobe. The girls had all decided that I was getting "hooched up." I had never expected the term to be applied to myself, but there wasn't a damned thing I could do about it. In shock, I was seated before a mirror as my friend, the leopardskin aficionado, searched for just the right skirt. She finally picked a short, black one out that had the correct mixture of pizzazz and, well, Lycra, and told me to put it on. I dumbly nodded my assent.

Even now, problems remained—shoes, makeup, and tights. The whole concept of tights was, however, abandoned quickly when I tried a pair on. A cautionary note to all would-be cross-dressers out there: NO ONE with protruding genitalia should attempt tights. They just hurt. A lot.

This seems a good time to give my ruminations on the whole cross-dressing experience. In my now enlightened state as a veteran cross-dresser, I still can't understand the appeal. The whole idea of putting women's clothes on a man seems inherently silly. Not only are women's clothes not made for me, but they're downright painful.

Anyhow, makeup did not constitute much of a problem. The girls were all too eager to paint my face as thickly as possible with the most ghoulish color combinations.

I was having difficulty finding footwear.

There are very few women with a size fifteen foot and none of them were in my dorm. The best we could do was my loafers, complimented by a pair of knee-length white stockings. I was now all ready to go to the ball.

I must admit I cut a fairly garish figure. The top half of me was hussy, the bottom half, Catholic schoolgirl. All this was topped off by a face that would have been cast as the archetypal Hideous Aging Prostitute.

So I made my way to Webster Hall, with naked legs and surrounded by a crowd of girls. Somehow I thought my companions would help to proclaim my heterosexuality. The door was "manned" by a gaggle of girls dressed up as men, with penciled-on mustaches and magicians' top hats. It looked like a third-grader's Halloween party. They let us in, giggling at my inappropriate attire.

The scene inside was nothing like I expected. There were maybe ten people inside, five of whom might have been in drag. I say "might" because the hall was so dark it was nearly impossible to see five feet away. As dim traces of techno music wafted through the hall, the cross-dressers huddled in the corners of the hall, not dancing, but muttering to one another and apparently hoping not to be seen.

I waited around for about an hour, waiting for something to happen. Nothing did, so, with all due fanfare, I slipped out the back with my coterie of female guards at about 11:30. I rushed home, secure in the knowledge that no one had recognized me.

Or so I thought. On Saturday night, I was at a Sigma Nu fraternity party, safely out of drag. Suddenly, I was approached by a man whom I vaguely recognized as one of the cross-dressers huddled in the corner the night before. He sauntered up to me, pinched my nipple, and asked my name.

Shocked, I explained to him that I was not only very heterosexual but a writer for the *Review*, and therefore an arch-heterosexual. He smiled, apologized for his mistake, and sauntered off.

Apparently, not all stereotypes of gays are wrong.

February 26, 1997

Have All the Sex You Want
by the Editors

A STUDENT went to Dick's House and met with Physician Assistant Anne Michaels. The student reported that she had not been taking her birth control pills regularly, but that she had been in a fight with her boyfriend and wasn't having sex, anyway. The night before, however, they reconciled—and had unprotected sex. She is concerned that she might be pregnant, the student told Michaels. The student did not ask for the morning-after pill; she just sought advice. After relating her problem, the conversation proceeded as follows.

ANNE MICHAELS: Let's look at this calendar. Tell me—here's today's date—when was the first day of your last period?

STUDENT: Umm. I think it was Wednesday, the 22nd.

AM: And you had a normal period?

STUDENT: Yes.

AM: And since you started your new pack of pills, how many days have you skipped them altogether? Have you taken them late?

STUDENT: No. I missed the last two days, and before that, I took a pill but I missed the day before that also.

AM: Since your last period, this is the only time you've had sex?

STUDENT: Yes.

AM: This is the only time you've had sex without any other protection?

STUDENT: Yes.

AM: And what were you guys using before your last period in addition to the pill, condoms?

STUDENT: Yes.

AM: One of the things we can do—I can feel how nervous you are. One of the options that we have is, if you had sex last night without a condom and you missed your pill, we can give you what's called the morning-after pill or emergency contraception, called Plan B. And what that does is that it's a hormone to try to stop you from ovulating. Okay?

So if, you know, if you were to ovulate while this medication is used, it can be used up to seventy-two hours after you had sex without protection or a condom breaks or anything like that. This hopefully will prevent you from ovulating. It's not an abortion pill; it's not going, you know, it's not going to get rid of a pregnancy. It's going to hopefully prevent you from—it makes everything kind of a hostile environment. That's what I recommend we do.

STUDENT: So, I don't understand. It's not an abortion?

AM: Yes. If you have a pregnancy there, it doesn't get rid of the pregnancy. It just stops you from ovulating, so that you don't have any eggs there, so that the sperm and the egg don't get together, if that makes sense. But it's not, you know—let's say, if you were pregnant now, it's not going to terminate a pregnancy, if that makes sense. But hopefully, because this happened last night, we're going to prevent you from getting pregnant. Does that make sense?

STUDENT: Yes.

AM: I would say that's what we need to do. Doing a urine test right now on you is not going to show us anything. But this is what I recommend: that you do Plan B now. Restart your pills—you know, start your pills again. You need to use condoms or abstain—no sex until your next period. If anything is different in your next period, you have to come back.

STUDENT: Okay.

AM: I'll go get it. We have it right here. But I want you—you need to read this—we can talk about it when I get back. You can have a seat right here. You will have to initial it, we'll go over it when I come back.

[Michaels gave the student a form entitled "Informed Consent for Emergency Contraception."]

AM: I'm going to have to give you a prescription. The pharmacy is closed but I'm going to give it to you now so you can take it today.

STUDENT: Okay. Great.

[Michaels read the form aloud and both signed at the bottom.]

AM: Any questions?

STUDENT: No.

AM: Listen, you're doing everything right. I totally understand why you're concerned. And my goal is that you get out of college and not have to worry about, you know. I want you guys to have all the sex you want.

The prescription is going to cost four dollars. You can come back and pay for it tomorrow so it doesn't go on your student account, but all it says is "pharmacy charge," anyway.

What time do you get up in the morning?

STUDENT: 8:30.

AM: Okay. This is how this goes: you take one now, and you take one twelve hours from now—you'll have to set your alarm clock for about 5:00.

And remember, don't have sex, or have sex with a condom and keep taking your pills, don't stop your pills, keep taking them and then come back and see us if you don't get a normal period. Even at anything the least bit strange, come back. All right? You feeling a little better? If you have any questions you can e-mail me. I have a little cup of water here if you'd like to take the first pill here so you don't forget.

STUDENT: I'd rather take it at home because I like to take any medications with food so that it won't upset my stomach.

January 15, 2001

Collis Sex Festival: Deviance on Tap

by Joseph Rago

D ESPITE THE REPUTATION of our nation's sex shops—seedy, private establishments where individuals in trench coats and dark sunglasses peruse the endless supply of smut, asking in quiet husky voices for the latest *Barely Legal* or *Transformations*—the academic elite are seeking to change all that. Never wanting to leave any deviant behavior private, lest it be oppressed, the common aim of administrators is to parade it around for all to see.

Perhaps it started at Cornell University, where students and faculty debated the need for vibrator sales through the campus Health Services. After all, "we know masturbation is healthy, so any tools that can help people discover their sexuality are positive. Any action by the University that gets the idea of sexuality out of the marginalized place that we're used to seeing it in is a good thing," said Orlando Soria, a Residential Advisor. But if any campus prudes got all huffy, a student health services worker explained, "Vibrators or personal massagers may have a broader appeal to people who use our massage therapy and physical therapy services for muscle relaxation. [Using a vibrator] can be a part of a holistic health approach." Nonetheless, never wanting to come second in the parade of idiocy, Dartmouth felt the need to one-up rival Cornell. Why just sell vibrators behind the veil of health services? Why not sell them next to the dining hall?

When I heard that the Center for Women and Gender was holding a "Sex Festival" to celebrate "sex, sexual expression, and sexuality in its myriad manifestations and complexities," my interest was piqued. "People of all genders" were invited to participate, and I heard that it would involve free stuff. I was there.

My heart pounded as I walked into Collis Commonground, festooned with festive colored flags and a swanky rotating discoball, all illuminated in seductive mood lighting. Hearts were a prominent theme. In short, the atmosphere beckoned for some sweet lovin'.

I was greeted by a young woman in a pink wig named "Moby," who handed me a ticket for raffle prizes and ushered me into the Sex Festival. In seconds, I was approached by an older woman flouncing with a hefty wicker basket of prophylactics. This condom fairy had a wide variety of latex to dole out, offering colors all shades of the rainbow, including glow-in-the-dark rainbows. I suggested that she should dump the cornucopia all over the floor and have people roll around seductively in them, but she ignored my request.

Tables lined both sides of the room, and an island in the center offered punch and cookies. A television played the film *The Truth About Cats and*

Dogs. Collis Commonground buzzed with a healthy crowd of students, and a gaggle of faculty and community members.

At the "Ask an Older Woman" table, older—and apparently fatter—women were chatting about a wide variety of subjects. One was instructing a young neophyte in the use of dental dams, repeatedly mentioning "the vulva area." Another dispensed free samples of flavored lubricants. Visitors could savor an ample spread of culinary delights, including "pina colada," "passion fruit," and "seedless watermelon." There was also a corpulent gentleman wandering about wearing a name tag broadcasting "Ask an Older Woman," but his services did not seem to be very popular.

A long table featured an extensive assortment of sex toys. The College says that it supports diversity, and, at least when it comes to vibrators and dildos, the statement is not mere lip-service. The station was a dazzling display of silicone—including, among others, a vibrator with a floral pattern, some lifelike latex penises, a variety of strap-on apparati, some weird black leather thing with a strap, a vibrator with a "Hello Kitty" head on it, a metal gadget, and a vibrator disguised as lipstick. Elinor, the rotund, effervescent woman running the table, explained that the vibrator was designed for the modern woman who needs a vibrator in an airport, but wants to remain discreet. When one male student lifted a limp three-pronged object, she explained, "You don't have places for these things to go." The station also exhibited "adjustable" nipple clamps and some other unmentionables. All the contraptions could be purchased from a provided Internet site.

But it was not all toys, games, and fun at the sex bacchanalia. There were also stations promoting abstinence and sexual abuse awareness run by the Sexual Abuse Peer Advisor (SAPA) organization. A couple of toothsome coeds manned an abstinence booth, which featured a bowl of strawberries and tub of chocolate sauce for dipping. "How Deep Do You Dip Your Strawberry," a sign read suggestively. They also presented several alternatives to sexual intercourse—they cleverly called it "outercourse"—including "cuddling," "holding hands," or even just "talking." The SAPA station centered around a prominent *Price Is Right*-style wheel, which disseminated information about sexual abuse.

There was also a station with information concerning eating disorders. These women were fighting to combat eating disorders and the judgment of people solely on the basis of their physical appearance. There was a sign that read, "Does anorexia make you have better sex?" Does it? Apparently, it does not.

They also offered a mimeographed memo entitled "Building Blocks: Self-Esteem Tips and Practices for All Women." I'm not exactly sure why this was handed to me, but I think it makes some points. For example, "Put your scale away. Beauty is NOT measured in pounds." And, "Find a picture of yourself you really like and put it in a beautiful frame. Keep it on display where you and others can see it." Or, "Respond to others thoughtfully when they criticize themselves. Don't let their negative remarks go unchallenged. Rather, tell them why their statements are untrue and self-defeating."

There were other more mundane issue-type tables that were not quite as popular as the more outlandish sex stations. There was a relationship abuse brainstorming station, a Student Global AIDS Campaign table, and a home base for the Students for Reproductive Rights club. The group VDAY was also in attendance, selling shirts and other paraphernalia. Students could also buy tickets to the *Vagina Monologues*.

Males also had their niche. The "Men's Project" was on hand, encouraging the male passersby to sign the "These Hands Don't Hurt" pledge, which sought to end "sexual violence against women" by changing the "attitudes and behaviors of men in our society."

There were not any actual intercourse demonstrations or even people making out on the couches by the fireplace, but a good time was had by all. Call me old-fashioned, but there is nothing quite like a College-sponsored carnival commemorating sex toys, fellatio, and promiscuity.

March 23, 2003

Barbie's Ethnic Friends
by Alexis Jhamb

W HEN I HEARD that the Center for Women and Gender was holding a discussion on "Becoming an Ally: White Women and Race," I was interested to see how the group would create "allies." The original e-mail invited the campus to come "if you think you might benefit from a discussion of race focused on the perspectives of white women." Even though I'm not strictly white or particularly interested in matters of race, I decided to check it out. I arrived to find that the discussion, moderated by a few Center for Women and Gender regulars, was held in a "safe and confidential place." How thoughtful of them!

Striking at first glance were the outlandish dress and styles of some of the participants. One wore overalls and purposefully mismatched striped socks, inevitably noticeable with their shades of neon. Another fashioned homemade earrings out of commonly used office supplies; she had paperclips dangling from her ears. Was she making a statement against the conformity and unambiguously impossible standards set by the fashion industry for women? Possibly, but I may not be thinking outside the box. I still feel that office supplies are no match for a pair of pearls.

To kick off the discussion, one of the moderators presented her view that white people—and white women specifically—often disown the existence of racism and assume that the egregious problems that may have occurred during earlier generations could not be attributed to them. What a shocker! I would dare say that anyone who chose to attend the meeting was predisposed to speaking about the negative effects of racism in modern society, likely with a heavy sense of white guilt. The centerpiece of the discussion was whether white women are "entitled" to discuss race. Naturally, since the participants were self-selected and yearning to be seen as "allies," the answer to this question was a resounding "yes."

The "plight" of white women was paralleled to that of white men. Can men take action when they overhear other men making disparaging comments about women or minorities? The question was broadened to relate to women: are they entitled to or obliged to do anything, especially when they cannot be a "spokeperson" for all white people, or is the notion of having a "spokeperson" for minorities inherently racist? None of these issues were explored as the discussion moved towards the most evident signs of racism.

Later it was suggested that "white people have to fix racism, not black people." The discussion seemed oddly centered on the white-black divide, ignoring that Hispanics now constitute the largest minority in America. Many of the participants gave an account of an epiphany in which they discovered they were white. Some of the more off-the-wall topics of discussion included the color of "flesh" crayons, bandages, and the skintones of Barbie dolls (versus Barbie's "ethnic" friends). While I do not have a distinctly white coloring, I cannot say that I sense the harm in using a Band-Aid of a different tone. Maybe I'm just callous to the feelings of those for whom bandages administer oppression.

The conversation shifted to talk of racism, and one woman noted her discomfort when those around her used phrases that carry negative emotional baggage. She noted her uneasiness when a friend from North Carolina commented that "the Negro women did my nails this afternoon." She described her attempt to understand why people use certain terms and to terminate them from her vocabulary. Still, talk of what white women can do to end racism and become an "ally" was avoided—curious for a discussion devoted to the subject.

The subject of race at Dartmouth College was broached with some trepidation. One participant noted that, attending high school in the South, she thought a Northern university implied a student body of "enlightened liberals"; she was deeply disappointed to discover Dartmouth's campus. Despite all the liberal and off-center "studies" programs that Dartmouth's academic departments provide, she felt there is an underemphasis on the role of race. Another woman brought up the scenario of a university with a solitary White People Studies department in which all other courses focused on the achievements of minority cultures. If the tables were turned, "I would feel so isolated," she told the group, practically in tears.

The conversation then took a turn towards feminism. It was suggested that many women declined to attend Dartmouth due to perceived gender bias. Some also said more women are involved in female-oriented writing and poetry publications than those politically aligned. This reinforces the notion that the "softer" sex naturally gravitates towards softer subjects. As a woman involved in a political publication, I disagree with the idea that Dartmouth's women lack the "politically aligned" bent of their male counterparts. Since I'm not an "enlightened liberal," however, I'm probably not the ideal "ally," either.

April 25, 2003

A Female-Gendered Anatomical Female
by Betsy Holder

A S I SAUNTERED into Silsby for the "My Butch Career: My Life as a Butch Lesbian" lecture, I felt out of place. I was neither butch—at the time, I was flaunting an adorable pink ensemble—nor was I a lesbian. I was confident about my sexuality, because I have a boyfriend, and, according to several sources, he is not a lesbian.

Imported from the State University of New York by the Center for Women and Gender, the lecturer was anthropology professor Ester Muster, who was in town to speak about her sensational life story. Ms. [?] Muster, as the title of her talk subtly implied, was a "butch lesbian." Her story checked out—her loutish demeanor left nothing to the imagination.

During her talk, she attempted to draw a parallel between her own sexual orientation and that of Gertrude Stein. She exhibited a pastiche of slides chronicling her life experiences and her quest for the holy grail of lesbianism: an "Alice" (Gertrude Stein's imagined female partner). After much soul-searching, Ms. Muster came to the conclusion that she must accept Sally Munt's belief that "the butch is either the magical sign of lesbianism or a failed, emasculated, and abdicated male." Whatever that means.

Ms. Muster felt that her mother, a mainliner from Greenwich, Connecticut, "had a thing for Jewish men." Despite her parent's erstwhile marriage, Ms. Muster's father, a European Jew, was her role model throughout her childhood. She found it hard to identify with her peers in upper middle-class Manhattan because she was a "WASP in Jewish clothing." She was also an athletic child who dreamed of becoming a boy and idolized male sports icons.

While Ms. Muster was unmistakably a "butch lesbian"—clad in lumberjack flannel, pressed khakis, and beefy hiking boots, in stark contrast to my darling tailoring—her path to "discovering her sexuality" did, in fact, involve several ill-fated heterosexual relationships, as well as an ill-fated encounter with a drag queen.

When she was ten years old, she became angered after engaging in "sex games" with a slightly older male friend. As a result, she concluded that heterosexual sexuality is "savage," while her lifestyle—and masculine self-awareness—is the more "civilized" alternative. Her comment evoked an outburst of chuckles from the predominately female audience. Mouth ajar, I could only envision the response had a white, heterosexual male suggested that Ms. Muster and her cohorts' lifestyles were "savage." The "civil" way of life, as she further elucidated, is rooted in the theories of Judith Butler. Butler, a post-modern gender theorist, believes that gender is socially constructed and not a product of an individual's biological sex. The world of the "savages" is a place where people ignorantly adhere to a belief that anatomical differences between females and males dictate a person's gender. One, apparently, can no longer be just a man or a woman. Rather, humans are anatomical males or females but can choose to conform to masculine or feminine gender roles. For example, Ms. Muster is a masculine-gendered anatomical female, just as I am a female-gendered anatomical female.

While the title of the Women's Studies Department has given way to the more verbose Women and Gender Studies, the department remains very much the same: ardent 1970s feminist wolves in postmodern flannel clothing. The abrasive tendencies of this department were highlighted during the question and answer session following Ms. Muster's presentation. While she only briefly discussed feminism in her lecture—as it pertained to her lesbian lifestyle in Manhattan during the Swingin' Seventies—the majority of the questions raised, from both students and faculty, related to feminist dogma. Ms. Muster, who appeared uncomfortable with many of these questions, was clearly attempting to avoid the subject, yet the audience was relentless in pressing her to discuss her views on feminism. This disrespectful behavior is all too typical of the Women's and Gender Studies Department.

June 2, 2003

Beautiful & Anatomical

by Alston Ramsay

O NCE UPON A TIME, Valentine's Day was a celebration of everything decent and pure between the sexes, with love and romance expressed through cards, flowers, chocolate, and whatever else the heart
could entertain and imagine. No longer.

The feminists' most recent usurpation has turned February 14, Valentine's Day, into V-day, whose three pillars—Vaginas, Victory, and Valen-
tines—seek to drag the rest of the world into the twisted world of radical
feminism. Ostensibly, the holiday is meant to first and foremost combat
global violence against women, but at Dartmouth and abroad the celebra-
tions focus on little more than sex and hedonism, and, even here, the
movement fails.

V-day, in its original incarnation, is the brainchild of Eve Ensler, the
latest golden calf in a long line of radical feminists. Ensler's *Vagina
Monologues*, now a venerable institution, made its first appearance in 1996
before spawning the inaugural V-day in 1998. Since then, V-day has seen a
rise in popularity and prominence; over 800 locales, many international,
hosted V-day in 2002, and over 2,000 events are expected this year.

In theory, the *Monologues* and V-day are synonymous; according to
www.vday.org, the goal is to "educat[e] millions of people about the
reality of violence against women and girls." This is to be accomplished
by spreading "V-energy," which will, hopefully, lead one day to the "v-
world," where all women are "free to thrive, not just survive."

The actual play, however, is far removed from these ambitions. In one
of the monologues at Dartmouth, Ashley Fisher '05 discussed pubic hair.
Any type of maintenance in that area was just "f*ck*ng weird" and a sign
of patriarchal dominance. The audience tittered when she cursed, much as
they did throughout the entire play. In fact, that seemed to be the primary
goal: desensitize the audience to any language that could be considered
inappropriate in public, from "vagina" and "p*ssy" to "tw*t" and "c*nt."

The feminist crowd will argue that the effusive use of the word "coochi
snorcher" allows women to reclaim their sexuality. For many, though,
using "vagina" as a metaphor for femininity, womanhood, etc., does
nothing more than objectify women. In Eve Ensler's world, vaginas equal
women. Sure, these vaginas may have all the trappings of humanity, but
they are the essence of women, or, as explained by "the woman who loved
to make vaginas happy": "I love vaginas. I love women. I don't see them
as separate things." Ensler—darling child of feminists—is the veritable
empress of V-world.

On the heels of "Hair" came "Crooked Braid," a sobering monologue describing an abusive American Indian relationship. Even within this topic, the last line berated the white man: "They took our ways, our land, our men, and we want them back." Somehow whites are responsible for domestic disputes within the Indian community. I guess this is to be expected from Ensler.

The *Monologues* continued with pontifications on what one's vagina would wear or what it would say ("rock me" and "enter at own risk," for example). Throughout, the vagina is its own entity, signifying womanhood.

This sentiment perhaps was most clearly expressed in "Because He Liked to Look at It." This story was prefaced by Amanda Bingel, the Community Director of the River Cluster dormitories, who explained, "This monologue is based on a woman who, surprisingly, had a good experience with a man." The anti-male sentiment elicited laughter from most corners. The monologue started with a woman describing the failings of her latest beau. Despite not liking him, she decided she would have him spend the night. So after removing her clothes, she's shocked as he implores time and time again, "I want to see you." He wanted to examine visually her vagina. After she relented, and after he gazed, he exclaimed, "you're so beautiful . . . you're elegant and deep and innocent and wild!" This, of course, all gleaned from staring at her nether-regions. The woman, who had characterized him as "not attractive," "not particularly bright," and "not very funny," was incredibly turned on. The dullard redeemed himself by seeing her as nothing more than a vagina. And that's the way it went; women are vaginas, and men are scum.

While this male-bashing didn't faze me, it was later juxtaposed with a rape scene that many schools performing the *Monologues* have axed, and for good reason. The monologue opens with a thirteen-year-old girl who is seduced by her school's female twenty-four-year-old secretary. The secretary serves the girl alcohol at her apartment; things get hot and heavy. A steamy description ensued—one uttered with such passion and heat that the audience almost forgot it was listening to a tale of rape and child molestation. This relationship was, in the words of the victim, a "surprising, unexpected salvation," mainly because, as her rapist cooed, the vagina was "untouched by man." The original, disturbing finale, however, was omitted. Ensler's text has the girl explain, "Well, I say if it was a rape, it was a good rape."

Ensler adheres to the school of feminist thought characterizing all men as vile, wife-beating brutes. She is, however, perfectly willing to condone an illegal and immoral act—provided it's girl-on-girl. Ensler's opus is nothing more than run-of-the-mill feminist rot interlarded with foul language. There are only so many times one can yell the word "c*nt" in public before it becomes old hat. Old hat about sums up the *Vagina Monologues*.

Ensler, in her interviews of over two hundred women, from which the *Monologues* were culled, even went as young as six years old. Following "Reclaiming C*NT," Ensler relayed the responses of six-year-old girls to questions such as, "What would your vagina wear?" The answers were just as vapid as those from older respondents.

Next came "The woman who loved to make vaginas happy," the story of a one-time lawyer turned female dominatrix—but only for women. She contrasted her previous work in the world of law with her new profession, explaining that she no longer had to wear business suits, and that there was "no moaning" in the profession. Afterwards, the actress, Khristina Gonzalez '04, demonstrated numerous moans, from those that characterized WASPs and Irish Catholics, to the specific moans associated with distinct areas of the female anatomy. Every so often, the *Monologues* came back to the issue of violence against women, but these discussions were sandwiched by pure whimsy, like "My Angry Vagina," a fiery denunciation of non-lubricated cotton tampons, gynecologists, and feminine hygiene products.

Despite the absurdities, the proceeds from the *Monologues* were put to good use; the money, minus the expenses of the show, was donated to a local shelter for battered women.

The *Vagina Monologues* and the associated V-day events continue to be the highlight of the Center for Women and Gender's programming. The CWG, it seems, is still obsessed with maximizing the sexual revolution, so that, as explained in "My Angry Vagina," "Women [will] be cumming all day long!" The *Monologues* are the logical extension of the CWG's prurient curriculum. Woman's Studies Professor Giavanna Munafo captured this sentiment when she silkily concluded the *Vagina Monologues*: "Sexuality freely expressed is truly beautiful."

If the *Vagina Monologues* typify freely expressed sexuality and the future of the women's movement, beautiful may be the wrong word. V-day may not have reached the entire world yet, but—be forewarned—it's coming.

March 23, 2003

God & Man at Dartmouth

How the Grinch Stole Christmas
by Conor Dugan & Ben Patch

I T IS A LONG-STANDING tradition that the Glee Club sings carols at the annual December lighting of the Christmas tree on the Dartmouth Green. But a week before this past Thanksgiving, 1997, Olivia Chapman, Assistant College Director of Public Programs, issued this message to Glee Club Director Leo Burkot: "The Office of Public Programs does not want the bulk of the offering to be traditional 'Christian' Christmas carols." Leo Burkot—who refused to comment to the *Review*—subsequently canceled the Glee Club gig altogether, explaining in an e-mail to the Glee Club on November 19: "Since there is not time to obtain and learn a whole new set of pieces, we will not sing this year."

The Glee Club's response was one of unanimous shock. One gleeker, as the members call themselves, wrote in an e-mail to the rest of the Club, "You're kidding me. What do they want, pagan carols?" Another gleeker went further: "From what I have been able to find out from various sources, the nixing of traditional Christmas carols at the tree lighting was a pretty direct request from President Freedman. The Dodecs will be singing in our place, merely because . . . there's not time for us to learn a whole bunch of new secular music." Still another member e-mailed, "I am a Buddhist, and I don't feel threatened when I sing Christmas carols or attend other religions' praying sessions." In protest, many of the gleekers planned a separate program of religious carols to sing unofficially the night after the lighting.

The weekend before Thanksgiving the Conservative Union sent an e-mail to a large number of students which explained the situation, declaring it "a poor decision that is insensitive to cultural and religious expression at Dartmouth." The letter directed students to e-mail Ms. Chapman and Gail A. Wolek-Osterhout, the Executive Assistant to the President's Office, and voice their opinions on the issue. Hundreds of students and other members of the Dartmouth Community responded. Professor Kuypers wrote in an e-mail, "If the administration wishes to have only secular events during the Holidays, then why is the College lighting a Jewish menorah every day during Hanukkah? And why is there going to be a Hanukkah party? Are these not religious expressions?"

In face of this heated opposition, Ms. Chapman changed her story. In a letter to the *Daily Dartmouth*, on November 27, she wrote, "The Director of the Glee Club declined the invitation to perform this year at the tree lighting because of a schedule conflict . . . our intention has been simply to encourage the inclusion of secular music—never to impose what should or should not be sung." Yet, in a response to an e-mail sent by *Review* contributor Michael Brigg, Chapman contradicted this claim: "Beginning in 1994 and again last year, we discussed with the Director of the Glee Club our interest in eliminating or at least reducing the proportion of religious music in the program in favor of secular music of the season."

The College hired the Dodecaphonics, a Dartmouth a cappella group, to sing in place of the Glee Club. According to Ms. Chapman: "We have asked the Dodecs to include some secular music in their program but have left the final choice of songs to them." The Dodecs' director followed suit writing in an e-mail message that, "The Dodecaphonics are singing what the Office of Public Programs would consider a 'balanced' program of songs." Another member e-mailed that, "Our repertoire has not been decided yet, but will consist of 'Christmas' songs as well as holiday songs, and Dartmouth songs." The actual performance on December 6, however, was decidedly unbalanced. The program consisted mostly of secular songs such as "Frosty the Snowman" and "Rudolph the Red-Nosed Reindeer."

The night after the official "Holiday Tree Lighting Ceremony," a large group of students followed through on their plans and gathered on the Green to sing religious carols such as "O Come All Ye Faithful," "Silent Night," and "Away in a Manger." To freshman Bruce Kennedy, "There could not have been a better place to carol, in front of the College Christmas tree on a snowy New Hampshire night. There was a sizable crowd, all very enthusiastic and disappointed at the administration's handling of the caroling."

January 22, 1997

KING FEATURES SYNDICATE
Some Good News from the Campus
by Jeffrey Hart

Y OU UNDOUBTEDLY will welcome some really inspiring news from the college campus, where students often think more clearly these days than their professors or administrators.

At Dartmouth College, year after year, for as long as anyone can recall, there has been a Christmas tree lighting ceremony in the middle of the gorgeous New Hampshire campus.

A large tree is brought in, not as large maybe as the one at Rockefeller Center, but large, and no doubt from the nearby New Hampshire or Maine woods.

The tree is established on the campus, in the middle of the so-called Green, which long ago was a sheep pasture. For as long as anyone can remember, as the lights of the tree are turned on each year, the Dartmouth Glee Club serenades the tree with Christmas carols.

No one had ever objected to the innocent and joyful ceremony until last month, when the Dartmouth administration intervened. It told the Glee Club that no religious carols were to be sung.

Thus "Silent Night," which had been sung around the tree almost forever, was now . . . officially verboten.

The operative ideology was "multiculturalism." The assumption behind the administration's directive was that the Asian, Jewish, Muslim, and agnostic students could be offended by such an outrage as "Silent Night."

As a longtime professor at Dartmouth, I can testify that no students would be offended by anything of the kind.

The Dartmouth administration, under the leadership of President James Freedman, has long been in the business of creating occasions for "offense."

A student who is "offended" can be richly rewarded.

Yale professor Harold Bloom has aptly characterized the official culture of the universities today as a "party of resentment." You had better not say, or indeed think, anything that would offend anyone.

So, at Dartmouth, as the lights on the tree went on last month, the Glee Club struggled with "Frosty the Snowman" and "Rudolph the Red-Nose Reindeer."

But the next day, normality rebelled against the culture of resentment. Glee Club members—acting informally and as individuals—conducted the first rebellious concert in Dartmouth history.

Despite final exams and a blinding snowstorm, club members gathered around the tree and sang unofficially.

Word had spread through the campus grapevine. As the singers gathered around the tree, some 300 students joined them as they sang Christmas carols.

That night, they performed in four-part harmony such really "offensive" songs as "God Rest Ye Merry Gentlemen," "Hark the Herald Angels Sing," and "Silent Night."

As the expert Glee Club members and their fellow students sang, they eventually linked arms, and they swayed gently with the rhythms. A strong snowstorm swirled around them.

It was not any sort of political protest. There were no charismatic student figures making incendiary speeches. What it amounted to was a rebellion on the part of the normal.

Before there was a Dartmouth Glee Club, an official organization, there were, maybe back in the 1920s, just some students who enjoyed singing.

Well, in their joyful protest, the members of the Glee Club de-officialized themselves.

It is possible that in today's culture of resentment on the campus, those who sang that night will be penalized in some way. They dared to sing songs they liked. They might be expelled from the official Glee Club. They might be required to take "sensitivity training."

Regardless, the "culture of resentment" and, I would say, the "culture of negation," cannot possibly prevail over the culture of normality and joy.

Printed in The Dartmouth Review *January 22, 1997*

SPEECH
Christianize Dartmouth?
by William F. Buckley Jr.

What follows is the text of a speech delivered at Rollins Chapel on January 21, 1998. Mr. Buckley's appearance was prompted by comments then Dartmouth President James O. Freedman made at the November 7, 1997 dedication of the Roth Center for Jewish Life and Culture—as reported in The New York Times *the following day—and Mr. Buckley's subsequent letter to the editor of the* Times, *published November 18, 1997.*

I WAS BOTH PLEASED and grateful when Dartmouth's Hillel group last week voted to co-sponsor my appearance tonight, and honored that the Roth Center has planned a reception for me after my talk.

I begin, in part for my own sake, by reviewing the circumstances of my visit here. It happens that my talk tonight is only the most recent—who knows, perhaps the last—in a series of occasional appearances on this campus that began in the mid 1950s, bespeaking a common disposition, Dartmouth's and my own, to endure pain. I am especially anxious to move step by step because I have felt the need to clarify my own thinking on the subject of Christianity and higher education. The invitation from Mr. [Craig] Parker [of Navigators Christian Fellowship] was to expand on a short piece I did for *The New York Times* in November. It was triggered by the inauguration of the Roth Center here and attendant revelations about Dartmouth's past. Had I, Mr. Parker asked me in his letter, weighed sufficiently the implications of what I wrote on that occasion? I had written that in seeking to amend past injustices to Jewish students, Dartmouth ought not to feel any need to forswear its own traditional mission, which is (was?), to use the freighted word I so innocently used a few weeks ago, to Christianize its students.

The response to my summons in *The New York Times* was at several levels. The first was silence. A silence here amused, there awestruck. The critical reaction was two generations more wizened than when I made my first onward-Christian-soldiers charge. That was done in my book *God and Man at Yale*. Back then (1951), the dismay of college spokesmen was that anyone should think there was any need to issue any such summons. The religious orientation of Yale, they insisted, was underway, uninterrupted; all flags flying. A committee was deputized to explore the question. Its chairman reported that "there is today [at Yale], more than ever, widespread realization that religion alone can give meaning and purpose to modern life."

But the reaction now is of a very different kind. My teaching assistant at Yale—in November I was teaching a seminar there in English composition—is himself a Yale graduate, son and brother of Dartmouth graduates. He wrote to me asking whether I could seriously envision the Jewish president of Dartmouth uttering distinctively Christian preachments on life and manners to Dartmouth's student body. His position was not entirely antagonistic. The young Jewish scholar derided what he labeled the "cartoonishly politically correct" practices at Dartmouth of in effect eliminating "Silent Night" as a Christmastime Glee Club offering. He deplores the contortionist lengths, as described in my current book, that my own prep-school alma mater, the Millbrook School, goes to conduct one hour's Christmas ceremonies without a single reference to Christmas, let alone to Christ.

At another level, the questions that arose were fundamental questions. The first was the sheer inconceivability that a university with feet so solidly encased in the concrete of secularism could be born again. Sure, one correspondent observed, it is true that as recently as in 1946 Dartmouth President Ernest Martin Hopkins reiterated his understanding that the continuing obligation of Dartmouth was to encourage Christian (Protestant) belief in its students. But since then, everything has changed. Yes, that's true. Almost everything has changed.

About the attitudes and conduct of universities that once hewed to the Christian line, quite a lot has been written. There is Professor George Marsden, whose title tells the story of his book: *The Soul of the American University: From Protestant Establishment to Established Nonbelief*. And there is Dan A. Oren's *Joining the Club: A History of Jews and Yale*, which tells of flat-out exclusion of tenure for Jewish faculty in the social sciences and the humanities in those benighted days.

But a trend in the multiculturalist direction was under way. Admissions policies broadened, as if to reflect internal reorientations. In my book on

Yale I had remarked the dilution of the Christian tradition. It was no longer the institutional lifeblood at Yale. I quoted from the inaugural address of the scholar who served as president of Yale during my undergraduate years. Charles Seymour had said in 1937, "I call on all members of the faculty as members of a thinking body, freely to recognize the tremendous validity and power of the teachings of Christ in our life-and-death struggle against the forces of selfish materialism." Could any president of a major American university today, even assuming he privately nursed the convictions Mr. Seymour expressed, use such language at an inaugural ceremony? Just imagine hearing such formulations from the next president of Dartmouth. The repercussions would be immense: perplexity and even outrage among the faculty; almost certainly a lawsuit backed by the American Civil Liberties Union, complaining that 15 percent of Dartmouth's budget was being sent in by the Federal Government, some of it wrested from the pockets of honest and hardworking skeptics, incensed now by their involuntary subsidy of that swinging evangelical, freshly installed as president of Dartmouth by a sleepy board of trustees ignorant of modern times.

A third response was simply curious. It asked, in effect, What can be done to advance Christianity—assuming the will to do anything at all? Can Christianity be practiced corporately at college level without engendering, at best, intercredal incivility; at worst, confrontational hostility?

For convenience, in this brief exploration, I omit mention of religions other than Christianity and Judaism. I ignore whatever complications Catholic Christianity could hypothetically present. No doubt there are curricular ambitions aborning from Buddhism and Islam. I intend no condescension in ignoring them. I do so purely for analytical convenience.

The spotlight, as focused last November by President Freedman, is on Christianity and Judaism, and I am supposed to contemplate the question: What in fact could be done? We return to what precipitated the exchange in *The New York Times*. It was at the formal opening of the Roth Center for Jewish Life and Culture that President Freedman disclosed the history of Dartmouth's quota on Jewish students. Now the presumed design of the Roth Center is to invigorate Jewish life and culture, which certainly includes Jewish religion. It was the official enthusiasm shown by Mr. Freedman and others for this enterprise that prompted me to ask whether, even as the Roth Center is designed to Judaize Jews, Dartmouth mightn't explore more vigorous means of Christianizing non-Jews. I asked, "In welcoming students from other creeds, is it expected that a college must forswear its own traditional creed?" I went on to ask the question which I judge it is my primary responsibility here tonight to explore. As I put it, "Is an effort to inculcate Christian values and Christian teaching a morphological act of anti-Semitism?"

That question needs to be probed at levels religious, social, and political. It is useful to begin by asking what it is that Judaism and Christianity have in common. The answer is a great deal. Irving Kristol put it succinctly: "Like the greatest Jewish theologian of this century, Franz Rosenzweig, I see Christianity as a sister religion to Judaism, as a form of Judaism for the Gentiles." The two faiths have in common the (monotheistic) belief in a single God. The Old Testament is the structural and historical springboard of Christianity. The division comes in primarily on the question of Jesus, revered by Christians as the Incarnation, ignored—or reviled—by Jews as a failed prophet at best, an impostor at worst.

Whether Franz Rosenzweig was correct in calling them sister religions is a matter of perspective. But it is useful to bear in mind that day-to-day differences are mostly liturgical. Moral codes, with differing emphases on faith and on the laws, are held in common by the two faiths. There is no sovereign social commandment spoken in the Old Testament that is profaned or defiled—how could it be so?—in the New Testament. The deportment of Jews obedient to their laws, and of Christians faithful to theirs, would expose no important differences in conduct.

But credal differences do tend to generate social differences, and some of these have political faces. The overwhelming datum here, dominating all emotion and much thought, is the history of racial and ethnic discrimination. From the practice of it in the United States, salutary lessons have been drawn. From the genocidal lengths to which discrimination has been practiced abroad, we learn terrifying truths. The memory of discriminatory practices, as for instance at Dartmouth and Yale, engendered credal fears and derivative political stands. Most conspicuous of them, in the past half-century, have been the fear of hegemonic concentrations of religious authority, and a lively concern for minorities. The relative unanimity of Jewish concern for the beleaguered Negro after the war is widely understood as an expression of fraternal support from one American group itself once beleaguered, to another still suffering. Conspicuous also, in this survey, is the relative solidarity of Jewish objection to Christian practices except when done under formally Christian auspices. In support of this bias, a whole constitutional vocabulary sprang up. The word Christian is not used, but Christianity is the special target of the judicial inquisition, even though it is ostensibly comprehensive in its anti-religious reach. It is a ban that extends equally to Jewish impertinences in public situations. Thus in 1989 the constitutional objection to an invocation at the Commencement ceremony of a public junior high school in Rhode Island—because it was pronounced, not by a minister or priest (their benedictions would also be forbidden), but by a rabbi. The Supreme Court solemnly weighed in—*Lee v. Weisman*, June 24, 1992—on the unconstitutionality of the rabbinical blessing and, even as we speak, is hearing the dolorous cries of an affronted petitioner in Alabama. There the objection is to the exposure of the Ten Commandments in a courthouse in Etowah County, a complaint that is chugging its way up the shadowy judicial ladder in serene expectation of coming, finally, on the liberating incandescence of that clause in the First Amendment that beams out its guarantees against an established national religion.

What is this strange commotion, in the name of protection from a national church? Six years ago, in my book *In Search of Anti-Semitism*, I relayed the views, once again, of Irving Kristol. Surveying the religion-in-schools scene he noticed a "tension now building up between Jews and Christians [which] has very little to do with traditional discrimination, and everything to do with efforts by liberals—among whom, I regret to say, Jews are both numerous and prominent—to establish a wall between religion and society in the guise of maintaining the wall between church and state." Mr. Kristol went on to say that he himself believes "the secular era [is] fading, that Jews (at least, as he put it, those who remain Jews) will become more Jewish, Christians more Christian, Moslems more Moslem, Hindus more Hindu, etc." He concluded: "There is a majority culture in this country, it is Christian, white, middle-class. Jews and nonbelievers (I am both) are outsiders to some extent in that culture."

If Irving Kristol is correct in saying that there is a majority culture and that it is Christian, what of the modern university? Is it only an enclave, pure and simple? Dartmouth, like so many of the elite universities, has Christian roots. Are these roots relevant to its current purposes? The temptation in answering that question—the easiest way out, and perhaps the only way out—is to say, No: they are irrelevant. But surely before we opt for instant deracination we should give a little thought to the Dartmouth of Ernest Martin Hopkins—as to the Yale of Charles Seymour—and ask: What happened? What happened that makes it somehow absurd even to hint at a corporate commitment to a religious faith, when to do so was commonplace in mid-century?

There have been two groundswells, one ideological, the second philosophical. On the first of these we have already touched, the idea that to show preference for any one religion is somehow unfair, aggressive, inconsistent with the very idea of equal rights for all religions. But that ideological perspective, an extension of the egalitarian imperative, brushes up against quite conventionally accepted rights of majorities, the right—cited, in this instance, by Irving Kristol—of a community to acknowledge the symbols and pronounce the ideals of the majority. This is of course the accepted practice in public life, in democratic politics, where the majority elects the leader and sets congregational rules that prevail during the tenure of that administration. It is not challenged that a college founded by evangelical Christians, or by and for observant Jews, should be free to organize college life and curriculum consistent with the indoctrinational ends of the institution. On the contrary, that is expected.

But the dividing line is quickly drawn. We begin by saying of a teaching institution that it is "secular," i.e., worldly, rather than spiritual. This inflection is not emasculating when narrowly applied. Nobody expects courses in Christian physics. The handiest next device for turning the curriculum loose is of course "academic freedom." The arguments for academic freedom are quickly marshaled and very persuasive. They include the doctrine's usefulness in academic research, an intellectual mobility we quickly appreciate for the most obvious reasons: If there is no stated objective to be achieved, no confining discipline to repress us, the researcher's freedom is enhanced. All very well, but of course at some point the offices of a teaching college assert themselves: there are one thousand students who enter Dartmouth as freshmen and will want, four years later, to be acquainted with some of the deposits of learning of the last three millennia, and perhaps with a few coordinates that enhance the meaning of life itself, and some knowledge of the religion that was an animating source of republican idealism. Any doubts we have on the matter can be settled by reading the speeches of Martin Luther King Jr., whose life we celebrate while tending to ignore what he always cited—as Abraham Lincoln did—as the ground of his idealism.

Academic freedom, fifty years ago, was most frequently acclaimed as protecting a scholar indifferent to or dissenting from establishmentarian religion or economics or politics. But more, really, was going on during this period. The academy's own establishment was gestating, and it is now pretty well fullborn. The new canon rules that religion is, well, appropriately left behind in our culture of science.

What evidence do we have of this progressive demotion of religion by the culture of science? Professor David Hollinger of the University of California at Berkeley has published a book—*Science, Jews, and Secular Culture*—from which much that is informative is conveniently derived. Jeffrey Hart, professor emeritus of English here at Dartmouth, summarizes one of Hollinger's points. It is that, at the moment, the secular perspective has "won the cognitive battle," to use the relevant language. The religious perspective has for the time being lost the battle to be thought of as "true," "in the sense that $E=mc^2$ is true," to use Professor Hart's language.

Now, Professor Hollinger is telling us—and he is a very learned sociologist—that in the substantive sense science is thought by academic thinkers to be "true" on a playing field where the religious world view is not true. That this is the academic consensus is hard to deny. The idea that Christianity might be true is not even entertained in most academic laboratories, let alone seriously explored. "Christianity marched into the modern era as the strongest, most institutionally endowed cultural program in the Western world," writes Hollinger. He continues, "The people in charge of this program tried through a variety of methods, some more coercive than others, to implant Christian doctrines and practices in as much of the globe as they could. Yet, as the centuries went forward, this extraordinary empire of power/knowledge lost some of the ground it had once held. Christianity at the end of the twentieth century—the 'Christian Century,' prophesied by the Protestant hegemonists at its start—is less triumphant in the North Atlantic West than it was in 1500 or 1700 or 1900."

Notwithstanding this dispiriting narrative, there is the perverse refusal, if the phrase is correct, of religion to perish by any sword, not physical, not archaeological, not anthropological, not biochemical, not historical, not, indeed, philosophical. Professor Hollinger appears, in passing, to acknowledge as much when he writes, "Christianity's continuing adherents include some of the most thoughtful and learned men and women in the world—as I believe they do—[but] the [secularist] trend is nonetheless real, and the historian's obligation to understand it is no less compelling."

He cites Thomas Kuhn's *Structure of Scientific Revolutions*. Mr. Kuhn argues that science has always been a collective enterprise. That is, scientific researchers do not go off in individual directions to discover this or that. Rather they pursue paths collectively agreed upon by what might be thought of as a "paradigm." The extant scientific paradigm is satisfied that present research "covers the facts." Most scientists, most of the time—we are to understand—pursue their research within the going paradigm. Researchers go happily forward, making advances and exacting refinements, until suddenly the circle comes up that won't fit in the square hole that stares them in the face.

The effort is then made to stretch the going paradigm, but finally a new one is needed to "cover the new facts," even as the Newtonian paradigm had to be changed to make way for subatomic particles and high-velocity physics, which amounted to a new "wing" on the Newtonian paradigm and a new direction for collective research, leading, I am reliably informed, to quantum mechanics. And now the question is at least tantalizing whether the anthropic paradigm will assert itself not merely as convenient to astrophysicists, but perhaps as undeniable.

I am ill at ease when dealing with physics, but I think that the question being raised is suitably addressed to the layman's generic curiosity. The question is, Which of two alternative explanations of human life is more plausible, that put forward by materialist evolution, or that which argues a superintending intelligence? The explorations are greatly varied, but notice is dramatically drawn to the conference of international scientists that met in Krakow in 1973 where Professor Brandon Carter rather timidly advanced the view that what we now know about the physical narrative of our cosmos is that one day it did in fact begin, with what they call the Big

Bang, and that multiple variables needed to play out in bizarre coordination with each other by which only a single apparent purpose was served, namely to make possible human life. He called this the anthropic principle. I am benumbed by numbers on galactic scales, but even minds primitively educated in science are arrested by some of the data currently going the rounds. What is the probability that a bullet randomly fired from the earth will hit a one-inch target at a distance of twenty billion light years? The answer, I'm told, is 10 to the 60th power. Do we know how many atoms there are in the known universe? Well, I know, because I've been told that the answer is 10 to the 80th power. I am then told that scientists consider any random event as unlikely as 10 to the 50th power to be, quite simply, impossible; which makes daunting the idea of the monkey randomly typing down the passage from *Macbeth* that closes with, "Told by an idiot, full of sound and fury/ Signifying nothing." The chances of that happening can be put down at 10 to the 50th power.

But all of this tells us nothing more than that there are paradigms on the move, and that alert scholarship must inevitably take these matters into account, or run the risk run by those blind to the demonstrations of Galileo. To be sure, to acknowledge that there was a Prime Mover is less than to certify either the God of Moses or the God of Christ. But it is heartening for those drawn to a religious view of the world to know that the operative paradigm is no reason for their current dishevelment. "I see it as one of the greatest ironies of this ironical time," Malcolm Muggeridge wrote fifteen years ago, "that the Christian message should be withdrawn for consideration just when it is most desperately needed to save men's reason, if not their souls. It is as though a Salvation Army band, valiantly and patiently waiting through the long years for Judgment Day, should, when it comes at last, and the heavens do veritably begin to unfold like a a scroll, throw away their instruments and flee in terror."

So we ask: What did President Hopkins mean when he spoke about Christianizing Dartmouth students? Presumably a little more than teaching them not to cheat at cards. One supposes that he had in mind the strength that especially attaches to idealism grounded in religious belief. The crime rate in Israel is lower among observant Jews than non-observant Jews. As a practical matter, what might the next president of Dartmouth do, if persuaded to revive Dartmouth's mandate? What has the retiring president done? The only time I have ever spent in the company of President Freedman was at a celebration of the 150th anniversary of Temple Emanuel in New York City. We were two of six speakers, no one of whom, if memory serves, spoke words disruptive of the evening's decorum. What are we afraid of? The coexistence of Judaism and Christianity is not imperiled in the United States. Why should we assume that a self-confident Jewish university president would be affronted by the recitation of a Christian prayer or the singing of a Christian hymn in his presence? We recall Yogi Berra's comment when told that a Jew had been elected mayor of Dublin: "Only in America," he exulted. Is it reasonable, in a country in which all parties are unambiguously united in the resolve to guarantee religious freedom, to affirm the freedom of religion by inhibiting its exercise? Should we, out of an unrealistic fear of giving offense, deprive ourselves of satisfactions to which the majority of a college community are entitled? Those deferences one rightly expects to enjoy when living in a society whose profile Irving Kristol accurately describes. Might a college president, in such circumstances, search out two or three learned scholars intending to situate them to teach pivotal courses in philosophy and history? Might not classes be suspended on Good Friday, and religious exhortations cited at convocations? Why sap the joy of a religious tradition, which is what we seem to be doing by pledging, on Christmas Day, not to let the image of the Christ-child pass through the mind or, on Easter, to shut off any inclination to dwell on the Resurrection?

But all of the foregoing is, in a sense, rhetorically detached, even desiccated, the talk of religion and academic freedom and institutional histories and wayward paradigms. I want to leave my hosts, the Protestant and Jewish ministries, with some sense of my shared partisanship with one understanding they absolutely have in common, those of you who believe. I close then with the final paragraph from Paul Elmer More's essay on Thomas Huxley. It caught my eye forty years ago, and I take from it now the undergirding confidence I share with your ministries. More wrote about the clash of the Darwinian model with the religious traditions of Oxford:

In 1864, there was a Diocesan Conference at Oxford. There chanced at this time to be in the neighborhood a man who was neither priest nor scientist, a man given to absurd freaks of intellectual charlatanry, yet showing at times also such marvelous and sudden penetration into the heart of things as comes only to genius. It was Disraeli. "He lounged into the assembly," so the scene is described by Froude, "in a black velvet shooting-coat and a wide-awake hat, as if he had been accidentally passing through the town. He began in his usual affected manner, slowly and rather pompously, as if he had nothing to say beyond perfunctory platitudes." And then, turning to the presiding officer, the same Bishop Wilberforce whom four years earlier Huxley had so crushingly rebuked, he uttered one of his enigmatic and unforgettable epigrams: "What is the question now placed before society with a glibness the most astounding? The question is this: Is man an ape or an angel? I, my Lord, am on the side of the angels." The audience, not kindly disposed to the speaker, applauded the words as a jest; they were carried the next day over the whole land by the newspapers; they have often been repeated as an example of Disraeli's brilliant but empty wit. I suspect [Professor More concluded] that beneath their surface glitter, and hidden within their metaphor, pointed to suit an Oriental taste, these words contain a truth that shall some day break to pieces the new philosophy which Huxley spent his life so devotedly to establish.

Printed in The Dartmouth Review *January 22, 1998*

Dartmouth's Anti-Semitism
by Steven Menashi

WHEN HE WAS PRESIDENT of Dartmouth, James O. Freedman visited the Hillel Jewish Students Association once a year for Friday night services. On his February 2, 1996 visit, he endeavored to explain why Jewish enrollment at Dartmouth is consistently the lowest among Ivy League schools. He mentioned Dartmouth's "reputation for anti-Semitism." He emphasized that Jews are "urban people," and less attracted to rural environments.

Freedman was known for grandstanding on Jewish issues. Despite his various rationalizations, however, there is a more obvious reason why Jewish students don't attend Dartmouth: they can't practice Judaism here.

For starters, they wouldn't be able to eat anything. Dartmouth remains the only Ivy League school without a kosher dining hall.

To be sure, there are a few sandwiches available in Food Court. But to keep kosher, students would have to commit to eating either a turkey or pastrami sandwich every day—for breakfast, lunch, and dinner—for four years. Recently, Dartmouth Dining Services started to provide microwavable TV dinners for kosher students; the meals are, to say the least, unappealing. To date, there are no dairy products offered for sale at Dartmouth that Jewish students who keep kosher can eat.

Even if they could eat, though, Jewish students would not be able to pray. There are no religious services anywhere in Hanover during the week. Even on the Sabbath, there are no services for Conservative or Orthodox Jews.

President Freedman made speeches about recruiting Jewish students and faculty; he gave interviews, wrote articles—even an introduction to his book—about his own Jewish identity. But Freedman's Dartmouth never took Judaism itself seriously.

Even the Roth Center for Jewish Life at Dartmouth, completed last year, acts primarily as a cultural, rather than religious, center for Jewish students. The Roth Center sanctuary doesn't even conform to basic requirements for such a structure—for instance, that it should face east toward Jerusalem.

Certainly, there's no discrimination against Jewish students at Dartmouth. Dartmouth is, however, hostile to religious expression. There is little accommodation for religion at Dartmouth, and improvements in the situation aren't forthcoming.

The only efforts to make Jewish students more welcome at the College have been rather juvenile and oppressive attempts to inhibit the expression of Christianity.

In 1997, before the lighting of the Christmas tree on the Hanover Green, Olivia Chapman, Assistant College Director of Public Programs, informed the Glee Club that Dartmouth would not allow the Club to sing Christmas carols at the tree-lighting ceremony, as it traditionally had in the past. The College "does not want the bulk of the offering to be traditional 'Christian' Christmas carols," she wrote. Dartmouth had an "interest in eliminating or at least reducing the proportion of religious music in the program in favor of secular music of the season." Without time to learn new songs, the Glee Club cancelled its program. In its place, a campus a cappella group sang "Frosty the Snowman."

The following year, in response to student outcry, Dartmouth again permitted Christmas carols at the tree-lighting. A different controversy ensued, however, over the placement of the Christmas tree in the center of the Green.

Then, after Campus Crusade for Christ, a student organization, purchased copies of *Mere Christianity* by C. S. Lewis as a Christmas gift for freshman students, Dean Scott Brown of the Tucker Foundation forbade distribution of the books via campus mail. "Our hope," explained Brown, "was that we could minimize the offense that some of our non-Christian minorities might feel from such an action."

The College clings to the infantile notion that the expression of Christian faith somehow threatens non-Christians. So, in lieu of actually accommodating minority religions, the College suppresses the majority religion.

Meanwhile, Jewish students find at Dartmouth an environment in which they cannot practice Judaism. So they don't come here.

"I have just been seething over the years that Dartmouth is seen as anti-Semitic," Freedman told the *Los Angeles Times* in a February 11, 1998 interview.

He may have been seething, but he never did much to improve the situation.

July 22, 1999

ON THE RIGHT
Church/State at Dartmouth
by William F. Buckley Jr.

T HE WHOLE BUSINESS of whether public schools can permit "intelligent design" to be acknowledged as an alternative to Darwinian evolution in explanation of human life will begin democratic exercises in a courtroom in Pennsylvania this week. There are regular flashpoints on this matter of the separation of church and state. Some of them test out constitutional questions, others merely modi vivendi. A week ago Noah Riner, the president of the Dartmouth Student Assembly, ran into the wrath of orthodox hardliners.

What happened was a convocation welcoming the freshman class to Dartmouth College. The student president traditionally speaks at these convocations, and this time it was the young man from Louisville, Kentucky, who uttered what turned out to be an inflammatory couple of sentences. He told the freshmen that the mere imparting of knowledge is less than what a college education should seek to do for students. The development of character is the higher goal. "Character has a lot to do with sacrifice, laying our personal interests down for something bigger. The best example of this is Jesus. . . . He knew the right thing to do. He knew the cost would be agonizing torture and death. He did it anyway. That's character."

That violation of secularist decorum brought on great indignation. A petition drive against the young student body president is contemplated. A vice president of the Student Assembly wrote to him, "I consider your choice of topic for the Convocation speech reprehensible and an abuse of power. You embarrass the organization, you embarrass yourself." A sophisticated defense was tendered by a Jewish student who wrote, "Many of us in the Dartmouth community proudly disagree with that and other aspects of Riner's religious beliefs, but our disagreements do not give us the right to limit his speech."

Riner himself gave a shrewd appraisal of the nature of the taboo. "The problem is not that Dartmouth has a formalized speech code. That would be easy to deal with, and easy for students to break. The problem is that Dartmouth has a speech culture, where some topics are off limits and some perspectives shouldn't be uttered. [Such] speech restriction is much more difficult to break—as I have recently discovered."

A few years ago the president of Dartmouth, dedicating the Jewish culture center, said that Dartmouth had a history of anti-Semitism, for which the college sought to shrive itself. Such prejudice was widespread before the Second World War, and the effort to expunge it engaged attention in the university world so high as to court the danger of drifting into a de facto prejudice against Christian expressiveness, as young Mr. Riner discovered. An effort was made (I wrote an op-ed for *The New York Times* and gave a lecture at Dartmouth) to make the sensible distinction: to eliminate anti-Semitic discrimination should not require the rejection of Christian traditions. The opposite could be held, inasmuch as a Christian who practices discrimination violates not only federal law, but also Christian law.

But as with the quarrel over the mere mention of intelligent design, the distinction struggles for air. The planted axiom being encouraged by the secular community is that an acknowledgment of biological evolution not only acquiesces in scientific certitudes, it cannot coexist with any thought of intelligent design. And this is true no matter how many metaphors are introduced ("we don't mean Noah actually got all living creatures into an ark . . .") to concede the morganatic difference between intelligent design and Darwinian evolution. Those at Dartmouth who objected to Mr. Riner's obeisance to Jesus acted as though he were bent on repealing the First Amendment. It wasn't as if he had been appealing to restore Dartmouth's original charter—which called for Christianizing the Indians.

Well, his experience helps him, and others, to develop the character, courage, and faith he sought to celebrate.

September 27, 2005; printed in The Dartmouth Review *October 7, 2005*

Rebel Yell

A Grand Opportunity for Reform: Alumni Vote for Trustee Representative
by Nathaniel Ward

J UST FOUR MONTHS after defeating a proposal to strip them of their governance rights, Dartmouth's alumni are faced with another election.

Trustee candidates are officially not supposed to campaign, but T. J. Rodgers '70 has nevertheless drawn considerable attention to his dark horse petition candidacy. Rodgers hopes to stave off the three "official" candidates, nominated by the College-influenced Alumni Council, and win the election. Balloting ends May 8, 2004.

Rodgers, chief executive of a Silicon Valley technology firm, says he hopes to reform the College's governance and leadership and return Dartmouth to a position of "academic superiority." As CEO of Cypress Semiconductor since 1982, Rodgers advocated then-radical programs like stock options for employees and other incentives to keep workers motivated.

"He is not a reiteration of stereotypical administration-selected trustees or the self-perpetuation which the Board produces for its own self-indulgence," said Quentin Kopp '49, a superior court judge in San Mateo, California. Instead, Rodgers was selected after a lengthy process to nominate a reform candidate, an effort led by an organization known as Dartmouth Alumni for Open Governance. Rodgers gathered nearly 2,500 signatures on his petition to be placed on the trustee ballot, five times the required minimum.

As a trustee, Rodgers wrote in a statement on the election website, he would look to overcome one obstacle in particular: the College's limits on free speech. Even trustees are unable to express dissenting opinions, he said, limiting the institution's ability to reform. Materials sent to alumni are simply "glossy infomercials" that avoid real debate, he continued, while the College's speech codes encroach on First Amendment rights.

Further battering the College and the board, Rodgers wrote that

Dartmouth's curriculum suffers a series of gaps "not only in math and science, but also in life's basics: thinking and reasoning, writing clearly, understanding the economy—and even understanding the basic principles and history of our American Democracy." The bureaucratic campus orthodoxy, which limits what opinions can and cannot be expressed at Dartmouth, further exacerbates these failings, he said.

Kopp noted that Rodgers is "grounded firmly in the value of a Dartmouth education, which is in turn not based on a smorgasbord of every contemporary educational fad." This variation from basic education is reflected in the roughly 350 courses Dartmouth offers, Kopp said, "the most superficial curriculum I've ever seen, since I first read a catalog of Dartmouth courses in 1945."

Rodgers also derided the College's approach to inclusivity, suggesting that efforts today do more harm than good. He proposed that Dartmouth admit students on the basis of merit rather than by quotas; a similar practice at Cypress has resulted in a racially diverse workforce, he said, where everyone understands they deserve to be there. "Diversity by mandate is wrong precisely because it demeans those it intends to help," he wrote. In the 1990s, he gained notoriety by dismissing a nun's criticism of the lack of women on Cypress's board by calling immoral any advancement except that based on merit.

Rodgers proposed a revision to Dartmouth's mission statement, emphasizing its liberal arts tradition of "educating America's leaders." This can only be achieved through academic superiority, he wrote, which in turn derives from a strong curriculum "taught by an exceptional faculty to small classes of the best students, who enjoy broad access to the faculty."

These proposals to remove academics from bureaucratic control have not gone unnoticed. Rodgers's candidacy has been featured in the *Wall Street Journal* and the *San Francisco Chronicle*. The *Journal* called Rodgers "a real choice" who would combat the "gooey Diversityspeak" of the other Trustee candidates, while the *Chronicle* presented Rodgers as a "crusader" for higher ideals.

Rodgers's petition candidacy is not unprecedented. In 1980, John Steel '54 successfully challenged an incumbent alumni Trustee through a petition campaign, becoming the first and only winning petition candidate. Most recently, a 1988 drive to elect Wid Washburn '48 to the Board by petition nearly unseated the sitting Trustee. The theme in each of the earlier elections, according to a statement from Dartmouth Alumni for Open Governance, "was the College's abandonment of its traditions, values and curriculum." DAOG last year successfully opposed a move to merge the Alumni Council and the 62,000-member Association of Alumni, which would have further limited the alumni Trustee selection process.

DAOG did consider other Trustee candidates, including Kopp, who declined because he didn't believe himself to be the strongest option. In-stead, he asked Rodgers if he would be willing to run. Rodgers, who met Kopp in December after the Alumni Association meeting, quickly agreed and set about organizing the petition drive.

Like Dartmouth, many Ivy League universities prohibit open campaigning for trustee positions, but politicization of elections is a growing (and yes, healthy) reality. Yale University's 2002 election for a place on the Yale Corporation saw the Reverend W. David Lee seek endorsements from politicians like Senator Joe Lieberman and other notable Yale alumni. Ultimately, Lee did not win the position despite a vocal campaign.

The other three Trustee candidates, nominated by committee, are not nearly as notable and are hard to readily distinguish. In contrast to Rodgers, the candidates very much follow the lead of many before them in academia: they boast their commitment to gender and racial diversity and, in rather dry language, explain their vague desire to expand Dartmouth's reputation as a leader in the liberal arts.

N. Bruce Duthu '80, the most interesting of the establishment candidates, brings with him long experience as a Dartmouth diversity-crat and anti-speech activist, starting with his position as director of the Native American Studies Program in the late 1980s. Later, he worked to degrade the quality of Dartmouth's academic offering by serving on a 1993 committee examining race relations at the College that recommended the creation of a full-time racial harmony administrator. The proposals the committee put forward later manifested themselves in the Office of Pluralism and Leadership (yes, that is a real title). He is the sole candidate to stand explicitly behind the 1999 Student Life Initiative. "I support the aspirations and values behind the College's Student Life Initiative," he said, perplexingly adding that the Initiative is "now operating to enhance the quality of students' out-of-classroom experiences."

When contacted by *The Dartmouth Review*, Mr. Duthu's office at Vermont Law School replied that he had taken a trip to China.

Perhaps the most nuanced of the "official" candidates, Daniel Papp '69, said in a statement on the elections website that "students must be exposed to diverse outlooks and positions on the issues of the day" and not only to racial variation.

The final candidate, Laura Stein '83, brings to the table years of experience running a ketchup company and the ability to speak a half-dozen languages. A vice president at H. J. Heinz, Mrs. Stein says she has experience at "reputation building, strategy development, operational oversight, investment and fiscal matters, risk management and education issues." Her vision for Dartmouth's future is of a strong University; she never neglected to mention the professional schools when discussing the College, and even proposed that Dartmouth invest more in those areas.

While the alumni are empowered to select half of the total members of the board, the candidates they choose do not necessarily sit as members. The board of trustees ultimately elects its own members, and the alumni only nominate candidates for the board's approval. Under an 1891 agreement, seven of the sixteen trustees shall be selected by alumni and seven directly by the board, with the other two consisting of the College President and the Governor of New Hampshire.

In early March, the board selected two new charter trustees, Putman Investments chief executive Charles Haldeman '70 and Albert Mulley '70 of Massachusetts General Hospital, both to take office in July. That month also marks the retirement of Chairwoman Susan Dentzer '77, who presided over much of the implementation of the Student Life Initiative that sought to impose on students from above a new, politically correct social order.

The board voted in November to add, over the next decade, six seats—three alumni trustees and three appointed charter trustees—after the New Hampshire legislature voted last summer to allow such changes to be made without explicit permission. Under the College's 1769 charter, the legislature must approve any changes to the charter, including changes in the composition of the board.

April 11, 2004

Rodgers Elected!
An Interview with T. J. Rodgers

by Nathaniel Ward

M ERE MONTHS after Dartmouth alumni scuttled College plans to restrict their voting rights, they dealt this administration another blow, electing darkhorse candidate T. J. Rodgers '70 to the Board of Trustees. A write-in candidate, Dr. Rodgers beat out three official candidates to win.

14,660 alumni—twenty-four percent of the total—cast their votes both online and by mail. Patricia Fisher-Harris '81 of the Alumni Leadership office said Dr. Rodgers was the "clear winner."

THE DARTMOUTH REVIEW: You are only the first candidate to win on a petition ballot after John Steele in 1980. What inspired you to make the attempt?
T. J. RODGERS: I was cruising along like about 75 percent of all alumni, living my life and ignoring the College when some alumni approached me

and said that I should run for the Board of Trustees. My first reaction was "I'm an extremely busy guy, who serves on seven boards of directors, and I run a company in Silicon Valley. I couldn't do it." But they prevailed in shaming me—I think that's a reasonable phrase—into doing it. The argument was along the lines of, "Either you ought to take the time and do something or stop griping." I chose A, because I love the College.

TDR: What are your fondest memories of Dartmouth?

TJR: There are really two categories of memories that overwhelm the others.

One is the school itself, the teaching. At the time I was there I didn't know I was in Heaven, but later on when I went to Stanford I realized I had been in Heaven. I hadn't appreciated enough the small classes. I studied physics and chemistry. The typical class size after my freshman year was ten. The professor was the person who wrote the book, and the professor was in his office every afternoon. You didn't need to make an appointment: you just showed up. Personalized instruction from a faculty that cared about teaching and world-class faculty, that's what characterized Dartmouth. That, I think, is still alive and well at Dartmouth, and it needs to be preserved.

Second is the fellowship, the fraternity of students at Dartmouth. And by that I don't mean a fraternity in the sense of a Greek organization, but the fellowship of your mates, to use the Australian phrase. That, of course, is something I think everyone at Dartmouth takes away with them.

TDR: How does this compare to Dartmouth today?

TJR: Students still benefit from the two attributes I described. I believe that if you properly select courses today you can still get great teachers, personal attention and small classes. You guys [at the *Review*] are conservative, I believe the College is left-liberal, and I'm a libertarian, so I'd argue with both sides on certain issues. I tried to keep my candidacy away from the Left-Right struggle because I believe the Left-Right struggle is at the wrong level; it's below the plane of where the debate should be. I deal with issues of freedom that transcend Left-Right politics.

One thing that I believe is distinctly different at Dartmouth today is the degradation of freedom of speech and the freedom of assembly—I'm deliberately using First Amendment language there—at the College today, by a lot, compared to when I was there. To me, any time that you lose the ability to be with whom you want, or to say what you want, then other bad things can happen. They happen by edict in the dead of night; they happen without announcement. You're in a precarious state when the freedom of speech is not robust. Obviously at Dartmouth people can make statements, but I don't believe the freedom of speech is as good as it was when I was there. That is one thing I'm going to work on; that is a sine qua non of a good school. Dartmouth should be leading the country as opposed to arguing in court, as it has on occasions, that it's a private institution and therefore not subject to all the laws of the country.

TDR: One area of particular concern to the *Review* is the College's insistence that students cannot deliver our publications in dormitories for an ever-changing slew of reasons. Other campus publications, even College-funded ones, are restricted just as the *Review* is. Does such a policy have any merits?

TJR: If a student signs up for a newspaper, they should have that newspaper delivered. A newspaper has the right to distribute its publication.

I thought that policy applied to [the *Review*] only. I'm a little relieved to find out that at least this bad policy is applied equally.

I think all newspapers should have the right to distribute. I believe that newspapers should be distributed freely at Dartmouth. I don't see why the administration feels the need to be involved at that nitty-gritty level of Dartmouth. That's command and control thinking and that's not appropriate for the College.

TDR: You were a member of a fraternity—Gamma Delta Chi—while at Dartmouth. What did that experience mean for you?

TJR: When I was a sophomore it was a very important thing for me to do. In 1966, the freshman social life was rather bleak. In my sophomore and junior years I enjoyed the fraternity life and standard fraternity stuff. As I understand it, the basics of fraternities haven't changed much, except that the College has pretty much put a wet blanket over everything.

I will talk directly and privately to fraternity members about their current environment. If they think their rights are being infringed upon, I will work with them. I believe the freedom of assembly is a right all Americans have.

At the very same time, I can tell you I got bored with my fraternity my senior year, and I quit Gamma Delta Chi. I didn't quit French Hall, the last dormitory down in the Wigwams. We had a fraternity down there, people who liked being in the furthest-away and ugliest building on campus.

TDR: As an alumnus and a fraternity member, what were your feelings when you first heard about the Student Life Initiative?

TJR: I've read about the Student Life Initiative, and I see it as an assault on the fraternities at Dartmouth, and I think it's abominable what's been done. If some of the stories I've heard are validated, some of the administration's tactics are a gross attack on rights of students, and I'm adamantly against it. I've read the attacks, I've read the political maneuvering that's been used to justify shutting them down. The concept that the school would demand that they be gender integrated.

TDR: The fraternities have resisted that at least, though it was implied in the wording of the original Initiative.

TJR: I've heard that you have to register a keg of beer to have it in a fraternity. I've heard that you need to have a College alcohol monitor at your parties. I don't like any of it. It sounds like I'm reading *1984*; it smacks of Big Brother. I think they ought to be left alone.

Over the years I have given my direct input to President Wright. I wrote a letter to him about repression of fraternities in 1998. About everything I wanted and said was right has gone wrong. At least with him as president, I've had someone who has listened to me. I have high regard for respectful disagreement; I have low regard for ignoring people.

TDR: One frequent criticism of the College is that it keeps its budget secret. Why is this bad?

TJR: I've heard that Susan Dentzer, the retiring Chairman of the Board of Trustees, was quoted along the lines of "T. J. will be assimilated by the Board." One thing that I will say is that I'm a fairly indigestible person. I think that openness leads to credibility, and that the College today has a credibility problem with the alumni body—and the faculty, assuming the views in Professor Iverson's letter on budget credibility are widely held.

June 1, 2004

The Connections of Strong Dartmouth
by Michael Ellis

T HIS YEAR'S ELECTION for the two open seats on Dartmouth's Board of Trustees has been marked by unusually vociferous public debate. The slate of candidates nominated by the Alumni Council, Sheila Cheston '80, Gregg Engles '79, Ric Lewis '84, and Curtis Welling '71 T '77, meet the usual politically correct requirements: one woman (Cheston), one minority (Lewis), and one corporate-suit-turned-do-gooder (Welling). Peter Robinson '79 and Todd Zywicki '88, following in the footsteps of T. J. Rodgers '70, were nominated by popular petition and are decidedly not politically correct. Robinson, a former Reagan speechwriter who penned the famous "Mr. Gorbachev, tear down this wall" speech, is currently a Fellow at the Hoover Institution and hosts the PBS program *Uncommon Knowledge*, while Zywicki, a professor of law at George Mason University, is a regular contributor to the conservative Volokh Conspiracy weblog.

Both Robinson and Zywicki share concerns about the state of undergraduate education at the College, the administration's suppression of free speech, and the Student Life Initiative. But while these views have won them support among many alumni, they have also provoked a sharp backlash from others. A shadowy group calling themselves "Alumni for a Strong Dartmouth" (ASD) has organized a website (strongdartmouth.org) to oppose the petition candidates and support the Alumni Council's hand-picked candidates.

Of course, the Alumni Association's prohibitions on campaigning prevent ASD from directly advocating for or against any particular candidates. So instead, their website uses a series of code words to make their points. They aren't opposed to Robinson and Zywicki, they just "remain supportive of the College and would like to ensure that responsible leadership remains on the Board of Trustees." They don't attack Robinson and Zywiciki's criticism of Dean of Admissions Karl Furstenburg belittling the Athletics Department, just note that "some people, even two in particular who weren't athletes themselves at Dartmouth, believe the College's commitment to athletics is waning." They don't criticize Robinson and Zywicki's petition candidacies, they just "believe that renegade campaigns that denigrate the good name and achievements of the College are divisive and do not contribute constructively to the debate."

But who are these Alumni for a Strong Dartmouth? Are they really just a group of "concerned alumni" who all coincidentally opposed the petition candidates and found each other through the magic of the Internet? Hardly. Many of the members of ASD are connected directly or indirectly to the Alumni Association, Alumni Council, the College's Alumni Relations Office, or the College itself. The man who organized ASD and designed its website is a Geoff Berlin, member of the class of 1984 and founder of Alums Online, a company specializing in alumni outreach. His op-ed piece in the March 1 *Daily Dartmouth* cleared up any doubt over his opposition to the petition candidates. In it, he calls Robinson and Zywicki's campaigns "alarming," "utterly mistaken," and "inclined to mislead their fellow alumni." Berlin has created the websites for the Class of 1982 and 1984, and is rumored to have done work for the Alumni Relations office as well. Nels Armstrong '71, the College's Director of Alumni Relations, said that he knew Berlin, and that he was "a wonderful entrepreneur," but denies that he has ever done work for Alumni Relations. Berlin did not return phone calls seeking comment.

Several Dartmouth College employees, including Elizabeth Meyer '96, the director of the Parents and Grandparents Fund in the College's Development Office, and Professor Susan Ackerman '80, chairwoman of the religion department, are also affiliated with the ASD. When contacted, Meyer was unavailable for comment and Ackerman refused to comment.

While no members of the Alumni Relations Office are directly connected to the group, Stan Colla '66, the Vice President of Alumni Relations, has a slightly more indirect link. His son, Geoffrey Colla '04, is a member of ASD. A complete coincidence, I'm sure. Two members of the *Alumni Magazine*'s editorial board, Julie Koeninger '81 and Patricia Berry '81, are affiliated with ASD. So are eight former trustees of the College: I. Michael Heyman '51, Henry Nachman, Jr. '51 T'55, Robert P. Henderson '53, Joe Mathewson '55, Robert Danzinger '56 T'57, Ronald Schram '64, Kate Stith '73, and Ann Fritz Hackett '76. The chance that all of these individuals gathered together to form ASD without the knowledge of administrators in Parkhurst and the Alumni Relations Office is so small that it makes the Powerball lottery look like an investment.

But it isn't just the College administration that has ties to ASD.: members of the Alumni Council and Alumni Association, the very bodies that nominate the candidates for Trustee and run the elections, are tied to ASD as well. Noel Fidel '66, Chas Carner '71, and Missy Attridge '77, former presidents of the Alumni Council (which nominates the official Trustee candidates) are all members of ASD, so too are J. Michael Houlahan '61, Robert Conn '61, Patricia Berry '81, and Karen Brown Letarte '84, all former or current members of the Alumni Council. Perhaps most troubling is Jeanhee Kim '90, a member of the Alumni Association's Executive Committee who is also a member of ASD. Three of Ms. Kim's colleagues on the Executive Committee also serve on the Ballot Committee, which oversees and establishes guidelines for the Trustee elections. Kim did not respond to attempts to contact her for comment.

While it seems highly unlikely that all of these individuals, with so many diverse ties to the College administration and the Alumni governing bodies gathered together of their own initiative, nothing about the group is against the election rules, per se. Since their members are affiliated with the alumni bodies that write the rules for the election, it comes as little surprise that ASD has taken great pains to stay within their bounds. But as much as the Alumni for a Strong Dartmouth might whine about returning responsible leadership to the Board of Trustees, the real cause of their opposition is fear—fear that the alumni will keep up the precedent set by Rodgers of nominating and electing the Trustees without the involvement of the Alumni Council or Association. The very existence of their organized opposition to Robinson and Zywicki is evidence that they are more concerned with maintaining power over their own personal fiefdoms among the alumni than with the future of the College.

March 11, 2005

The Dartmouth Review, *Volume 1, Issue 1.*
Distributed at the 1980 Dartmouth commencement ceremonies, the newspaper became
instantly recognizable thanks in part to this cover cartoon by Steve Kelley '81—
soon to be an award-winning cartoonist for the San Diego Union-Tribune *and*
The Times-Picayune *in New Orleans.*

Review *founders Gordon Haff
and Gregory Fossedal '81
celebrate at a Hanover election-
night party for Ronald Reagan,
top, as Steve Kelley tallies the
returns and draws one for the
Gipper, right.* © *Gordon Haff.
Below, Charlton Heston
becomes an early reader
of the* Review.

A letter from President Ronald Reagan to Gregory Fossedal upon Fossedal's appointment following his tenure at the Review, *right. Below, Fossedal leaving a meeting at the Reagan White House.*

THE WHITE HOUSE
WASHINGTON

27 August 1981

Greg Fossedal,
Staff writer for
    Education Policies,
E.O.B. 102

Dear Greg:

Lyn Nofziger informed me of your appointment a few weeks ago, and I'm delighted to have you on board.

While he was in the office, he slipped me a few copies of *The Dartmouth Review*. I must say, it's an impressive paper. You should be proud to have started this important movement; let's hope that your fine efforts will be imitated elsewhere.

Sincerely,

Ronald Reagan

Ronald Reagan

Review *editors hire an airplane to carry a banner above Commencement with their editorial on the Indian symbol controversy, top. Steve Kelley, upper left, and Benjamin Hart '81, upper right, show Dartmouth spirit while tempting College discipline. A pro-Indian banner at the Homecoming bonfire, lower right. Inset: The Dartmouth Indian. © Gordon Haff.*

Gamely Response To A Rally

By Bill Scoville

Croquet, a game which has always appealed to the aristocratic has been receiving a lot of publicity lately. At last week's meeting of the Hanover Mallet Society, the current president and a two year member of the club, said, "Of course croquet players have always been polished and dignified ourselves, but we do have problems with the spectators."

Croquet is a game borrowed from England, it was popular in the eighteenth century, and certain novelists used it for lubricious symbolism. The word "croquet" is a misnomer, accidentally derived from the French "croquer," which means "to crunch." In a particularized sense, however, that was precisely the effect last Friday's game had on anti-Review ralliers.

You do not have to be a member of the Hanover Mallet Society to play croquet, though: there are two fraternities on campus which include the sport among its most arduous physical activities. A good game of croquet, said one player at Theta Delt, helps to relieve the pressure in the classroom as well as to provide a needed social outlet other than the basements of houses.

"Croquet can be much more relaxing than ping-pong," said Al Segal, the Grand Krükon at Theta Delt. Other houses, however, have other reasons for playing croquet ranging from just having the space to play the game to the fact that carrying up a ping pong table is too difficult.

The college will probably never give college status to the traditional sport because of the propensity for alcoholic beverages at the matches. "Without suitable drinks," giggled one player, "you would not be able to play a spirited game." Theta Delt and Zeta Psi, moreover, would not be able to play their matches of beer-croquet if the game were to be put under the auspices of the college.

Bill Scoville is a sophomore at Dartmouth and staff writer for The Review.

STAFF PHOTOS BY NATE LEVENSON

The Dartmouth Review

Vol. 4 Issue 6
October 31, 1983
The Hanover Review, Inc.
P.O. Box 343
Hanover, N.H. 03755

Nemo me impune lacessit

FREE

The INDIAN: Here to Stay!
-p. 8

- **Former Castro supporter Armando Chardiet '39 on Communism in Latin America** -p. 9
- *The Spike* **co-author Arnaud de Borchgrave on KGB disinformation** -Interview p. 6

The lighter side of the Review: *newspaper founders inaugurate Dartmouth's croquet club, top, including Keeney Jones '83 with a* Brideshead-*inspired Aloysius teddy bear; professor Jeffrey Hart, right, in formal wear, prepares to defend the* Review *against Government professor Roger Masters; the* Review *celebrates the (unsanctioned) return of the Indian symbol to the 1983 Homecoming game.*

Resolved: That The Dartmouth Review has a deleterious effect on the intellectual and social life of the college.

Roger Masters vs Jeffrey Hart

Thursday, November 19 at 8:30 p.m. in Cook Auditorium

Clockwise from top left: William Cattan '83 and Dinesh D'Souza '83 on "Nightline" in 1982; Deborah Stone '87 on "Donahue"; Cattan with George Champion '26, a major supporter of the newspaper; Stone and Laura Ingraham '85 with Freedom Fighters in El Salvador; Ingraham kisses Jerry Falwell; William Grace '89; Teresa Polenz '89 in disguise; Hart and Jones; D'Souza interviews George Gilder.

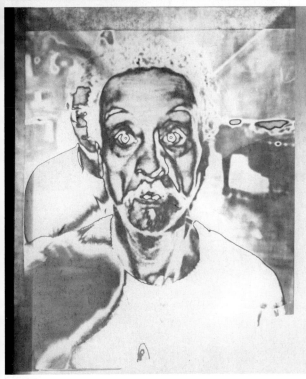

The controversies. Clockwise from upper left: two images of the divestment protest and aftermath; President James O. Freedman (left) spots a Reviewer; Kevin Pritchett '91 (with flag) and other victims of the AAm; Bill Cole moments before striking a Review photographer; a Harvard Lampoon parody of The Dartmouth Review following the "Hitler Quote incident"; the last image of Bill Cole taken before he destroyed the Review's photography equipment.

The Review *today: a meeting of the board of trustees of* The Dartmouth Review, *spring 2004, with Harry Camp '04, Steven Menashi '01, Joseph Rago '05, and William Grace;* Review *reporters prepare for an undercover bust of the 2004 Dartmouth Drag Ball; the two faces of Dartmouth—James O. Freedman leads a room in song (right) while Maceo Parker (left) performs on the porch of Phi Delt fraternity on Green Key weekend 1995; James Panero '98 emcees the 1998 Psi Upsilon Winter Carnival Keg Jump, soon to be a victim of the College crackdown on Greek life; Stefan Beck '04 competes in the* Review*'s first annual Rigoberta Menchú Memorial Pong Tournament (2003).*

The Lone Pine Revolution

by Michael Ellis & Scott Glabe

T WO BESPECTACLED, suit-wearing academics make for unlikely revolutionaries. However, the election of Hoover Institution fellow Peter Robinson '79 and George Mason University law professor Todd Zywicki '88 to Dartmouth College's Board of Trustees, announced Thursday, is perhaps the most significant event in the institution's recent history.

Most trustee elections at Dartmouth, like those to most corporate boards, are low-key affairs, marked by apathy. But not this one. Just to earn a place on the trustee election ballot, Robinson and Zywicki each had to collect 500 alumni signatures on a petition. They next fought back a spirited opposition from the four "official" candidates nominated by the administration-controlled Alumni Council, all the while fending off attacks from rogue groups of alumni trying to scuttle their campaigns.

Many dismissed as a fluke last year's triumph by another conservative petition candidate, Cypress Semiconductors CEO T. J. Rodgers. Rodgers won easily after a low-key campaign. Zywicki and Robinson would not have it nearly so easy.

As the balloting got under way, Dartmouth President James Wright embarked on an expensive tour of Dartmouth alumni clubs around the nation, delivering speeches ad infinitum that implicitly endorsed the establishment candidates. More sinisterly, a shadowy organization composed largely of College administrators—and wishfully titled "Alumni for a Strong Dartmouth"—set up a website openly attacking Robinson and Zywicki. Meanwhile, Professor Susan Ackerman, chairman of Dartmouth's religion department, penned a particularly malicious e-mail asserting that "the two petition candidates both represent, as far as I can tell, the same sorts of reactionary ideologies as were represented in last year's elections by T. J. Rodgers."

The petition candidates were up against a barrage of institutionally sponsored criticism, yet they were prohibited from campaigning except in two e-mails and one letter to alumni. Then, a series of "glitches" befell their campaigns: one of Zywicki's e-mails was mysteriously "lost" for several days; many alumni never received their ballots in the mail; and, to top it off, the election was suddenly extended for two weeks just as the petition candidates seemed at their strongest.

What was it about these two men that provoked such vitriol and so many irregularities? Robinson campaigned on three issues: small classes (paid for by eliminating superfluous bureaucrats); free speech; and strong athletics. Zywicki's platform was nearly identical. All of these issues are highly salient; each, when explored, casts the current College administration in an extremely bad light.

Dartmouth's administrators claim an "average" class size of eighteen, but the actual value is upwards of forty in many of the most popular departments. Courses are chronically over-subscribed, even as the College continues to employ literally dozens of deans.

The Foundation for Individual Rights in Education (FIRE), a nonpartisan advocacy group, gave the College its worst rating for free speech in 2003. Dartmouth's speech code was detailed in a 2001 letter from Dartmouth President James Wright in response to some particularly ill-advised expression by some fraternity members. He wrote that students lack "'rights' [which] trump the rights, feelings, and considerations of others."

At the same time, Dartmouth's athletics have been suffering. Last year, ten of the College's thirty varsity teams finished either in last or second-to-last place in the Ivy League—and it is little wonder. In 2002, the administration attempted to cut the swimming and diving teams before widespread alumni and student protest forced them to reverse the decision. More recently, a letter surfaced from Dean of Admissions Karl Furstenberg declaring that the football program had a mission "antithetical" to that of the College (perhaps no one told him that last year's commencement speaker, General Electric CEO Jeffrey Immelt '78, played football during his time at the College).

With further study, it becomes clear that Robinson and Zywicki's issues were not those of a reactionary minority, Professor Ackerman's claims notwithstanding. In a poll of current students conducted by the student government—a bunch probably more sympathetic to College bureaucrats than relatively conservative alumni—only a quarter of respondents agreed that "the administration is responsive to concerns of the student body." Just 11 percent claimed to "understand the administration's visions for Dartmouth in ten years." These are shocking numbers.

As heartening as Robinson and Zywicki's victory may be, nothing has been accomplished yet. Indeed, the most pressing issue at the College has barely been addressed: improving the quality of education and restoring some semblance of a core curriculum. It is practically impossible for a student to receive an education in the Western tradition these days.

Robinson and Zywicki's campaigns and subsequent victory have awakened student and alumni alike to the challenges Dartmouth faces. Campus newspapers and weblogs have been alive with talk of free speech, class sizes, and administrative deception for weeks on end. Just last Tuesday, FIRE improved its rating of free speech at Dartmouth after the administration spent months backpedaling—a move for which the trustee election is directly responsible.

Over a half century ago, William F. Buckley Jr.'s *God and Man at Yale* asked whether the education provided at that university corresponded with the wishes of its alumni, to whom its administrators ultimately report. The answer at Dartmouth, as it was at Yale, has always been a resounding "no." However, with Robinson and Zywicki's upset win, the answer at one Ivy League institution could soon be "yes."

May 14, 2005

An Interview with Todd Zywicki '88

by Nathaniel Ward

TODD ZYWICKI '88 is one of Dartmouth's two new trustees. A petition candidate running against determined opposition from the College establishment, Mr. Zywicki garnered the support of 45 percent of alumni.

THE DARTMOUTH REVIEW: What made you decide to run for trustee?
TODD ZYWICKI: Two things. First, the proximate cause was obviously Rodgers's winning last year and showing it can be done, that the alumni were ready for change. Secondly—I'm sure a lot of alumni have thought about this—general dissatisfaction with the direction of the College over the past decade.

TDR: Are you surprised you won?
TZ: I am surprised. It's only happened twice before in history [that a petition candidate has won]. Although I share many of the same concerns as T. J. Rodgers did last year, he was a very different sort of person and candidate than I was.

TDR: What are your goals? Where do you see Dartmouth in ten years?
TZ: I think that my goals are pretty clear. First, I'd like to see the College recommit itself to undergraduate education in particular. The most tangible way is to clarify its financial goals, to make sure that money and resources are going into educational programming—not into bureaucracy and not into expenditures of dubious education value, like the infamous Sustainability Director post.

Secondly, I've talked to a lot of recent alumni in particular, and one thing I think I'd like to do is rebuild Dartmouth's community and the affection and loyalty that students and alumni have for the institution. I think that in terms of recruiting and educating more well-rounded leaders, people who are concerned about the community who are willing to give of themselves for Dartmouth and who will go out and represent Dartmouth as opposed to people who are just preoccupied with narrow interests and that sort of thing.

Finally, I'd like to increase the transparency and the accountability of College governance. I feel, as many alumni do, that the College has a tendency to patronize us and to make alumni feel like they have nothing to contribute to College governance. I would like to have a greater transparency in College governance so people have more of a sense of what the College is doing and why they're doing what they do, as opposed to whitewashed communications from the College that come down as if from on high. [I propose] a more collaborative process between the College and its stakeholders: students, alumni, faculty, and parents alike.

TDR: Do you think that Dartmouth should have a core curriculum?
TZ: Yes.

TDR: What do you make of the recent decision by the Foundation for Individual Rights in Education to upgrade Dartmouth's free speech ratings?
TZ: I think that Dartmouth's repeal of its speech code is a step in the right direction. From that perspective, I was very pleased to see FIRE's tentative steps in that direction. It's also a first step. A next step is for Dartmouth, in both word and deed, to come out unambiguously in favor of free speech. I would like to see Dartmouth as a leader on this issue in modern academia, to hold Dartmouth up as a model for freedom of speech and freedom of expression on college and university campuses. From that perspective, I think that what Dartmouth has done so far—I'm cautiously optimistic it is a good step in the right direction. I'd like to see us continue moving in that direction and build on that.

TDR: You spoke about rebuilding the Dartmouth community. Do you see fraternities playing a role in this community?
TZ: I believe so, yes. The College would do better to have a more balanced attitude towards fraternities and be more cooperative with students in arranging social and other residential alternatives. The College should continue to invest in alternative social arrangements, but it must also respect students' rights of freedom of association and freedom of speech.

TDR: One of the major issues addressed during the campaign was the state of the athletics program. What do you think could be done to improve sports at Dartmouth?
TZ: Ivy League athletics strikes the correct balance between academics and athletics. Not only is [the balance] appropriate, but every other conference and institution in the country tries to match it. I think the Ivy League is the gold standard.

The concern that there's going to be an anti-intellectual culture spawned by college athletics at Dartmouth is frankly absurd.

TDR: Many wrote off T. J. Rodgers's election last year as a fluke. But now there have been three petition candidates elected to the Board of Trustees in two years. Do you think it's now a trend?

TZ: It's clearly more than a fluke, but it's hard to say whether or not it is a trend. Each election is different, but it's quite clear that there's deep-seated concern about the direction of the College, not only reflected in this, but also in alumni contribution rates.

TDR: Do you think the rules governing the Trustee elections, in particular the campaigning, are fair? Do they need reform?

TZ: They need to be largely abolished. In the modern era where information is so valuable and so difficult to control, the idea of trying to control information seems to be largely absurd. What it ends up doing is controlling those of us who can be sanctioned by failure to follow the rules. It does not place any limitations—nor should it place any limitations—on others. What you end up with is the kind of situation you saw here, where you can have alumni—many of them, astoundingly to me, campaigning in the name of their various Alumni Association officers, attacking properly qualified petition candidates—and us not having the opportunity to respond in any way. I think that is really, fundamentally unfair.

Any effort to try to enforce those rules, which are so counterproductive and silly, were going to be rife with inequality because the rules themselves don't make any sense. Any way you try to enforce it is going to be largely arbitrary. I think we saw that this time around.

June 2, 2005

SUMMATION

SEVEN SPECIALLY COMMISSIONED ESSAYS ON
TWENTY-FIVE YEARS OF *THE DARTMOUTH REVIEW*

Dartmouth's J-School

by Jeffrey Hart

Jeffrey Hart, who holds a B.A. and Ph.D. from Columbia University and served in U.S. Naval Intelligence during the Korean war, is the author of nine books, including Acts of Recovery: Essays on Culture and Politics, Smiling through the Cultural Catastrophe: Toward the Revival of Higher Education, *and* The Making of the American Conservative Mind: National Review and Its Times. *A longtime senior editor at* National Review, *he is Professor Emeritus of English at Dartmouth College, and advisor to* The Dartmouth Review.

M ORE OR LESS, *The Dartmouth Review* was launched in the living room of my house in Lyme, New Hampshire. There should be a bronze plaque on the house because a) the *Review* has been Dartmouth's School of Journalism, and b) it became and remains the flagship example of independent college conservative newspapers across the country.

I myself had nothing to do with launching the newspaper and was only a benign spectator. Living in my house at the time were my son Ben '81 and Dinesh D'Souza '83, two founders of the *Review*. Other students came and went. Sometimes things turned into a party. As a freshman D'Souza had been a reporter for the *Daily Dartmouth*, the regular student newspaper. There he had shown conspicuous talent, marked especially by humor. One notable article covered a talk given by the novelist William Styron in the Wren Room at Sanborn House, home of Dartmouth's English Department.

During the question period, as covered by D'Souza, Professor Donald Pease of the English Department, widely known as a man of many words, asked Styron a question consisting of about 136 words. Styron answered, "No." D'Souza wrote this up with a straight face. Thus a major talent hove into view. When the *Review* was being launched, D'Souza saw it, correctly, as an opportunity to write longer and more wide-ranging articles.

As I remember it, he was not especially political as a freshman, but experience moved him in a conservative direction.

That the *Review* has been Dartmouth's School of Journalism is obvious. Dinesh D'Souza is now famous, emerging in the public arena with two important books, *Illiberal Education* and *The End of Racism*. He has, of course, published many more, and become famous as a debater on public platforms, scoring well against such as Stanley Fish and Jesse Jackson. Laura Ingraham '85 became a reporter for MSNBC, a best-selling author, and radio host. Deborah Stone '87 went to work for John Stossel at ABC News. As for the editors of this present volume: James Panero '98 is now Managing Editor of *The New Criterion*, our leading journal of the arts, where Stefan Beck '04 is Associate Editor. Joseph Rago '05, a recent *Review* editor, won an internship at the *Wall Street Journal*, and then, as almost never happens, was appointed to a permanent position in the editorial department. Kevin Pritchett '91 also became an editor at the *Wall Street Journal*, while Hugo Restall '92 went from *The Dartmouth Review* to the *Wall Street Journal* in New York to the *Asian Wall Street Journal* in Hong Kong. Now he is Editor of the *Far Eastern Economic Review*, another Dow Jones publication, also in Hong Kong. Benjamin Wallace-Wells '00 is an editor at the *Washington Monthly*. Steve Menashi '01 has worked as Associate Editor of *Policy Review* and served on the Editorial Board of *The New York Sun*. Andrew Grossman '02 now works for the Heritage Foundation. Alston Ramsay '04 is an editor at *National Review*. Michael Ellis '06, the most recent Editor of the *Review*, has worked for the Republican National Committee while taking a full schedule of courses. His future is unlimited. The *Review* now has a startling number of gifted writers, any one of whom might emerge as an important journalist.

The Dartmouth Review got launched because of converging circumstances. Little known is the importance of a very liberal assistant priest at Aquinas House, the Catholic student center. This priest's liberalism took several forms, but most conspicuous was his donning of vestments incorrect for the Mass to be celebrated. The group of students who objected to this and other extravagances planned a newsletter to express their protest against the deviations of this priest.

There was also the candidacy of Ronald Reagan and the conservative—reaction to the Kemeny presidency—trustee candidacy of Dr. John Steel. At this time in mid-1980, Greg Fossedal '81 was editor of the regular student newspaper, the *Daily Dartmouth*. He supported Reagan, and in a signed column endorsed Steel. This proved indigestible. He was removed from his editorship, evidence that that paper is anything but independent.

That event was pivotal for *The Dartmouth Review*. An editor without a newspaper, Fossedal brought to the *Review* idea the practical skills necessary to putting out an actual newspaper rather than the hypothetical newsletter. He even put up some of his own money to finance an initial issue, which duly appeared at Commencement 1980 with a cover cartoon by Steve Kelley '81, now nationally known as the cartoonist SKelley. With that first issue out, it was possible to raise money from alumni, who have been the principal support for the paper ever since. Fossedal designed the format of the newspaper along the lines of *National Review*: letters, then short editorial paragraphs, articles, and "culture," here including sports.

On the *Review*'s success, one point is impossible to stress too much. Tax-deductible status was essential, as it facilitated alumni support. Most colleges' imitations of the *Review* foundered on that vital matter. Rep. Jack Kemp became interested in Dartmouth through his son Jeff, quarterback on the football team, and helped out with achieving tax-deductible status.

With the appearance of *The Dartmouth Review*, which flourished on into the fall of 1980, when Reagan won in a landslide over Carter, and far beyond, it was widely thought among faculty members that I was writing for it. I was known as a conservative. In 1968 I had been a speechwriter, first for Reagan, taking leave to go to Sacramento out in Lotusland, and then for Nixon in his successful 1968 run, as he slid swivel-hipped between Humphrey and Wallace.

It was not widely known, however, that I never introduced current politics into my courses, considering that to be unprofessional and otiose. That I had time to write for the *Review* would have been a preposterous notion for anyone who knew my schedule. Since 1969, I had been flying twice a month to New York for my duties at *National Review*, and during this period wrote two commercially successful books inspired by college tuition bills for sons and daughters. Otherwise, I was more than fully occupied with my teaching and writing on literary subjects.

My benign relation to the *Review* has exacerbated my relations with some on the faculty. But, as Dartmouth football coach Earl "Red" Blaik said, and made the title of his memoir: *You Have to Pay the Price*. It was not much of a price to pay. And even without the *Review* I would have created trouble, I suppose, some of it comical.

For example, I recall a faculty cocktail party where, during a conversation with a Government professor, the subject of South Africa unfortunately came up, apartheid a matter on which moral superiority was delightfully easy, cost-free, to achieve. I observed, mischievously, that more or less all of the countries in Africa were dominated by one tribe or another, that the white tribe was running South Africa, and, except for a few Bushmen, had been there first, the Zulus pushing south later. The Government fellow drew himself up to his six-foot-three height or something like that and with matchless pomposity actually declared, "No gentleman would defend South Africa."

Secure in my own status as a gentleman, I didn't care. It's possible that this attitude communicated itself rather widely. I knew some reporters for Ruppert Murdoch's right-wing tabloid the *New York Post*, especially a Murdoch investigative reporter who was trying to dig up Mafia connections involving then-Governor Mario Cuomo. It must have been through his agency that the editorial cartoonist for the *Post* made an ink drawing of my supposed coat-of-arms. It featured the usual shield in the middle, plus symbols representing my interests, a pair of skis on one side, crossed tennis rackets on the other, a quill in a bottle of ink on the shield, and, as a spectator interest, a football helmet at the top, no doubt in place of the usual knight's helmet. Where the usual motto should be on the shield, instead of *Lux et Veritas*, *Excelsior*, *E Pluribus Unum*, or some such respectable thing, it said "I Don't Give a Shit."

That is not exactly how I see myself, and I would have preferred something maybe from Emerson's essay "Self-Reliance." There, he is urging Americans to resist the tyranny of the majority, a feature, as Tocqueville and Emerson saw, of post-aristocratic societies in which there are few or no barriers to mass opinion.

About the football helmet a word might be in order. My father graduated from Dartmouth with the class of 1921, and my first connection otherwise with the College was through football. Every year, from about the age of five, he took me to the Dartmouth-Princeton game at Palmer Stadium. The train going back to Nassau Hall left from Penn Station and was always packed with Dartmouth people celebrating the expected victory, celebrating to the extent that some, I feel sure, failed to make it off the train at Princeton Junction. A couple of beautiful sentences written by Francis Russell epitomize for me my recollection of those distant afternoons at Palmer Stadium: "It is that hushed moment before the two teams surge onto the empty field and the rival captains walk toward each other for the toss-up. Any hushed moment, however, is apt to be shattered by the crash of a hip flask inadvertently dropped on the concrete."

The mention of Emerson and "Self-Reliance" focuses for me the quality I have admired at *The Dartmouth Review* from the start in 1980. If you don't like the existing newspaper, well, start a better one. It is that quality of self-reliance, independence of spirit, that has always characterized the *Review*, despite repeated attempts to crush that spirit through intimidation and even official calumny. Such independence is an indispensable quality for anyone who would be a writer, that is, indispensable for finding one's own voice. The *Review* has exposed scandals, as with the "teaching" of Music Professor Cole; it has taken risks, hilarious sometimes, as with the performance journalism of Keeney Jones. In the early days of the *Review*, the influence of *Brideshead Revisited* was palpable, not so much the novel as the television movie, narrated by Bill Buckley.

That influence showed up in croquet matches on the lawn in front of San-born House, with gin and tonics catered from the Hanover Inn, and, once, lobster and champagne on the Inn porch to protest the self-congratulation of World Hunger Week. Sebastian Flyte should have been there, and perhaps he was, in spirit.

For all the joking, during this first Reagan-era period of the *Review*, the talent of its student editors became recognized. The White House mess looked like a *Review* staff meeting.

The faculty, to be sure, no doubt objected all along to the *Review*'s regular "course guide" characterizations of individual teachers and courses. But, where I have had knowledge of the individual, these have been pretty much on the mark. One definition of good journalism is printing things that someone does not want printed.

It is both remarkable and not remarkable that the *Review* has now flourished for twenty-five years. The *Review* has had a great many talented and courageous editors and staff members, and, in my judgment, is now in a spectacularly successful phase.

January 2006

Lessons from Jeffrey Hart

by Peter Robinson

Peter Robinson, Dartmouth class of 1979, an author, television host, and former Chief White House Speechwriter for President Ronald Reagan, is a Fellow at the Hoover Institution. While studying in Oxford after Dartmouth graduation, Robinson served as correspondent for the first issues of The Dartmouth Review.

In 2005, Peter Robinson was elected by petition vote to the Dartmouth Board of Trustees.

W HILE JOHN STEEL was attempting a revolution here in Hanover, Ronald Reagan was starting one in Washington, and if you supposed the two had nothing in common, you'd need to reconsider. A startling number of people served as firebrands in both. First, they used the pages of *The Dartmouth Review* to support John Steel's efforts to turn Dartmouth upside-down—or, rather, right-side-up. Then they used positions in the Reagan administration to help the fortieth chief executive do the same to the world.

At the Reagan White House, I wrote speeches for the President, Will Cattan '83 wrote speeches for the Vice President, and Dinesh D'Souza '83 helped administer the Office of Domestic Policy. Within a few blocks, Gregory Fossedal '81 held a senior position at the Department of Education, Benjamin Hart '81 produced position papers for the Heritage Foundation, Michael [Keeney] Jones '82 wrote speeches for the Secretary of the Treasury, and Laura Ingraham '85 served as an assistant to the Secretary of Transportation. So many Dartmouth students went from the *Review* straight to positions of responsibility in the nation's capital that Sidney Blumenthal, a reporter for the *Washington Post*, composed an article about us in which he hinted darkly at some sort of conspiracy.

How did this happen? How did so many twenty-somethings from an upstart student newspaper at a small college find ourselves working for the

The Early Days

by Dinesh D'Souza

Dinesh D'Souza, Dartmouth class of 1983, a former Editor-in-Chief of The Dartmouth Review, *is the Robert and Karen Rishwain Fellow at the Hoover Institution at Stanford University. He is the author of, most recently,* What's So Great About America *and* Letters to a Young Conservative. *His 1991 book* Illiberal Education *spent fifteen weeks on the* New York Times *bestseller list and has been acclaimed as one of the most influential books of the 1990s.*

I ARRIVED AT DARTMOUTH in the fall of 1979, having come to the United States the previous year as a Rotary exchange student from Bombay, India. I started out as a pretty typical Asian American student. I was not a conservative. In fact, I didn't see myself as political. In retrospect, I realize that by the end of my freshman year my views were mostly liberal. If you had said "capitalism," I would have said "greed." If you had said "Reagan," I would have said "washed-up former actor." If you had said "morality," I would have said, "can't legislate it." These were not reasoned convictions. Rather, I was carried by the tide.

My plans were to major in economics and to earn an advanced degree in business, either in the United States or in London. I enjoyed writing, however, and I signed up to write for the *Daily Dartmouth*. Toward the end of my freshman year, a major schism occurred at the *Daily D*. The editor of the paper, Greg Fossedal, came out of the closet as a conservative. He began to write editorials supporting the candidacy of Ronald Reagan for president; the other editors, scandalized by this offense, began the process of getting him fired. They succeeded, and Fossedal resolved to start an alternative weekly newspaper.

I joined *The Dartmouth Review* for two reasons: one aesthetic, the other intellectual. The first was that I found a style and a *joie de vivre* that I had not previously associated with conservatism. The best example of this was

323

advisor Jeffrey Hart, a professor of English (now emeritus) and a senior editor of *National Review*. Hart was exactly the opposite of the conservative stereotype. He wore a long raccoon coat around campus, and he smoked long pipes with curvaceous stems. He sometimes wore buttons that said things such as "Soak the Poor." In his office he had a wooden, pincer-like device that he explained was for the purpose of "pinching women that you don't want to touch."

Even more outrageous than Hart's attire and equipment was his mind. Hart's writing was striking for its lyricism and candor. His most controversial column about Dartmouth was called "The Ugly Protesters." He wrote it during the time of the protests against white rule in South Africa, when the Green was regularly occupied by a horde of angry young men and women shouting various slogans. Hart wrote that he was puzzled by the intensity of the protesters. What possible interest could they have in events so remote from their everyday lives?

Observing the protesters, Hart noted that their unifying characteristic was their state of dishevelment. Exploring the connection between their demeanor and their political activism, Hart decided they were protesting their own ugliness! Hart's column caused a sensation on campus. Walking to class the next day, I saw a remarkable sight on the Green. In an attempt to disprove Hart's characterization, the protesters had shown up in suits and long dresses. But they had made a strategic blunder because their suits were so ill-fitting that they looked even more ridiculous. Watching the scene from his office in Sanborn, Hart blew billows of smoke from his pipe and chuckled with obscene pleasure.

In part because of his political incorrectness, Hart was one of the few people I have met whose jokes made people laugh out loud. Consider a contest that *National Review* held among its editors following the publication of a controversial Bill Buckley column that suggested those with AIDS receive a small tattoo on their rear ends to warn potential partners. Buckley's suggestions caused a bit of a public stir, but the folks at *National Review* were animated by a different question: What should the tattoo say? A contest was held, and the winner by unanimous consent was Hart. He suggested the lines emblazoned on the gates to Dante's *Inferno*: "Abandon all hope, ye who enter here."

I remember some of those early dinners at the Hart farmhouse. We drank South American wine and listened to recordings of Ernest Hemingway and F. Scott Fitzgerald, of Robert Frost reading his poems, and Nixon speeches, of comedian Rich Little doing his Nixon imitation, George C. Scott delivering the opening speech in *Patton*, some of Winston Churchill's orations, and the music from the BBC version of Evelyn Waugh's *Brideshead Revisited*. There was an ethos here, and a sensibility, and it conveyed to me something about conservatism that I had never suspected. Here was conservatism that was alive; that was engaged with art, music, and literature; that was at the same time ironic, lighthearted, and fun.

The second reason I joined *The Dartmouth Review* was that I was greatly impressed by the seriousness of the conservative students. They were passionate about ideas, and they argued vigorously about what it meant to be a conservative, and what it meant to be an American, and who was a liberally educated person, and who should belong to a liberal arts community, and whether journalism could be objective, and whether reason could refute revelation, and whether corporations should give money to charity, and why Joseph Stalin was a worse man than Adolf Hitler, and why socialism was not merely inefficient but also immoral. Once, in the middle of a serious argument, I proposed a break for dinner and was greeted with the response, "We haven't resolved the morality of U.S. foreign policy and you want to *eat*?"

I realized that these students, who were not much older than I was, had answers before I had figured out what the questions were. Their conversations, peppered with references to classical and modern sources, revealed how much I could learn from them, and how much I had to learn on my own. Thus I began to read voraciously, not just my classroom stuff but also Edmund Burke, David Hume, Adam Smith, F. Scott Fitzgerald, Evelyn Waugh, Freidrich Hayek, and Aleksandr Solzhenitsyn. Gradually, I found myself developing a grounded point of view. For the first time, disparate facts began to fit together, to make sense. Conservatism provided me with a framework, durable and yet flexible, for understanding the world. And having the world, at the tender age of twenty, I was ready to change it—as a member of *The Dartmouth Review*.

The first thing I should note is that we were an outrageous bunch. I didn't start out that way; in fact, for the first year I was considered a moderating influence on the paper. The reason I became radicalized is that I saw how harshly the conservative newspaper was treated by professors and by the administration. No sooner had the first issue appeared on campus than the administration threatened to sue *The Dartmouth Review* for using the name "Dartmouth." The College maintained that it owned full and exclusive copyright to the name. Never mind that Dartmouth is a town in England. In fact, some two dozen establishments in Hanover all used the name. These were commercial operations unaffiliated with the College. By contrast, we were a group of students publishing a non-profit weekly about the College and distributing it to the Dartmouth community. Clearly the motive of the lawsuit was ideological.

The administration did not stop with legal threats. In 1982, founder Ben Hart was distributing copies to the Blunt Alumni Center when administrator Sam Smith went berserk, attacked Ben, and bit him! Smith grabbed Ben from behind, Ben attempted to free himself by wrapping his arm around Smith's neck, and Smith proceeded to bite him on the chest. When Ben—who is the son of Jeffrey Hart—entered his dad's office and explained the bloody gash, his father's terse response was, "Thank God you didn't have him in a scissors hold." Smith was eventually convicted of assault and paid a small fine.

Such incidents point to the larger dilemma facing conservative students in a liberal culture. The dilemma can be stated this way. Typically, the conservative attempts to conserve, to hold on to the values of the existing society. But what if the existing society is liberal? What if the existing society is inherently hostile to conservative beliefs? It is foolish for a conservative to attempt to conserve that culture. Rather, he must seek to undermine it, to thwart it, to destroy it at the root level. This means that the conservative must stop being conservative. More precisely, he must be philosophically conservative but temperamentally radical. This is what we quickly understood at the *Review*. We recognized that to confront liberalism fully we could not be content with rebutting liberal arguments. We also had to subvert liberal culture, and this meant disrupting the etiquette of liberalism. In other words, we had to become social guerillas. And this we set out to do with a vengeance.

Reading over old issues of the *Review*, and sharing recollections with my former colleagues, I am sometimes amazed to realize what social and intellectual renegades we were. We were not above using *ad hominem* attacks. We described one professor as sporting "a polyester tie and a rat's-hair moustache." When he wrote to complain, claiming we were inaccurate on both counts, we printed an apology: "We regret our error. In reality Professor Spitzer has a rat's-hair tie and a polyester mustache." Feminists and homosexuals were a regular target of satire. Founder Keeney Jones, now a Catholic priest, wrote that "The question is not whether women should be educated at Dartmouth. The question is whether women should be educated at all." The *Review* also printed an alumnus's Solomonic observation that "any man who thinks a woman is his intellectual equal is probably right." And the Last Word featured the observation: "Homosexuality is fine," said Bill, half in Ernest.

That some of these quips are in bad taste goes without saying. But is this scorched-earth approach effective? Let's consider an example. When Dartmouth refused to stop funding the Gay Students Association, despite numerous *Review* editorials questioning why funds should be awarded based on sexual orientation, we decided to test the consistency of the administration's policy. We founded the Dartmouth Bestiality Society. We appointed a president, a vice president, a treasurer, and a zookeeper. We wrote up an application and developed a budget. Then we went before the Committee on Student Organizations.

The administrators were appalled, of course. "There is no interest in, ahem, bestiality at Dartmouth," one said. To which the president of the Bestiality Society gamely replied, "That may be true, Dean Hanson, but it is because of centuries of discrimination! Those of us who are inclined toward animals have been systematically excluded and ostracized. Our organization will provide a supportive atmosphere in which people of our particular sexual orientation are treated with respect. At Dartmouth, if not in society, let us put an end to beastophobia." No, we didn't get recognition or funding. But we did make our point, and the point was well-covered in the local media. One newspaper printed a hilarious feature titled, "Students Go to the Dogs."

As I recount some of the sophomoric things we did, you must keep in mind that, during this time, we were sophomores! Having turned forty a few years ago, I now have a somewhat different perspective than I had when I was twenty. Thus, in bringing back adventurous times, it seems worthwhile to ask what we accomplished. Conservative newspapers like the *Review* have sprung up on college campuses across the nation, in large part following the example we set in those early days of the Reagan Revolution at Dartmouth. Conservatism isn't just a doctrine for stuffy reactionaries; on the contrary, it is vibrant and timeless. The *Review* could not have survived for twenty-five years without so sturdy of a foundation, and it is a testament to those early days that it is today every bit as intelligent, irreverent, and insightful as it was then.

September 22, 2005

The *Review* & the Olin Foundation

by James Piereson

James Piereson was executive director of the John M. Olin Foundation from 1985 to 2005. Following longstanding plans, and the wishes of the donor, the Foundation allocated its assets and closed its doors at the end of 2005.

T HE JOHN M. OLIN FOUNDATION began its association with *The Dartmouth Review* in 1981, barely months after the newspaper was launched. According to the Foundation's files, Benjamin Hart, then the editor of the *Review*, sent an appeal for assistance to William E. Simon, president of the Foundation, who was delighted to endorse the request. He (along with the trustees and staff of the Foundation) was encouraged by the example of students with the courage and moxie to take on the campus establishment and to raise the banner of liberty and reason on the Dartmouth campus. The trustees quickly approved a contribution of $10,000 for the fledgling conservative publication. They hoped that the *Review* would become a force on the Dartmouth campus, and also that a conservative publication at such a prominent college would encourage students at other institutions to establish their own newspapers.

This initial grant in 1981 was followed up by annual contributions of $5,000 in 1982 and 1983. These grants were made as a way of lending support to the enterprise and of giving encouragement to the editors. But as the *Review* began to establish itself as a conservative voice at Dartmouth, the College administration, goaded on by left-wing faculty and radical campus groups, raised the stakes by trying to silence and suppress the publication entirely. "Free speech for me but not for thee," cried the administration and faculty in a near chorus. Campus leftists openly published their own papers and pamphlets, brought speakers to campus, staged demonstrations, and even illegally occupied College buildings to make their ideological points. Yet a conservative newspaper on campus was regarded as beyond the pale.

There is no great mystery as to why this was so. Like many colleges, Dartmouth had embarked on a crusade to promote diversity on the campus, which meant in practice that traditional academic and scholarly standards had to be sacrificed in order to give representation on campus to members of preferred groups, all of which were affiliated with the Democratic party. Conservatives, not being Democrats, counted for less than nothing in the College's calculus of representation, and were in fact regarded as something of a nuisance. The students on *The Dartmouth Review*, with good reason, criticized the administration's efforts to put the diversity ideology into practice, as they understood more clearly than their elders that the representation of interest groups on the faculty and in the curriculum was antithetical to the ideals of liberal education. The paper attacked the collapse of standards at the College, the introduction of trendy courses designed to appeal to left-wing groups, the hiring of faculty whose main qualifications were that they could teach such courses, and the promotion of radical causes on the campus. It was precisely the *Review*'s opposition to these diversity policies that convinced the administration that the paper had to be suppressed.

Over the next several years, from roughly 1983 to the early 1990s, the College steadily escalated its attacks on the publication, trying at times to discredit the editors and at other times to intimidate them with threats of suspension or expulsion. The trustees of the John M. Olin Foundation, for their part, saw an important principle at stake, and sought to support and defend the editors at every opportunity.

There were, however, some ominous rumblings coming from the administration and faculty from the very day the publication was launched. In April of 1981, in one of its early issues, the *Review* published a long interview with William Simon in which editors Greg Fossedal and Wendy Stone raised a host of questions dealing with national politics and economic policy. Near the end of that interview Simon noted that he and other supporters had received calls from Dartmouth administrators and alumni discouraging them from donating funds to the *Review*. Simon, of course, rightly disagreed, as he felt that this kind of publication was precisely what was needed to add intellectual balance to that campus. It was thus obvious to Simon that the Dartmouth administration was trying to strangle the infant conservative paper in its crib. Moreover, such calls reflected the wildly erroneous view among some in Hanover that the paper was merely a front for conservatives in New York and Washington and would not exist save for their financial support. The paper, according to this paranoid view, was inserted into the Dartmouth scene by "outside agitators."

Two episodes, one in 1988 and a second in 1990, brought these conflicts out into the open, and generated national controversies that brought the John M. Olin Foundation and *The Dartmouth Review* into closer collaboration. In both cases, the controversies were created by irresponsible and imprudent conduct by Dartmouth's trustees and administration. The campaign to silence the *Review*, it is plain in retrospect, was among the most unwise and destructive enterprises undertaken by any college administration in modern times. It brought lasting damage to Dartmouth and disgrace to the trustees and administrators who participated in it.

The first episode was sparked in 1988 when the editors of the *Review* taped the classroom remarks of a radical professor and published them in the paper. The transcripts revealed that the professor's classroom presentations were stocked with fulminations against racism and ideological rants unrelated to the subject matter of the class. The professor, who happened to be black, took umbrage at the publication of his remarks, it being a presumption of radical professors that it is unfair to hold them accountable for their own statements. The administration, viewing such remarks as an acceptable form of diversity, defended the professor's right to free expression. Some weeks later, editors of the *Review* approached the professor outside his classroom with an invitation to defend his views in the paper. The student journalists, after all, were merely covering a story by seeking comments from a controversial figure on the campus. The professor, however, was not amused by such journalistic methods. Harsh words were exchanged and, according to the students, the professor shoved one of the editors.

In a bizarre Orwellian turnabout, the College responded, not by reprimanding the professor, but by suspending the journalists from school on trumped up charges of "vexatious oral exchange." When the students appealed these suspensions in a state court, the John M. Olin Foundation stepped in to pick up some of their legal expenses. As the proceedings dragged on for some months, with the College defending its strange conduct all the way, these expenses were substantial and beyond the means of the students involved. The court eventually vindicated the student journalists by overturning the suspensions, and ordering the College to readmit them. Yet this black eye for the College only stimulated the administration's appetite for revenge.

The second and certainly climactic episode occurred in the autumn of 1990 when an unknown student, probably not even a member of the *Review*'s staff, sought to sabotage the paper by inserting an anti-Semitic quotation into its masthead after this particular edition had been put to bed by the editors. When they discovered the sabotage, the editors quickly recalled the papers and issued an apology for their oversight. It was plain to any fair-minded person that the editors never intended to publish these hateful comments, for if this had been their intention they would have published them openly instead of burying them in the masthead of the paper. The episode should thus have ended with the apology by the editors.

Yet the College administration, led by the new president, James Freedman, seized on the episode as a pretext for getting rid of the *Review* once and for all. Freedman, a former law school professor well versed in the First Amendment, certainly should have known better than to highlight this unfortunate event on his campus. Yet, like too many in leadership roles at Dartmouth, he was in thrall to left-wing ideology, which undermined any sense of prudence and responsibility he might once have had. In the cocoon-like environment of Hanover, it was perhaps too easy to conclude that the ravings of left-wing interest groups reflected the mature judgment of the wider world. Freedman thus responded to critics, like the editors of the *Review*, by alternately whining that he had been unfairly treated or by thundering irrationally that they must be censured and driven off campus.

Freedman's presidency brings to mind the familiar scene in Woody Allen's film *Sleeper*, which is set many hundreds of years in the future. Allen's character relates the fact that late in the twentieth century the earth was blown up in a nuclear holocaust. When queried as to how this had happened, he explained with wry humor that "a man by the name of Albert Shanker got a hold of a nuclear warhead"—a reference to the head of the New York City Teachers' Union, who led a series of teacher strikes in 1968. This comment was most unfair to Mr. Shanker, who was a distinguished and level-headed union leader. Yet for those familiar with Dartmouth's history, the quotation would be perfectly understandable if Freedman's name were substituted for Shanker's.

Freedman's recklessness was quickly displayed when he called a campus "Rally Against Hate" to denounce the editors of the *Review* for publishing those comments and for encouraging a climate of "hate" at Dartmouth. He was not moved by the fact that the comments were published unintentionally, that the offending publication had been withdrawn, or that sincere apologies had been made. Nor, apparently, did he see any irony in calling a rally against hate in order to promote hate against the editors of *The Dartmouth Review*, who, after all was said and done, were still students of the distinguished college over which he exercised responsibility. It was especially perplexing to those familiar with the paper who knew that its editor at the time was a black student, and that among previous editors were Jewish and Indian students. Outsiders, meanwhile, looked in on these developments at Dartmouth with a mixture of surprise and incomprehension.

Freedman next poured still more gasoline on the inferno he had started by taking his case to *The New York Times* in an effort to embarrass the off-campus supporters of the *Review*, including, most especially, the trustees of the John M. Olin Foundation.

He had decided to make a national issue of an event that any sensible administrator would have tried to contain at the local level. The head of the Boston bureau of the *Times* was no doubt surprised to hear from the public affairs office that the College wished to promote across the nation the idea that bigotry was rampant on the Dartmouth campus. Yet this reporter was happy to oblige the College, no doubt thinking naively (as Freedman did) that public opinion might be focused with surgical precision against the *Review* and its backers. In one of the many ironies of this episode, the distinguished newspaper that took pride in its devotion to the First Amendment was about to join a campaign to suppress another newspaper. In fairness to the journalist involved, however, the decision to publish such an article may have been influenced by the fact that the chairman of Dartmouth's board was then a director of the New York Times Company. When the article appeared in the national edition of the paper, filled with news about the "Rally Against Hate" and accusations back and forth of bigotry and suppression of free speech, Freedman had gotten his wish. The public was now aware that something was wrong at Dartmouth.

There then followed an exchange of op-ed columns in the *Times* between Freedman and Simon, along with follow-on articles and editorials in other leading publications. Freedman pointedly criticized the John M. Olin Foundation for assisting the *Review*, even though the funds at issue were used to cover legal expenses for students the College had wrongly suspended (a bizarre position for a legal scholar to take). Along the way, he also advanced scurrilous charges of bigotry against the editors of the paper and its supporters. Simon, for his part, defended the *Review* along with the Foundation's support for it, and blasted Freedman for "demagoguery" in the service of left-wing orthodoxy. George Munroe, chairman of Dartmouth's Board of Trustees, went so far as to suggest in the *Wall Street Journal* that the *Review* should be suppressed because it interfered with the College's efforts to recruit a "diverse" student body. Thus, while the College respected the First Amendment, no one could be allowed to criticize its diversity policies. The controversy thus gave the public an early window into what would later be called "political correctness" on the campus: the idea, in other words, that open debate on important subjects must be suppressed in the name of "diversity."

The College soon reaped the damage that Freedman had so irresponsibly sowed. Soon the opinion settled across the nation that there were problems at Dartmouth, that the faculty was filled with left-wing zealots, that conservatives or Republicans were not welcome on campus, that bigotry was rampant, that the president of the institution was given to making wild accusations. Parents wondered if it was really safe to send their youngsters to Hanover. Freedman's public relations campaign had backfired against the College. Now Freedman and his enablers were forced to backtrack, to reassure the public that all was in order at Dartmouth, that cries of bigotry and anti-Semitism were exaggerated and had been blown out of proportion.

It was true that such cries had been blown out of proportion, but they had been done so by no one other than Freedman himself. He was the arsonist who now had to put out the fire he had ignited. A few on campus, most notably Jeffrey Hart, distinguished professor of English, called for Freedman's dismissal, which was clearly in order. Freedman was without a doubt the worst president in Dartmouth's long and distinguished history, more embarrassing to the College even than Nathan Lord, who was forced out by the trustees in 1863 for his pro-slavery views and because he refused to approve an honorary degree for Abraham Lincoln. The only difficulty here was that the trustees who would have to dismiss Freedman were themselves implicated in his destructive policies. No academic institution in modern times had been more badly served by its president and trustees than was Dartmouth in these years.

The trustees of the John M. Olin Foundation, for their part, were duty-bound to stand behind the editors of *The Dartmouth Review* during these troubled times. To have done otherwise would have betrayed fundamental principles of fair play, and would have left conservative students at Dartmouth and elsewhere at the mercy of activist faculty and administrators. Fortunately, the newspaper survived these efforts to kill it on the part of the College administration and national institutions like *The New York Times*. Today the paper continues to be a vital voice for conservative ideas on the Dartmouth campus.

The Dartmouth Review as an institution has much to be proud of as it celebrates its twenty-fifth anniversary. Many of its editors and writers have moved on to distinguished careers in journalism, business, and other fields. Perhaps just as important, *The Dartmouth Review* spawned a movement to establish conservative newspapers on college campuses across the nation. Today there are to be found conservative newspapers and magazines on nearly one hundred campuses, all of them outgrowths from the original example of *The Dartmouth Review*. The John M. Olin Foundation has allocated funds to support these papers, just as it did for *The Dartmouth Review* in its formative years. In this sense, the collaboration between the paper and the Foundation continues. Thus, despite these controversies and difficult times or, rather, because of them, the influence of *The Dartmouth Review* lives on.

January 2006

Delhi, *Deliverance* & Dartmouth

by Harmeet Dhillon

After leaving Dartmouth and following a career as a journalist, Harmeet Dhillon, class of 1989, a former Editor-in-Chief of The Dartmouth Review, *attended the University of Virginia School of Law, after which she clerked for the Hon. Paul V. Niemeyer of the United States Court of Appeals for the Fourth Circuit in Baltimore, Maryland. She has practiced law in London, New York, and California, and her commercial and civil rights litigation and general commercial practice is currently based in northern California and New York City.*

W HEN I ARRIVED at Dartmouth twenty years ago, I was a sixteen-year-old naïf whom fate had delivered from my birthplace in the Punjab to a public school education in the backwoods of rural North Carolina. My father had chosen to start his medical practice there, without apparent concern for the signs on the highway proclaiming "the Ku Klux Klan welcomes you to Smithfield, North Carolina." It was from this somewhat bizarre juxtaposition of cultures—"Delhi meets *Deliverance*"—that I traveled to the Hanover Green, where things were stranger still: "safe sex kits," mock shanties where the Winter Carnival sculpture was supposed to be, rich kids dressing in rags and pretending to understand the hardships of apartheid, the politics of divestment, and the efficacy of economic sanctions as a tool of international diplomacy (which, incidentally, the selfsame leftists now loudly decry when the target is Castro's Cuba, the retro last bastion of communism).

While I sympathized with the noble anti-apartheid sentiments of the divestment proponents (who didn't?), I quickly realized that something was very rotten in the state of Dartmouth. The lawlessness of the shanty-dwellers, their pseudo-righteous posing, their strained efforts to distance themselves from their mostly privileged upbringings, and their desire to project the evils of Dutch colonialism onto Dartmouth, all belied any sense of proportion or rationality. Yet even more striking was the fact that the College administration—rather than giving the miscreants the disciplinary equivalent of a good spanking or, today, a "time out"—patiently indulged the jejune antics of the radical chic protestors, answering their spoiled behavior with total inaction other than effete hand-wringing. This disconnect between actions and consequences was new to me, and only *The Dartmouth Review* was brave enough to point out that the emperor had no clothes. This early (to me) example of the *Review* as a "vox clamantis in deserto" championing an unpopular, but morally and logically correct, viewpoint, was like a siren song to my rebellious soul. I never looked back.

In retrospect, it is no surprise to me that in the balkanized and Orwellian world of Dartmouth in the late 1980s, the only place that I experienced complete meritocracy and egalitarianism was on the staff of the *Review*. It was the only place in my Dartmouth experience (with the possible exception of some of my three-and-four-student Greek and Latin classes with some outstanding and apolitical Classics professors) where my background—be it gender, ethnicity, or religion—was irrelevant to my role and my potential. All that mattered was how well I could report, write, edit, and reason. I had the great privilege to work alongside and learn from four of the *Review*'s finest editors—Debbie Stone, Chris Baldwin, Bill Grace, and Kevin Pritchett. I learned courage and discipline from the peerless Jeffrey Hart and the quirky Douglas Yates—at the time, the only two professors on campus with the intestinal fortitude to defend the *Review* in public. I was privileged to know and work with great and generous alumni such as George Champion, whose support made the *Review* possible. Along the way I made some lifelong friends and learned some painful and hard-won lessons about writing, politics, the First Amendment, and the art of war.

I no longer remember the names of most of the professors, student leaders, and College administrators who were the subjects or targets of many articles, exposés and editorials . . . but I can barely suppress a smile at the memory of my and my fellow reporters' wintry antics.

One of the more vivid lessons that I learned during my editorship was that not everything is a laughing matter—or at least, not a laughing matter fit for public, front-page consumption. Memorable satire often flirts with the boundaries of good taste, as Jonathan Swift makes clear. Having crossed that boundary on more than one occasion—perhaps most strikingly by comparing James Freedman to Hitler during a controversy about the campus police's tackling, handcuffing, and arresting freshman attempting to form their class numerals on the football field during halftime—I would like to think that I now know better. Most of the time, anyway. (My new-age-style-parenting brother likes to ask his misbehaving three-year-old son the possibly illuminating question *in media res*: "Son, is that a good idea or a bad idea?" I wish someone wiser had asked me that question a couple of times during my editorship. Much gnashing of teeth might have been averted all around.)

What are the lasting effects and memories of my four years at *The Dartmouth Review*? I've assembled this partial list, in no particular order: love for underdogs; a passion for freedom of speech; an almost visceral distrust of authority; respect for debate; tolerance for honestly held and well-articulated views that differ from my own; a withering disdain for anodyne and characterless school mascots; defenestration (inside joke). In retrospect, things were rarely as black-and-white as they appeared to be when I was eighteen. After all, I have evolved into a San Francisco-dwelling ACLU board member; an elected Republican official who actively participates in the Federalist Society yet also devotes a substantial amount of time to pro bono legal work on behalf of political refugees, battered women, and religious minorities; and who reviews litigation discovery documents while listening to rap—but prefers John Coltrane and Miles Davis for writing appellate briefs.

The Harmeet Dhillon who edited *The Dartmouth Review* might have looked upon such a person and mocked her "diversity" of viewpoints. Yet it is precisely the trial by fire, strange bedfellows at the ACLU, attempts to explain to an instransigent Morley Safer on *60 Minutes* that I was, in fact, a bona fide immigrant even though I spoke English passably well, and innumerable other sublime and ridiculous milestones of my *Review* tenure that ultimately engendered the complex, contrarian, and sometimes contradictory woman I have become. I hope that I will always be proud to call myself a Reviewer. A "wah-hoo-wah" shout-out to my fellow Reviewers past and present, and I hope to many generations of them to come. May they all cherish their *Review* experiences as much as I have.

January 2006

Shut Up,
I Explained

by Joseph Rago

Joseph Rago, Dartmouth class of 2005, a former Editor-in-Chief of The
Dartmouth Review, *is an assistant editorial features editor at the* Wall
Street Journal.

AMID THE PARAPHERNALIA that's accumulated in our offices
over the past twenty-five years, there's wheat and there's chaff. For
instance: we claim a mechanical wooden hand that Jeff Hart used to crank
when faculty meetings grew tedious, so that its fingers would drum loudly
and impatiently against the boardroom mahogany. But *The Dartmouth
ReView* [sic] is also guilty of possession, it pains me to note, of a "Student
Activist Award" by way of David Horowitz. The distinction, so far as I'm
concerned, is mortifying—not least of all for its association with a thing as
unsavory as Activism.

Mr. Horowitz is a conservative Activist himself and, not surprisingly,
he's a controversial figure in contemporary higher education. Some years
ago he installed himself as Viceroy of young conservatives and began
steeling his soldiers for combat (which probably accounts for the
provenance of the *ReView*'s war medal); now, he'd like to deliver a great
coup de main against the leftist regimes he believes are ruining the nation's colleges and universities.

The central fieldpiece in the campaign is his "Academic Bill of Rights."
If adopted—several state legislatures are considering it—the Bill would
mandate "intellectual diversity" in faculty recruiting and tenure decisions;
require "viewpoint-neutral" and "politically balanced" reading lists, lectures, and assignments; and create bureaucracies to handle accusations of
"bias," "unfairness," and "marginalization." It's only fair, the thinking
goes, because conservatives are an "underrepresented minority" on campus these days, and ever so sensitive about it.

That the climate of academia is overwhelmingly left-liberal shouldn't send anyone rushing for his defibrillator. It's so blatant that only a fool or a liar could dispute it—leading many professors to acknowledge it themselves, often with the most indulgent of justifications. In 2003, Dartmouth English Professor Ivy Schweitzer asked, "Is the general atmosphere here 'liberal'? Yes, because we are a liberal arts institution, and liberal arts education is supposed to produce 'liberal' attitudes that encourage forward-thinking ideas about inclusion, equality, and innovation." Well, no—but never mind.

Yet, while it's one thing to sympathize with the efforts of Mr. Horowitz and his legions, it's quite another to support them. The last thing conservatives should be joining is the ranks of the perennially indignant. I'd expect the campus conservative to have more fortitude than a shucked oyster.

I don't have any more patience with the state of academia than Mr. Horowitz does. But I don't want to get a more conservative education as a trade-in for my biases—a part of my very constitution, after all—in the name of intellectual or political neutrality, and I don't want anyone else to either. I didn't go to Hanover for a convalescent education or for people to agree with me all the time—neither of which makes for a keen mind, or, for that matter, a very lively college experience.

Besides, simply because the prevailing winds at Dartmouth are liberal—the administration's interminable shilly-shallying, the baying of the loudest professors, the gutter patois of the *Daily Dartmouth*—doesn't mean all the details are. The Economics Department, to cite one example, is consistently excellent, hardly a bastion of liberal thought, and perpetually oversubscribed; while year after year Education, say, is on the brink of foreclosure. A few of the most progressive departments (History and English come to mind) can be very, very good. Dartmouth has some terribly silly professors, but it has some tremendous ones, too. Some of *them*, believe it or not, are liberals.

The real task, then, is to separate the wheat from the chaff. This is done best not by appropriating the academic liturgy or by wallowing in victim culture or even by Activism but through robust, intelligent criticism—the reasoned exercise of judgment, discrimination, and taste.

Might I suggest a venue? Consider writing for *The Dartmouth Review*. What you'll find is an independent counterweight to all the nonsense at Dartmouth today; that takes the issues seriously but never so itself; whose animadversion is spirited, articulate, sharp-witted. What you'll find is a critical voice in a pitched contest of ideas about what the College should and should not be—the sort of conversation that is the only legitimate way to straighten out the politics of higher education. And most importantly, should you be inclined to contribute to our pages, the only oysters you'll encounter are the ones at our raw bar.

September 20, 2004

The *Review* Today

by Michael Ellis

Michael Ellis, Dartmouth class of 2006, is Editor-in-Chief of The Dartmouth Review. *Following his tenure at the newspaper, and upon early graduation from Dartmouth this spring, Mr. Ellis will be an Associate Director in the White House's Office of Strategic Initiatives.*

S OME MIGHT WONDER why today's *Review* seems more sedate than its predecessors, which, of course, it is. Circumstances are different now than they were in the 1980s: During my editorship, not many staffers have been bitten by enraged professors, let alone suspended or expelled from Dartmouth by an administrative kangaroo court. To be sure, there are still attacks on the *Review* in some corners: our offices were vandalized and burglarized two years ago, and there's been an effort to keep the newspaper out of the dormitories. Dartmouth has changed a great deal over the past twenty-five years—for the better and for the worse—and the *Review* has changed with it, staying all the while true to its original mission. It is with irony that we note that the same people who once attacked the *Review* for its supposed offensiveness now attack it for not being attacked by them enough.

James Wright is no James Freedman. Wright is more indirect, discreet, perhaps underhanded. The situation on the ground simply doesn't warrant the kind of tactics the *Review* employed during the eighties and early nineties, which would ring hollow today.

The *Review* today, then, faces a new challenge. How can we reconcile our original mission of providing a conservative perspective on campus affairs with an academic environment that is less ideological, less easily offended, than ever? By less ideological I mean several things. Liberalism on campus remains, but it is not quite so loud. Most professors are professional, and leave their politics to the antiwar protests and the teach-ins.

The faculty and administrators may still be as doggedly liberal as ever, but they are quieter in their zealotry. These changes are testament to battles won, early on, by *The Dartmouth Review*. There hasn't been another Professor Cole because the *Review* stared down—twice—Cole's first incarnation.

In light of those changes, today's *Review* relies less on theatrics and more on the fundamentals of conservative journalism: the depth and detail that long-form journalism can lend to complex subjects, its willingness to raise issues that other campus publications are too lazy to approach, its devotion to Dartmouth's history and traditions that might otherwise fall by the wayside, its unswerving devotion to a core vision of a College that provides a superior liberal arts education, and its ability to do all of these things while simultaneously introducing an air of levity and humor into the campus and alumni debate.

This formula continues to drive campus debate. For instance, last year the *Review* invited Harvard professor Harvey Mansfield to campus; he was to take part in a debate on manliness and masculinity. When we asked the Center for Women and Gender to field a suitable opponent, its representatives informed us that CWG does not believe "public debate to be a method conducive to furthering its aims on campus."

This response seems to be largely representative of the new campus atmosphere. When I noted that the campus atmosphere was less ideological, perhaps it would be more accurate to say ideologically comfortable or ideologically settled. This is why the *Review* remains important today. Almost every substantive issue the *Review* raises—library funding, the Student Life Initiative, new campus construction, a core curriculum, the opacity (or lack thereof) of the administrative budget, Dartmouth's Speech program, the state of freshman writing, Dartmouth's admissions standards and their effect on athletics, the recent rash of faculty departures, and perhaps most importantly, alumni Trustee elections—would go unscrutinized and undiscussed without the *Review*'s influence. Whenever the administration is on the cusp of making a major change that will indelibly affect Dartmouth's future, they can count on the *Review* to analyze it from a reasoned, detached, and conservative perspective.

It is perhaps in the realm of alumni Trustee elections where the *Review* has had its greatest impact over recent years. The election of T. J. Rodgers '70, Peter Robinson '79, and Todd Zywicki '88 to Dartmouth's Board of Trustees were landmark events. They were positive proof that the ultimate aim of William F. Buckley's *God and Man at Yale*—increased alumni control over how contribution dollars are spent—is ultimately attainable. We are hanging on now to that goal by our fingertips; but soon it could be in our grasp. Additionally, their election has led to a welter of important changes at the College. The moratorium on new Greek houses has been lifted. A stultifying speech code has been repealed. The workings of College finances are gradually becoming more apparent, though slowly, like a photograph in the developing bath.

The *Review*'s role in the successful candidacies of Rogers, Robinson, and Zywicki was indisputable: the paper thoroughly outlined their campaign agenda, and provided in-depth coverage of ongoing election stories and issues on our website (which was garnering 2,500 unique hits a day at the height of the election). It was a spur for thousands of alumni to participate. The election showed the *Review*'s agenda moving from the fringes of the campus debate to the mainstream.

As the College moves ahead, then, we remain cautiously optimistic. There have been many recent changes for the better. It would be naive to believe, however, that the trends will continue unless the *Review* and others who care about the College continue their hard work. The gains of the past few years could easily slip away if the *Review* does not continue to be vigilant in its work. In the immediate future, the stakes could hardly be higher—the Greek system is still on tenuous footing, the effects of the new construction on campus life have yet to be seen, and the alumni will be called upon to fill more seats of the Board of Trustees. Fittingly enough, the first twenty-five years of the *Review*'s history closes just as it began, with a traditionally minded alumni body and student base galvanized by events.

I have no doubt future *Review* staffers will continue to cover all of those developments and more in their quest to make Dartmouth a better place—and neither do I doubt they will face today's same mix of scornful and welcoming reactions on campus when they do so.

January 2006

Contributors

Peter Arnold, Dartmouth class of 1986, is a former editor of *The Dartmouth Review*.

Christopher Baldwin '89 is a former Editor-in-Chief of *The Dartmouth Review*. He is now a Managing Director of Merrill Lynch Investment Banking. Mr. Baldwin is married and raising four children in Manhattan.

Stefan Beck '04 is a former editor of *The Dartmouth Review*. He is now the Associate Editor of *The New Criterion*.

Mark Behnam '90 is a former contributor to *The Dartmouth Review*.

Dorn Bishop '86 is a former editor of *The Dartmouth Review*.

William F. Buckley Jr. is Editor-at-Large of *National Review*. He is the author, most recently, of *Miles Gone By: A Literary Autobiography*.

William Cattan '83 is a former Editor-in-Chief of *The Dartmouth Review*. A former speechwriter for President Ronald Reagan and Vice President George H. W. Bush, Mr. Cattan is an attorney at Patton Boggs, LLP.

M. Ryan Clark '01 is a former editor of *The Dartmouth Review*. He is now pursuing an MBA at the Kellogg School of Management following two years in the financial sponsors group at Goldman Sachs.

L. Gordon Crovitz began as an editorial writer for *The Wall Street Journal* in 1981, and became a member of its editorial board in 1986. He is now senior vice president of Dow Jones & Company and president of the Company's Electronic Publishing group.

Harmeet Dhillon, '89 is a former Editor-in-Chief of *The Dartmouth Review*. A former clerk for the Hon. Paul V. Niemeyer of the United States Court of Appeals, Ms. Dhillon's commercial and civil rights litigation and general commercial practice is currently based in northern California and New York City.

Dinesh D'Souza '83 is a former Editor-in-Chief of *The Dartmouth Review*. He is now the Robert and Karen Rishwain Fellow at the Hoover Institution at Stanford University. The author, most recently, of *What's So Great About America* and *Letters to a Young Conservative*, Mr. D'Souza's 1991 book *Illiberal Education* spent fifteen weeks on the *New York Times* bestseller list and has been acclaimed as one of the most influential books of the 1990s.

Conor Dugan '00 is a former editor of *The Dartmouth Review*.

Michael Ellis '06 is Editor-in-Chief of *The Dartmouth Review*. Following his tenure at the newspaper, Mr. Ellis will be an Associate Director in the White House's Office of Strategic Initiatives.

Robert Flanigan '87 is a former President of *The Dartmouth Review*. He is now President of Educate LLC, an educational consulting company.

Gregory Fossedal '81 is a founder and former Editor-in-Chief of *The Dartmouth Review*. A senior fellow of the Alexis de Tocqueville Institution, he is the author, most recently, of *Direct Democracy in Switzerland.*

James Garrett '88 is a former contributor to *The Dartmouth Review.*

Scott Glabe '06 is an editor of *The Dartmouth Review*. Following his tenure at the newspaper, Mr. Glabe will be an intern in the governor's office in Missouri, after which he plans to live in Washington, D.C.

William Grace '89 is a former Editor-in-Chief of *The Dartmouth Review*. He is a founder and partner of MDRxFinancial, which provides online healthcare data and analytics for mutual and hedge funds.

Andrew Grossman '02 is a former Editor-in-Chief of *The Dartmouth Review*. He is now Senior Writer at the Heritage Foundation.

Gordon Haff, Dartmouth Thayer School of Engineering class of 1981, is a founder of *The Dartmouth Review*. He is now Deputy Research Director at Illuminata.

Benjamin Hart '81 is a founder and former President of *The Dartmouth Review*. The founder of DirectMailCopywriters.com, Hart's

direct mail letters have generated more than $500,000,000 in sales and donations since 1990. He is the author of five books, including *Poisoned Ivy, Faith & Freedom, Fund Your Cause With Direct Mail, How To Write Blockbuster Sales Letters*, and *Automatic Marketing.*

Jeffrey Hart is Professor of English Emeritus of Dartmouth College, Senior Editor of *National Review*, and advisor to *The Dartmouth Review*. He is the author, most recently, of *The Making of the American Conservative Mind: National Review and Its Times.*

Betsy Holder '03 is a former contributor to *The Dartmouth Review*. She and her husband are now students in Vermont Law School.

Gerald Hughes '88 is a former editor of *The Dartmouth Review*. He now lives with his wife and four children, working as a strategy consultant to the media and marketing industries, and skirmishing with the leftist and pseudo-Republican baby boomers trying to ruin his suburban, conservative haven.

Christian Hummel '01 is a former editor of *The Dartmouth Review*. After a Fulbright Scholarship and a masters degree from the University of Chicago, Mr. Hummel helped start the American University of Kuwait and now works as an administrator at a Catholic, liberal arts college.

Laura Ingraham '85 is a former Editor-in-Chief of *The Dartmouth Review*. A former law clerk to Supreme Court Justice Clarence

Thomas and Ralph K. Winter on the U.S. Court of Appeals for the Second Circuit, Ms. Ingraham is now the host of the nationally syndicated "Laura Ingraham Show." She is the author of *The Hillary Trap* and, most recently, *Shut Up & Sing: How the Elites in Hollywood, Politics . . . and the UN are Subverting America.*

Alexis Jhamb '03 is a former contributor to *The Dartmouth Review.*

Keeney Jones '83 is a founder and former editor of *The Dartmouth Review.* He is a former speechwriter for William Bennett.

Steven Menashi '01 is a former Editor-in-Chief of *The Dartmouth Review.* Formerly an editorial writer at *The New York Sun*, associate editor of *Policy Review*, and a public affairs fellow at the Hoover Institution, Mr. Menashi is now a student at Stanford Law School.

Arthur Monoco '98 is a former Editor-in-Chief of *The Dartmouth Review.*

Catherine Muscat '02 is a former contributor to *The Dartmouth Review.*

Sean Nolan '91 is a former contributor to *The Dartmouth Review.*

Dave Pan '00 is a former contributor to *The Dartmouth Review.*

James Panero '98 is a former Editor-in-Chief of *The Dartmouth Review.* He is now the Managing Editor of *The New Criterion.*

Ben Patch '00 is a former Editor-in-Chief of *The Dartmouth Review.* He is now the owner of Ben Patch Digital Design.

James Piereson was executive director of the John M. Olin Foundation from 1985 to 2005. Following longstanding plans, and the wishes of the donor, the Foundation allocated its assets and closed its doors at the end of 2005.

Teresa Polenz (Delany) '89 is a former editor of *The Dartmouth Review.* She is now an associate in the law firm Hughes Hubbard & Reed, LLP.

Kevin Pritchett '91 is a former Editor-in-Chief of *The Dartmouth Review.* Mr. Pritchett still writes (infrequently), spends time on airplanes (too frequently), enjoys wine (currently taken with the Symphony grape), and worries about China. He works and lives with his wife in Arizona.

Joseph Rago '05 is a former Editor-in-Chief of *The Dartmouth Review.* He is now a features editor for the *Wall Street Journal* editorial page.

Alston Ramsay '04 is a former Editor-in-Chief of *The Dartmouth Review.* He is now Associate Editor of *National Review.*

Frank Reichel '86 is a former President of *The Dartmouth Review.*

Hugo Restall '92 is a former Editor-in-Chief of *The Dartmouth Review.* A former member of the editorial board of *The Wall Street Journal*, and editorial page editor for *The Asian Wall Street Journal*, Mr. Restall became the editor of the *Far Eastern Economic Review* in October 2004.

Roland Reynolds '87 is a former Editor-in-Chief of *The Dartmouth Review.* He is now partner in the law firm Pfeifer & Reynolds, LLP.

Contributors

Peter Robinson '79 is a former correspondent for *The Dartmouth Review*. A former Chief White House Speechwriter for President Ronald Reagan, he is now a Fellow at the Hoover Institution. In 2005, Peter Robinson was elected by petition vote to the Dartmouth Board of Trustees.

Jeff Rosenthal '89 is a former contributor to *The Dartmouth Review*.

J. Lawrence Scholer '04 is a former Editor-in-Chief of *The Dartmouth Review*. He is now Editor of *The Insider*, a publication of the Heritage Foundation.

Suzanne Schott (Reichel) '85 is a former editor of *The Dartmouth Review*.

Deborah Stone (Colloton) '87 is a former Editor-in-Chief of *The Dartmouth Review*. She is now a producer for John Stossel of ABC News.

Jim Sullivan '89 is a former contributor to *The Dartmouth Review*.

William Sushon '92 is a former editor of *The Dartmouth Review*. He is now a partner at O'Melveny & Myers, LLP.

John Sutter '88 is a former editor of *The Dartmouth Review*.

Alexander Talcott '04 is a former editor of *The Dartmouth Review*. He is now a second year student at Notre Dame Law School and engaged to former *Review* President Kristin Steinert '04.

Darren Thomas '04 is a former editor of *The Dartmouth Review*.

Matthew Tokson '02 is a former editor of *The Dartmouth Review*. He is now a first year student at the University of Chicago Law School.

Benjamin Wallace-Wells '00 is a former Editor-in-Chief of *The Dartmouth Review*. He is now an editor of the *Washington Monthly*.

Nathaniel Ward '05 is a former editor of *The Dartmouth Review*. He now works as a writer and fundraiser at the Heritage Foundation.

Kenneth Weissman '93 is a former Editor-in-Chief of *The Dartmouth Review*. He is now Corporate Counsel for Sony Corporation of America.

Chris Whitman '89 is a former Editor-in-Chief of *The Dartmouth Review*.

Alexander Wilson '01 is a former editor of *The Dartmouth Review*.

Acknowledgments

T HE EDITORS owe thanks first and foremost to the board of *The Dartmouth Review* for encouraging them to undertake this anthology.

For both their mentorship and the use of their columns, the editors thank Jeffrey Hart and William F. Buckley Jr. Thanks are also due to *The Forward* and the *Wall Street Journal* for permission to reprint material from their archives. The story of *The Dartmouth Review* would not have been complete without their exegesis.

To this the editors add thanks to the seven essayists who not only shaped *Review* history, but also have contributed to this volume their own commentary on this history: Jeffrey Hart, Peter Robinson, Dinesh D'Souza, James Piereson, Harmeet Dhillon, Joseph Rago, and Michael Ellis.

This book would not have been possible without the enthusiasm of the Intercollegiate Studies Institute and the Collegiate Network. The CN has been a supporter of *The Dartmouth Review* from the paper's inception, and its tradition of generous support has carried over to the production of this book. The editors are indebted to Steve Klugewicz of CN and Jeremy Beer and Jennifer Connolly of ISI for their stewardship.

For their patience and good cheer throughout the production of this book, the editors are grateful to their colleagues at *The New Criterion*: Hilton Kramer, Roger Kimball, David Yezzi, Cricket Farnsworth, Dawn Steeves, and Gabbe Grodin. The editors are particularly thankful to Roger Kimball, no stranger to book publishing, for his technical assistance.

The editors would never have attended Dartmouth, much less edited *The Dartmouth Review*, without the support of their parents. This fact is not lost on them.

The editors are obliged to Gordon Haff, Michael Ellis, Joseph Rago, and Courtney Andree for graciously giving their time to read through this manuscript. James Panero is especially grateful to his fiancée, Dara Mandle, for both her unwavering support and her liberal insight into the conservative arguments of *The Dartmouth Review*.

Finally, this anthology would not exist without twenty-five years of reader support for *The Dartmouth Review* and twenty-five years of unpaid student labor.

To the editors and writers of *The Dartmouth Review*, this is your story.

Index

AAm
  See Afro-American Society
ABC, 117, 208, 316
ACF
  See Asian Christian Fellowship
Ackerman, Susan, 238, 305, 307, 308
ACLU
  See American Civil Liberties Union
*Acts of Recovery: Essays on Culture and
  Politics* (Hart), 315
Adams, Roland, 220
ADL
  See Anti-Defamation League of B'nai
  B'rith
The Adventures of Huckleberry Finn
  (Twain), 34, 77
African-Caribbean Students Organization,
  202
Afro-American Society (AAm), 25, 35, 84,
  132, 135–41, 143, 144, 148–50, 153,
  164, 183, 193, 200
Akamu, Aaron, 252, 253
Alien, Jacqueline, 138, 139
Allen, Woody, 331
Al-Nur, 202
Alpha Chi Alpha, 245, 252, 253, 255, 256
Alpha Delta fraternity, 5, 253
Alpha Kappa Alpha, 243
Alpha Phi Alpha, 243
Alpha Xi Delta, 245, 250, 254
Alumni for a Strong Dartmouth (ASD),
  305–6
Alvarez, Richard, 82
Alverson, Hoyt S., 51, 188
American Civil Liberties Union (ACLU),
  65, 147, 287, 336

Amherst College, 245–46
Anderson, Doug, 159
Anderson, John, 8
Andrews, T. Coleman, 14
Anti-Defamation League of B'nai B'rith
  (ADL), 193, 194, 205, 218, 220–21, 225,
  231
AP
  See Asian Power; Associated Press
Appleton, John, 49, 51, 131, 143, 146, 147,
  200
Archambault, Jodi, 200
Armstrong, Nels, 305
Arnold, Benedict, 71
Arnold, Peter, 54
ASD
  See Alumni for a Strong Dartmouth
Asian Christian Fellowship (ACF), 257
Asian Posse (AP), 256–57
Asian Power (AP), 256–57
Asian Wall Street Journal, 316
Associated Press (AP), 208, 251
Astin, Alexander, 262–63
Astor, Hewlett, 181
Attridge, Missy, 306

Back to Basics (Pines), 188
Bader-Meinhof, 95
Baer, Andrew, 205–7, 234
Baldwin, Christopher, 84, 109, 112, 115,
  122, 131, 135, 142, 148, 151, 154–56,
  163, 166, 176, 216, 335
Baldwin, Marilyn, 63, 65, 68
Bass, Jaqueline, 74, 75
Beard, Malcolm, 14
Beatty, Jack, 76, 77

Beck, Stefan, 316

Becker, David, 147

Behnam, Mark, 166

Belloc, Hilaire, 175

Bennett, William, 84, 145, 176

Berkow, Daniel Jay, 60, 62–63, 66–67

Berlin, Geoff, 305

Bernhardt, Sarah, 174

Berolzheimer, Alan, 88

Berra, Yogi, 293

Berry, Patricia, 306

Bestiality Society, 59, 326

The Best 331 Colleges (Princeton Review), 263, 267

Better than Sex: Confessions of a Political Junkie (Thompson), 230

Billings, Franklin S., Jr., 54

Bingel, Amanda, 280

Birch, John, 176, 179

Bishop, Dorn, 47, 75

Black Caucus, 164

Black Panthers, 40, 95

Black Praxis, 133

Blaik, Earl "Red," 317

Blake, Merriweather, 181

Bloom, Allan, 161

Bloom, Harold, 284

Bloom, Randall, 138, 139

Blumenthal, Sidney, 320

Boghosian, Varujan, 76

Bok, Derek, 83, 90

Bonz, Margaret, 79, 85, 110, 111, 112, 114–15

The Boston Globe, 40, 137, 153, 164, 184, 205, 208, 211, 244

Bowdoin College, 242

Bowdon, David, 138, 139

Bradford, Lisa, 251

Bradley, Edward, 36, 39

Braun, Charles, 49

Brawley, Tawana, 194

Breeden, James, 116, 171

Brideshead Revisited (Waugh), 318, 324

Brigg, Michael, 283

Bromann, Ed, 180

Brown, Scott, 295

Bruce, Lenny, 149

Brudnoy, David, 188

Bryan, Kieron, 260

Bryn Mawr, 251

Buchanan, Patrick J., 233

Buchanan, Peter, 199–200

Buckley, William F., Jr., 9–10, 11, 39, 41, 52, 106, 117, 145, 148, 151, 162, 176, 188, 199, 208, 210, 212, 213, 233, 248, 285, 296, 308–9, 318, 321, 324, 340

Budd, David, 222, 225

Burke, Edmund, 159, 325

Burke, Kate, 136, 137

Burkot, Leo, 282

Burnett, Larry, 67

Burns, Ray, 80

Bush, George, 183, 204

Bush, Ian, 20, 21-22

Butler, Judith, 278

Butterfield, Fox, 210–11, 215, 216–18

Byfield, Bryan, 109–10

Calder v. Jones, 55

California, University of, Berkeley, 107, 290

California, University of, San Diego, 40

Camp, Cathy, 25

Campus Crusade for Christ, 295

Cannell, Michael, 231

Canty, Trecia, 200

Capote, Truman, 224

Carey, Jull, 254

Carner, Chas, 306

Carter, Brandon, 291–92

Carter, Gwendoline, 89

Carter, Jimmy, 8, 205, 317

Carter, Stephen, 67, 69

Cassidy, Margaret, 105

Castro-Klaren, Sara, 49

Cattan, E. William, 45, 47, 48–49, 54, 55, 56, 88, 320

CBS, 56, 117

CCSC

See College Committee on Standing and Conduct

Center for Women and Gender (CWG), 273, 275, 277, 281, 340

CFSC

See Coed Fraternity Sororities Council

Champion, George, 335

Champion, John, 199

Chapman, Olivia, 282, 283, 295

Chen, Pang-Chung, 221, 222–25

Cheston, Sheila, 304

Chi Gamma Epsilon, 245, 254

Chi Heorot, 245

China: Alive in the Bitter Sen (Mao), 211

Christo, 76

Churchill, Winston, 324

Clark, Gary, 6, 8, 63, 64, 66, 68, 241

Clark, M. Ryan, 244

Clausen, William, 19–20, 23, 24, 28, 29, 48–50, 109, 110

Cleghorn, Mildred, 85

Cleveland, Sara, 44, 123

The Closing of the American Mind (Bloom), 161

CNN, 200

Coed Fraternity Sororities Council (CFSC), 244, 250–56

Cohen, Andrew, 254

Cohen, M. H., 176, 177, 178

Colby College, 242

Cole, William, 43–58, 122–36, 142–43, 146, 148–55, 164–65, 184, 186, 196, 202, 216, 218–19, 318, 340

Colla, Geoffrey, 306

Colla, Stan, 206

College Committee on Diversity and Community, 247

College Committee on Residential Life, 247

College Committee on Standing and Conduct (CCSC), 18, 23–24, 25, 26, 27, 28–29

College News Service, 220

Collis Commonground, 273–74

Collis Student Center, 265–66

Coltrane, John, 336

Columbia University, 40, 86

Committee for Palestinian Rights (CPR), 183, 190, 196–97

Committee on Standards (COS), 64–70, 99, 101–3, 108–10, 112–15, 118–20, 135, 137, 142, 147–50, 156, 157, 163, 181, 230

Committee on Student Organizations, 132, 326

Como, Perry, 209

Conn, Robert, 306

Conservative Union, 282

Cook, William W., 51

Cornell University, 78, 107, 261–62, 273

Cortez, Jayne, 44, 123, 126

Corum, Richard, 130, 134

COS

See Committee on Standards

COSO

See Council on Student Organizations

Council on Student Organizations (COSO), 59, 241

CPR

See Committee for Palestinian Rights

Craig, Anne, 26

Crossfire, 200

Crovitz, L. Gordon, 151, 155, 203

Crown, Theodore, 59

Csatari, Thomas, 63, 64

Cuomo, Mario, 318

Custer, George Armstron, 12

CWG

See Center for Women and Gender

DAGLO

See Dartmouth Area Gay and Lesbian Organization

The Daily Dartmouth, 13, 17, 24, 25, 28, 67, 110, 185, 192–93, 196, 198, 218, 235,

241, 243, 254, 258, 283, 305, 315, 316, 323, 338

Daily Princetonian, 58

Damon Runyon (Lardner), 34

Danzinger, Robert, 306

DAO

  See Dartmouth Asian Organization

DAOG

  See Dartmouth Alumni for Open Governance

Dartmouth Alliance Against Racism, 202

Dartmouth Alumni Council, 199, 298

Dartmouth Alumni for Open Governance (DAOG), 298, 299–300

Dartmouth Alumni Magazine, 5, 42, 148, 154, 159, 162, 176, 177–79, 183, 227–28, 229, 230, 306

Dartmouth Area Gay and Lesbian Organization (DAGLO), 132, 138, 164, 201, 202

  See also Gay Students Association (GSA)

Dartmouth Asian Organization (DAO), 202, 257, 258

Dartmouth Commitee for Divestment (DCD), 99

Dartmouth Committee to Beautify the Green Before Winter Carnival (DCBGBWC), 98–104, 106, 108, 109, 110, 110–12, 113, 133

Dartmouth Community for Divestment (DCD), 95–97, 100–102, 105, 106, 109, 110, 114, 116

Dartmouth Rainbow Coalition, 268

Dartmouth Rowing Club, 79

Dartmouth United Against Hate Rally, 203, 219, 226, 229

Dartmouth Women's Association, 240

Darwin, Charles, 30, 52, 293

Davidson, Stephen, 113

Davies, Laurence, 109

Davis, Angela, 183, 188, 190, 196

Davis, Miles, 336

Davison, Stephen, 109

DCBGBWC

  See Dartmouth Committee to Beautify the Green Before Winter Carnival

DCD

  See Dartmouth Community for Divestment

Deadrick, Marc, 138–39

Delta Delta Delta, 251, 252, 253, 254, 255

Delta Sigma Theta, 243

Dentzer, Susan, 178–79, 259, 301, 304

Desir, Anthony, 27

Dhillon, Harmeet, 140, 144, 155, 156, 166, 182, 189, 334, 336

Dick's House, 166–71, 270–72

Dieckmann, Yale, 245

Disraeli, Benjamin, 293

Dragoon, Alice, 110

Drexel, Allen, 201

D'Souza, Dinesh, 9, 16, 18, 28, 30, 45, 47, 48, 50, 54, 55, 73, 155, 176–77, 203, 205, 216–17, 220, 231, 234, 315–16, 320, 323

Duegger, Arthur, 156

Dugan, Conor, 282

Duggan, Timothy, 49

Duncan, Bruce, 49

Duthu, N. Bruce, 300

EC

  See Executive Committee

Edwards, Arthur, 138

Ehrlich, Chris, 188

"Ein Reich, Ein Volk, Ein Freedmann" (Garrett), 180–91, 221

Eisenhower, Dwight D., 87

Eliot, T. S., 227

Elliott, Rogers, 49

Ellis, Michael, 304, 307, 316, 339

Ellner, Brian, 197, 203

Emerson, Ralph Waldo, 318

The End of Racism (D'Souza), 316

Engles, Gregg, 304

Ensler, Eve, 279–81
Epsilon Kappa Theta, 252
Ernest Martin Hopkins Institute, 148
Etu, Eric, 254
Everhart, Henry, 35
Executive Committee (EC), 136

Fahey, Peter M., 259
Fanelli, Alexander, 7
Far Eastern Economic Review, 316
Farrakhan, Louis, 183, 188
Fayard, Caroline, 251
Fear and Loathing in Las Vegas
    (Thompson), 230
Feder, Don, 188
Federalist Society, 336
Feey, Father, 211
Fidel, Noel, 306
Field, Robert, 13, 14–15
Finnegan, Jim, 143, 144
FIRE
    See Foundation for Individual Rights in
    Education
Firespitters, 123
Fish, Stanley, 316
Fisher, Ashley, 279
Fisher-Harris, Patricia, 301
Fitzgerald, F. Scott, 324, 325
Flanigan, Robert, 100, 103, 109, 112, 133
Flyte, Sebastian, 319
Fogelin, Robert J., 51
Food and Drug Administration, U. S., 166
Ford, Henry, 89
Forgey, Ben, 76-77
Forward, 207
Foss, Perkins, 76
Fossedal, Gregory, 3, 5, 18–29, 316–17,
    320, 323, 329
Foundation for Individual Rights in
    Education (FIRE), 308, 310
Founding Fathers, 119
Fowler, Mary, 71
Franco, Francisco, 7

Frankenberry, Nancy K., 51
Franklin Pierce College, 133
Freccero, Carla, 138, 139, 150, 151, 196
Freedman, Bathsheba, 136
Freedman, James, 135–37, 143–50, 153,
    155–59, 180–96, 198, 204–15, 218–22,
    226–29, 232–38, 247–48, 282, 285, 287,
    292, 293, 295, 331–33, 335, 339
French, John, 5, 6, 7, 16, 17
Friedan, Betty, 39
Friedman, Milton, 39
Frost, Robert, 324
Fryer, Charles, 176, 177, 178
Funk, Tom, 111
Furstenburg, Karl, 305, 308

Galileo, 292
Gamma Delta Chi, 303
Garling, David, 67, 68
Garrett, James, 180, 182, 183, 185, 186,
    189–90
Garthwaite, Gene, 104–-5
Gaudin, Collette, 49
Gay Students Association (GSA), 59–70,
    105, 132, 215–16, 326
    See also Dartmouth Area Gay and
    Lesbian Organization (DAGLO)
Gelfant, Blanche, 49
George III, King, 72
George Mason University, 89, 246, 304
German, Sean, 156, 186
Gert, Bernard, 49
Giaccone, Nick, 222–25
Gilder, George, 212, 213
Glabe, Scott, 307
Glee Club, 282–85, 295
God and Man at Yale (Buckley), 9, 286,
    308–9, 340
Godcheaux, Steven, 28
Goebbels, Joseph, 42
Goering, Hermann, 186
Gold, Allan, 159
Golden, Soma, 217

Gonzalez, Khristina, 281
Gorbachev, Mikhail, 304
Gordon, Jim, 84–85
Gorman, Sean, 177
Grace, William, 171, 172, 335
Graham, Robert, 19, 20–21, 23
Grand Met, Inc., 13
Grant, Leslie, 109, 112
Green, Donald, 116–17
Green, Michael, 18, 19–20, 21–22, 23–24,
    24–25, 26–27, 28, 33
Green, Ronald, 27, 51
Grossman, Andrew, 241, 316
GSA
    See Gay Students Association
Guthrie, Philippa, 19, 28

Hackett, Ann Fritz, 306
Haffner, Michael, 109, 112
Hager, Nicole, 202
Haldeman, Charles, 301
Hall, Melvin, 138
Hamm, Charles E., 51
Hannigan, Thomas, 65
Hanover Review Corporation, 47, 54, 56,
    132
Hanson, John, 26, 327
Harding, Vincent, 199, 221
Harris, Kiki, 181
Hart, Benjamin, 5, 7, 24, 35–36, 38, 39, 42,
    320, 325–26, 328
Hart, Jeffrey, 11, 12, 22, 86, 120, 137, 146,
    147, 150, 161, 176, 177, 178, 183, 200,
    207, 221, 222, 241, 283, 290, 315,
    321–22, 324, 326, 335, 337
Hart, Nancy, 222
Harvard University, 41, 78, 90, 107
Hayek, Friedrich, 325
Heffernan, James, 49, 147
Heinrichs, Jay, 176, 177, 178, 230
Heinz, H. J., 300
Held, Robert Peter, 187
Hemingway, Ernest, 324

Hemphill, Julius, 126
Hena, James, 82
Henderson, Robert P., 306
Henken, Matt, 223
Henry, Claude, 151
Heritage Foundation, 316
Hernandez, Michele, 259–60
Herndon, Marsha, 127
Herpel, Jack, 25
Hertzberg, Arthur, 185, 199-200
Heston, John, 75
Heyman, I. Michael, 306
Hicks, Ort, 178
Hill, Herald, 128
Hillel Jewish Students Association, 285, 294
Himmler, Heinrich, 40, 186
Hitler, Adolf, 42, 118, 176, 177, 179-83,
    195, 196, 198, 204, 208-12, 220, 222,
    224, 231, 232, 325, 335
Hoffmeister, Wemer, 204
Hokupa'a, 252
Holder, Betsy, 277
Hollinger, David, 290–91
*The Hollow Men: Politics and Corruption in
    Higher Education* (Sykes), 34
Holocaust, 186–87, 193
Homer, 32
Hoover Institution, 304, 323
Hopkins, Ernest Martin, 78, 286, 289, 292
Hopkins Foundation, 199
Horowitz, David, 188, 337, 338
Horton, Sherman, 23, 111
Houlahan, J. Michael, 306
Huggins, Elisha, 19, 28
Hughes, Gerald, 13, 67, 109, 112, 113
Hume, David, 325
Hummel, Christian, 244
Humphrey, Gordon, 120
Humphrey, Hubert, 317
Humphrey, Walter, 75
Huppe, Alex, 156, 157, 159, 192, 218, 221
Hutchins, Peter, 137
Hutchins, Robert, 41

Hutensky, Brad, 47
Huxley, Thomas, 293

Illiberal Education (D'Souza), 316, 323
Immelt, Jeffrey, 308
Ingraham, Laura, 43, 46, 47, 49, 52–56, 58,
    64, 67, 71, 78, 79, 131, 133, 316, 320
In Search of Anti-Semitism (Kristol), 289
International Students Association (ISA),
    198, 201, 202
In Your Face, 201
Iowa State University, 107
ISA
    See International Students Association
Ives, Almon, 19, 28

Jackson, Jesse, 94–95, 187, 316
Jefferson, Thomas, 8, 41
Jhamb, Alexis, 275
Jim, Roger, 82
Johnson, Blind Willie, 44
Johnson, Dee, 241
Johnson, Luzmila, 143
*Joining the Club: A History of Jews and
    Yale* (Oren), 286
Jones, Keeney, 27, 31, 32, 34, 38, 39, 49,
    240, 318, 320, 326
Jones, Marsha, 136
Jordan, Vernon, 89
Joseph, Richard, 148
*Journal of the American Medical
    Association*, 21

Kafka, Franz, 18, 147
Kagan, Donald, 228
Kaplitt, Steve, 188
Kappa Alpha Psi, 243
Kartalopoulos, Bill, 230
KASA
    See Korean American Student
    Association
Kasfir, Nelson M., 51
Katz, Steven, 49

Keitt, Taylor, 260
Kelley, Eric, 253
Kelley, Steve, 13–15, 27, 317
Kemeny, John G., 4, 6–7, 8, 17, 25, 73, 75,
    78, 236, 316
Kemp, Jack, 145, 317
Kennedy, Bruce, 283
Kennedy, Edward, 208
Kennedy, John F., 86
Kent State University, 107
Khmer Rouge, 208
Khomeini, Ayatollah, 18
Kim, Jeanhee, 306
Kimball, Roger, 228
King, Deborah, 184
King, Gwendolyn, 174
King, Julia, 21
King, Martin Luther, Jr., 99–101, 118, 133,
    141–42, 290
Kinsley, Michael, 162
Kirschner, Jim, 28
Klinghoffer, David, 188
Koch, Carla, 180
Koeninger, Julie, 306
Kondracke, Morton, 159, 161–62
Kopp, Quentin, 298–300
Korean American Student Association
    (KASA), 258
Korean Posse (KP), 256
Korean Power (KP), 256
KP
    See Korean Power
Kristol, Irving, 288, 289, 293
Kuhn, Thomas, 291
Ku Klux Klan, 42, 141, 148, 150, 184, 334
Kuypers, Professor, 282–83

La Alianza Latina, 202
Lahr, Dwight, 131, 135, 136, 143, 183
Lamb, Scott, 59
Lambda Upsilon Lambda, 252, 253
Lancaster, Mark, 110, 112
Lang, Richard, 77

Lardner, Ring, 34

Larimore, James, 255, 259, 261

La Valley, Albert, 111, 157, 161, 163, 164

Lee, W. David, 300

Leek, Joe, 136

Leek, Rob, 135

Lee v. Weisman, 288

Lenox, Kimberly, 253

Leo, John, 246

Letarte, Karen Brown, 306

Letters to a Young Conservative (D'Souza), 323

Levi, David, 234

Lewis, C. S., 295

Lewis, Ric, 304

Lincoln, Abraham, 86, 290, 333

Lipsky, Seth, 207

Llacer, Lillian, 103, 110–11, 114–15

Long, John L., Jr., 48, 51, 53-55, 57

Lopez, Melinda, 104

Lord, Nathan, 333

The Los Angeles Times, 233–34, 235, 295

Louisiana State University, 248

Lucas, William, 206

Lupo, Alan, 211

McBennet, Tara, 198

McCarthy, Joseph, 41, 176, 208

McCormick, Alex, 110, 111

McCullough, Norman "Sandy," 159

McFall, Lynne, 60

McGean, Michael, 6, 7

McGeehan, Michael, 3

McGovern, George, 40

MacGovern, John, 211

McGowan, Daniel, 117

McGrath, Robert, 49, 75–76

McKee, Patricia, 37, 39

MacLam, Helen M., 51

McLaughlin, David, 23, 35, 49, 66, 74–79, 83–84, 97, 99, 104–8, 112, 113, 118, 123, 133, 241

McMullen, Joanne, 17

The Making of the American Conservative Mind: National Review and its Times (Hart), 315

Malcolm X, 193, 200

Manchester Union Leader, 19, 21, 23, 143, 144, 220

Man-Child in the Promised Land (Henry), 151

Mandell, Harvey, 186

Mansfield, Harvey, 340

Manuel, Ralph, 19, 22, 26, 27

Mao Tse-tung, 211

Marsden, George, 286

Marshall, Karim, 237

Marshall, Thurgood, 238

Masters, Roger D., 51

Mathewson, Joe, 306

Mein Kampf (Hitler), 176, 179, 208, 209, 210, 212

Menashi, Steven, 233, 235, 252, 294, 316

Menon, Rajiv, 105

Mere Christianity (Lewis), 295

Merrow, Robert, 241

Meyer, Elizabeth, 305

Meyer, Werner, 109, 112

Meyers, Michael, 261

Meyerson, Adam, 188

Michaels, Anne, 270–72

Middlebury College, 242

Milan, 202

Milton, John, 130

MIT, 248

A Modest Proposal (Swift), 182

Mohl, Bruce, 152, 154–57, 159–60, 162–64

Monoco, Arthur, 230

Montgomery, William, 199

Moody, JoAnne, 260–61

Moore, Douglas, 109

More, Paul Elmer, 293–94

Morrison & Foerster, 69

Mosseau, Peter, 67

Moyers, Bill, 44

Muggeridge, Malcolm, 292

Mulley, Albert, 301

Munafo, Giavanna, 281

Munroe, George, 185, 215, 217, 332

Munt, Sally, 277

Murdoch, Rupert, 318

Muscat, Catherine, 250

The Music Man, 128

Muster, Ester, 277–78

Mvubelo, Lucy, 90–95

Myerson, Harvey, 152, 153, 156–57, 164

Nachman, Henry, Jr., 306

NAD

   See Native Americans at Dartmouth

Nader, Ralph, 39

National Endowment for the Arts, 223

National Lampoon, 34

National Panhellenic Conference, 251

National Review, 176, 188, 316, 317, 321, 324

National Union of Clothing Workers, 90

National Urban League, 89

Native American People (Herndon), 127

Native Americans at Dartmouth (NAD), 25, 26, 74, 80, 138, 164, 200–202, 202

Navarro, Marysa, 51, 146–47, 183

NBC, 117

NEBHE

   See New England Board of Higher Education

NEC, 208

Nelson, Bruce, 199

The New Criterion, 316

New England Board of Higher Education (NEBHE), 260

The New Republic, 76, 159, 161–62

Newsweek, 29, 178

Newton, Douglas, 234

New York Daily News, 211

The New York Post, 118, 151, 318

The New York Sun, 316

The New York Times, 64, 159, 164, 184, 195, 204, 208, 209, 210, 211, 213, 215, 217,

222, 227, 228, 229, 235, 237, 244, 285, 286, 287, 297, 322, 331–32, 333

Niedermeier, Jerome J., 55

Niemeyer, Paul V., 334

Nixon, Richard M., 317, 324

Nolan, Sean, 130, 135, 142

Nolan, William, 171

Nova, Scott, 120

Oberlin College, 30

Obomsawin, Alanis, 123

Occom, Samson, 71–73

O'Hearn, Sean, 105

Olin, John M., Foundation, 199, 212–13, 216, 328–33

O'Neal, Melinda, 131

Oppenheimer, Matthew, 237

Oren, Dan A., 286

Orr and Reno, 12, 13

Orwell, George, 18, 143, 240

Palestine Liberation Organization (PLO), 183, 188, 193

Paley, Michael, 171

Palmer, Barry J., 218–20

Pan, Dave, 256, 257

Panero, James, 227, 230, 316

Papp, Daniel, 300

Paradise Lost (Milton), 130

Parker, Craig, 285

Partners in Health (Sloane), 166, 167, 168

Patch, Ben, 282

Patton, 324

Paul, Jaimie, 250–51

Pease, Donald, 228, 315

Pelton, Lee, 233

Penner, Hans, 45, 46–47, 49

Pennypacker, Steve, 42–43

Peretz, Martin, 162

Peterson, Walter, 133

Petrosemelo, Art, 241

Phillip, Kevin, 223

Phinney, John, 254, 256

Index

Pickard, Lennie, 25

Piereson, James, 328

Pierpoint, Rutherford, 186

Pines, Burt, 188

Pinochet, Augusto, 7

Pittsburgh, Unviersity of, 45

Pius XII, Pope, 211

Playboy magazine, 61

PLO

   See Palestine Liberation Organization

Poisoned Ivy (Hart), 42

Poison Ivy, 266

Polenz, Daryl, 109, 112

Polenz, Teresa, 63–70, 97, 100, 109, 112, 133

Policy Review, 188, 316

The Politics of Rich and Poor (Phillip), 223

Porteus, Kim, 102, 114

Prince, Gregory, 183

Princeton Review, 263

Princeton Unviersity, 40, 58, 186

Pritchett, Kevin, 137, 155–56, 164, 192,
   195, 203, 204, 206, 209, 210, 213, 222,
   224, 228, 316, 335

Prospect magazine, 58

Provost, Daniel E., III, 13, 14

Psi Upsilon, 248

Quilhot, John, 131, 134, 135, 142, 171–72

Rafat, Roham, 245

Rago, Joseph, 273, 316, 337

RAID

   See Responsible AIDS Information at
   Dartmouth

Ramsay, Alston, 279, 316

Rasenberger, Raymond, 3, 8, 9, 14

Rashid, Omar, 252, 253

Raspberry, William, 89

Rath, Thomas, 12, 13

Raube, Avery, 6, 13, 14, 177

Reagan, Ronald, 8, 12, 17, 39, 96, 97, 118,
   145, 231, 304, 316, 317, 319, 320, 321,
   322, 327

Reardon, Judy, 24

Redman, Martin, 255

Reed, Christopher, 111

Reichel, Frank, 56, 97, 109, 112, 113, 115, 133

Reiners, William, 49

Responsible AIDS Information at Dartmouth
   (RAID), 172–75

Restall, Hugo, 223, 316

Reynolds, Roland, 56, 67, 102

Rieser, Leonard, 49

Rimer, Sara, 228-29, 232, 233, 237-39

Rinfret, Pierre, 209

Ringer, Noah, 296–97

Rivkin, David, 135

Robinson, Peter, 15, 57, 304–9, 320, 340–41

Rockefeller Center, 240

Rockwell, George Lincoln, 188–89

Rodgers, T. J., 298-304, 307, 309, 311,
   340–41

Rogers, William, 57

Rogers and Wells, 54

Roos, Thomas, 184

Roosevelt, Franklin D., 86

Roosevelt, Theodore, 195, 204, 208, 209

Roots, 32–33

Rosenthal, Jeff, 98

Rosenthal, Seth, 186

Rosenzweig, Franz, 288

Roth, Amanda, 200

Roth Center for Jewish Life, 233, 235, 236,
   285, 287, 294

Russ, Joseph, 82

Russell, Bertrand, 41

Russell, Francis, 318

Rutland Herald, 47

Safer, Morley, 336

SAGE

   See Sexual Awareness through Greek
   Education

Sakharov, Andrei, 64

The San Diego Union, 13

San Francisco Chronicle, 299

SAPA
    See Sexual Abuse Peer Advisor
    organization
Saumweber, Philipp, 253
Scheu, Edmund, 13, 14
Scholer, J. Lawrence, 237
Schram, Ronald, 13, 14, 306
Schott, Suzanne, 79
Schwartzkopf, Norman, 268
Schweitzer, Ivy, 338
Science, Jews, and Secular Culture
    (Hollinger), 290
Scott, George C., 324
Screed, 230
Segal, Bernard, 109
Seldes, George, 225
"Self-Reliance" (Emerson), 318
Sexual Abuse Peer Advisor (SAPA)
    organization, 274
Sexual Awareness through Greek Education
    (SAGE), 251
Seymour, Charles, 287, 289
Shakespeare, William, 32
Shanahan, Edward, 47, 64–66, 68–70, 84,
    96, 99, 103, 105, 108, 112, 131, 135–36,
    137, 142, 148, 154, 157, 163–64, 166,
    169
Shanker, Albert, 331
Sharpton, Al, 194, 205, 234
Sheldon, Richard, 49, 183
Sheppard, Alexandra, 236
Shula, Dave, 28
Siegal, Rabbi Daniel, 186
Sigma Nu, 270
Sigma Phi Epsilon, 254
Silberman, Laurence, 64, 65, 66, 69, 162,
    195
Silver, Brenda R., 51
Simon, William, 39, 212, 214, 328, 329, 332
Sinnott-Armstrong, Walter, 116
Sisters of Chanty, 215
Sitting Bull, 11
60 Minutes, 164, 336

Sleeper, 331
SLI
    See Student Life Initiative
Sloane, Beverly Conant, 166, 167, 171–72,
    172–73
Smallwood, Ann, 19, 20, 28
Smiling through the Cultural Catastrophe:
    Toward the Revival of Higher Education
    (Hart), 315
Smith, Adam, 87, 325
Smith, David, 138
Smith, Peter, 42
Smith, Samuel, 35–40, 325–26
Smith, Warren, 126
Smithsonian Institution, 77
Solzhenitsyn, Aleksandr, 325
Sophocles, Alexandra, 253
Soria, Orlando, 273
The Soul of the American University: From
    Protestant Establishment to Established
    Nonbelief (Marsden), 286
Sowell, Thomas, 33
Soyster, Blair, 54, 55, 56, 57
Spaeder, Deborah, 223
Spengemann, William, 130
Spitzer, Leo, 88, 326
Sports Illustrated, 122
Stalin, Joseph, 325
Stanford University, 323
Starzinger, Vincent, 49
State University of New York, 277
State v. Sheedy, 68
Stearns, Russell, 20, 22
Steel, John, 3–7, 12–14, 16, 301, 316
Steele, Shelby, 262
Stein, Gertrude, 277
Stein, Laura, 300
Stet, 190, 197
Stevenson, John, 238
Stith-Cabrane, Kate, 251, 306
Stokes, Michael, 139
Stone, Deborah, 83, 95, 97, 100, 101, 109,
    112, 114–15, 131, 133, 316, 320, 335

Stone, Wendy, 329
Stossel, John, 316
Struckhoff, Gene, 68
Structure of Scientific Revolutions (Kuhn),
    291
Student Assembly, 230
Student Handbook, 101
Student Life Initiative (SLI), 259, 263–68,
    300, 301, 303, 305, 340
Styron, William, 315
Sullivan, Jim, 104
Sununu, John, 120, 133, 144
Supreme Court, U. S., 288–89
Sushon, William J., 215, 223, 224
Sutter, John, 128–29, 131, 134, 135, 137,
    142, 148, 149, 155, 156, 163, 176, 216
Swarthmore College, 30
Swift, Jonathan, 182, 335
Sykes, Charles J., 34

Talcott, Alexander, 259
Tapper, Jack, 198, 202–3
Tatum, James, 49, 51
Taylor, Lucy, 82
Teachers Insurance and Annuity Association
    (TIAA), 115–17
Technology Review, 8
Teevens, Shaun, 24, 25
Teitz, Richard, 76
Telerico, Chip, 142
Theresa, Mother, 215
Thomas, Clarence, 206
Thomas, Darren, 259
Thompson, Hunter S., 230
Thompson, P. Esmé, 51
TIAA
    See Teachers Insurance and Annuity
    Association
Tokson, Matthew, 263
Tocqueville, Alexis de, 318
Tom, Uncle, 33
Tomockham, 71
Trade Union Council of South Africa, 90

Trexler, Marie, 109, 112
Trilling, Lionel, 121
Tucker Foundation, 295
Turco, John, *167–68*, 171
Turner, Tina, 172
Twain, Mark, 34

UGC
    See Undergraduate Council
Uncommon Knowledge, 304
Undergraduate Council (UGC), 37, 38
Upper Valley Committee for Free South
    Africa (UVCFSA), 88
UVCFSA
    See Upper Valley Committee for Free
    South Africa

Vagina Monologues, 275, 279–81
Valley News, 21, 47
V-day, 279
Vickers, Nancy, 105
Volokh Conspiracy weblog, 304

Walker, Keith, 28
Wallace-Wells, Benjamin C., 268, 316
The Wall Street Journal, 64, 66, 68, 103,
    144, 159, 209, 299, 316, 332, 337
Walsh, Barbara B., 51
Ward, Nathaniel, 298, 301, 309
Washburn, Wid, 299
Washburn, Wilcomb, 77–78
Washington, Booker T., 238
Washington, George, 86, 101
Washington Monthly, 316
The Washington Post, 76, 89, 192, 196, 204,
    208, 320
Washington Times, 188
Waugh, Evelyn, 318, 324, 325
Webster, Daniel, 214
Weissmann, Kenneth, 218
Welch, Joseph, 208
Wellesley, 251
Welling, Curtis, 304

West, Diana, 188

Westmoreland, General, 56

What's So Great About America (D'Souza), 323

Wheelock, Eleazar, 8, 71, 75, 87, 181

Whitman, Chris, 132

Whitaker, Nathaniel, 72

Wiencke, Matthew, 75–76

Wilberforce, Bishop, 293

Wilkens, Math, 253

Williams, Walter, 89

Wilson, Alexander, 233, 241

Wolek-Osterhout, Gail A., 282

Wolland, Elyse, 201

Women for Peace movement, 91

Women's Issues League, 132, 138, 164

Wood, Professor, 231

Woodward, Cynthia, 19, 28

World Affairs Council, 183

Wright, James, 237–38, 241–44, 247, 248, 259, 264–65, 304, 308, 339

Yale Law School, 207

Yale University, 40, 107, 119, 250, 286–87, 300

Yates, Douglas, 135, 177–78, 335

You Have to Pay the Price (Blaik), 317

Zacharski, Leo, 19, 20, 21, 28

Zion, Sidney, 188

Zywicki, Todd, 15, 246, 304–11, 340–41